FAIRY TAIL

43

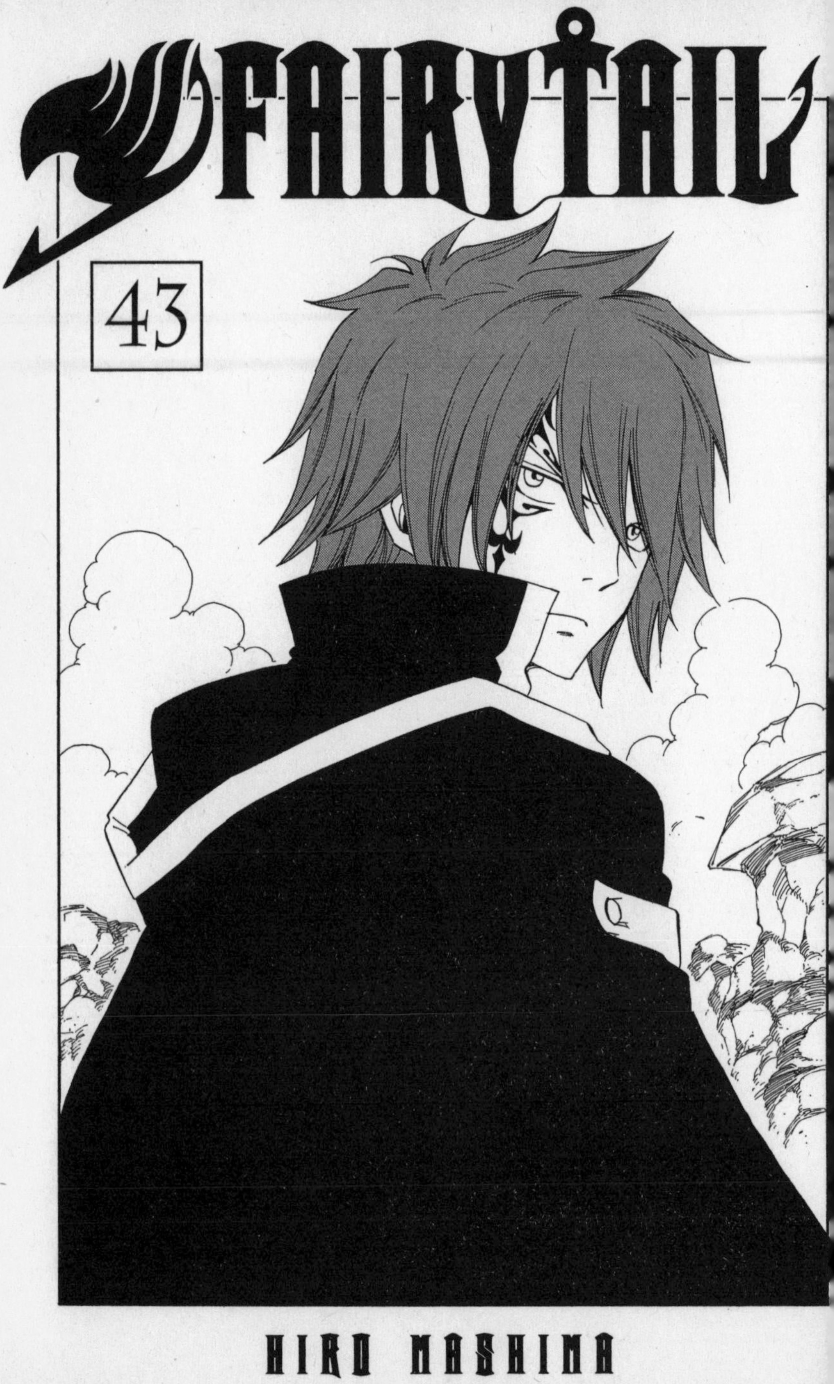

HIRO MASHIMA

FAIRY TAIL 43 CONTENTS

FAIRY TAIL

Chapter 362: Natsu vs. Jackal

BLUE PEGASUS

Name: Jenny Realite **Age:** 25

Magic:
Takeover (Machina Soul)

Likes: **Dislikes:**
Shopping Black coffee

Remarks

The top pinup model for Weekly Sorcerer. Seven years ago, she and Mirajane were rivals for the top model spot, and now they are both good friends and good rivals. Her magic is Machina Soul, which allows her to transform into an outfit armed with heavy weaponry. Whenever she touches a machine, she can make its power her own.

She lost a bet with Mira during the Grand Magic Games and had to pose nude for Weekly Sorcerer Magazine, but when the time came, she wasn't as embarrassed about it as everyone thought she would be.

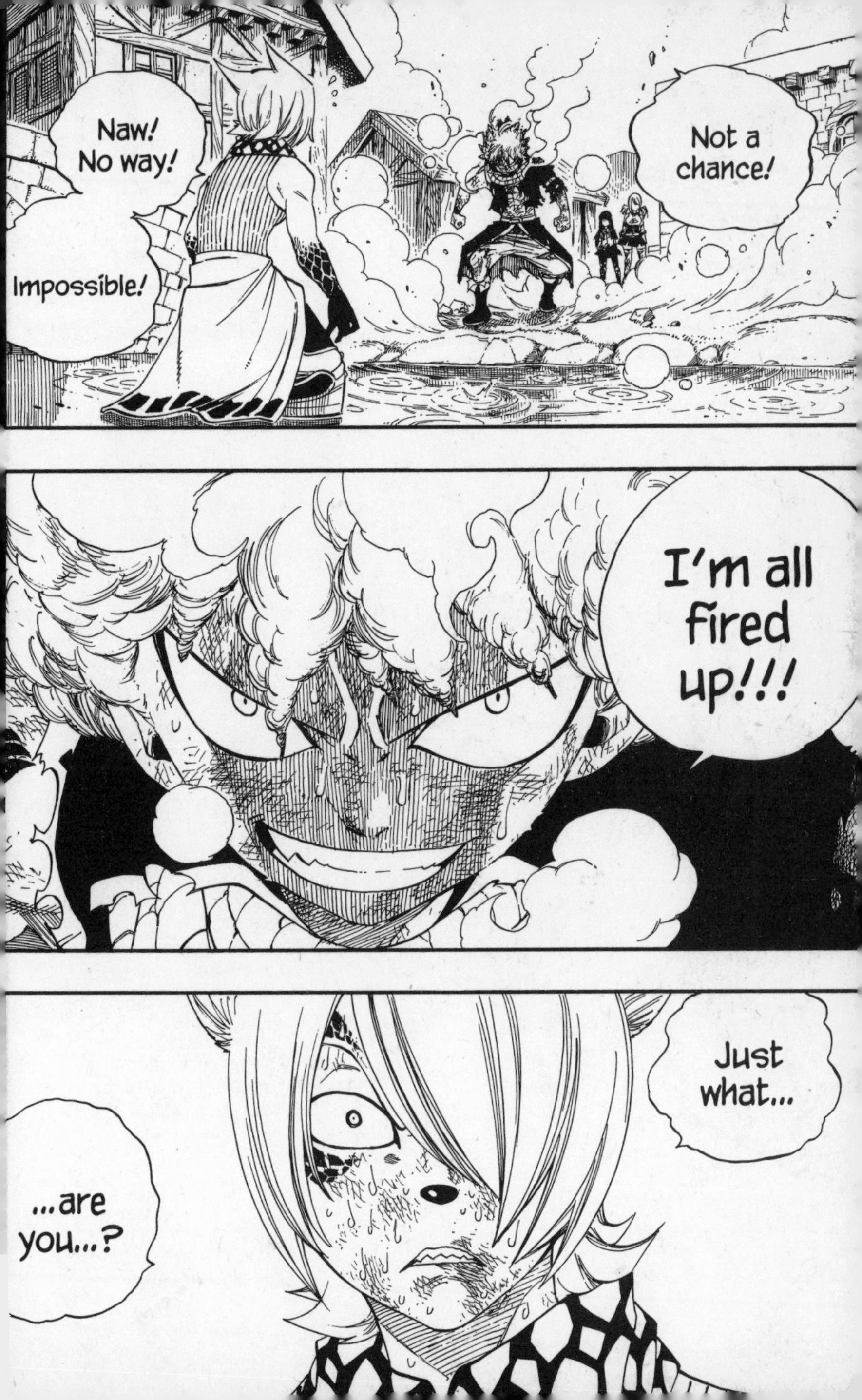
Not a chance!
Naw! No way!
Impossible!
I'm all fired up!!!
Just what...
...are you...?

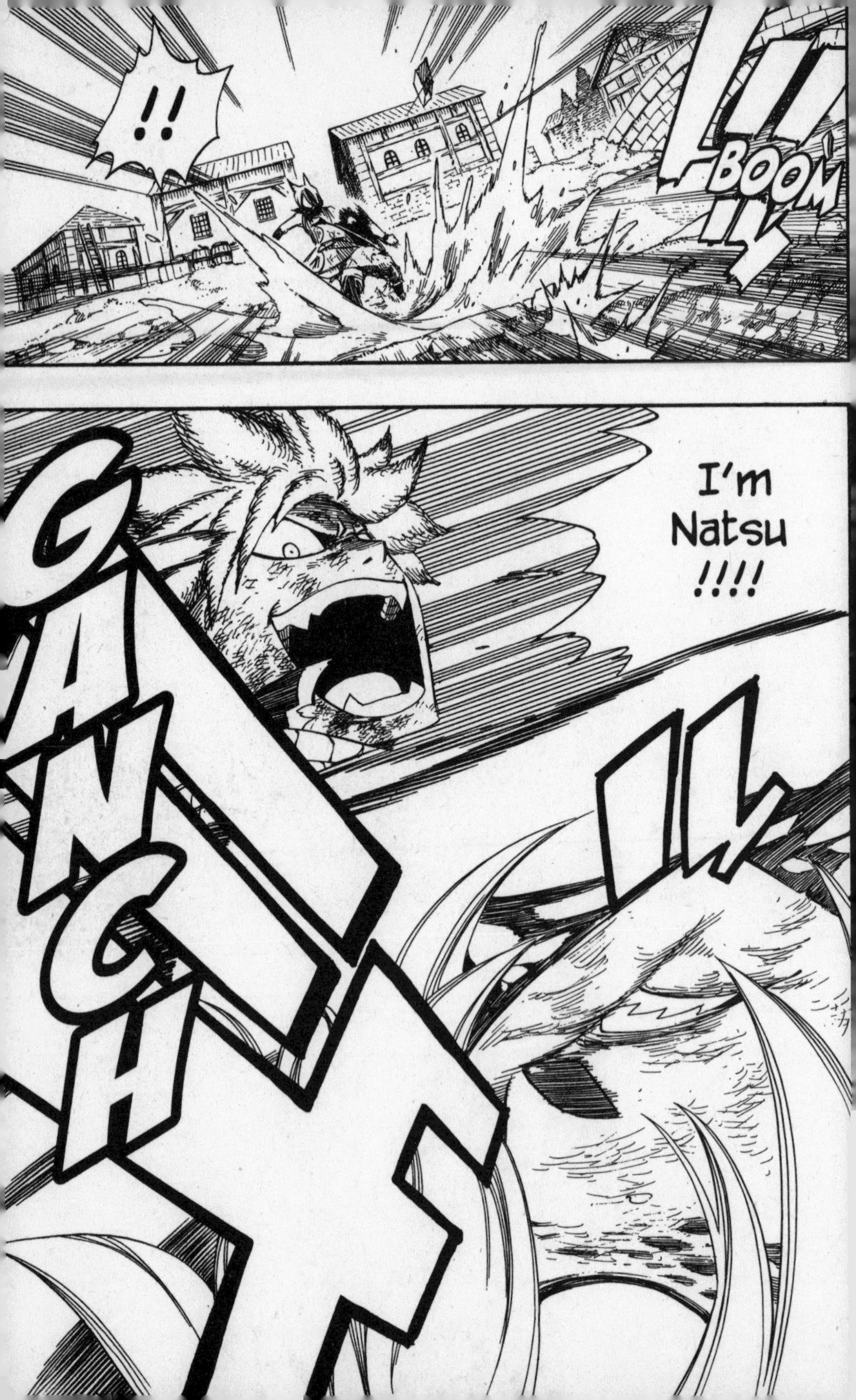
BOOM
!!
I'm Natsu!!!!
GANCH

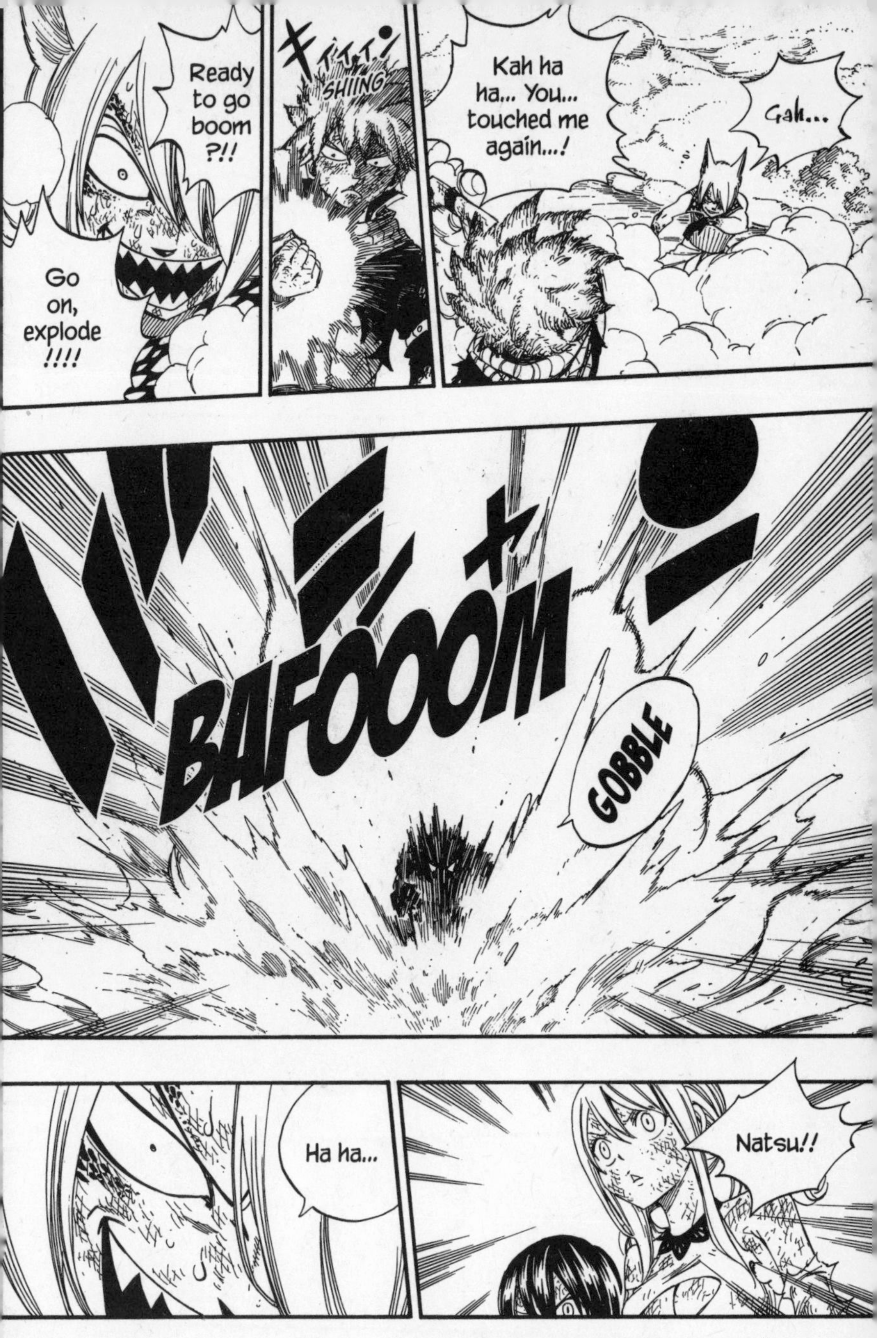
Gah...
Kah ha ha... You... touched me again...!
SHIING
Ready to go boom ?!!
Go on, explode !!!!
BAFOOOM
GOBBLE
Natsu!!
Ha ha...

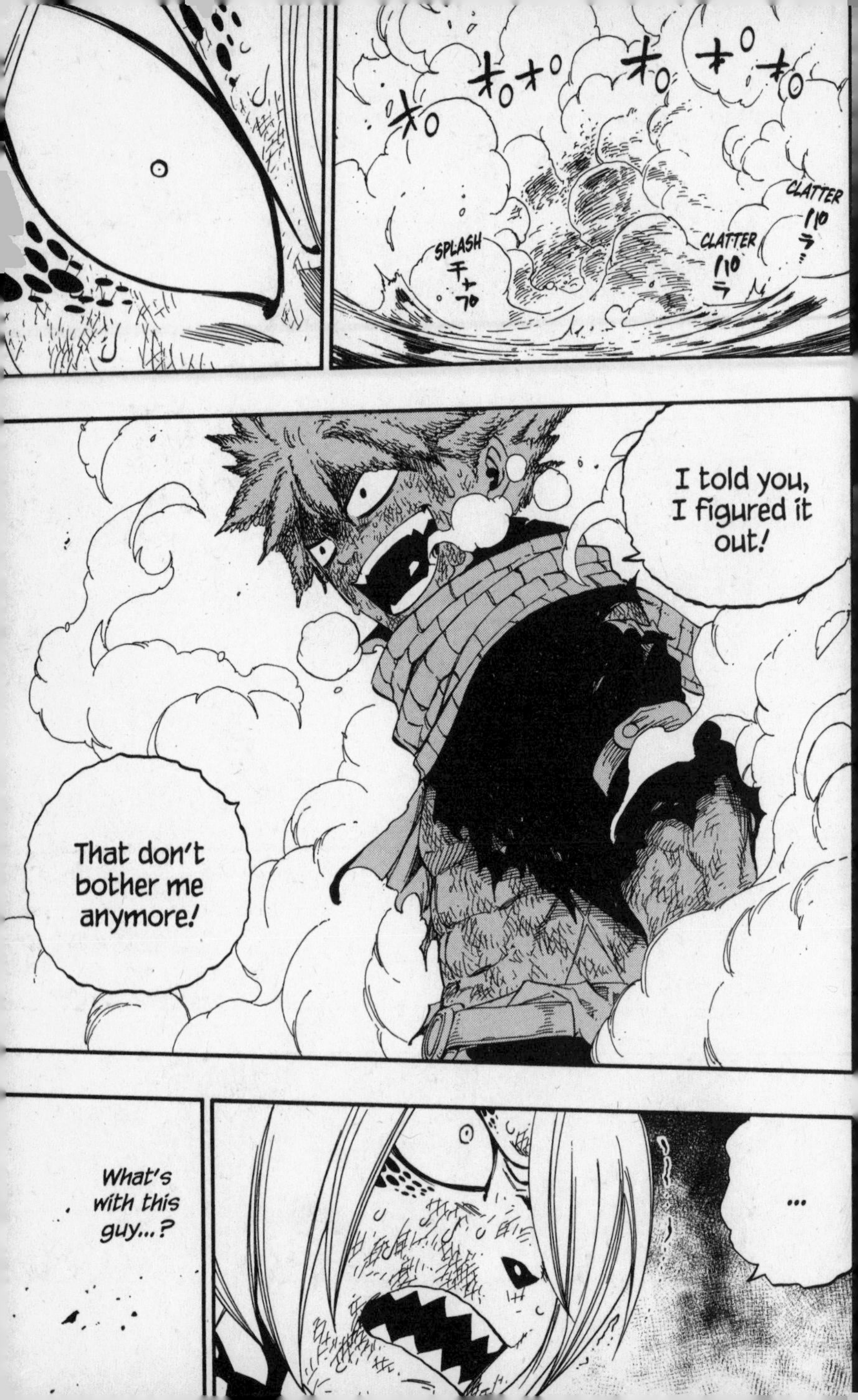
CLATTER
パラ
CLATTER
パラ
SPLASH
チャプ
I told you, I figured it out!
That don't bother me anymore!
...
What's with this guy...?

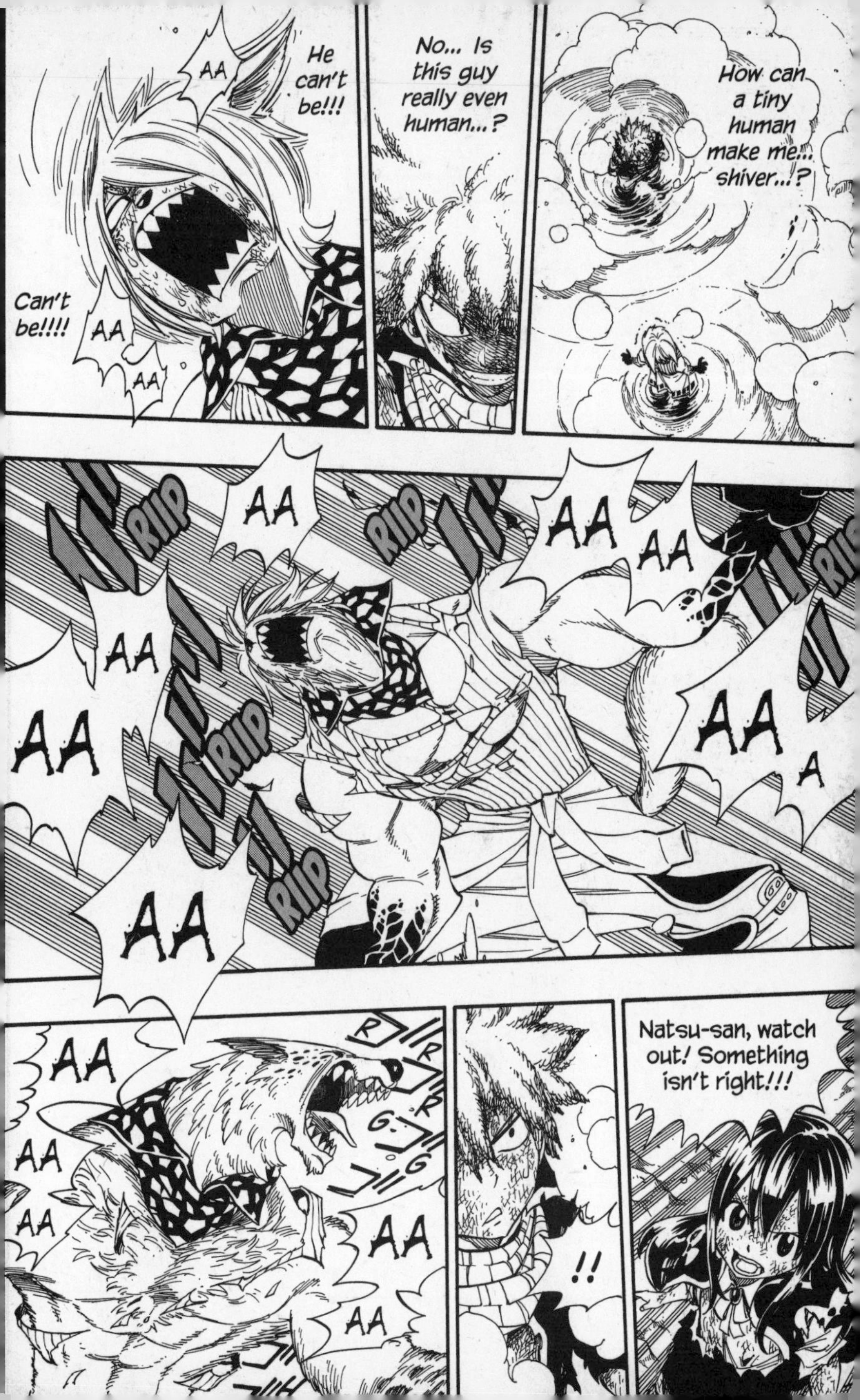
How can a tiny human make me... shiver...?
No... Is this guy really even human...?
AA
He can't be!!!
Can't be!!!!
AA
AA
RIIP
AA
AA
RIIP
AA
A
RIIP
AA
AA
RIIP
AA
AA
Natsu-san, watch out! Something isn't right!!!
!!
R
R
R
G
G
AA
AA
AA
AA
AA

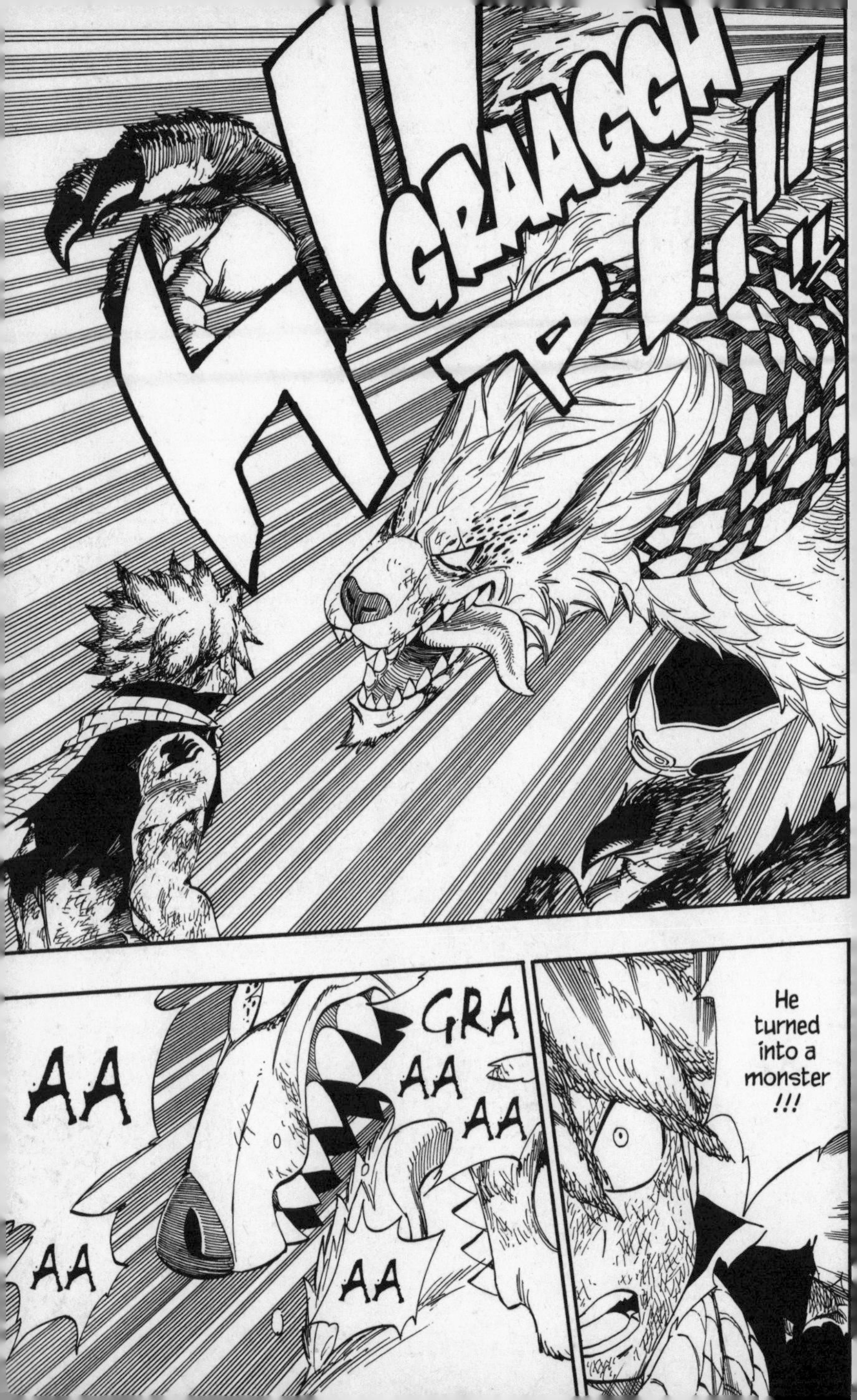
GRAAGGH!!
He turned into a monster!!!
GRA AA AA
AA
AA
AA
AA

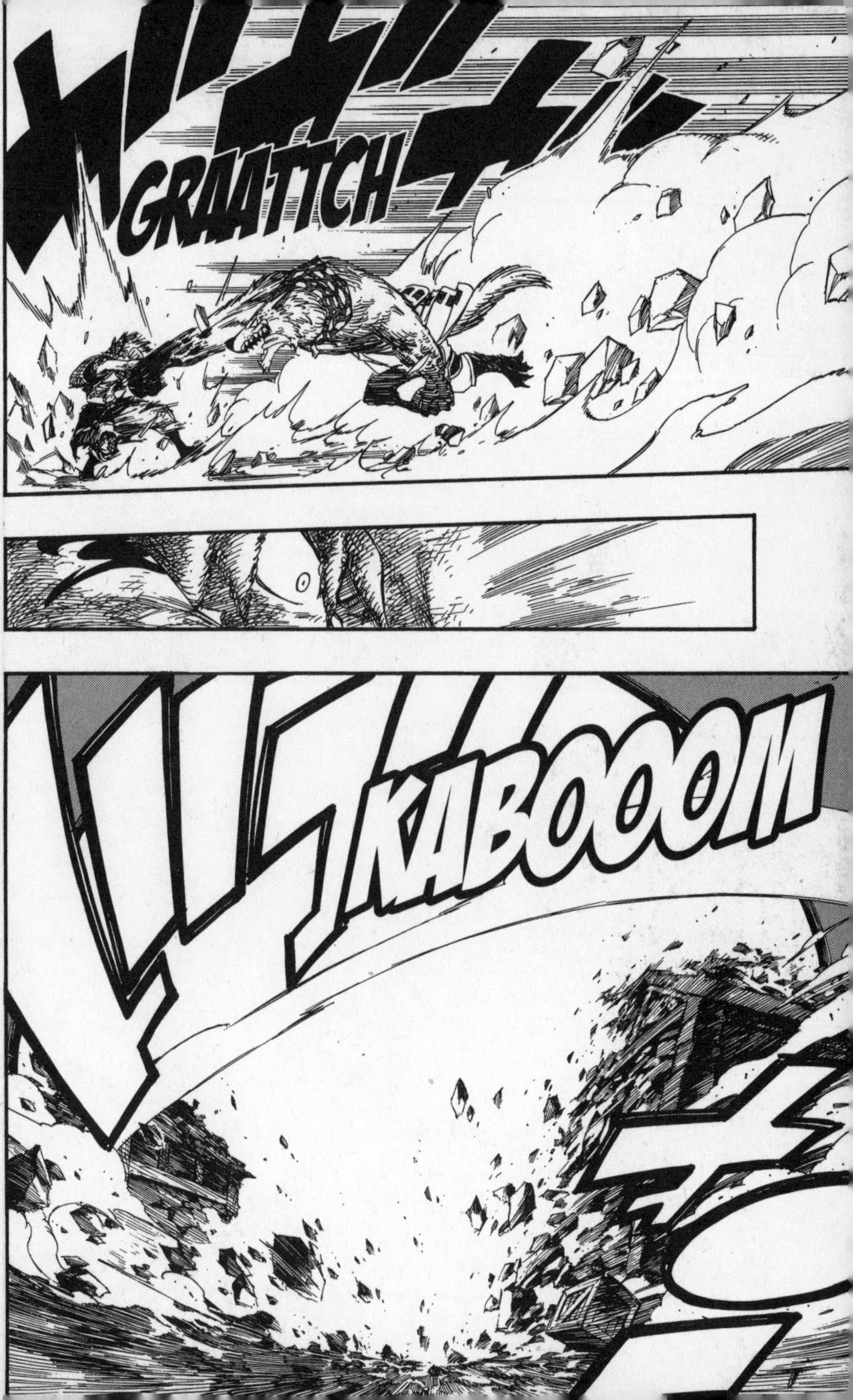
GRAATTCH
KABOOOM

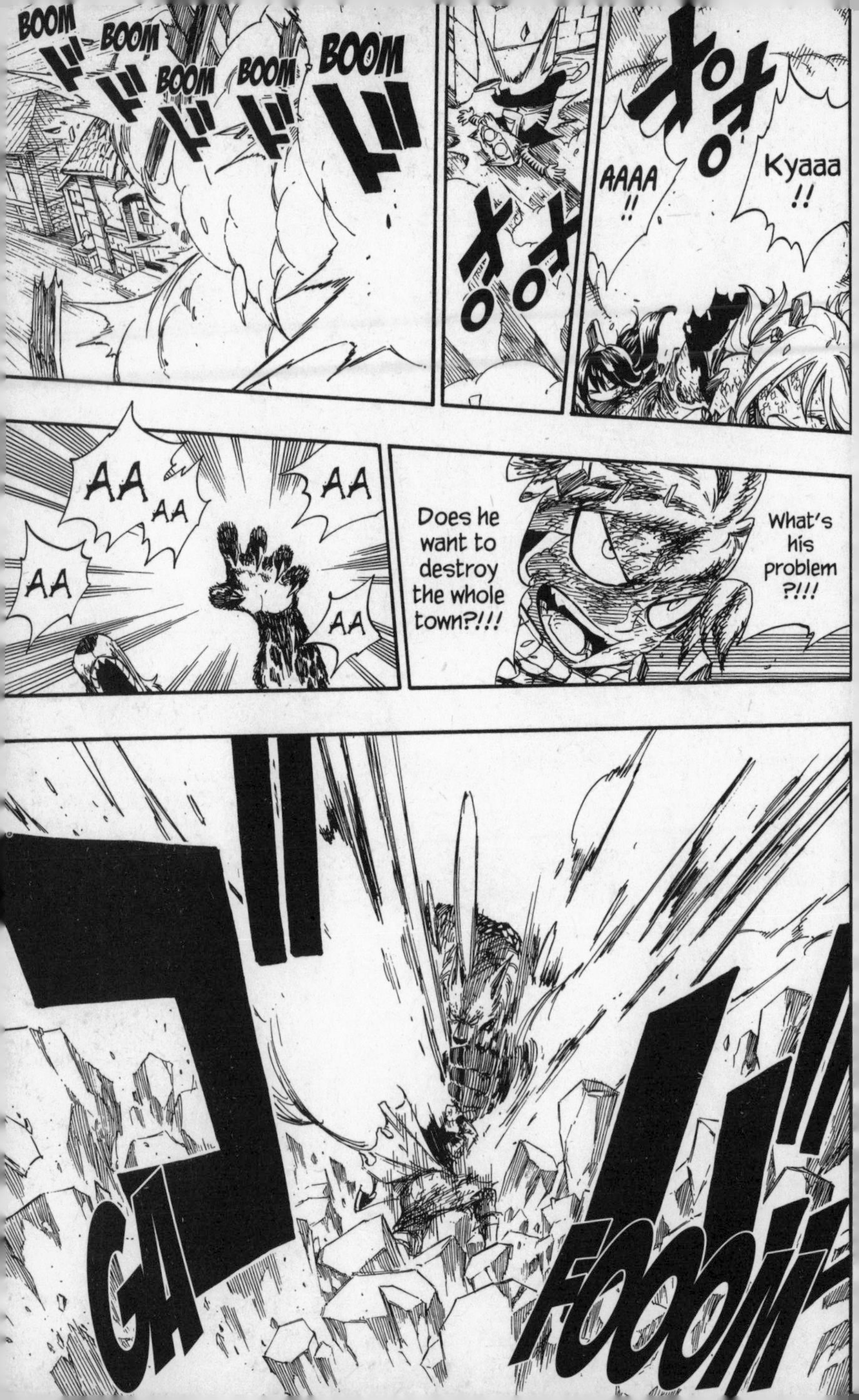
オォォ
Kyaaa!!
AAAA!!
オォォ
BOOM
ド
BOOM
ド
BOOM
ド
BOOM
ド
BOOM
ド
What's his problem?!!!
Does he want to destroy the whole town?!!!
AA
AA
AA
AA
AA
GA
FOOOM!!

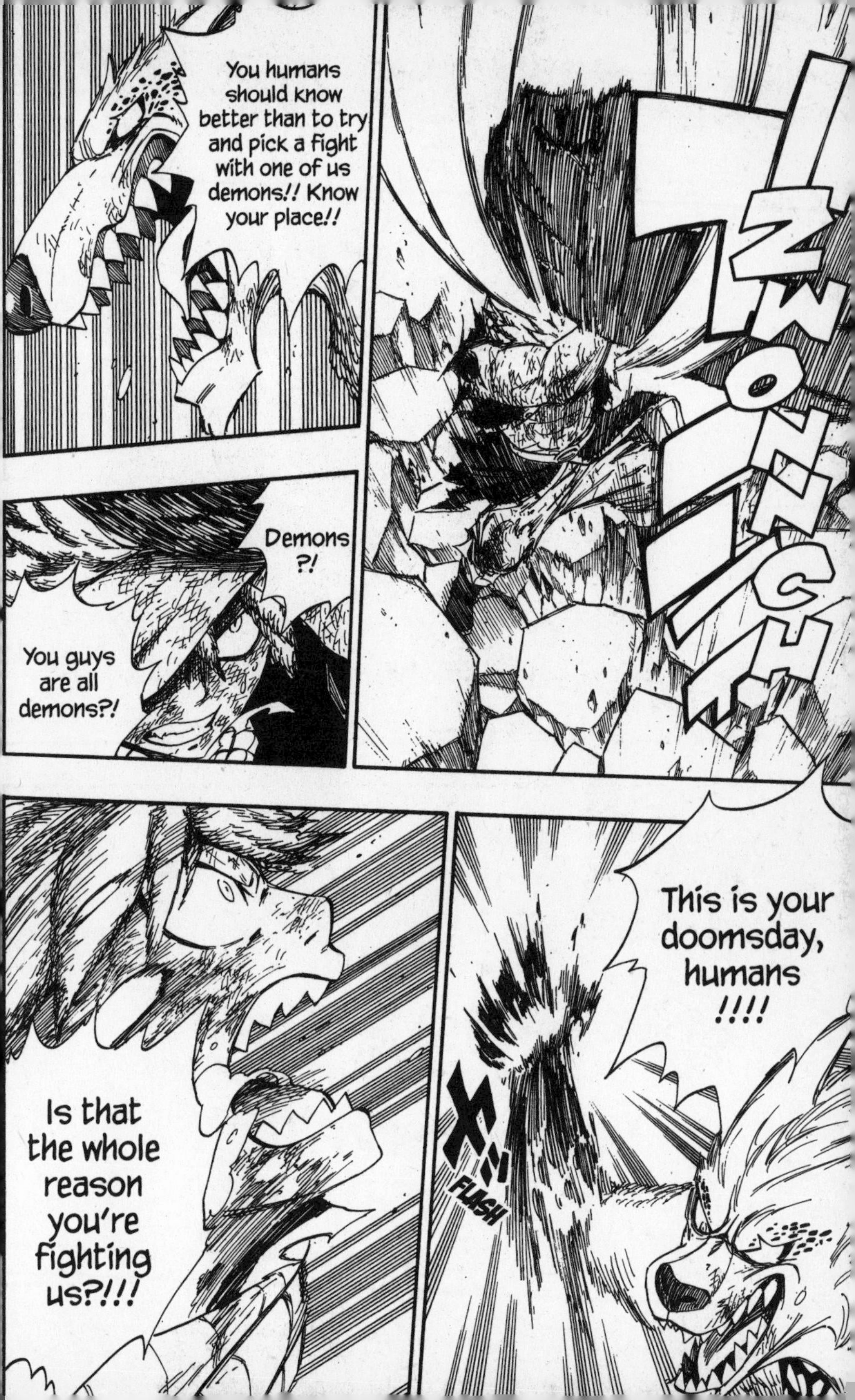
You humans should know better than to try and pick a fight with one of us demons!! Know your place!!
Demons?!
You guys are all demons?!
This is your doomsday, humans!!!!
FLASH
Is that the whole reason you're fighting us?!!!

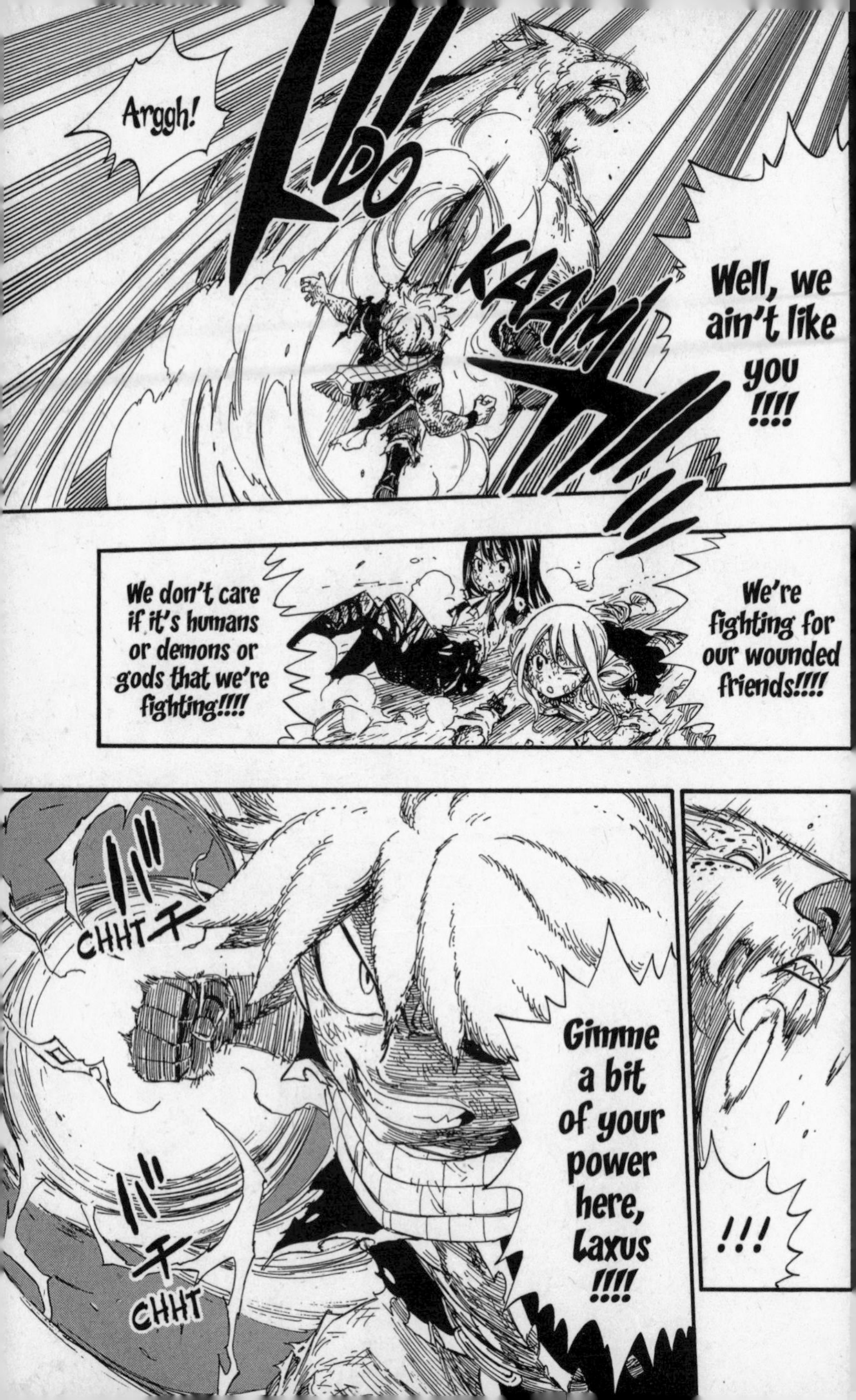
Well, we ain't like you!!!!
DO KAAM
Arggh!
We're fighting for our wounded friends!!!!
We don't care if it's humans or demons or gods that we're fighting!!!!
!!!
Gimme a bit of your power here, Laxus!!!!
CHHT
CHHT

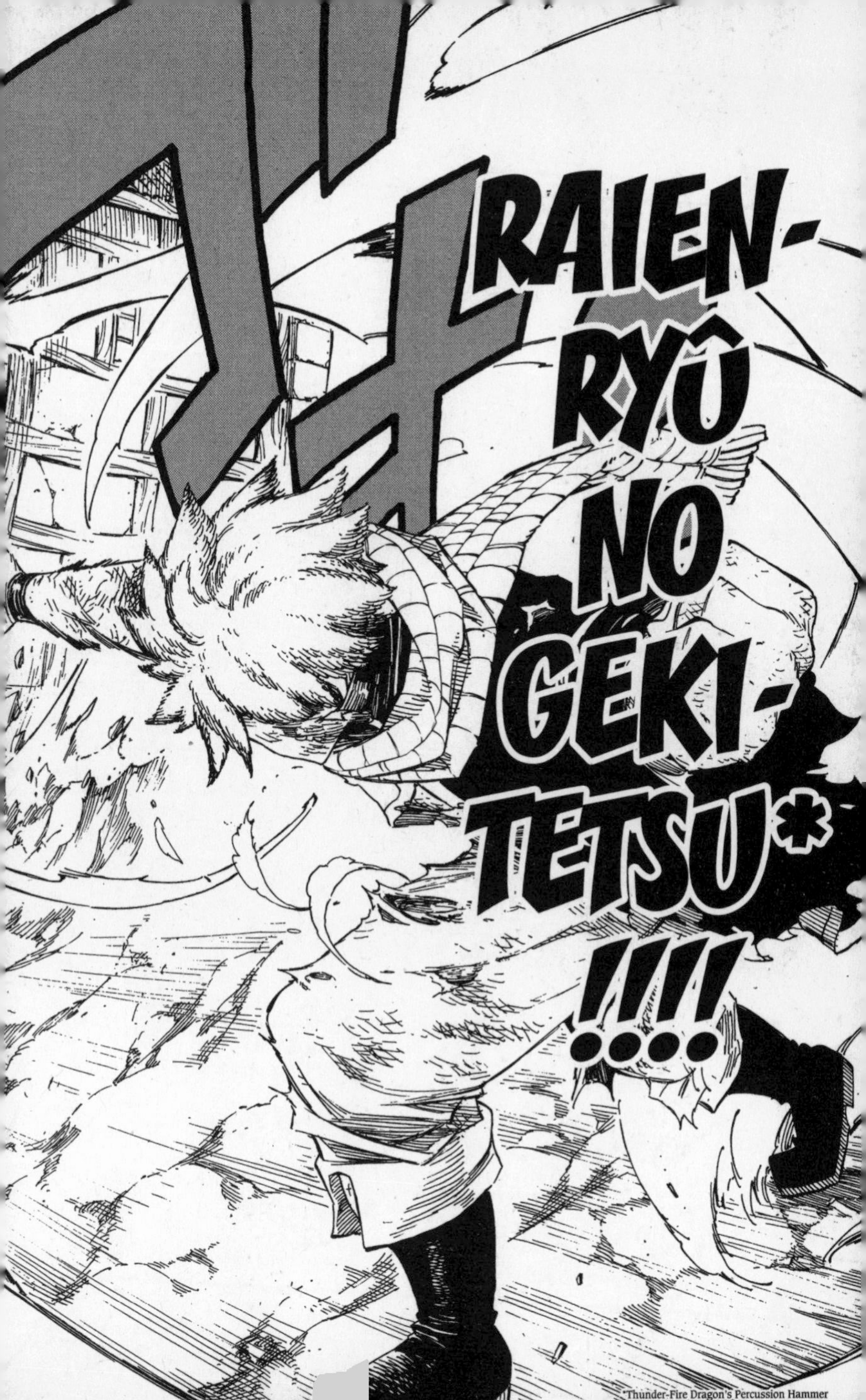
RAIEN-RYÛ NO GEKI-TETSU* !!!!

*Thunder-Fire Dragon's Percussion Hammer

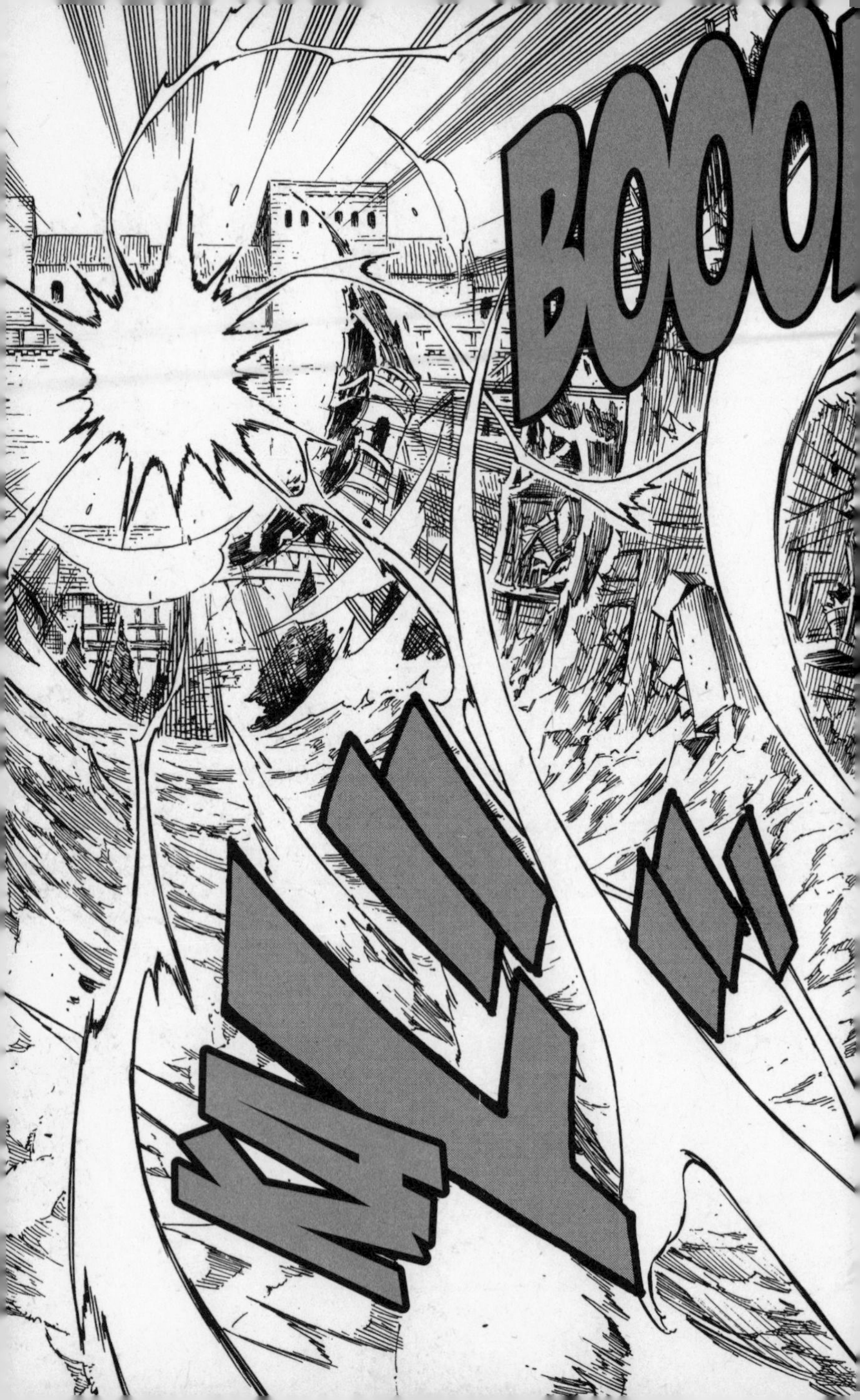
BOOO

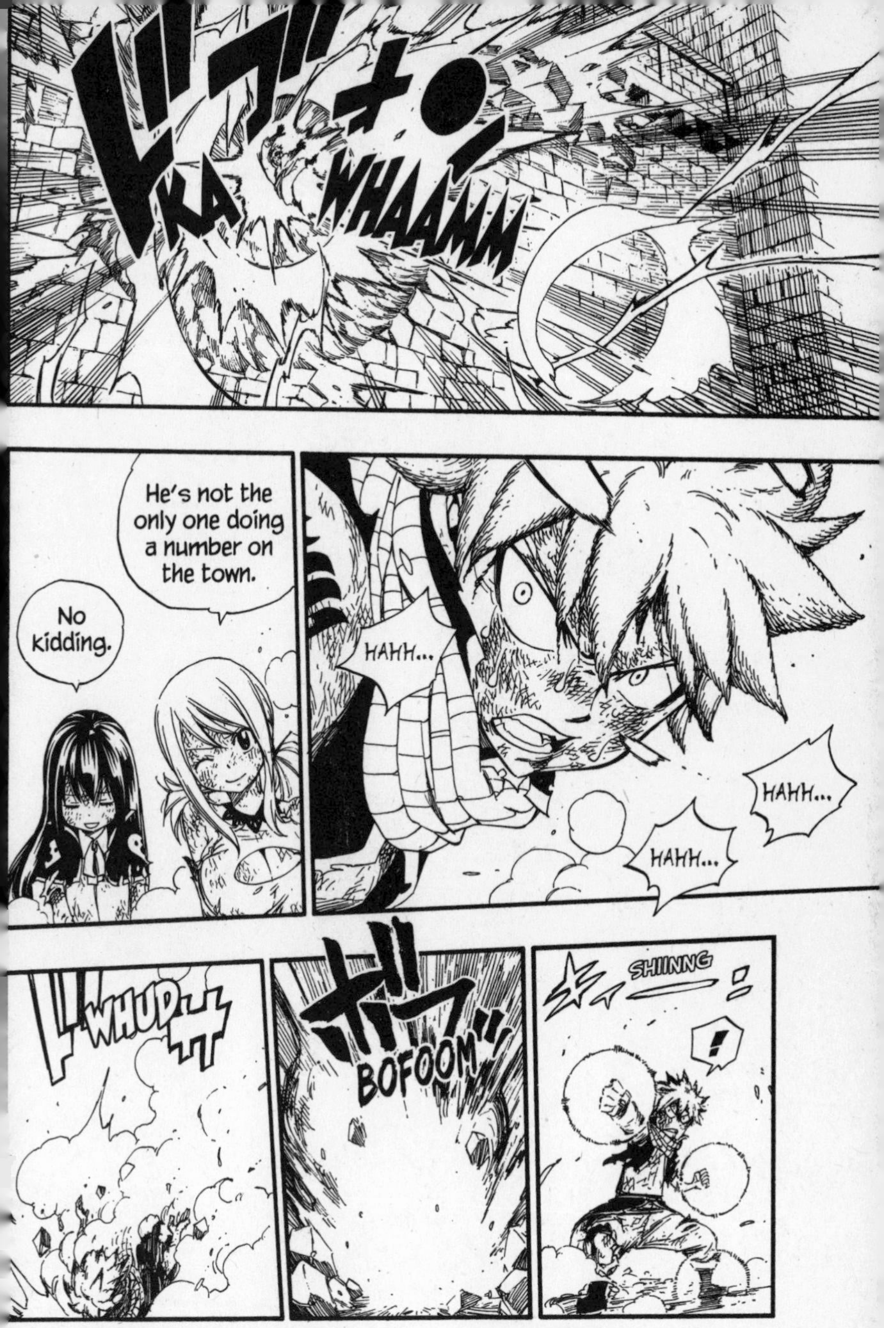
KA-WHAAMM
HAHH...
HAHH...
HAHH...
He's not the only one doing a number on the town.
No kidding.
SHIINNG
!
BOFOOM
WHUD

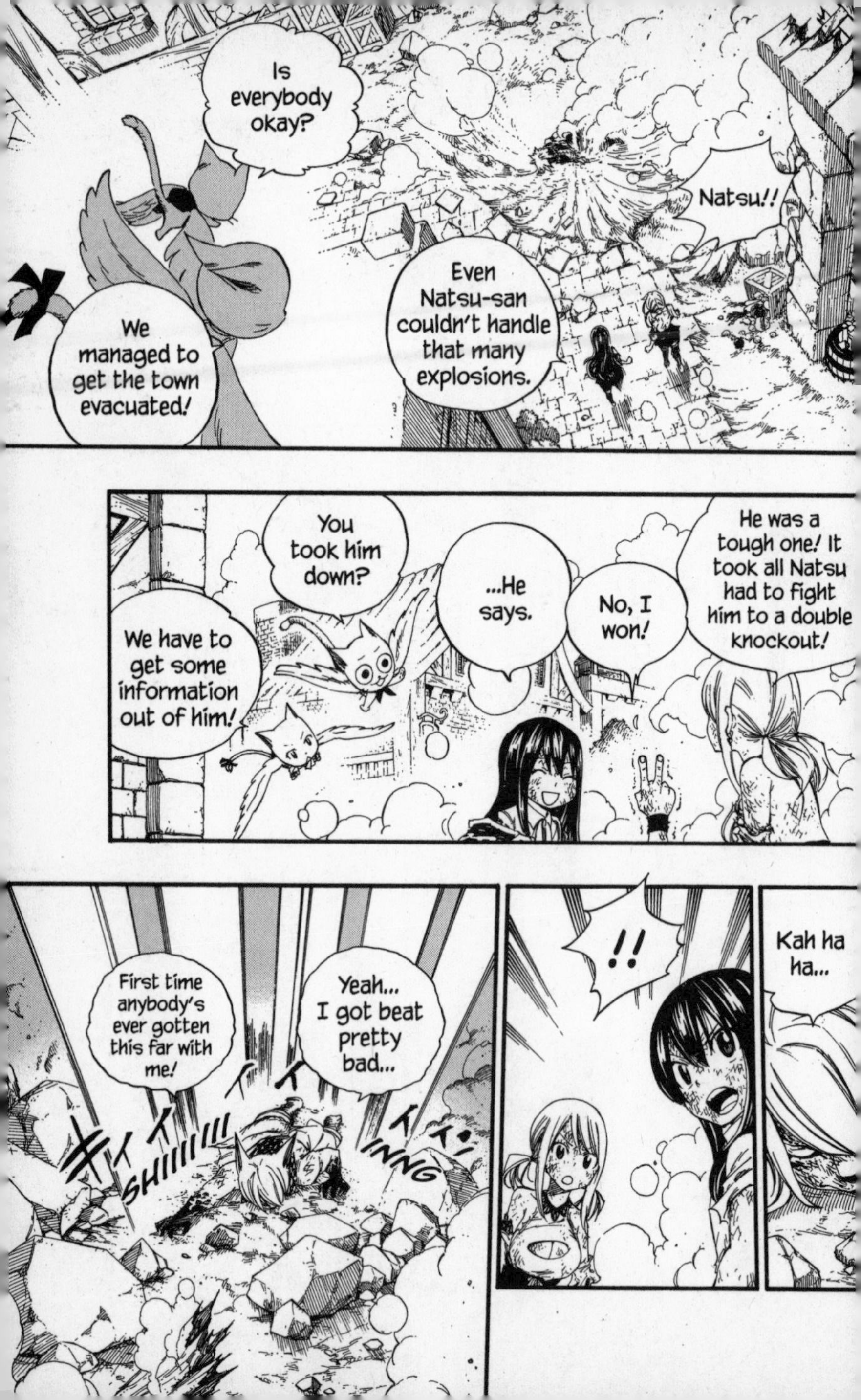
Natsu!!
Is everybody okay?
Even Natsu-san couldn't handle that many explosions.
We managed to get the town evacuated!
He was a tough one! It took all Natsu had to fight him to a double knockout!
No, I won!
...He says.
You took him down?
We have to get some information out of him!
Kah ha ha...
!!
Yeah... I got beat pretty bad...
First time anybody's ever gotten this far with me!
SHIIIIII
INNG

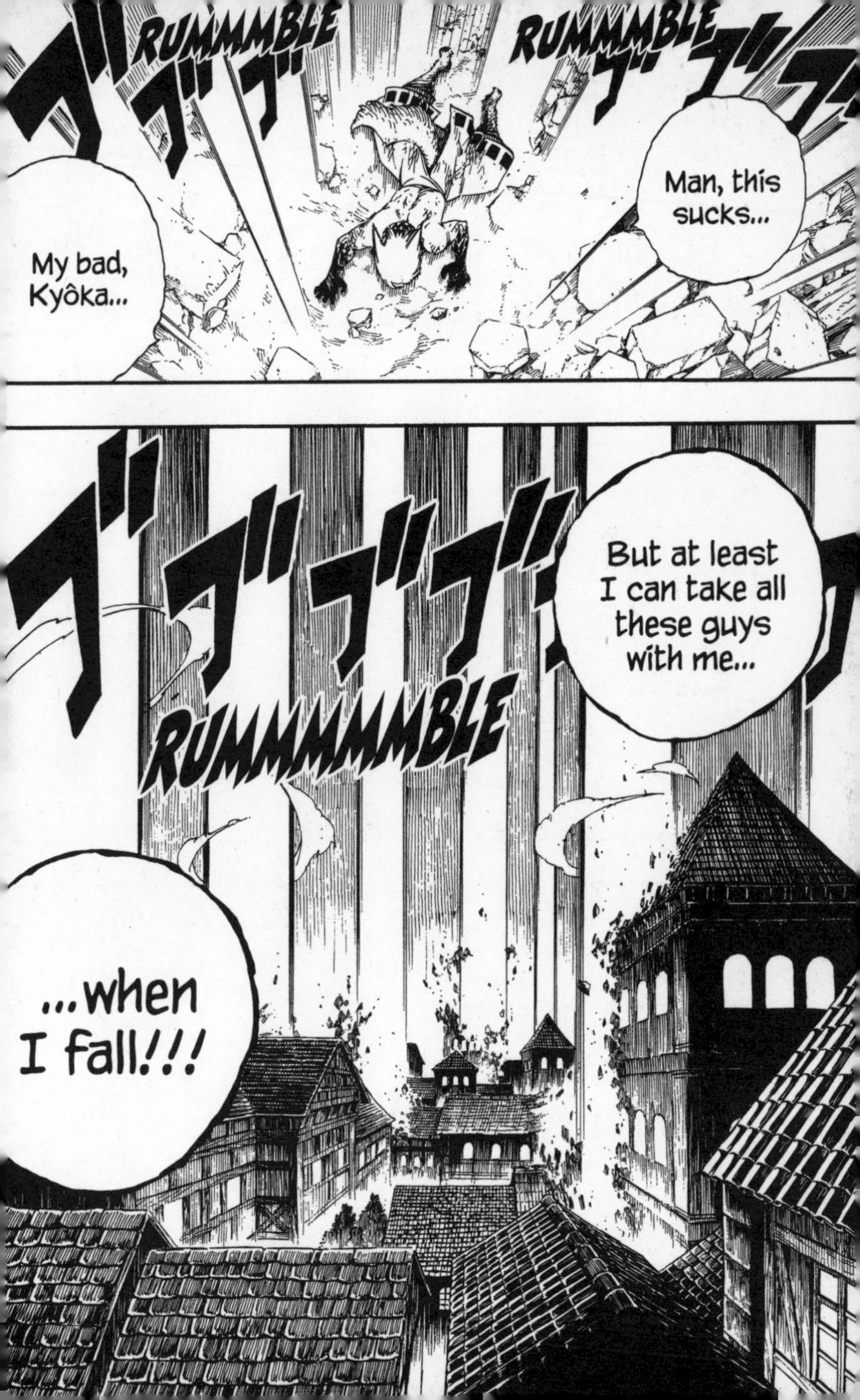
RUMMMBLE
RUMMMBLE
Man, this sucks...
My bad, Kyôka...
RUMMMMMBLE
But at least I can take all these guys with me...
...when I fall!!!

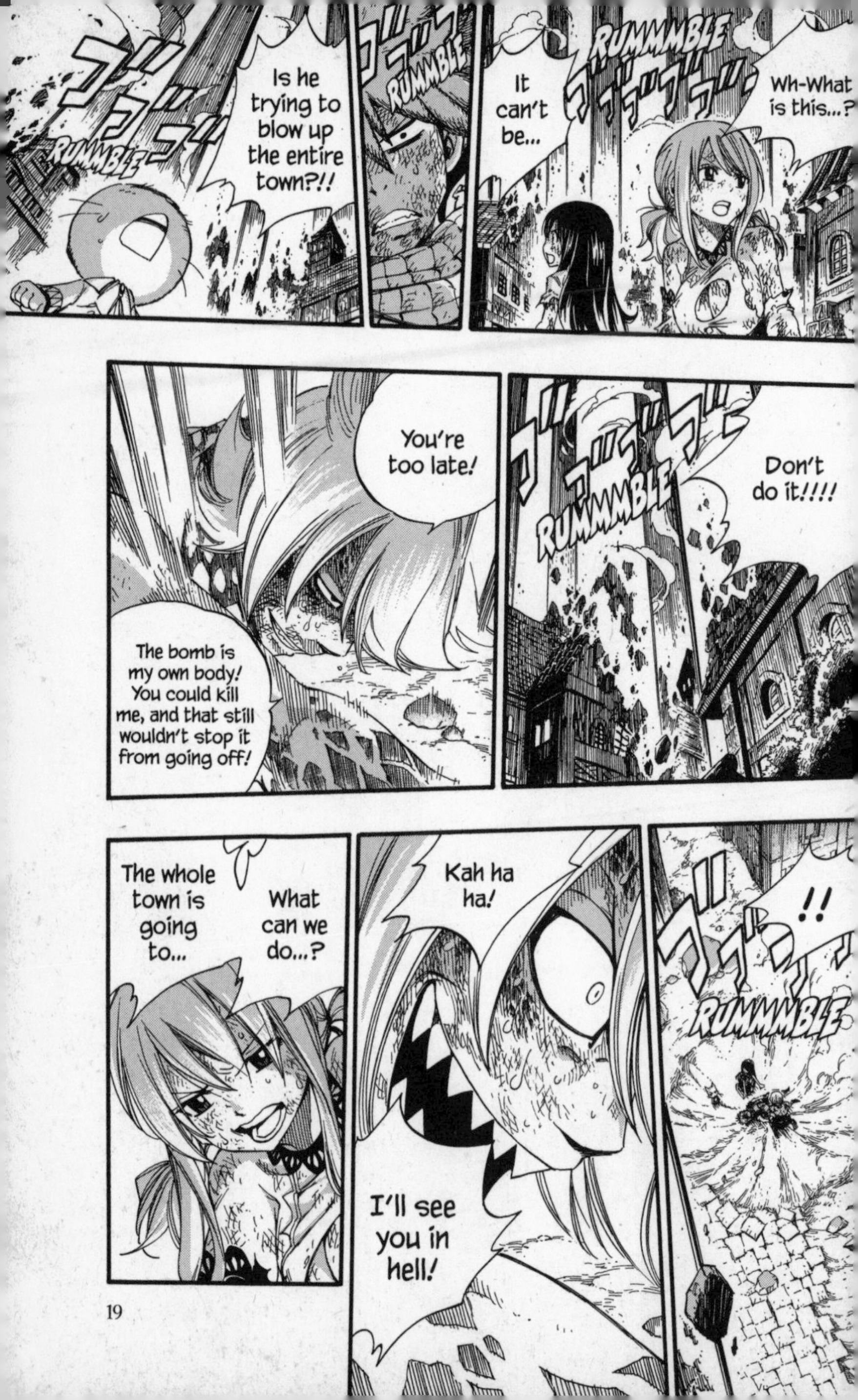

Wh-What is this...?
RUMMMBLE
It can't be...
RUMMBLE
RUMMBLE
Is he trying to blow up the entire town?!!
Don't do it!!!!
RUMMMBLE
You're too late!
The bomb is my own body! You could kill me, and that still wouldn't stop it from going off!
!!
RUMMMBLE
Kah ha ha!
I'll see you in hell!
What can we do...?
The whole town is going to...

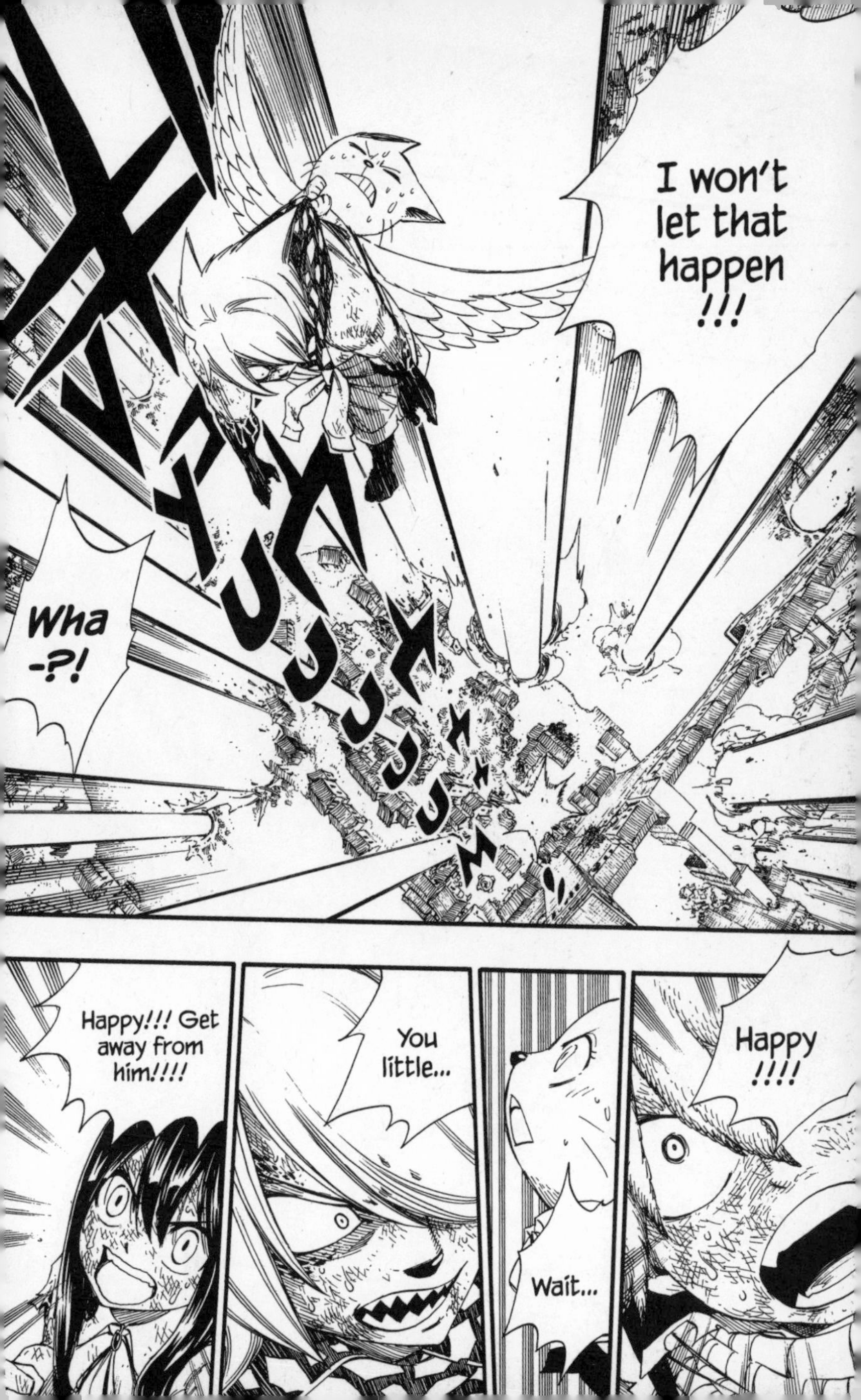
I won't let that happen!!!
Wha-?!
Happy!!!!
Wait...
You little...
Happy!!! Get away from him!!!!

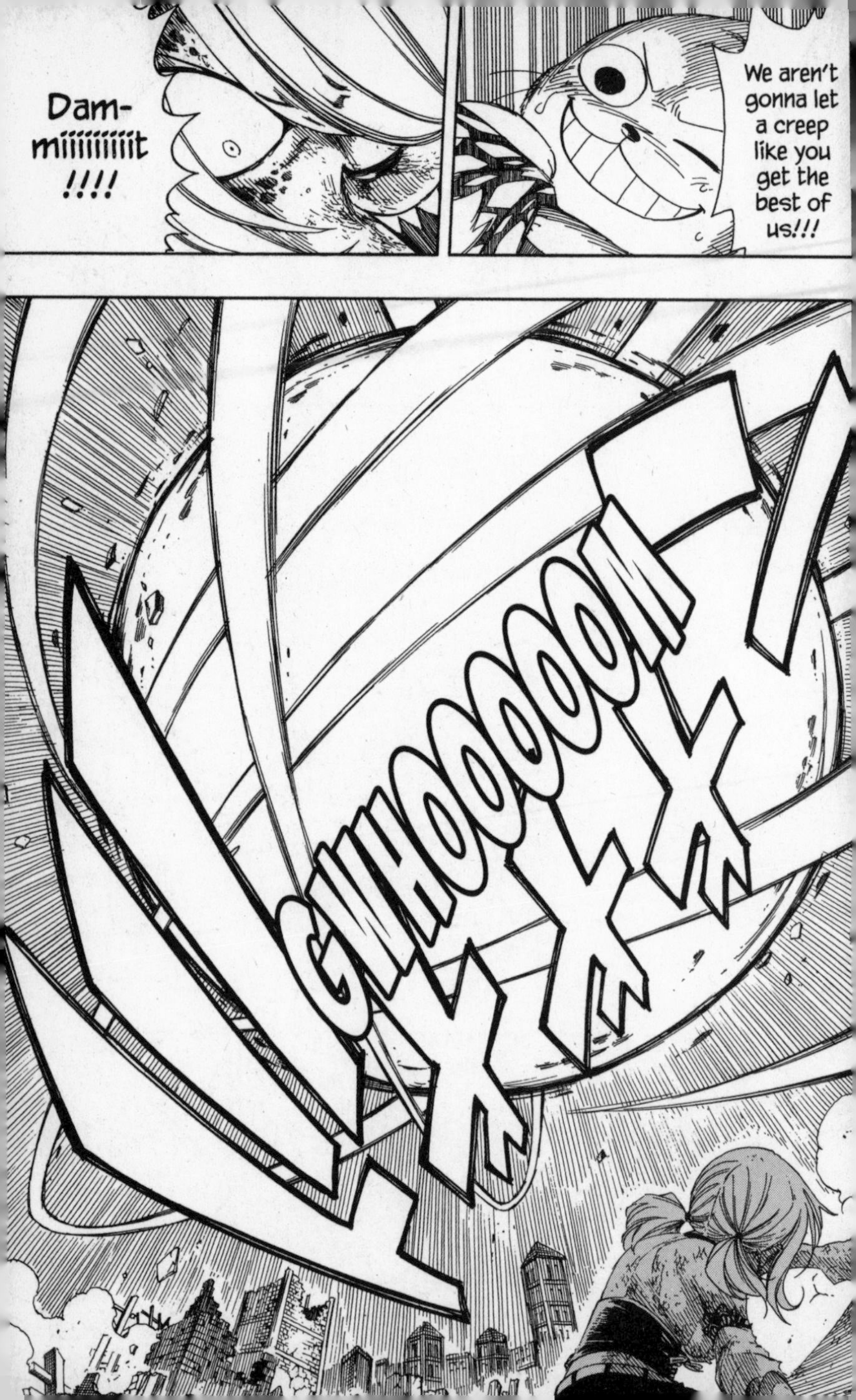
We aren't gonna let a creep like you get the best of us!!!
Dam-miiiiiiiiiit!!!!
GWHOOOOON

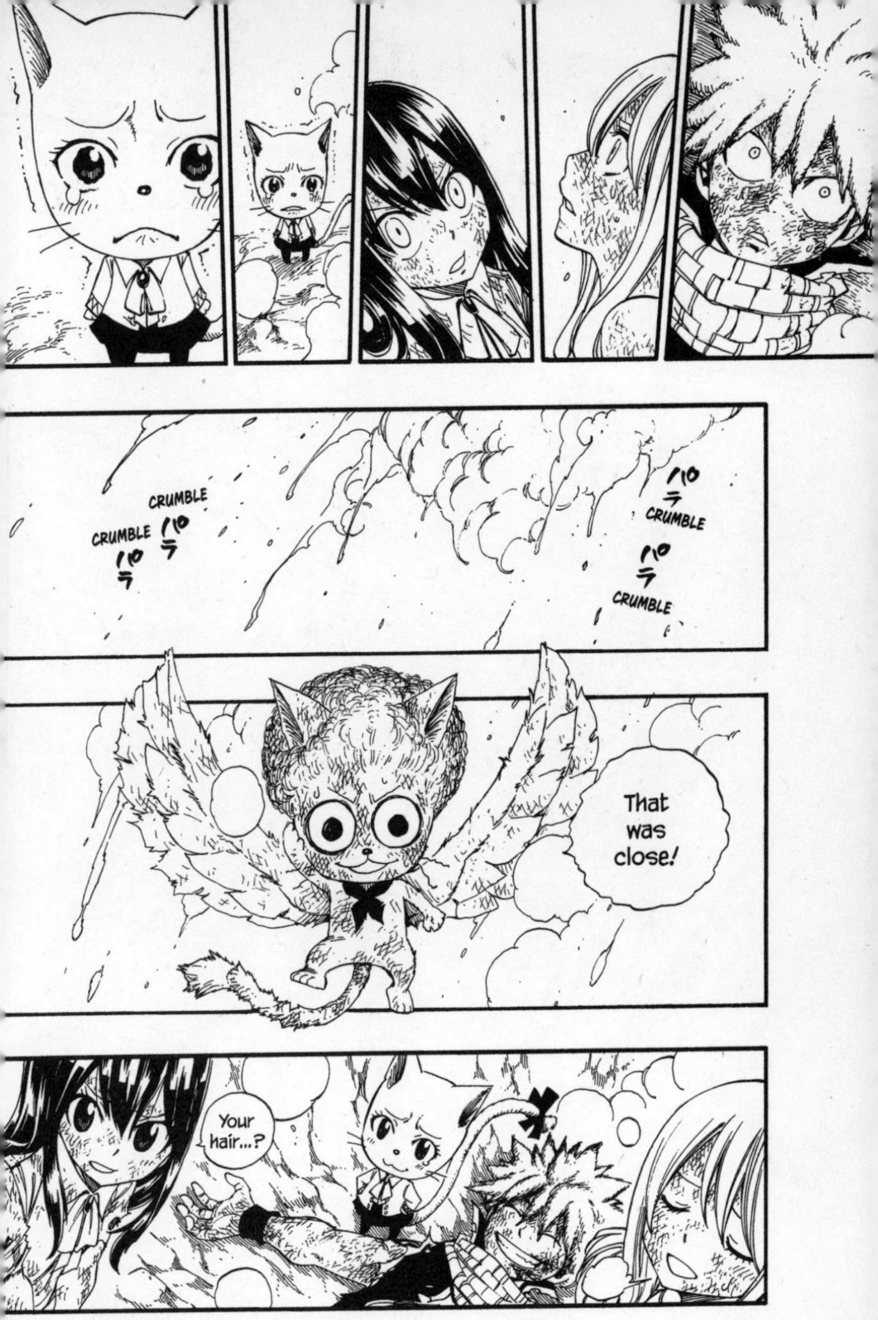
パラ
CRUMBLE
パラ
CRUMBLE
CRUMBLE
パラ
CRUMBLE
パラ
That was close!
Your hair...?

FAIRY TAIL

Chapter 363: Stories that Demons Read

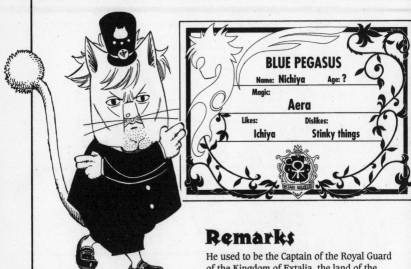

BLUE PEGASUS

Name: **Nichiya**   Age: **?**

Magic:

Aera

Likes: Dislikes:

Ichiya   **Stinky things**

Remarks

He used to be the Captain of the Royal Guard of the Kingdom of Extalia, the land of the Exceed (cats). Even after he arrived in this world, he remained captain of the guard for the group of Exceed, but when he learned how many beings out there were stronger than he was, he stepped down from the position. After that, he met Ichiya, and he left the Exceed's group to take a place with Blue Pegasus.

Before his appearance at the Grand Magic Games, he, Ichiya, and Master Bob were the only ones who knew he had joined.

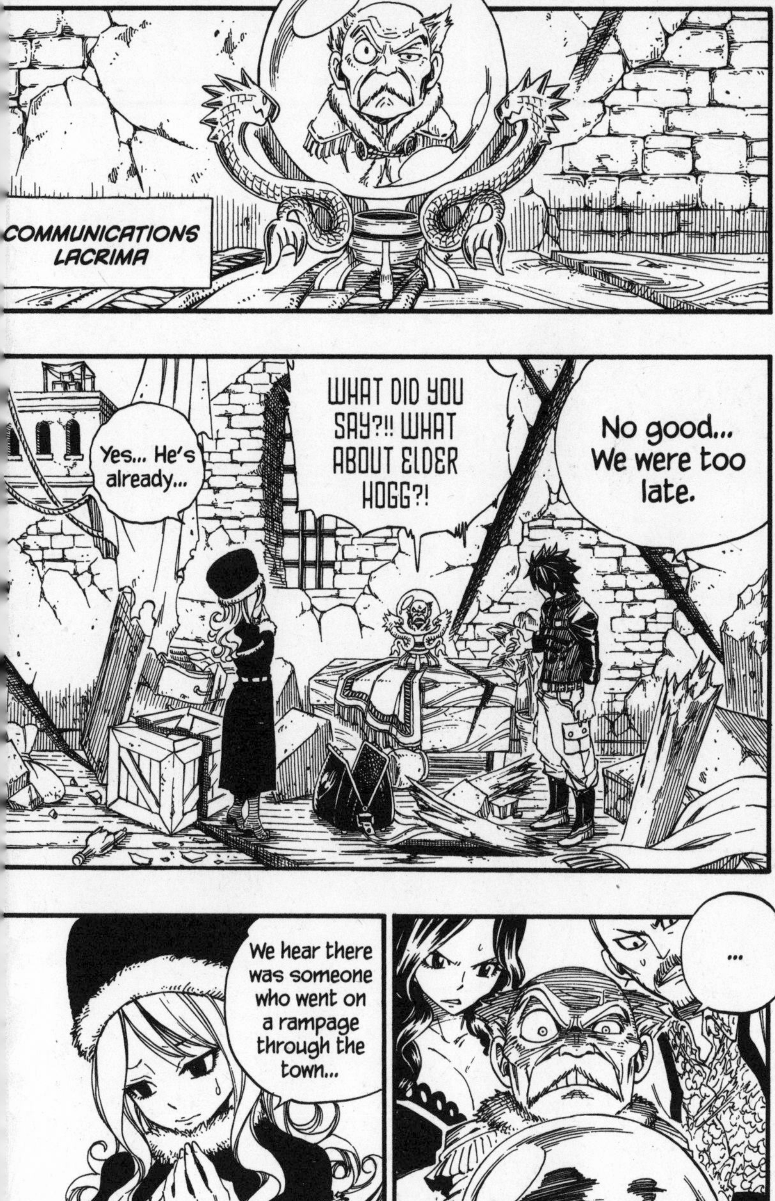
COMMUNICATIONS LACRIMA
No good... We were too late.
WHAT DID YOU SAY?!! WHAT ABOUT ELDER HOGG?!
Yes... He's already...
...
We hear there was someone who went on a rampage through the town...

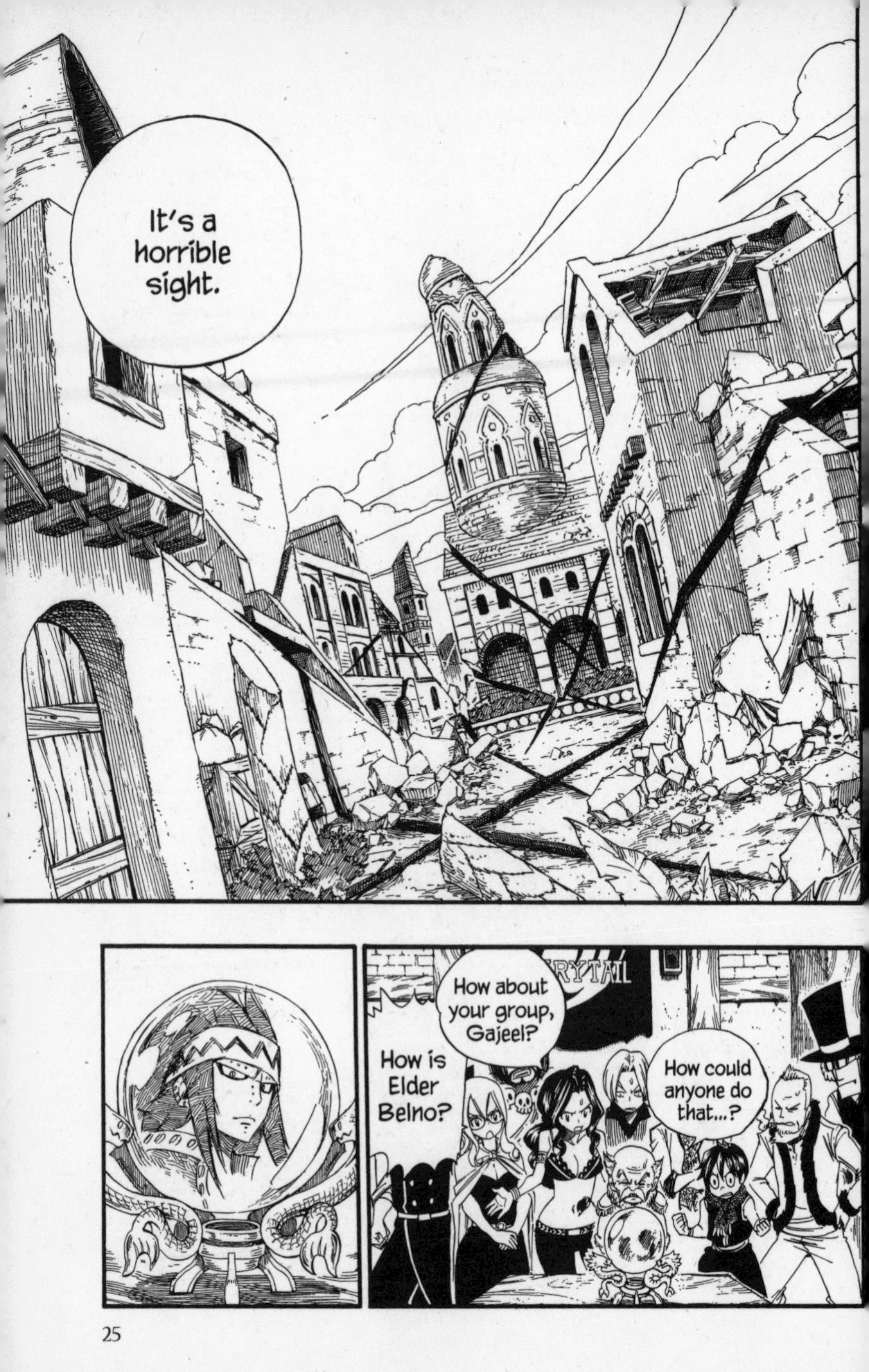
It's a horrible sight.
How could anyone do that...?
How about your group, Gajeel?
How is Elder Belno?

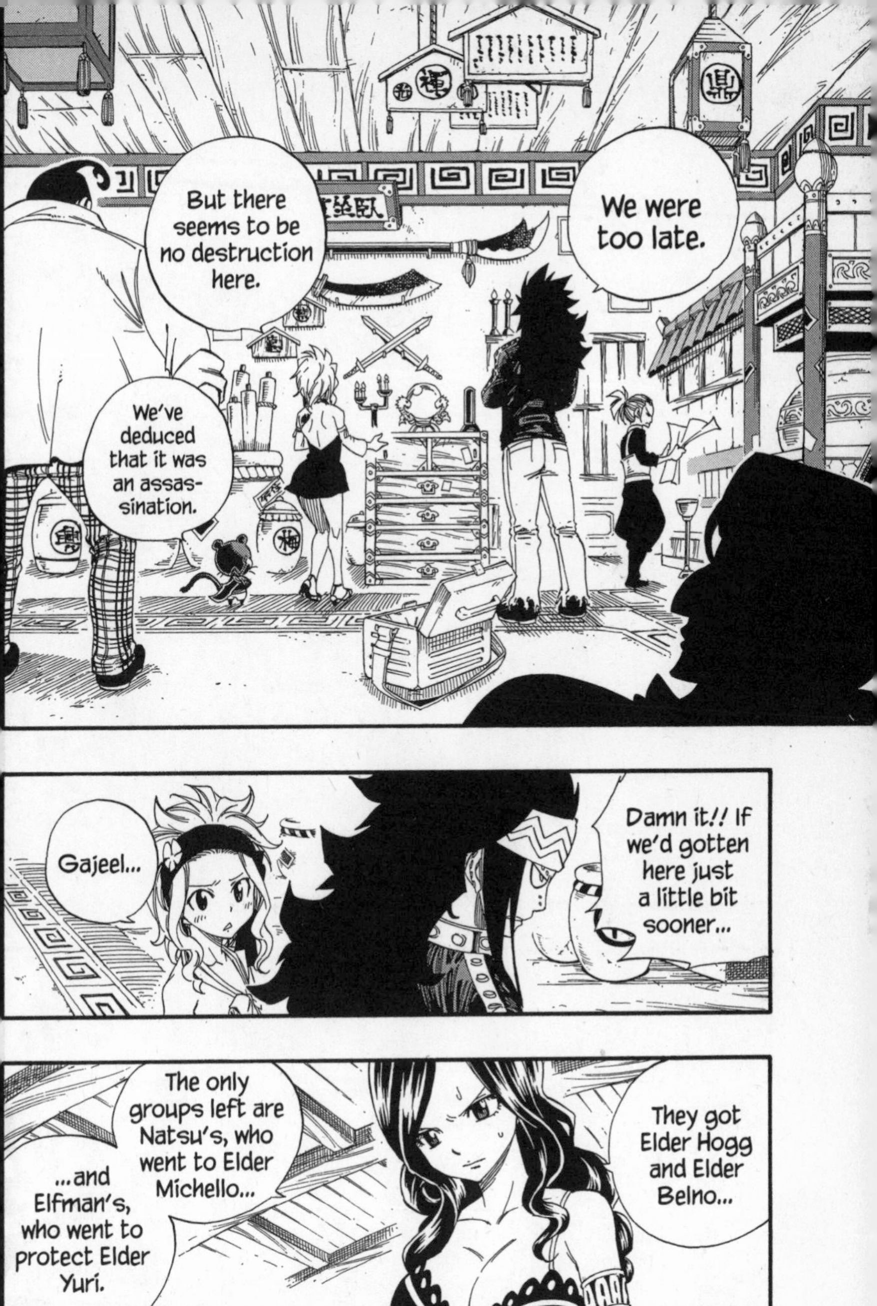
We were too late.
But there seems to be no destruction here.
We've deduced that it was an assas-sination.
Damn it!! If we'd gotten here just a little bit sooner...
Gajeel...
They got Elder Hogg and Elder Belno...
The only groups left are Natsu's, who went to Elder Michello...
...and Elfman's, who went to protect Elder Yuri.

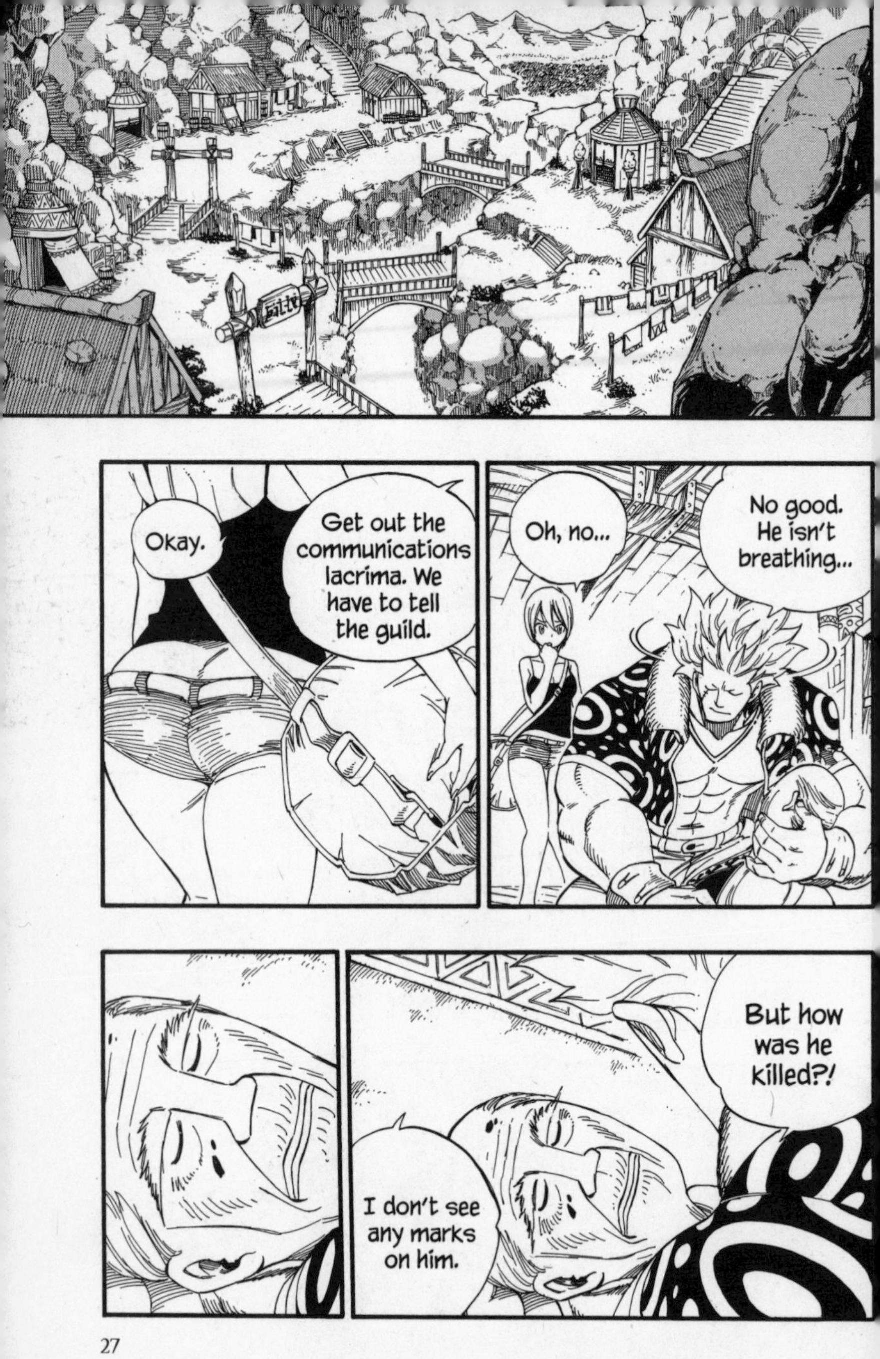
No good. He isn't breathing...
Oh, no...
Get out the communications lacrima. We have to tell the guild.
Okay.
But how was he killed?!
I don't see any marks on him.

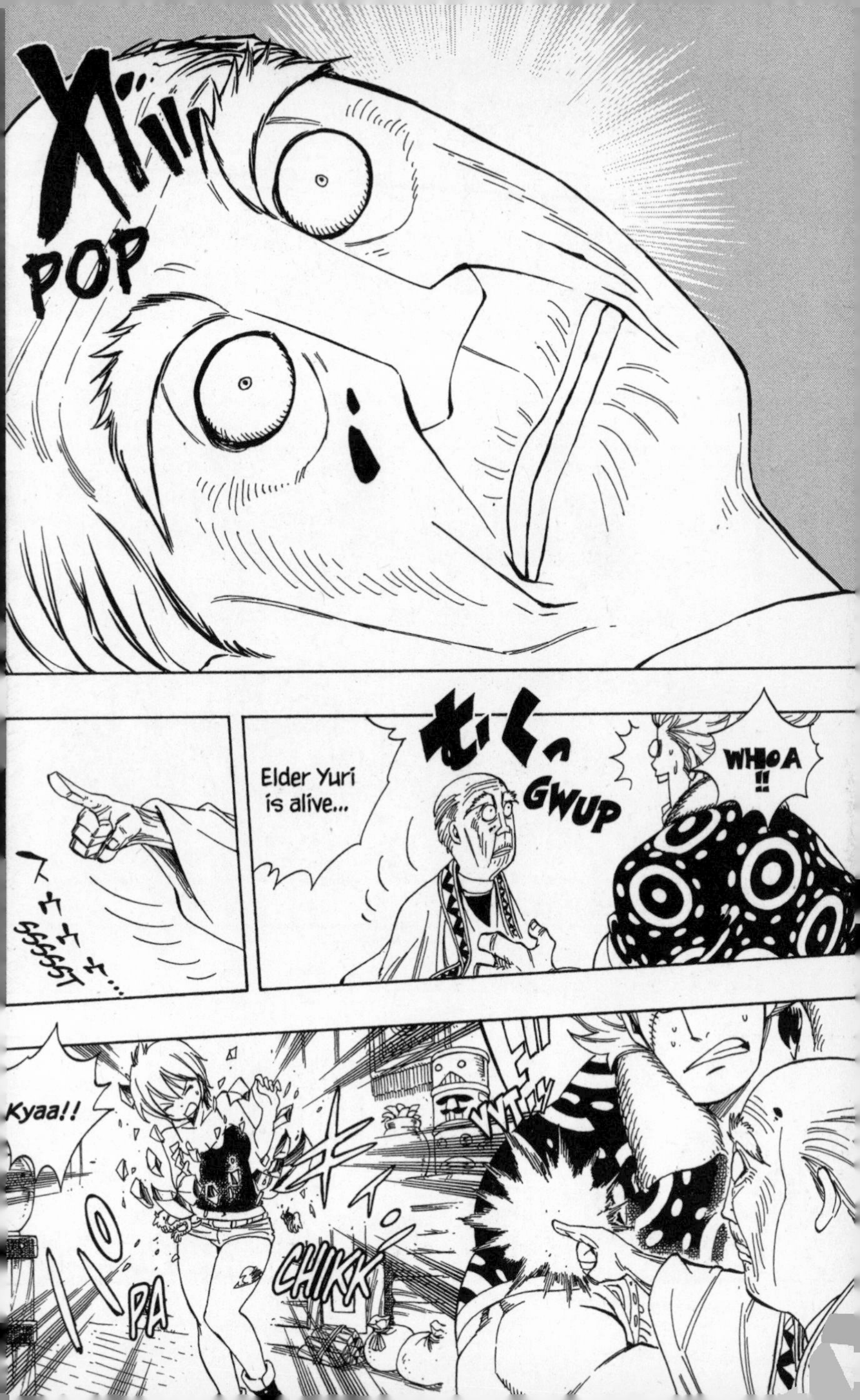

POP
WHOA !!
GWUP
Elder Yuri is alive...
SSSSST...
CHIKK
PA
Kyaa!!

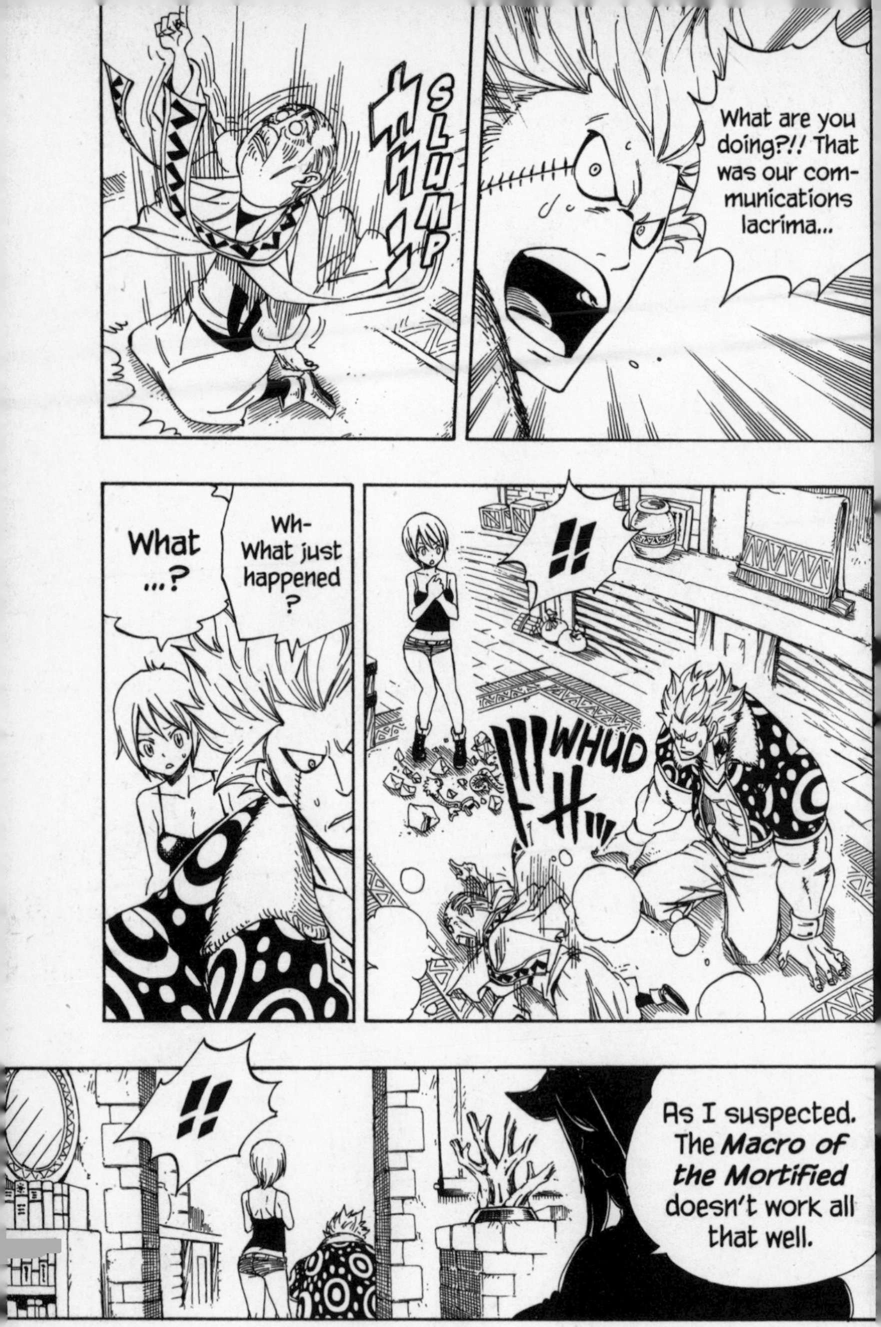
What are you doing?!! That was our communications lacrima...
SLUMP
!!
WHUD
Wh- What just happened?
What ...?
As I suspected. The Macro of the Mortified doesn't work all that well.
!!

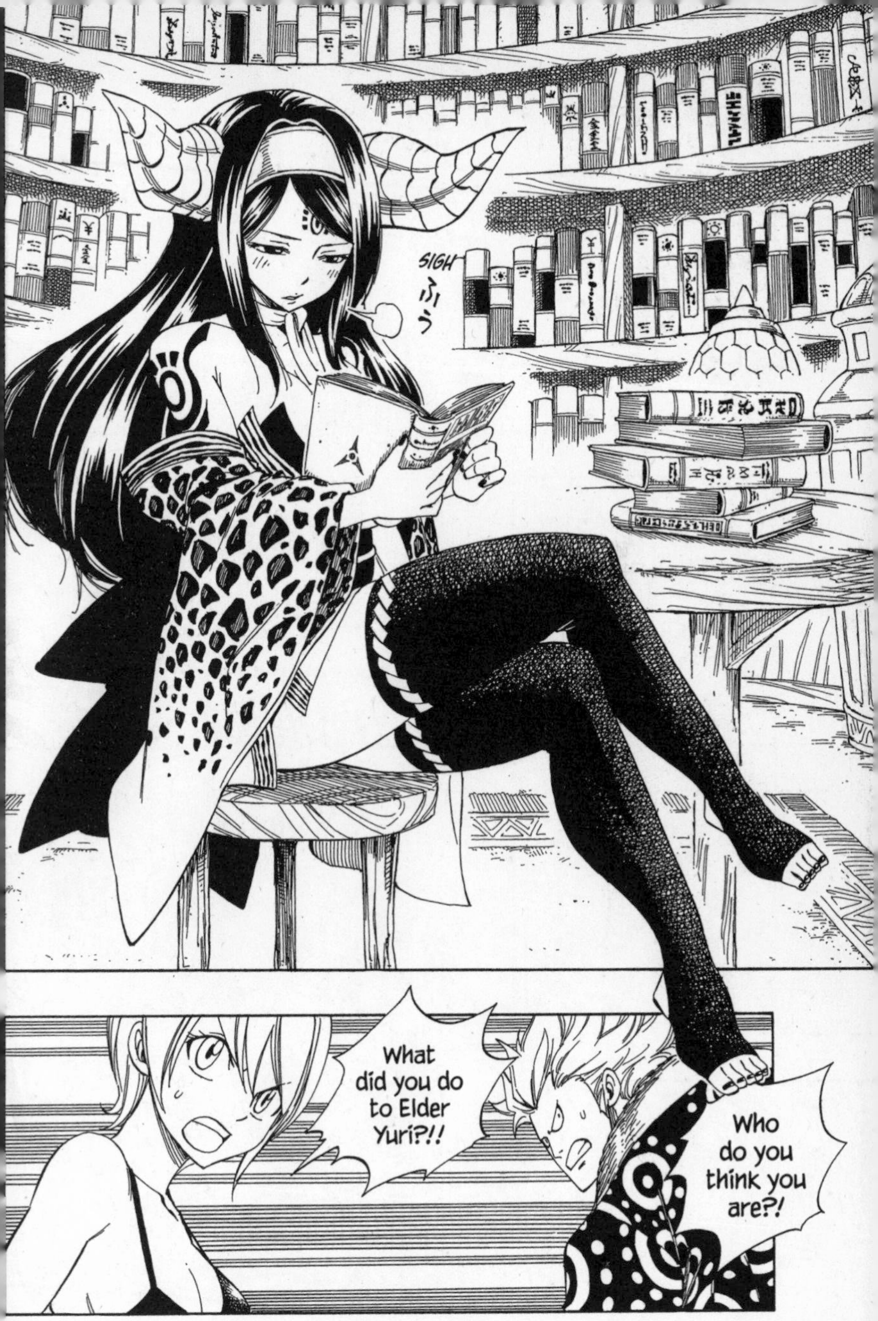
SIGH
ふう
Who do you think you are?!
What did you do to Elder Yuri?!!

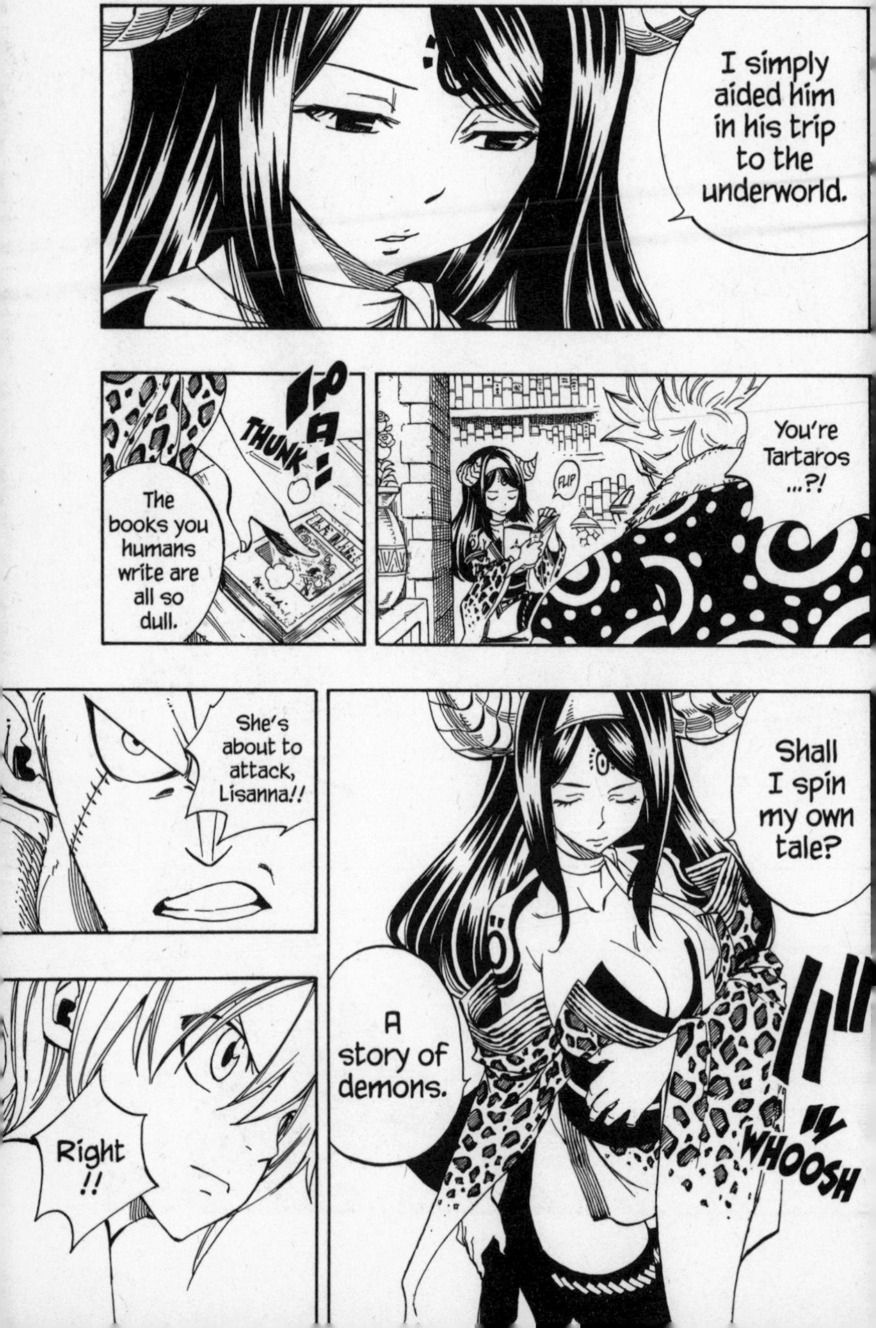
I simply aided him in his trip to the underworld.
You're Tartaros ...?!
FLIP
THUNK
The books you humans write are all so dull.
Shall I spin my own tale?
A story of demons.
WHOOSH
She's about to attack, Lisanna!!
Right !!

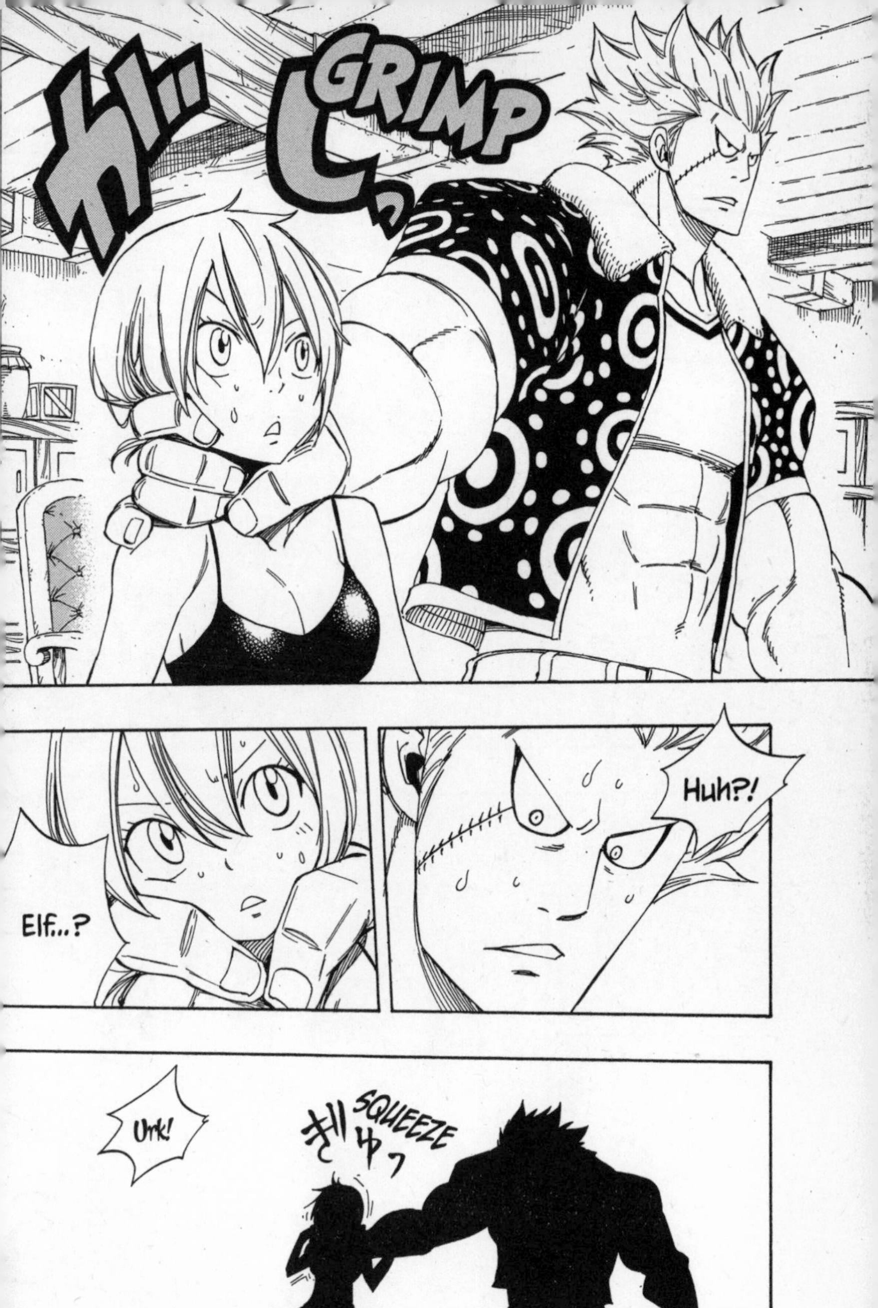
GRIMP
Huh?!
Elf...?
SQUEEZE
Urk!

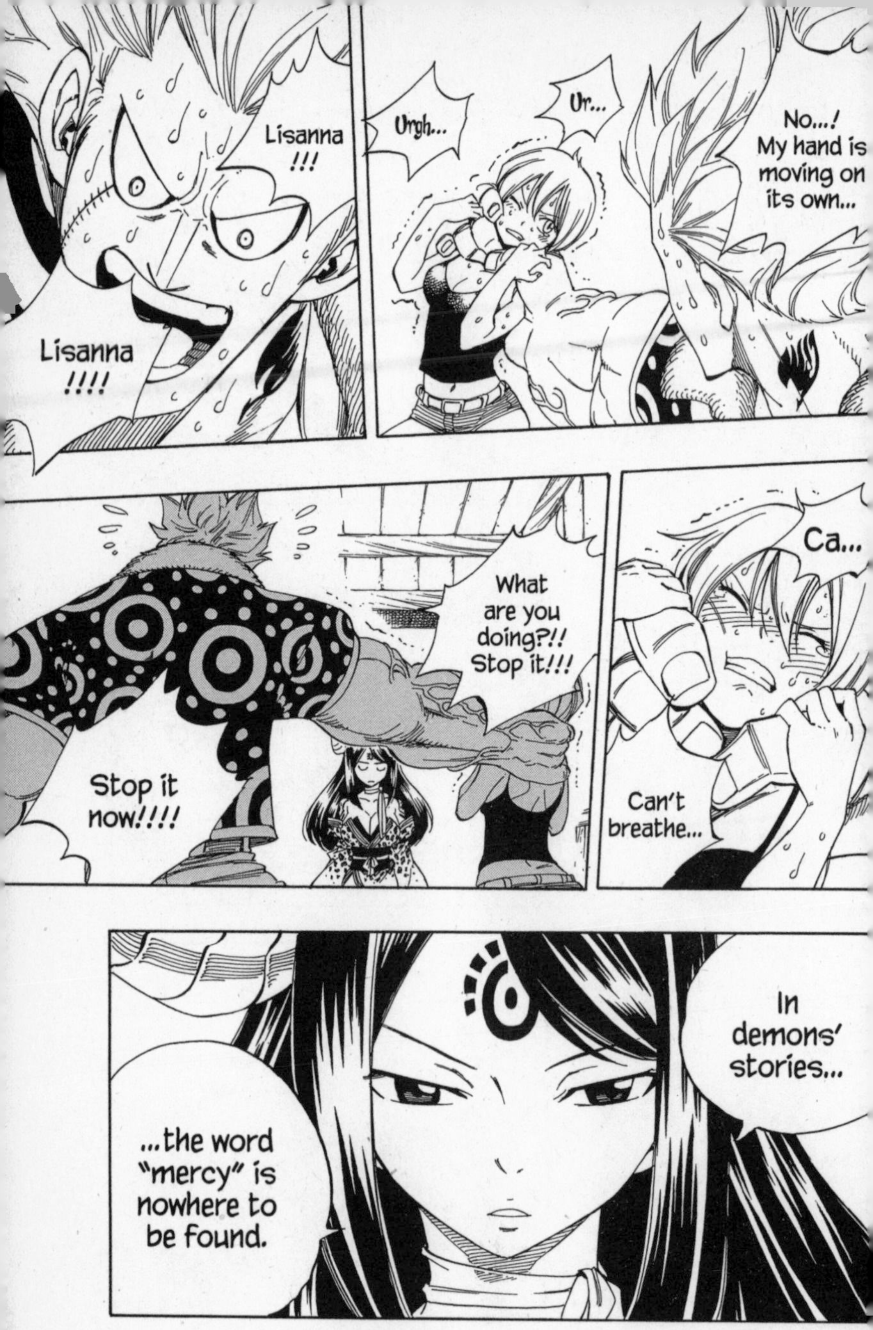

No...! My hand is moving on its own...
Ur...
Urgh...
Lisanna!!!
Lisanna!!!!
Ca...
Can't breathe...
What are you doing?!! Stop it!!!
Stop it now!!!!
In demons' stories...
...the word "mercy" is nowhere to be found.

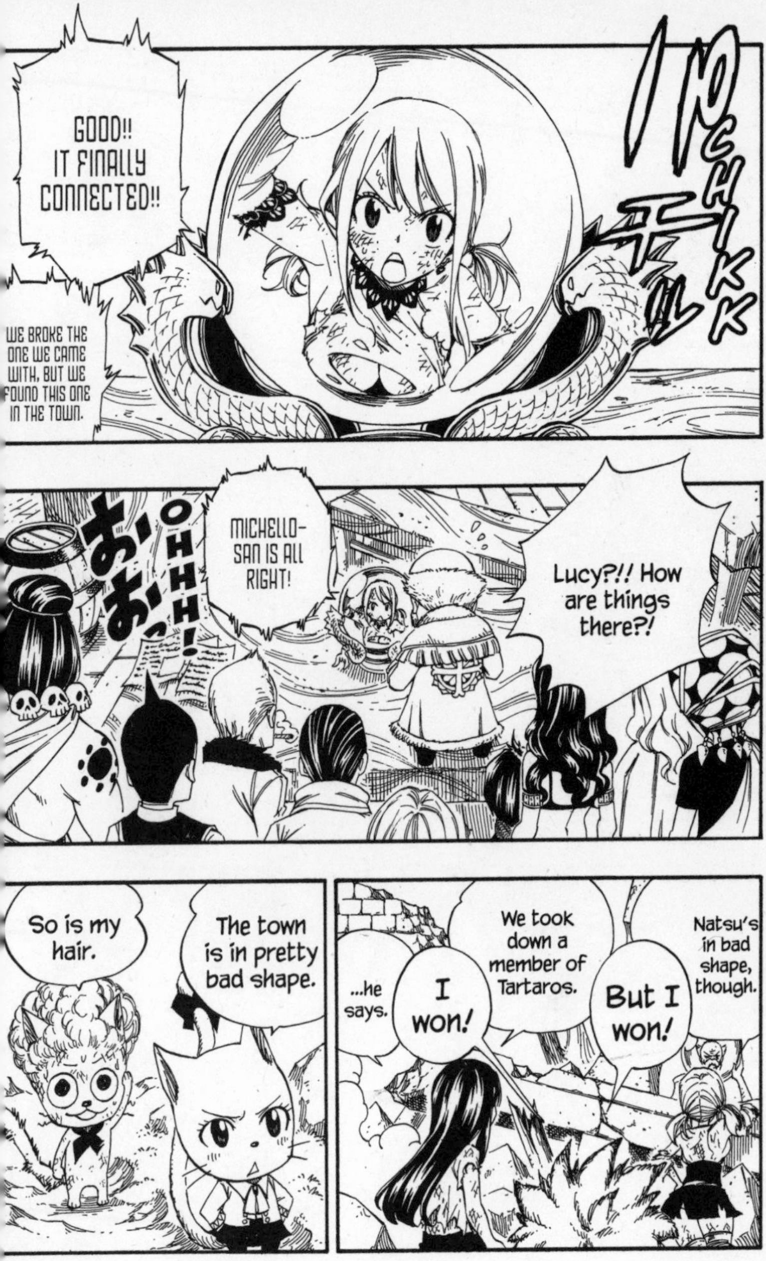
CHIKKK
GOOD!! IT FINALLY CONNECTED!!
WE BROKE THE ONE WE CAME WITH, BUT WE FOUND THIS ONE IN THE TOWN.
Lucy?!! How are things there?!
MICHELLO-SAN IS ALL RIGHT!
OHHHH!
Natsu's in bad shape, though.
But I won!
We took down a member of Tartaros.
I won!
...he says.
The town is in pretty bad shape.
So is my hair.

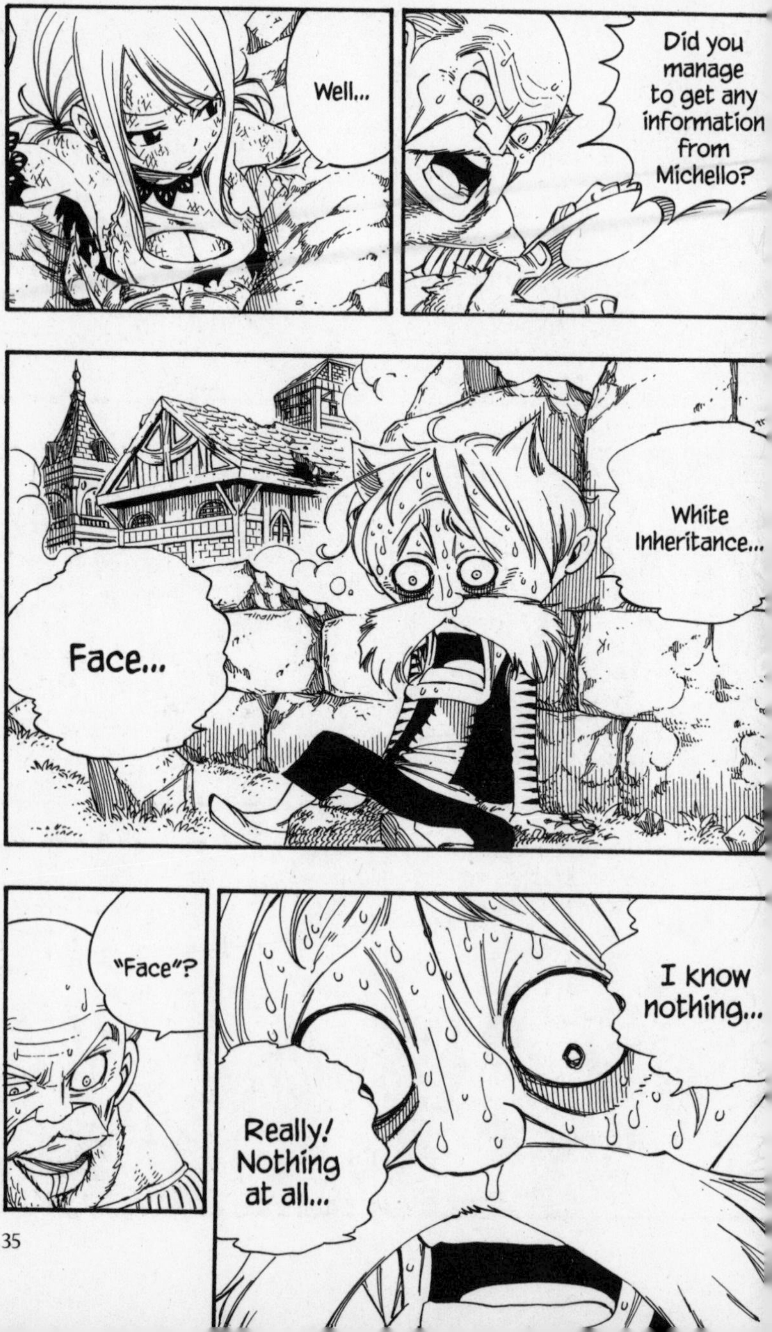
Did you manage to get any information from Michello?
Well...
White Inheritance...
Face...
I know nothing...
Really! Nothing at all...
"Face"?

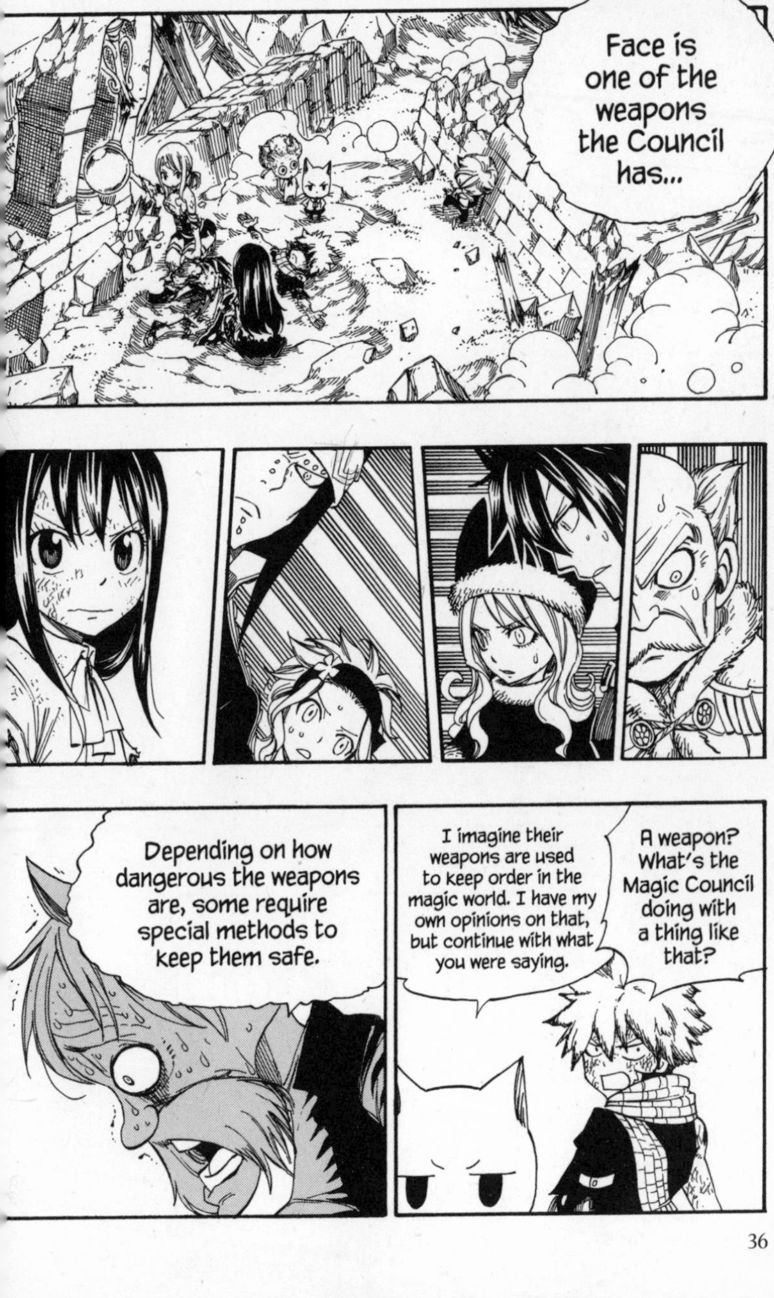
Face is one of the weapons the Council has...
A weapon? What's the Magic Council doing with a thing like that?
I imagine their weapons are used to keep order in the magic world. I have my own opinions on that, but continue with what you were saying.
Depending on how dangerous the weapons are, some require special methods to keep them safe.

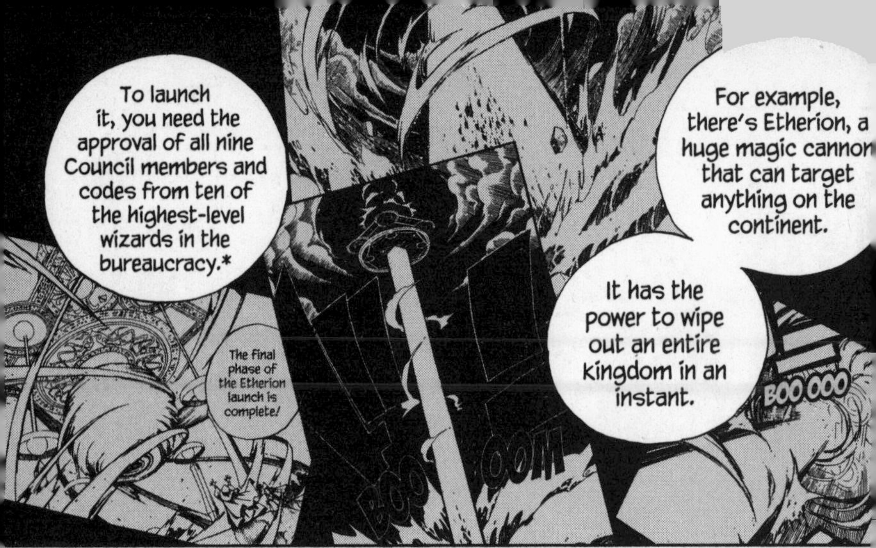
For example, there's Etherion, a huge magic cannon that can target anything on the continent.
It has the power to wipe out an entire kingdom in an instant.
BOO OOO
To launch it, you need the approval of all nine Council members and codes from ten of the highest-level wizards in the bureaucracy.*
The final phase of the Etherion launch is complete!
BOO OOM

* Seven years ago, it only took the agreement of five members of the Council to fire it.

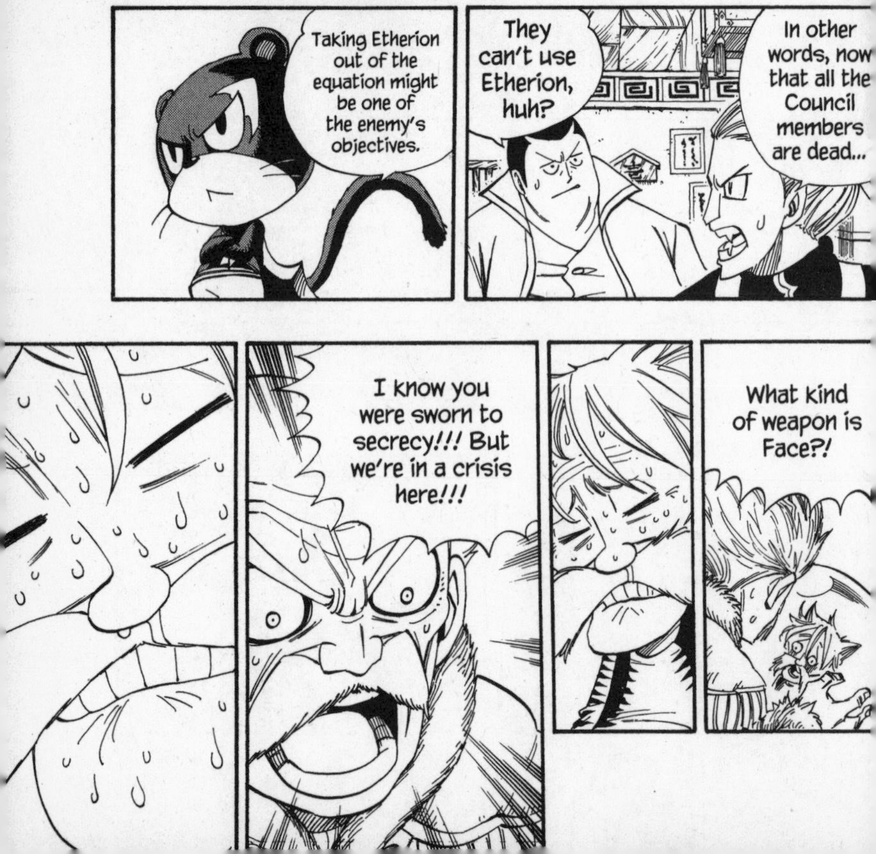
In other words, now that all the Council members are dead...
They can't use Etherion, huh?
Taking Etherion out of the equation might be one of the enemy's objectives.
What kind of weapon is Face?!
I know you were sworn to secrecy!!! But we're in a crisis here!!!

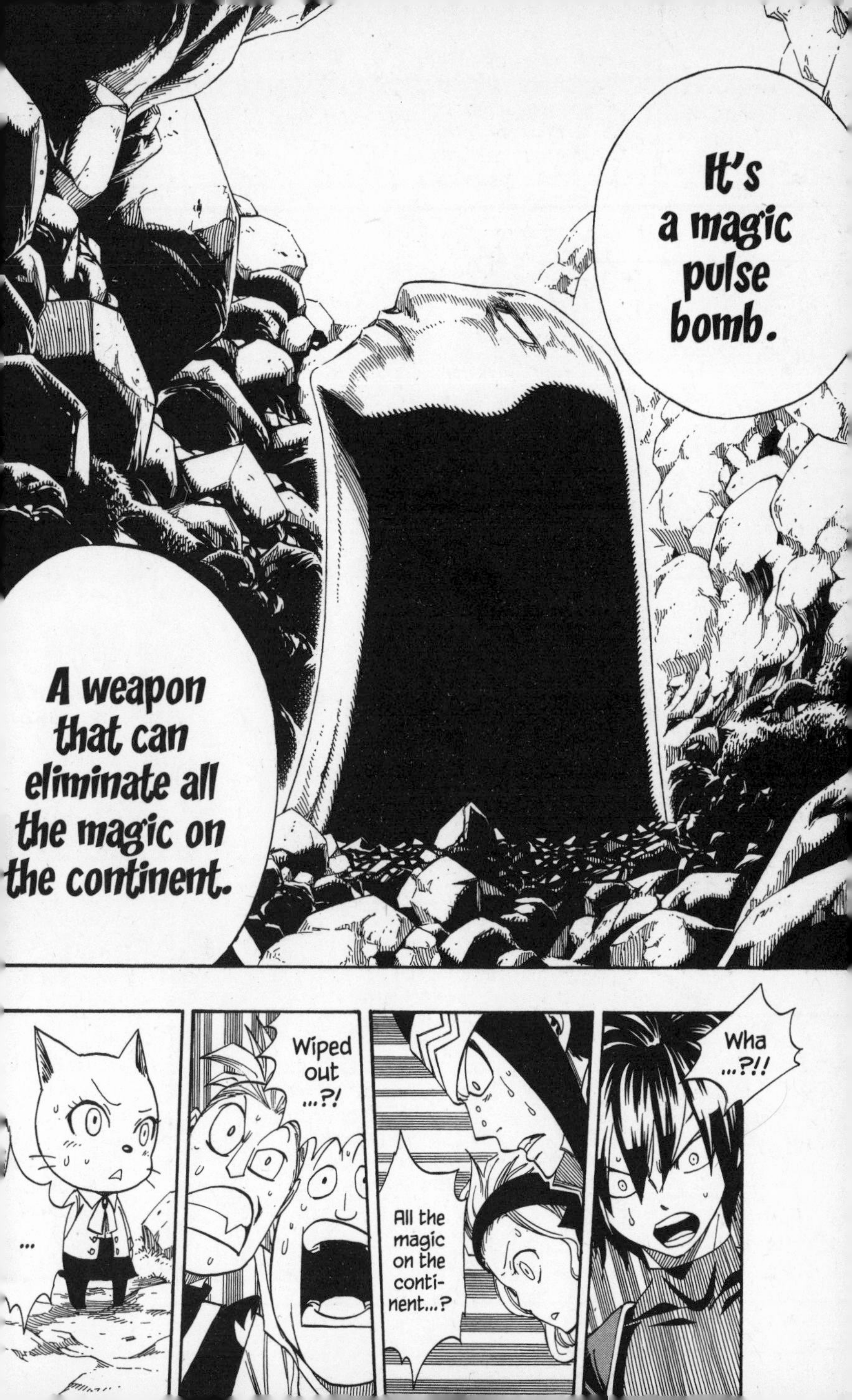
It's a magic pulse bomb.
A weapon that can eliminate all the magic on the continent.
Wha ...?!!
All the magic on the continent...?
Wiped out ...?!
...

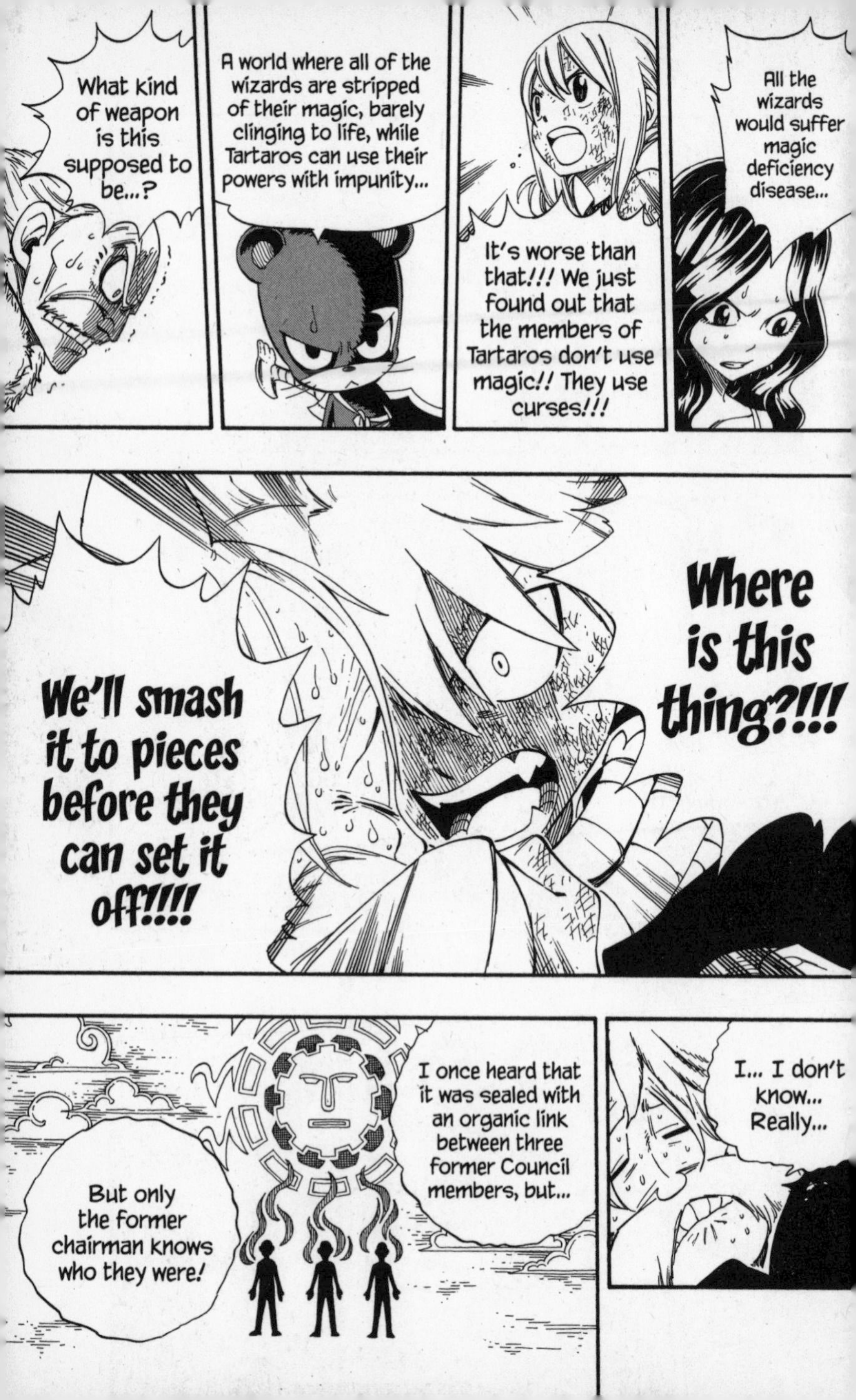
All the wizards would suffer magic deficiency disease...
It's worse than that!!! We just found out that the members of Tartaros don't use magic!! They use curses!!!
A world where all of the wizards are stripped of their magic, barely clinging to life, while Tartaros can use their powers with impunity...
What kind of weapon is this supposed to be...?
Where is this thing?!!!
We'll smash it to pieces before they can set it off!!!!
I... I don't know... Really...
I once heard that it was sealed with an organic link between three former Council members, but...
But only the former chairman knows who they were!

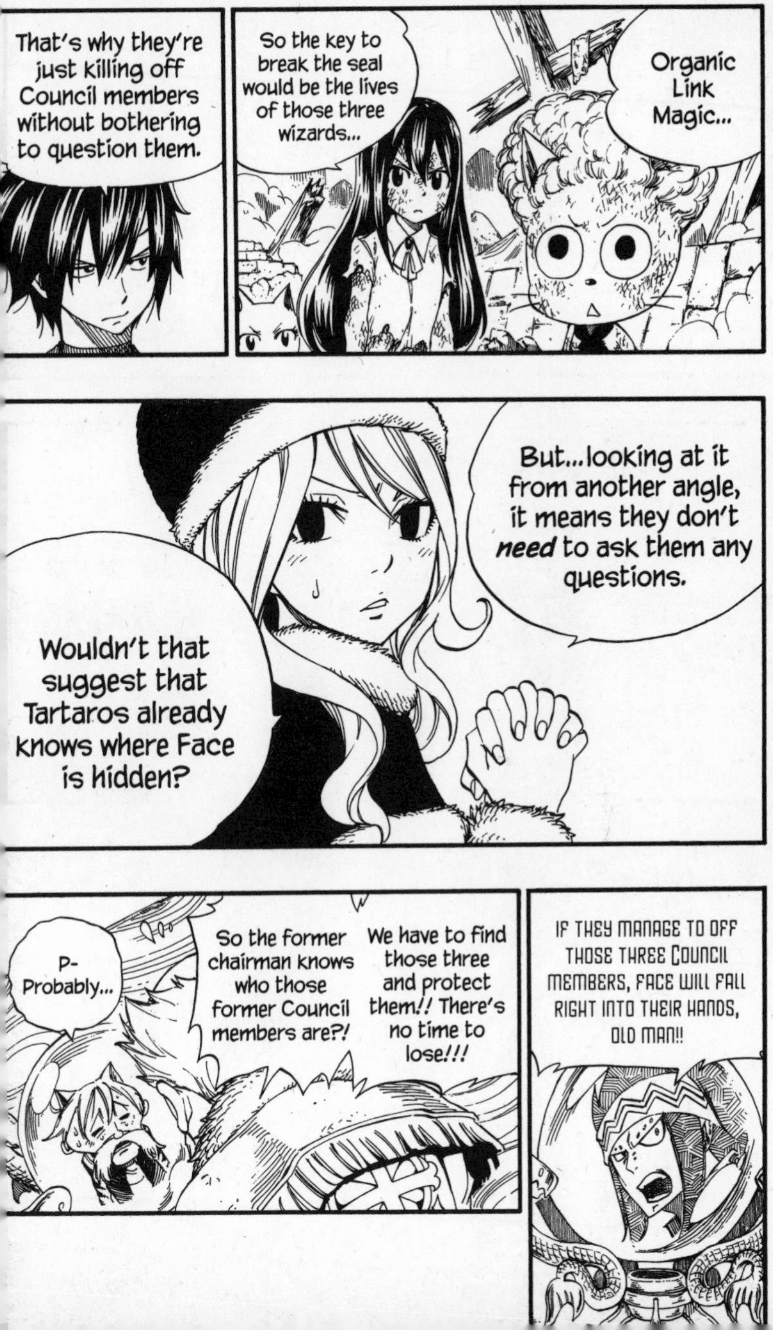

Organic Link Magic...
So the key to break the seal would be the lives of those three wizards...
That's why they're just killing off Council members without bothering to question them.
But...looking at it from another angle, it means they don't *need* to ask them any questions.
Wouldn't that suggest that Tartaros already knows where Face is hidden?
IF THEY MANAGE TO OFF THOSE THREE COUNCIL MEMBERS, FACE WILL FALL RIGHT INTO THEIR HANDS, OLD MAN!!
We have to find those three and protect them!! There's no time to lose!!!
So the former chairman knows who those former Council members are?!
P-Probably...

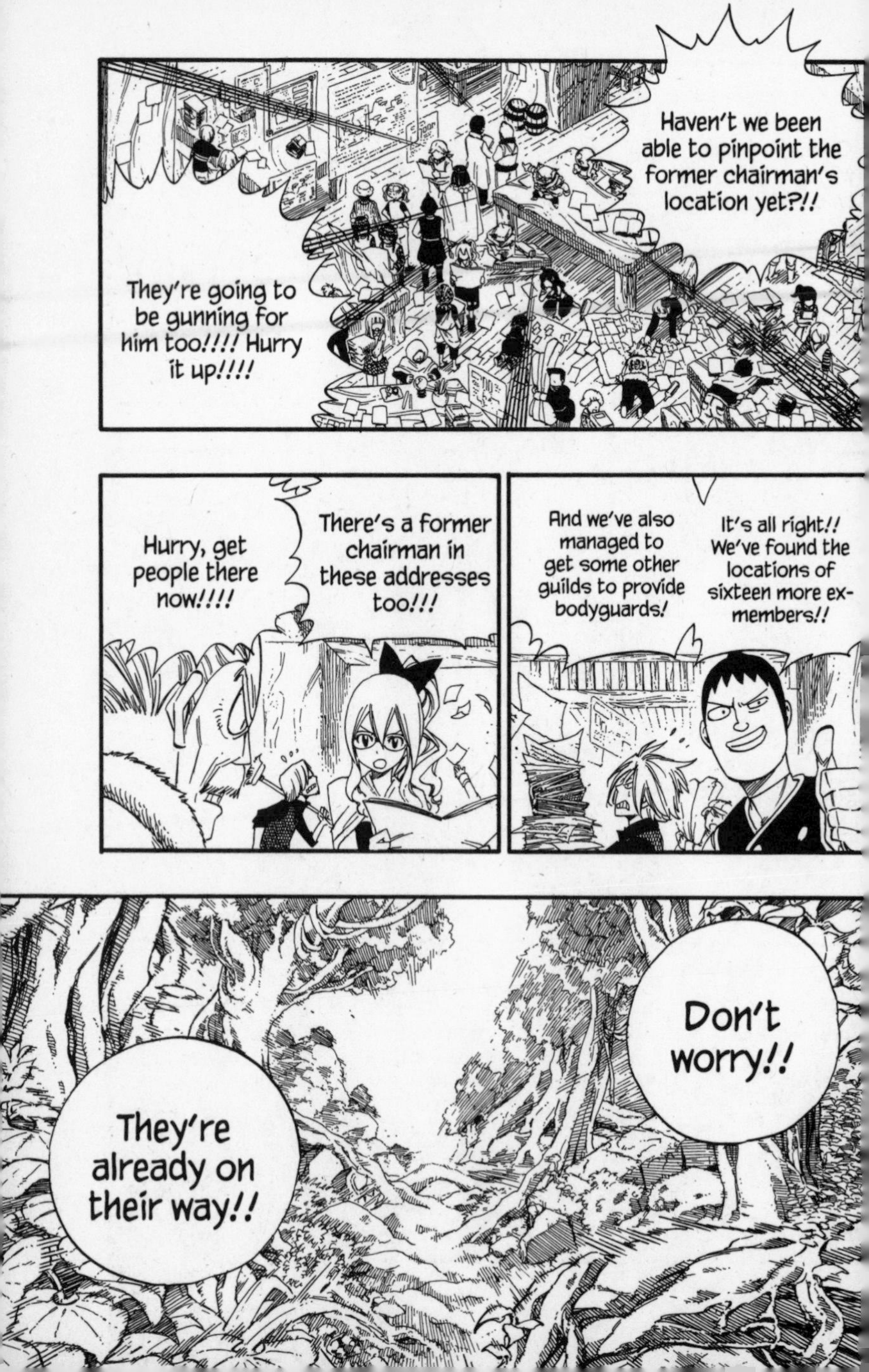
Haven't we been able to pinpoint the former chairman's location yet?!!
They're going to be gunning for him too!!!! Hurry it up!!!!
It's all right!! We've found the locations of sixteen more ex-members!!
And we've also managed to get some other guilds to provide bodyguards!
There's a former chairman in these addresses too!!!
Hurry, get people there now!!!!
Don't worry!!
They're already on their way!!

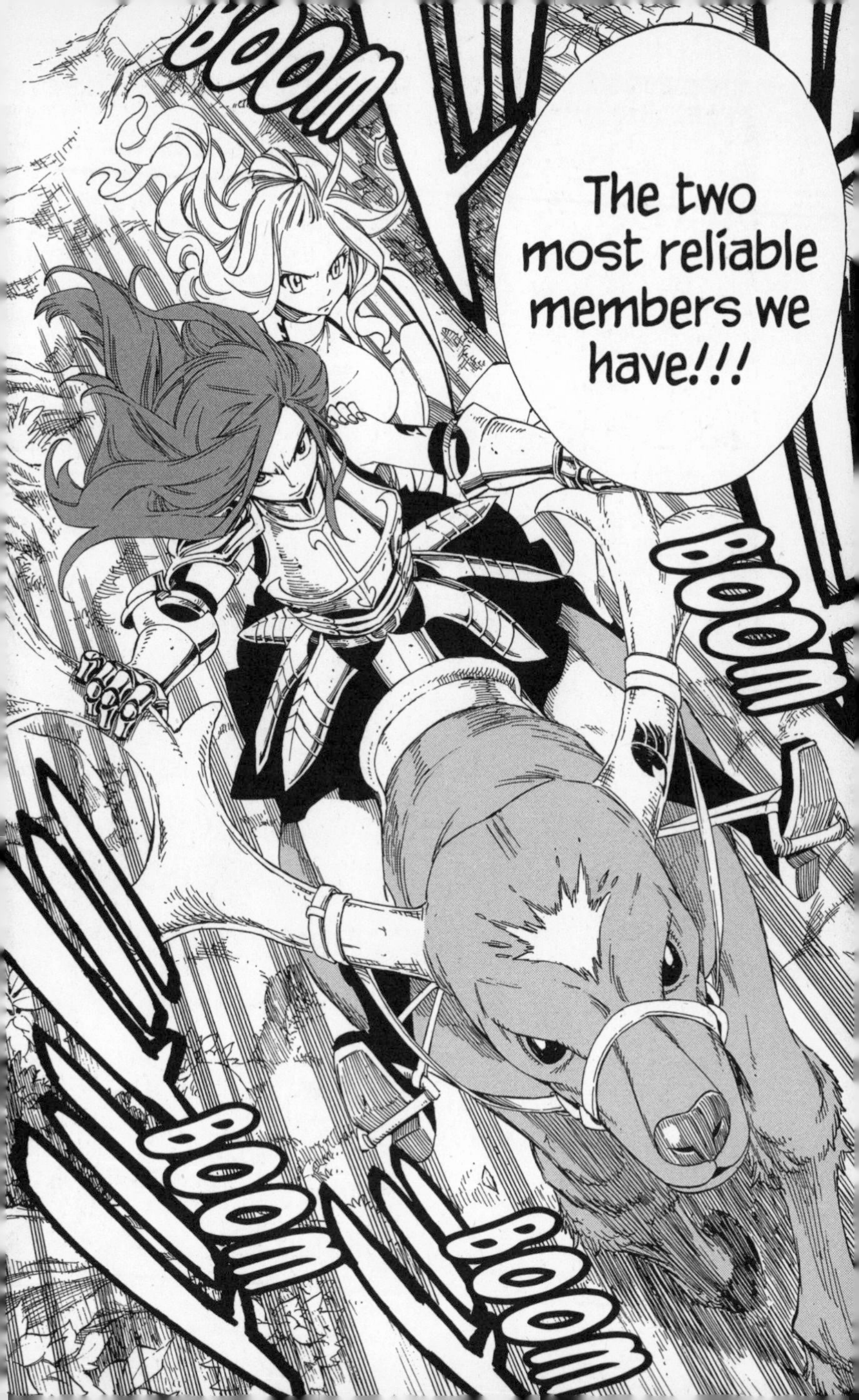
BOOM
The two most reliable members we have!!!
BOOM
BOOM
BOOM
BOOM

Chapter 364:
Tartaros Arc, Part 1: Immorality and Sinners

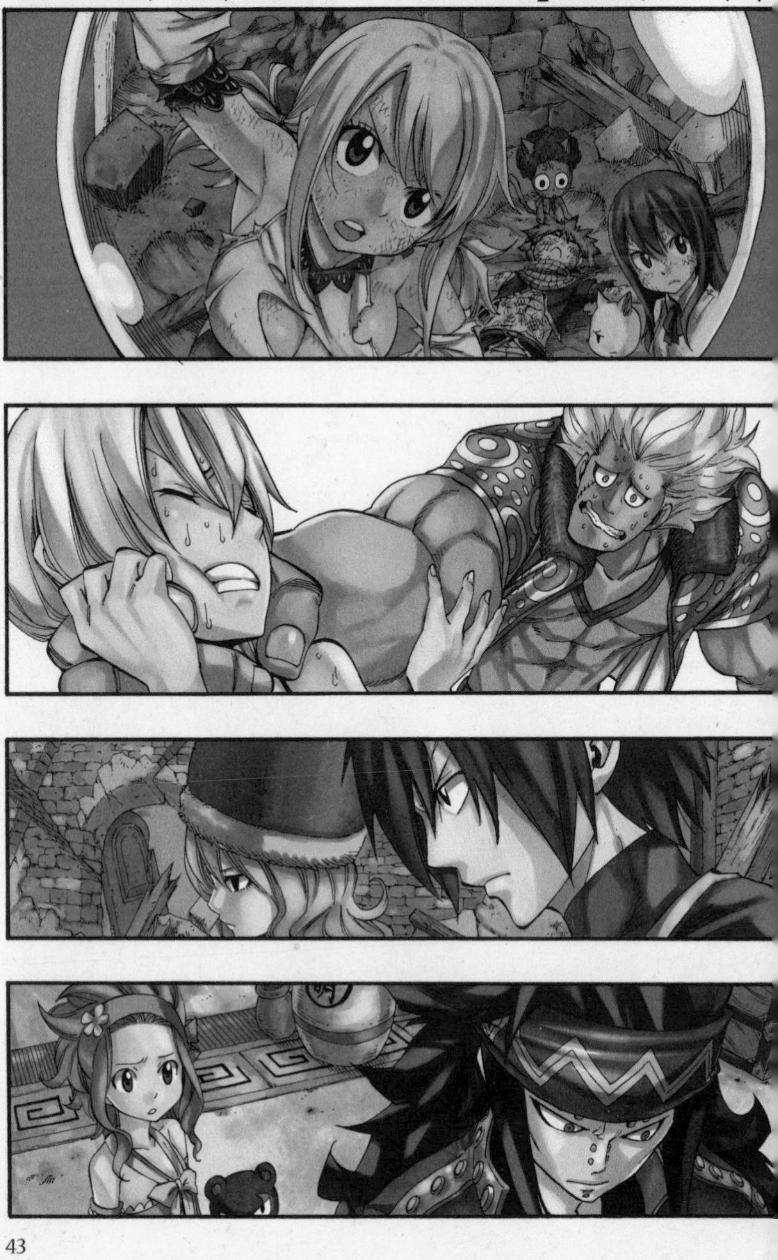

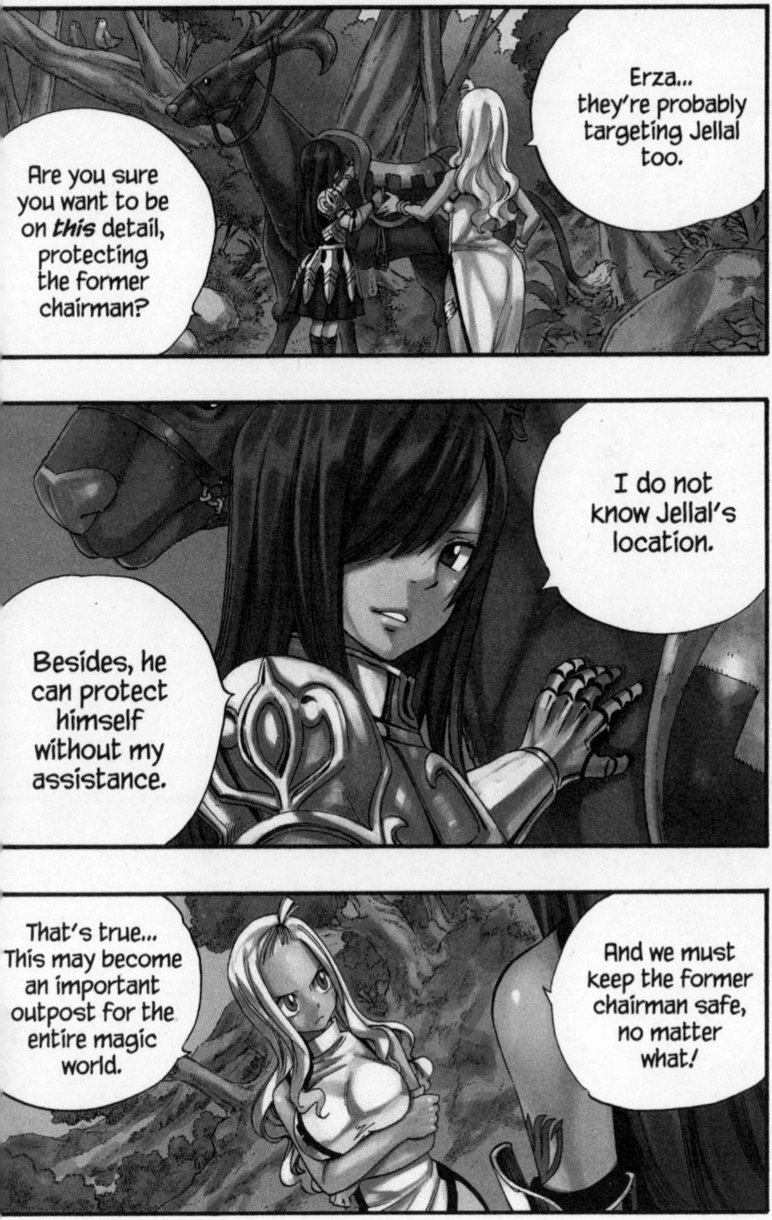
Erza... they're probably targeting Jellal too.
Are you sure you want to be on *this* detail, protecting the former chairman?
I do not know Jellal's location.
Besides, he can protect himself without my assistance.
And we must keep the former chairman safe, no matter what!
That's true... This may become an important outpost for the entire magic world.

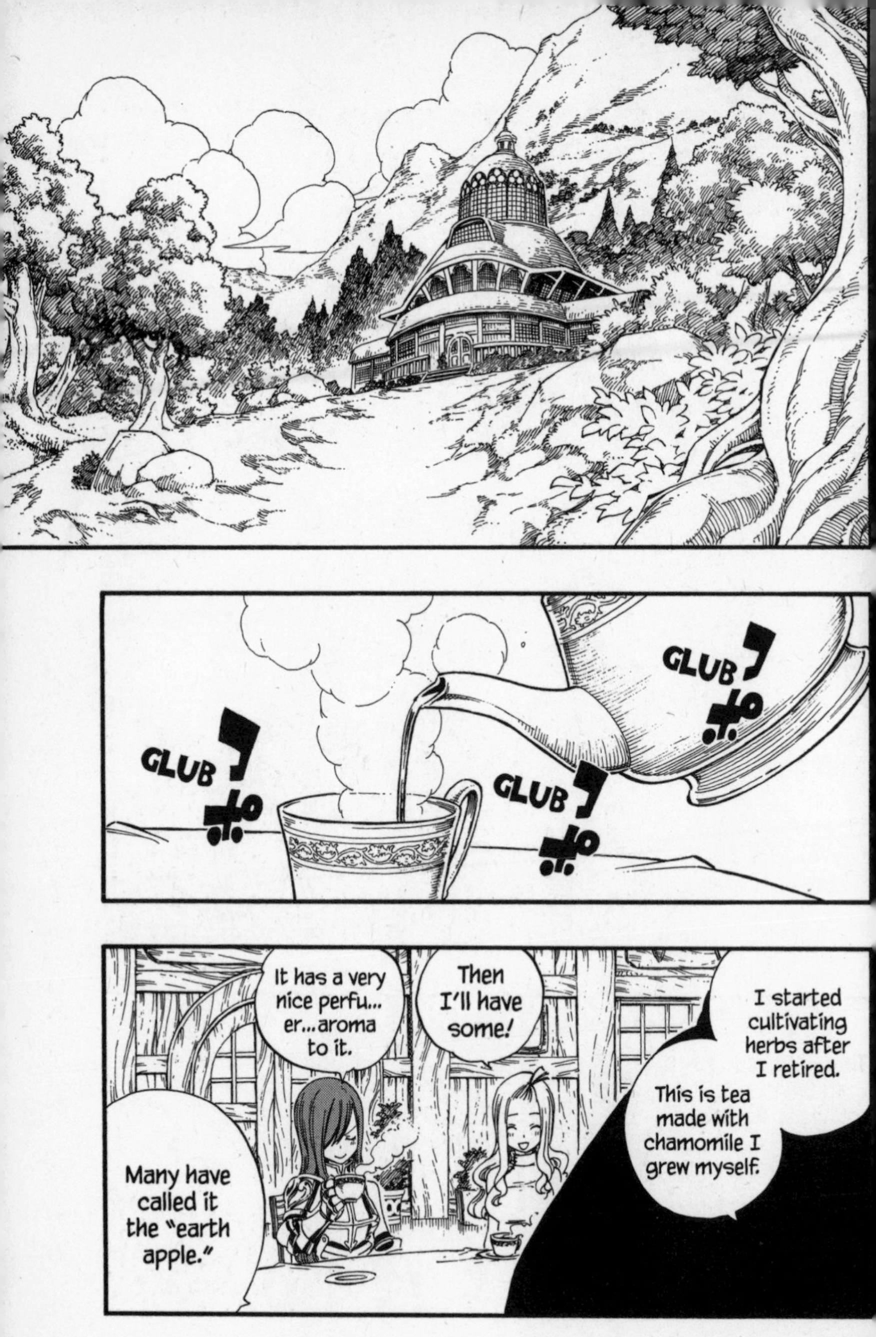
GLUB
GLUB
GLUB
I started cultivating herbs after I retired.
This is tea made with chamomile I grew myself.
Then I'll have some!
It has a very nice perfu... er...aroma to it.
Many have called it the "earth apple."

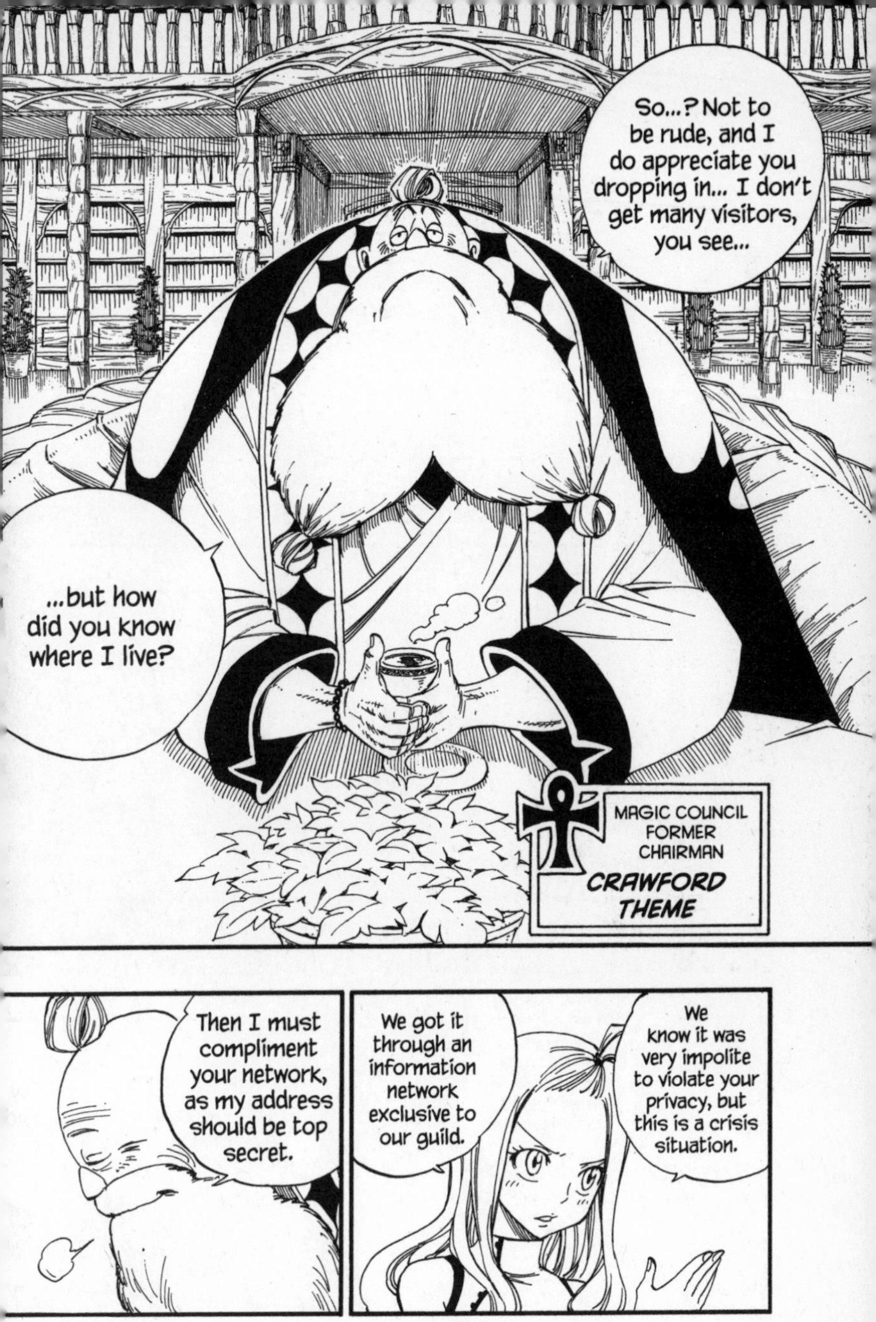
So...? Not to be rude, and I do appreciate you dropping in... I don't get many visitors, you see...
...but how did you know where I live?
MAGIC COUNCIL FORMER CHAIRMAN
CRAWFORD THEME
We know it was very impolite to violate your privacy, but this is a crisis situation.
We got it through an information network exclusive to our guild.
Then I must compliment your network, as my address should be top secret.

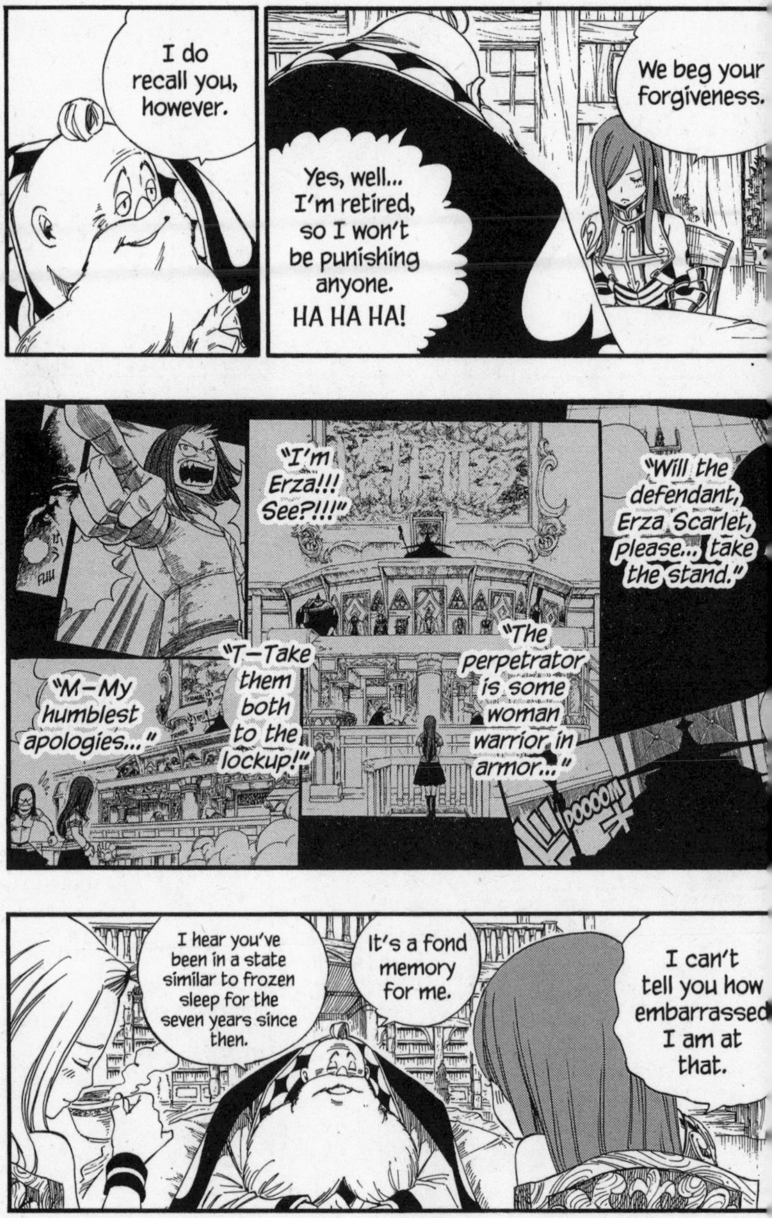
We beg your forgiveness.
Yes, well... I'm retired, so I won't be punishing anyone. HA HA HA!
I do recall you, however.
"Will the defendant, Erza Scarlet, please... take the stand."
DOOOOM
"The perpetrator is some woman warrior in armor..."
"I'm Erza!!! See?!!!"
"T—Take them both to the lockup!"
"M—My humblest apologies..."
I can't tell you how embarrassed I am at that.
It's a fond memory for me.
I hear you've been in a state similar to frozen sleep for the seven years since then.

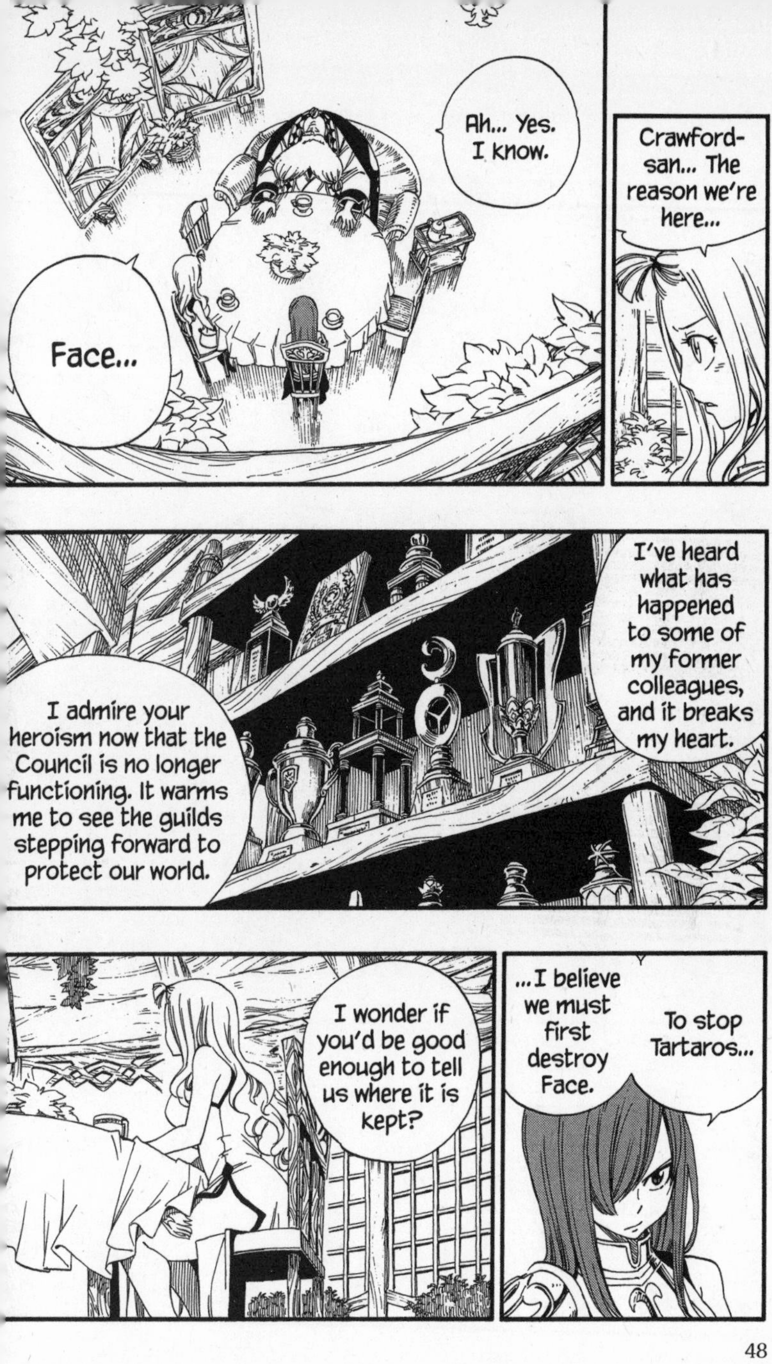
Crawford-san... The reason we're here...
Ah... Yes. I know.
Face...
I've heard what has happened to some of my former colleagues, and it breaks my heart.
I admire your heroism now that the Council is no longer functioning. It warms me to see the guilds stepping forward to protect our world.
To stop Tartaros...
...I believe we must first destroy Face.
I wonder if you'd be good enough to tell us where it is kept?

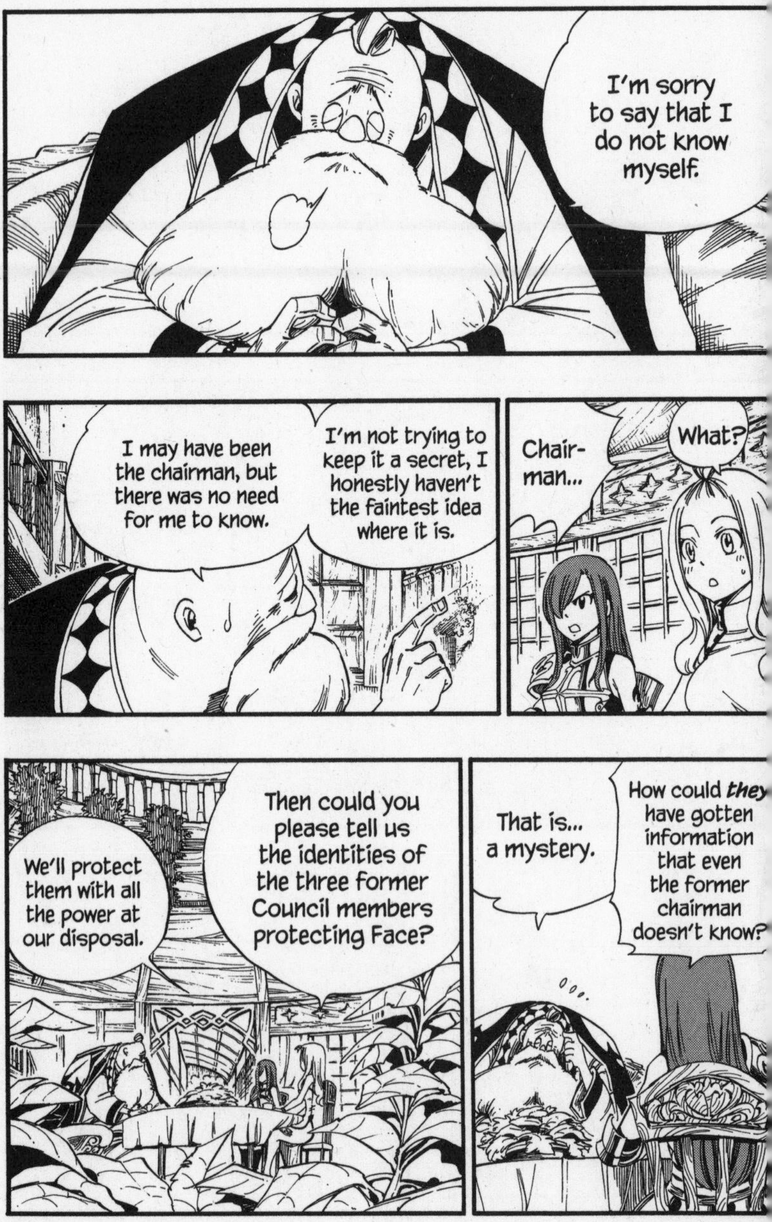
I'm sorry to say that I do not know myself.
What?
Chair-man...
I'm not trying to keep it a secret, I honestly haven't the faintest idea where it is.
I may have been the chairman, but there was no need for me to know.
How could *they* have gotten information that even the former chairman doesn't know?
That is... a mystery.
Then could you please tell us the identities of the three former Council members protecting Face?
We'll protect them with all the power at our disposal.

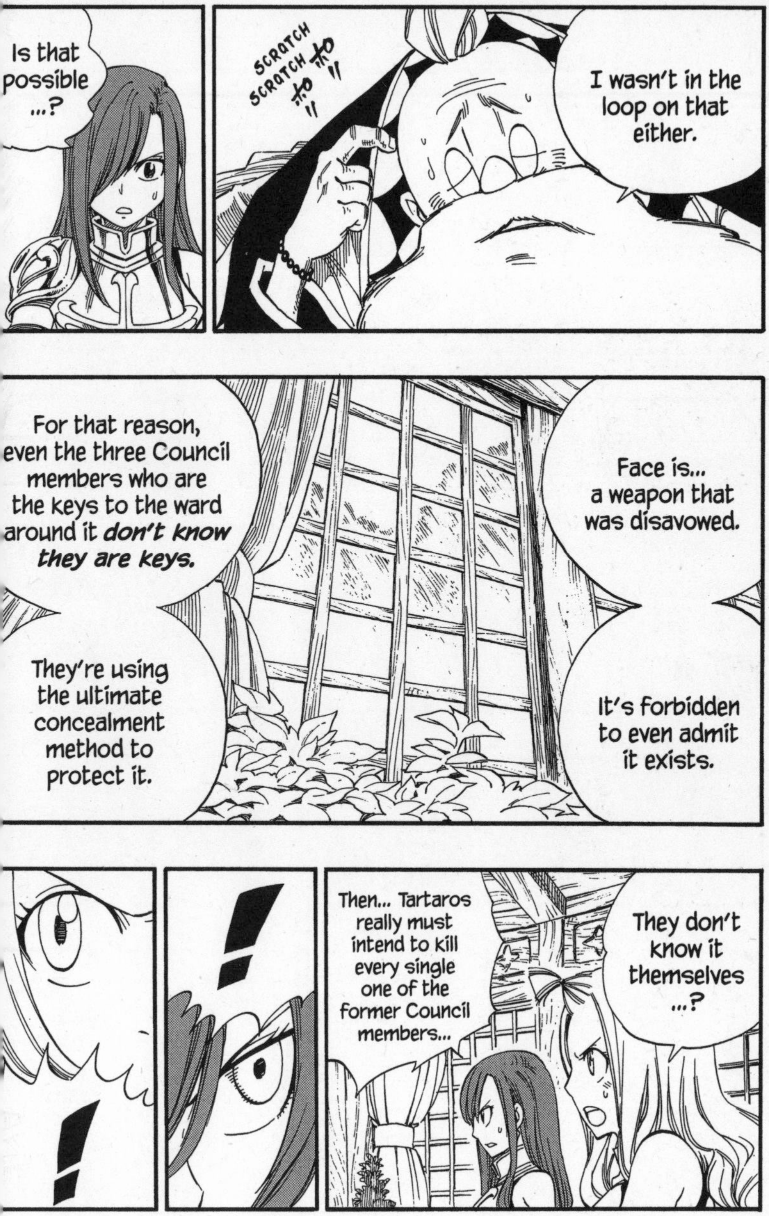
SCRATCH SCRATCH
I wasn't in the loop on that either.
Is that possible ...?
Face is... a weapon that was disavowed.
It's forbidden to even admit it exists.
For that reason, even the three Council members who are the keys to the ward around it ***don't know they are keys.***
They're using the ultimate concealment method to protect it.
They don't know it themselves ...?
Then... Tartaros really must intend to kill every single one of the former Council members...
!
!

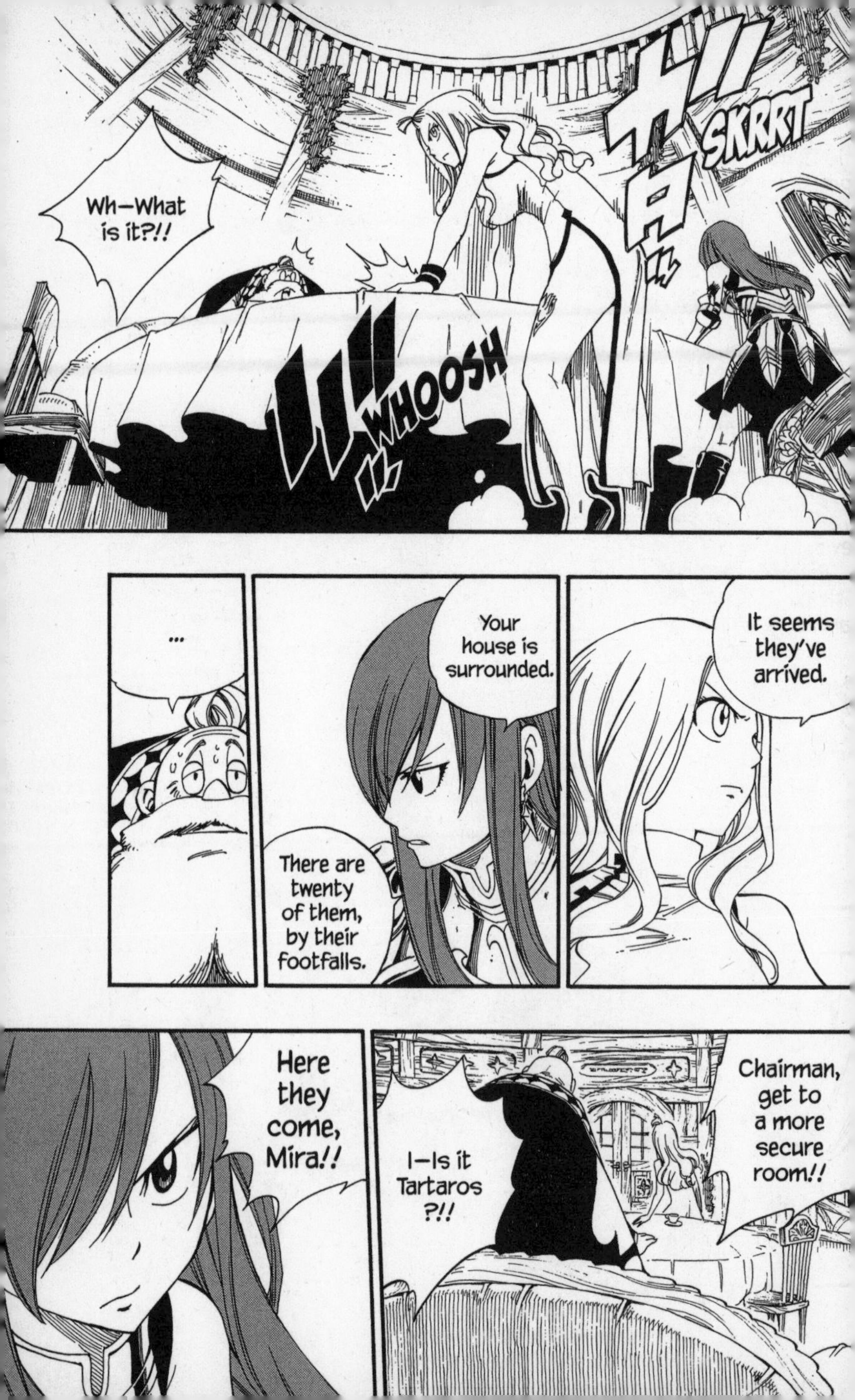
SKRRT
Wh—What is it?!!
WHOOSH
It seems they've arrived.
Your house is surrounded.
There are twenty of them, by their footfalls.
...
Chairman, get to a more secure room!!
I—Is it Tartaros?!!
Here they come, Mira!!

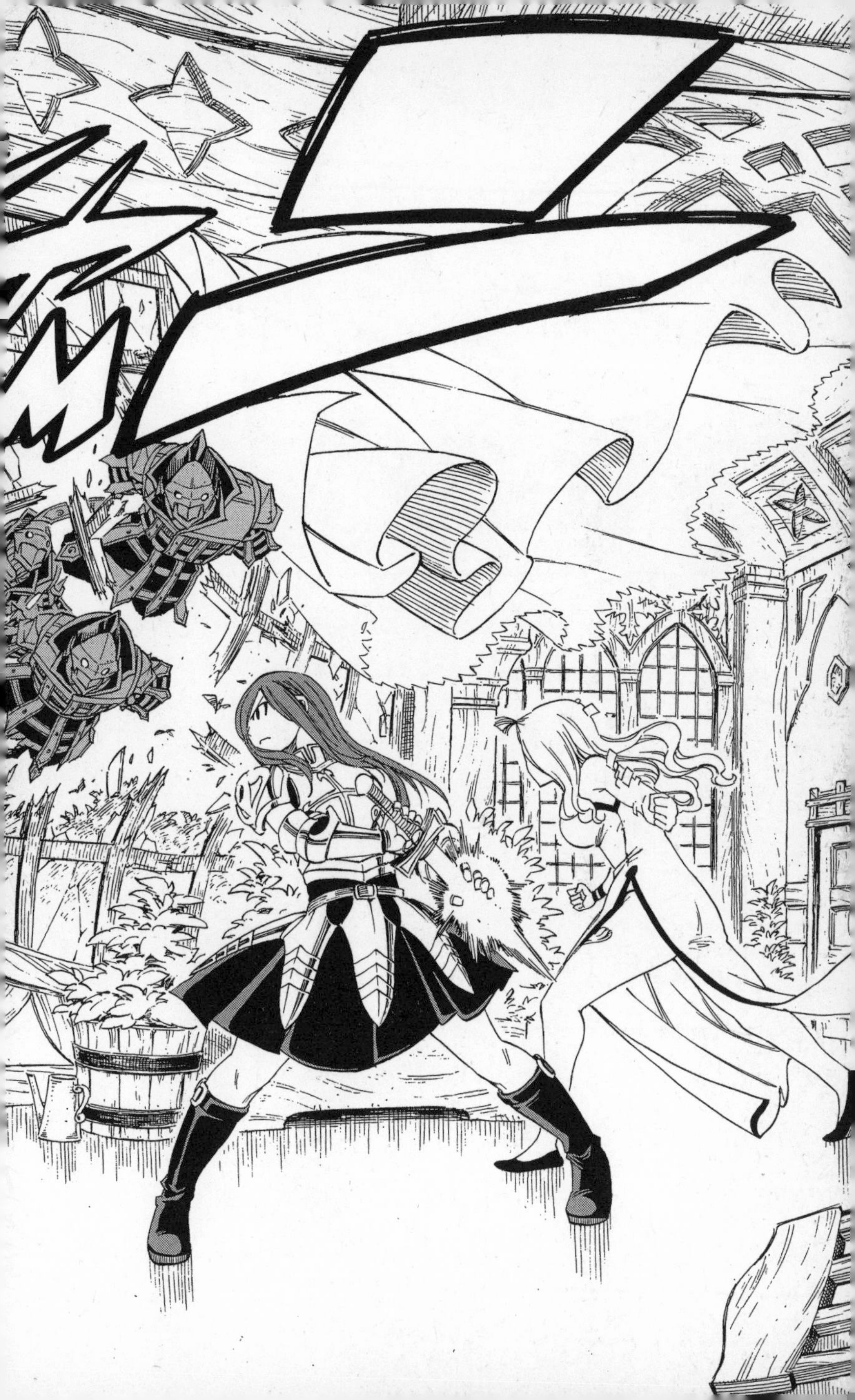

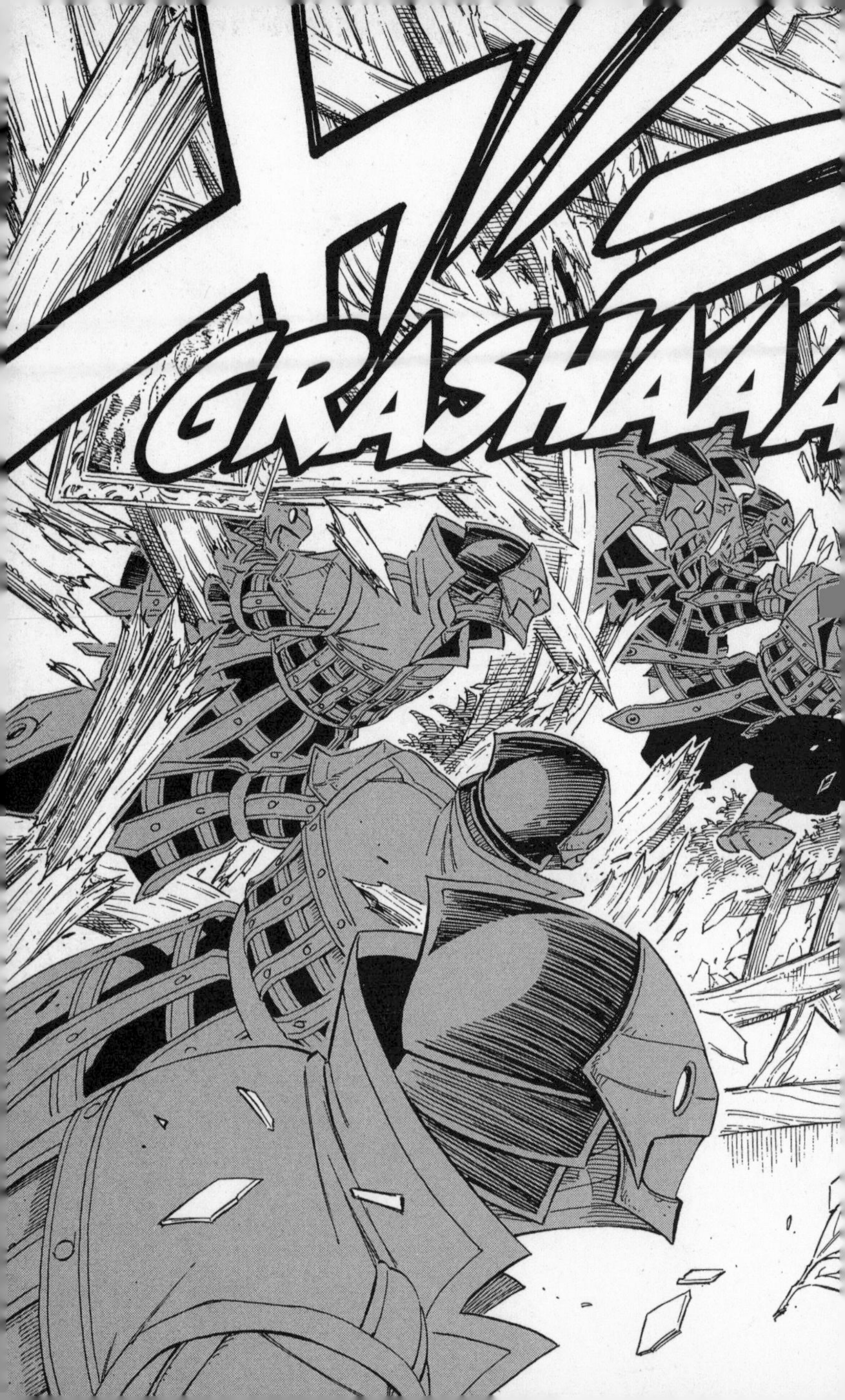
GRASHAA

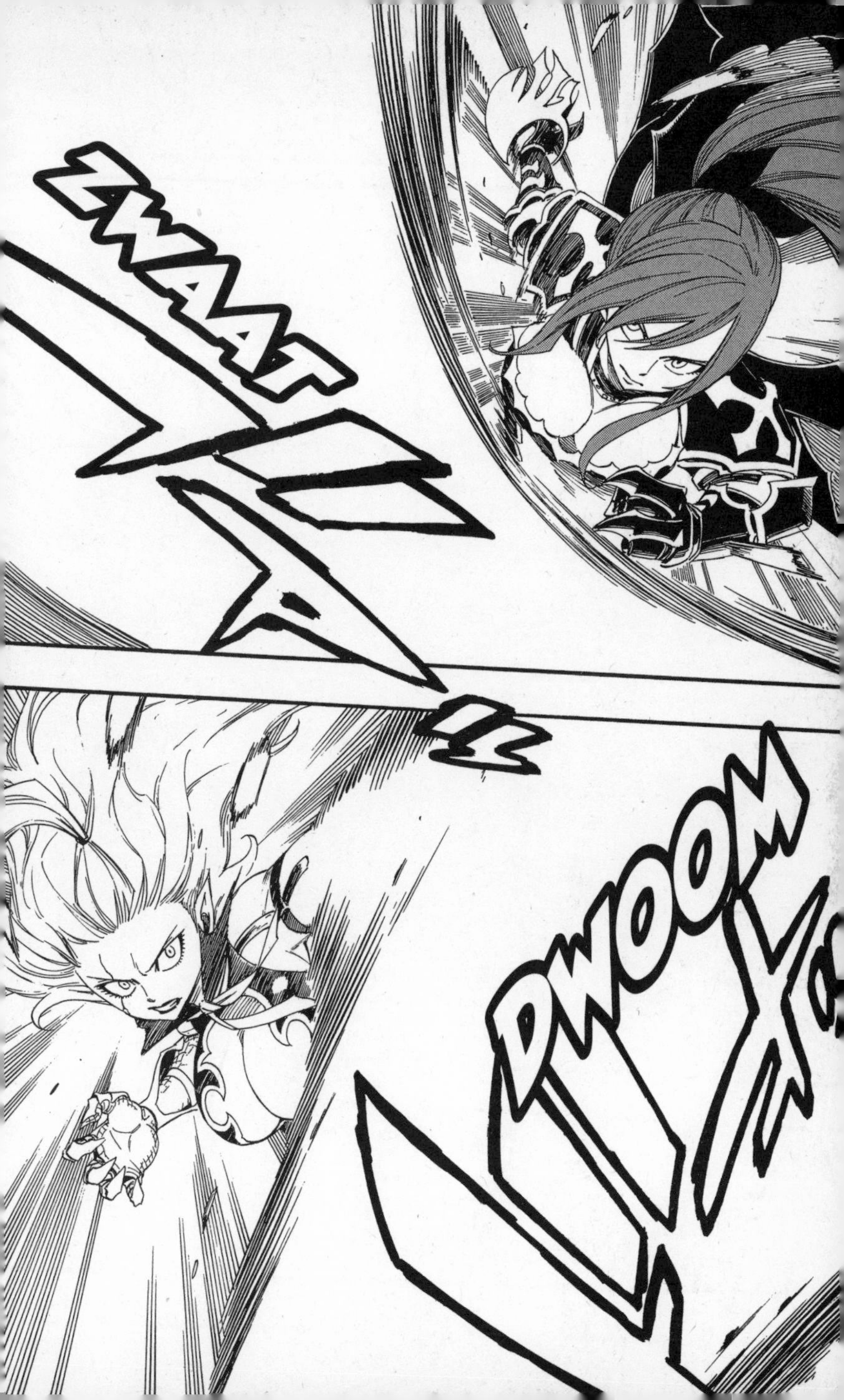
ZWAAT
DWOOM

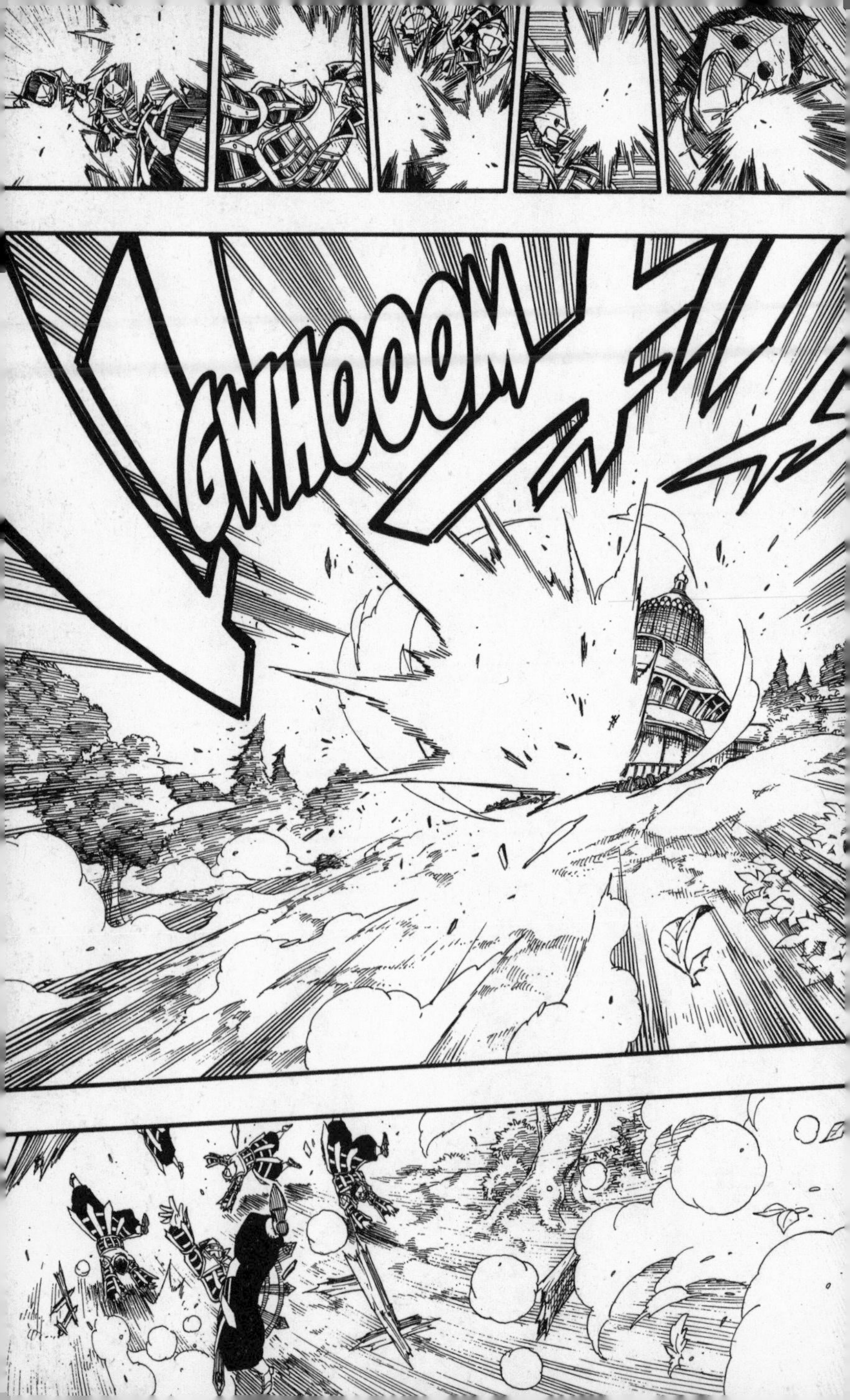
GWHOOOM

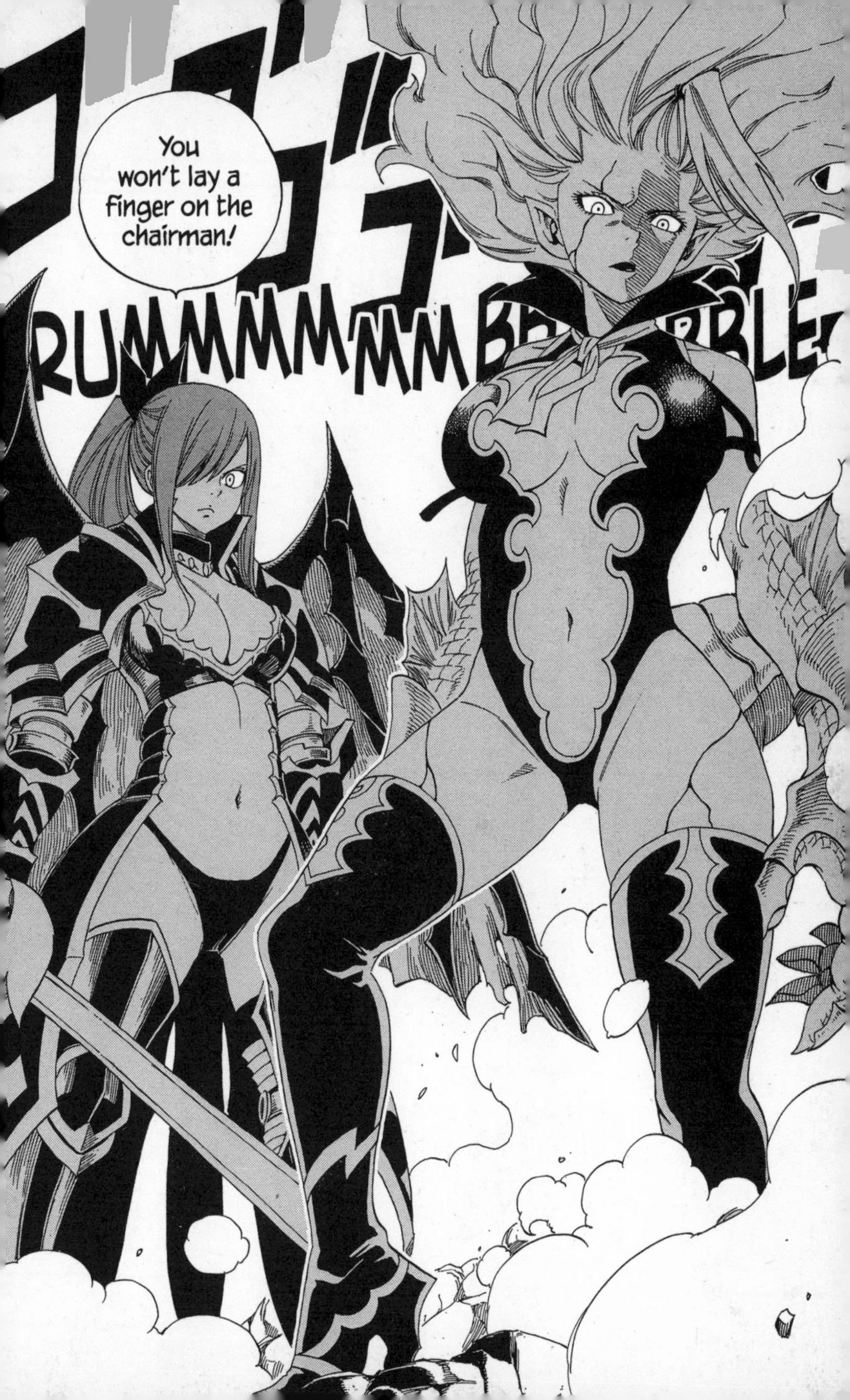
You won't lay a finger on the chairman!

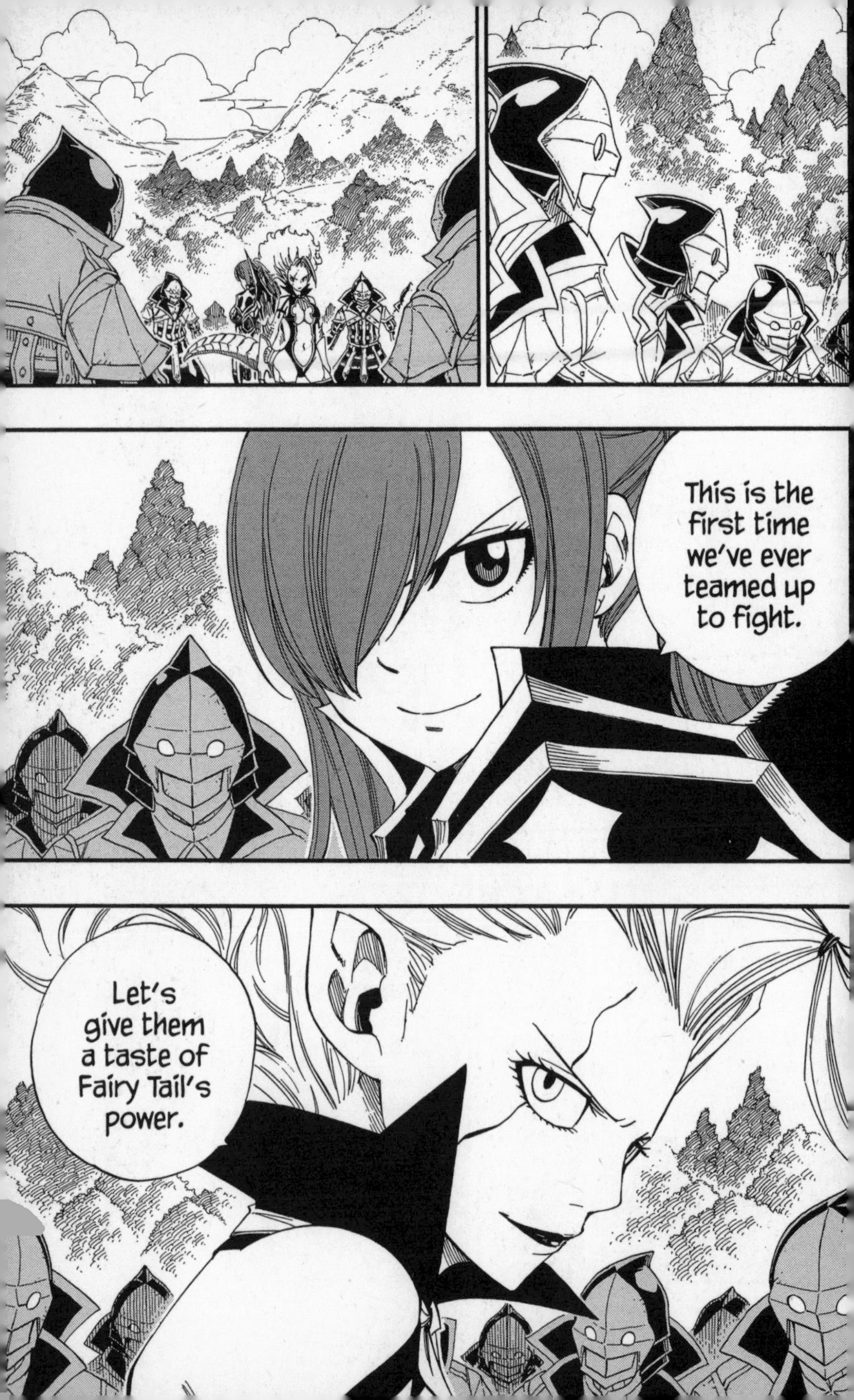
This is the first time we've ever teamed up to fight.
Let's give them a taste of Fairy Tail's power.

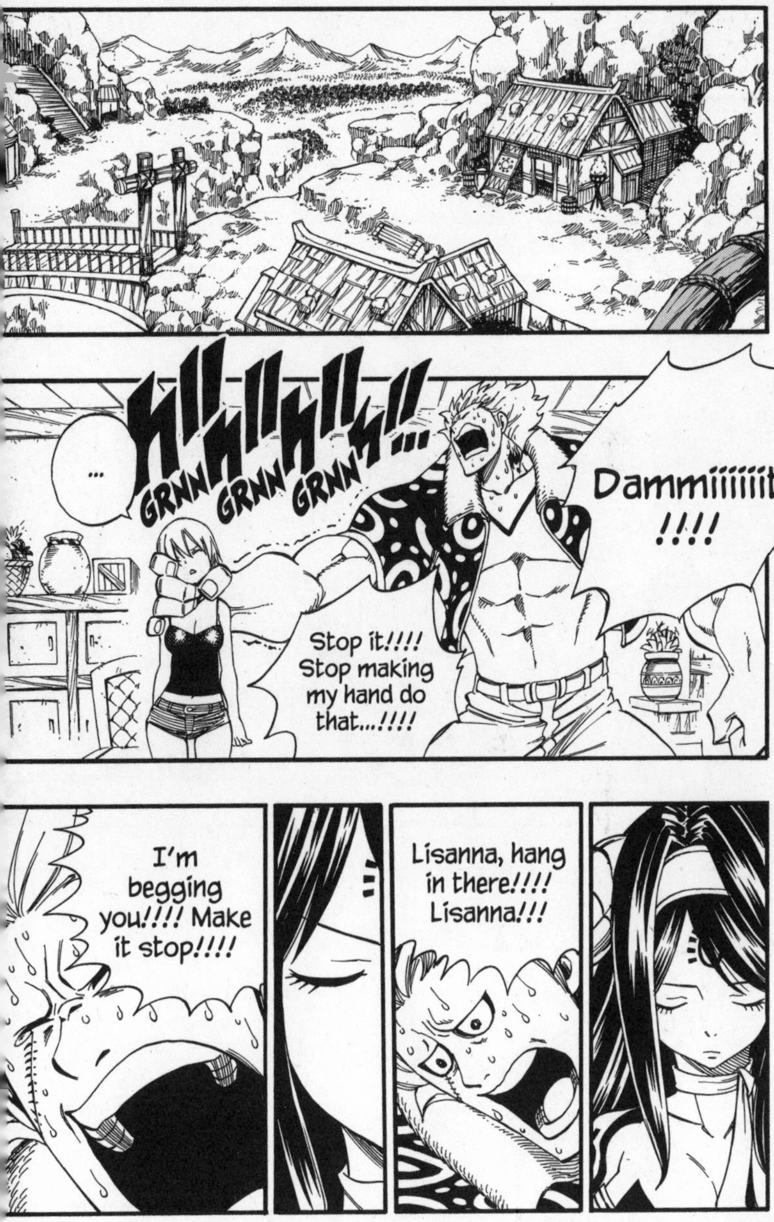
Dammiiiiiit !!!!
GRNN GRNN GRNN
...
Stop it!!!! Stop making my hand do that...!!!!
Lisanna, hang in there!!!! Lisanna!!!
I'm begging you!!!! Make it stop!!!!

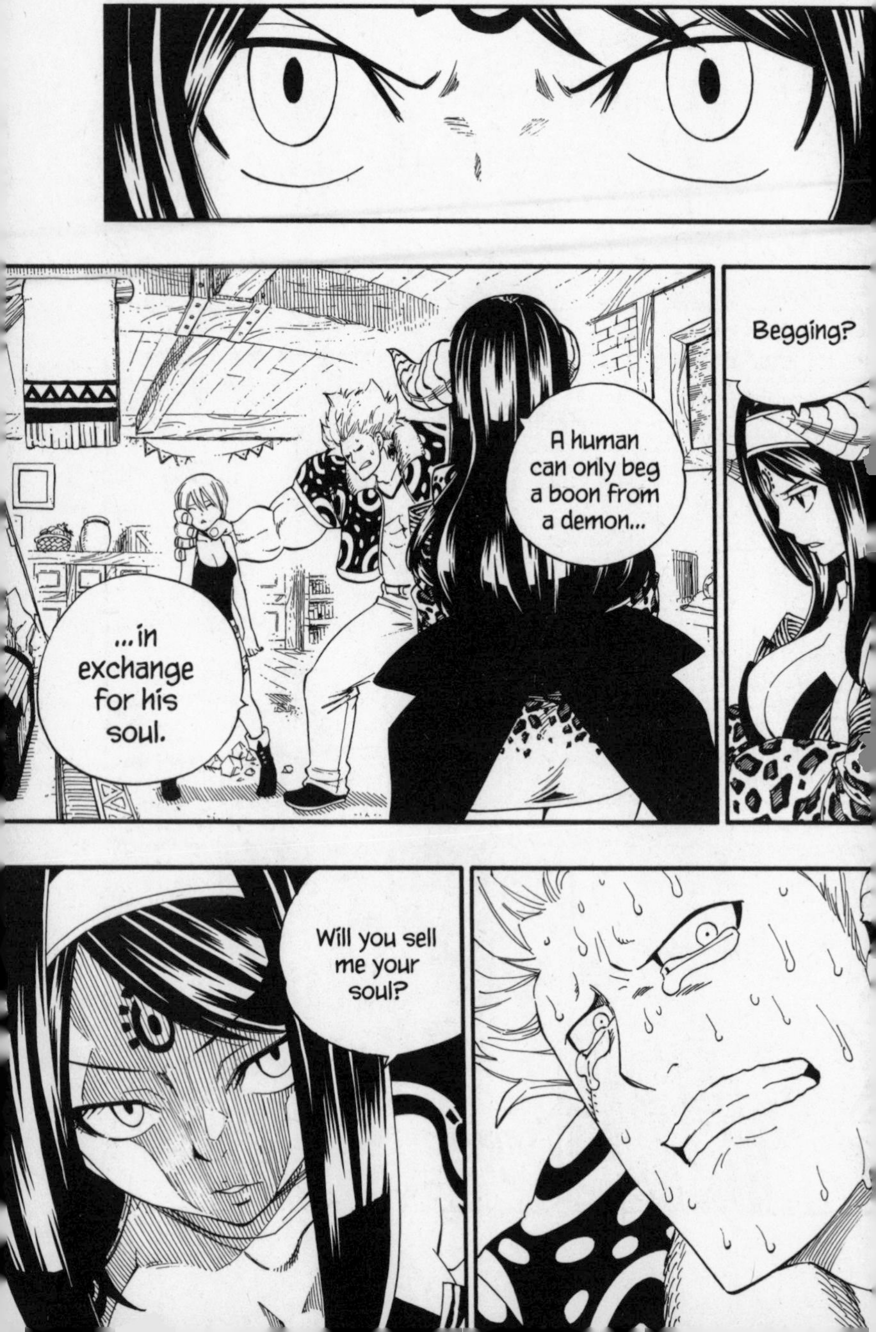
Begging?
A human can only beg a boon from a demon...
...in exchange for his soul.
Will you sell me your soul?

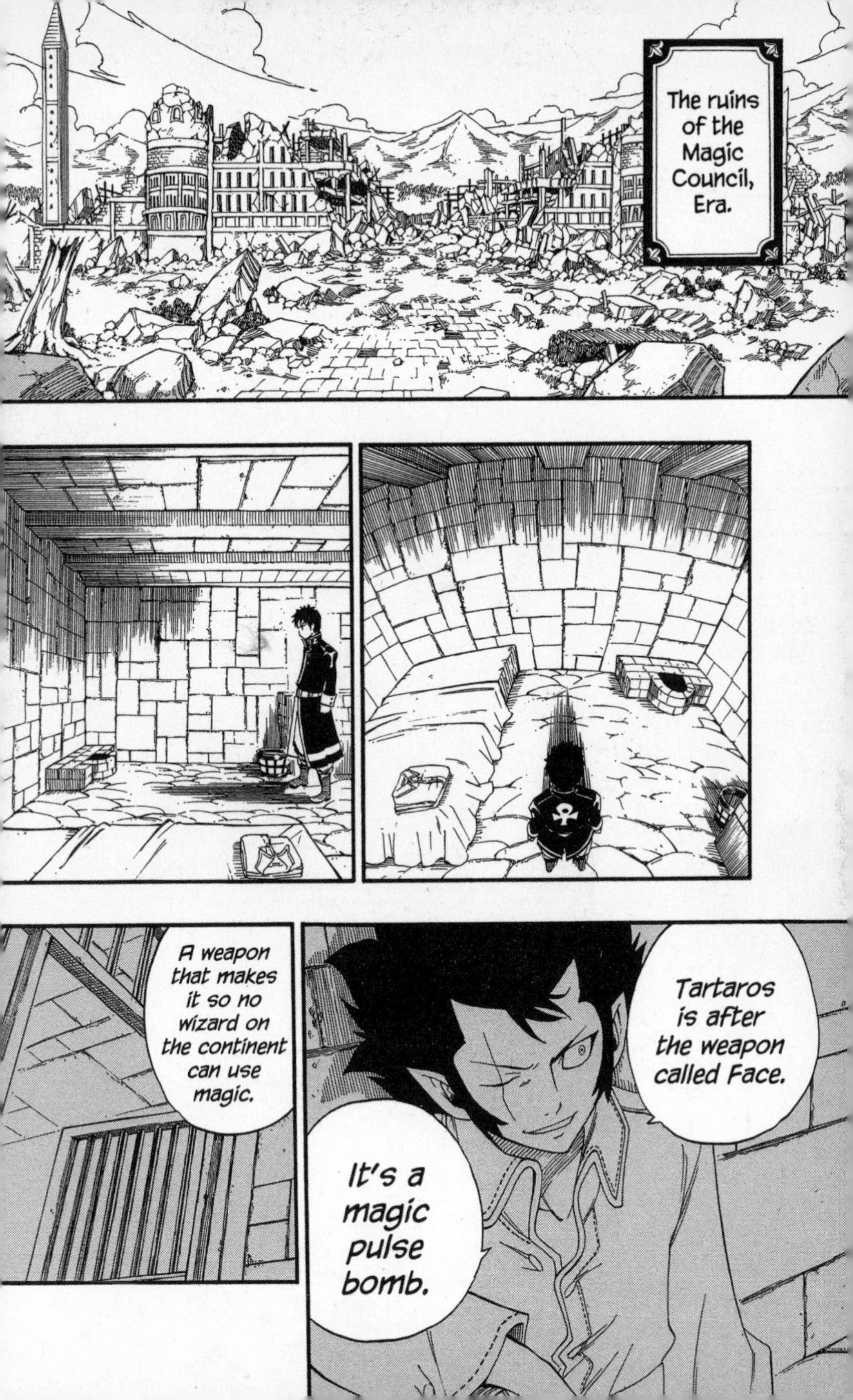
The ruins of the Magic Council, Era.
Tartaros is after the weapon called Face.
It's a magic pulse bomb.
A weapon that makes it so no wizard on the continent can use magic.

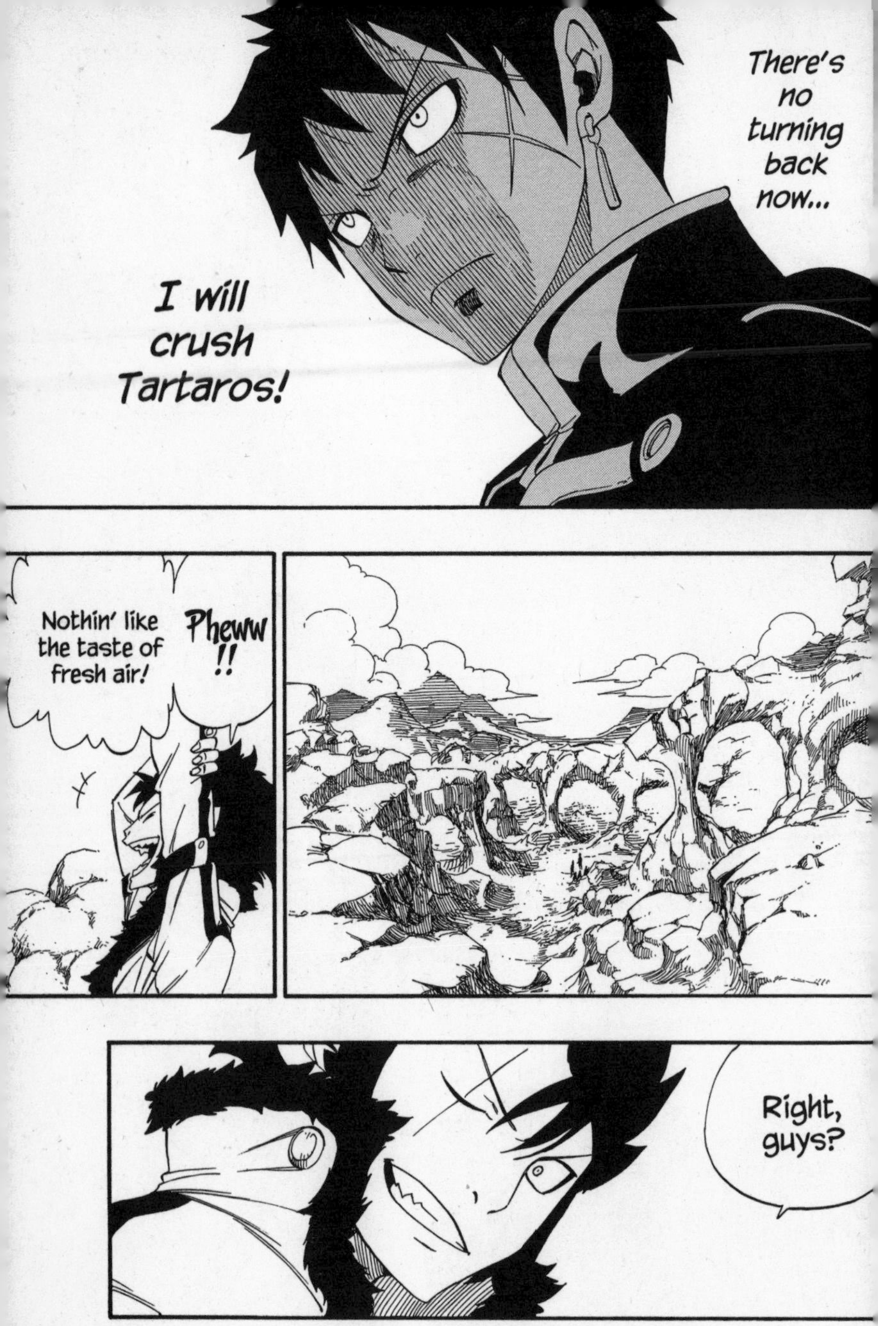
There's no turning back now...
I will crush Tartaros!
Pheww!!
Nothin' like the taste of fresh air!
Right, guys?

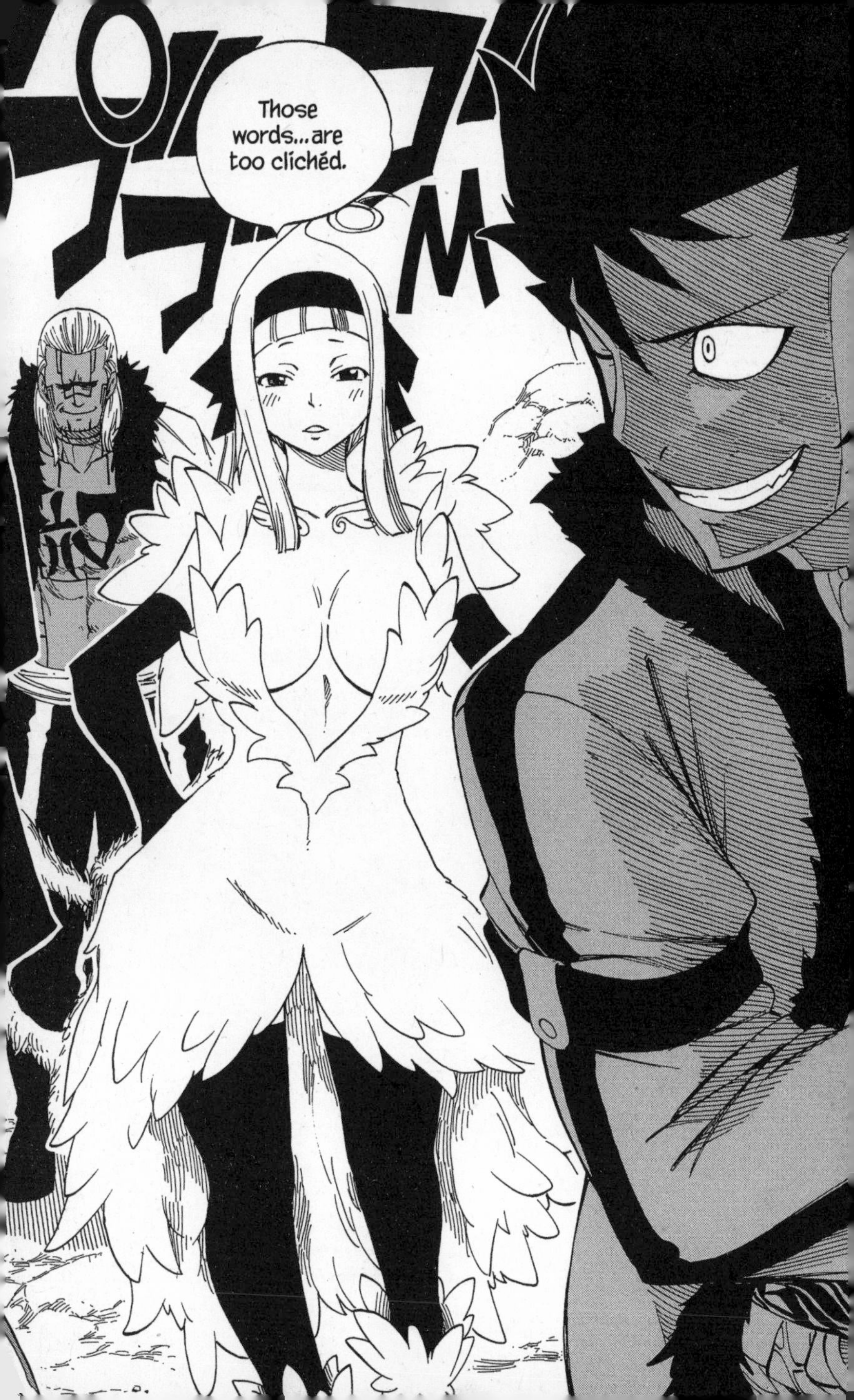
Those words...are too clichéd.
M

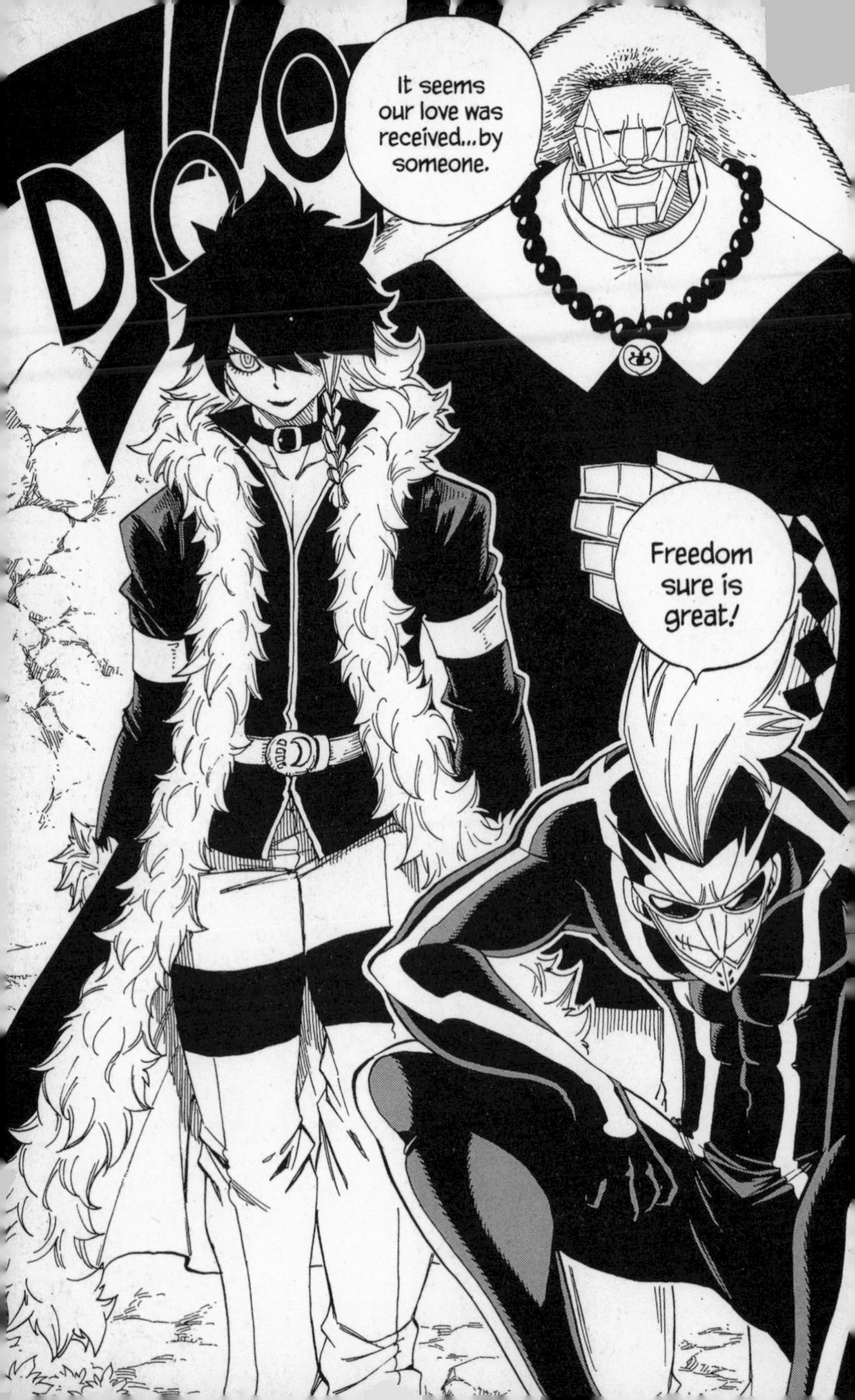
It seems our love was received...by someone.
DOOO
Freedom sure is great!

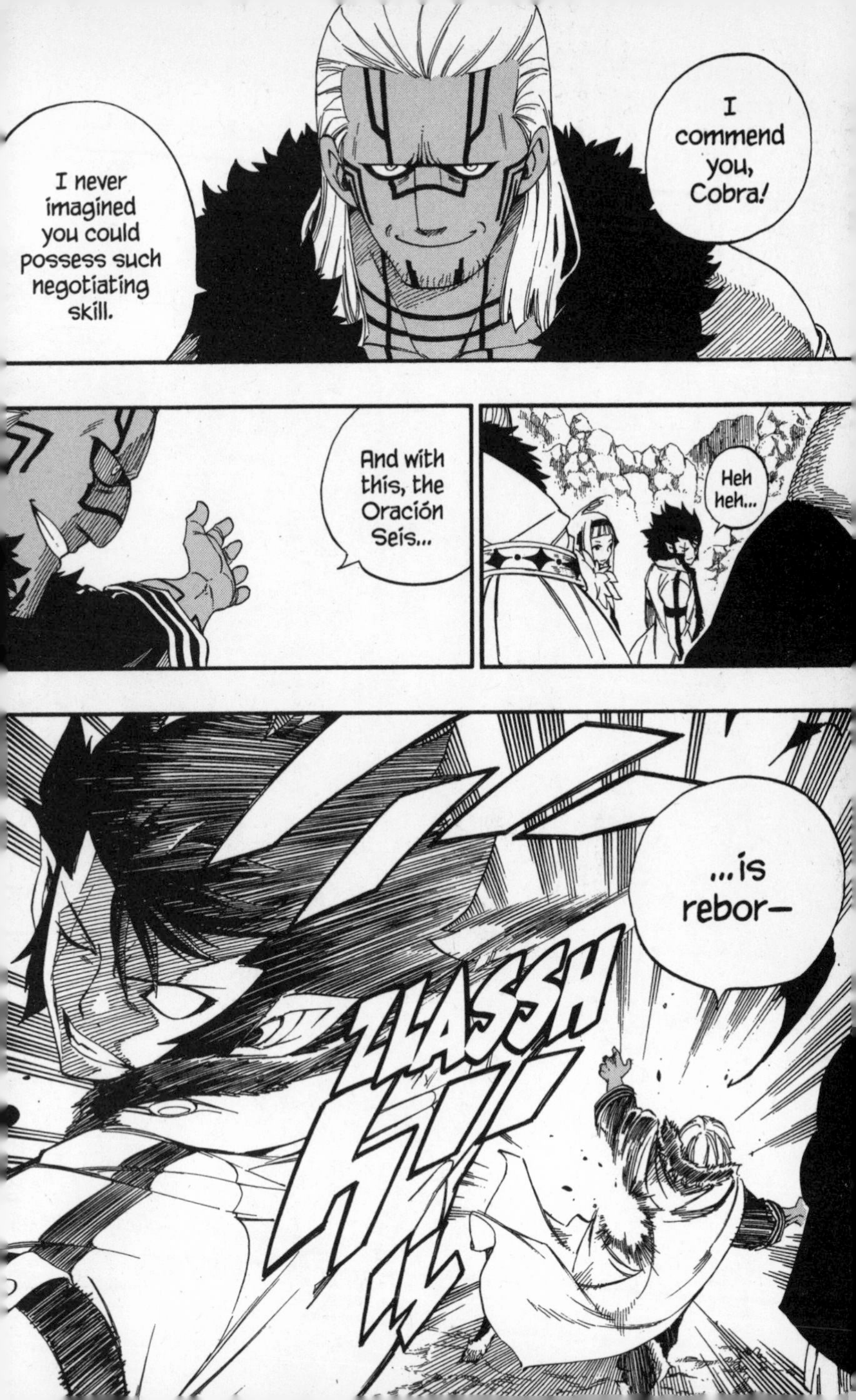
I commend you, Cobra!
I never imagined you could possess such negotiating skill.
Heh heh...
And with this, the Oración Seis...
...is rebor–
ZLASSH

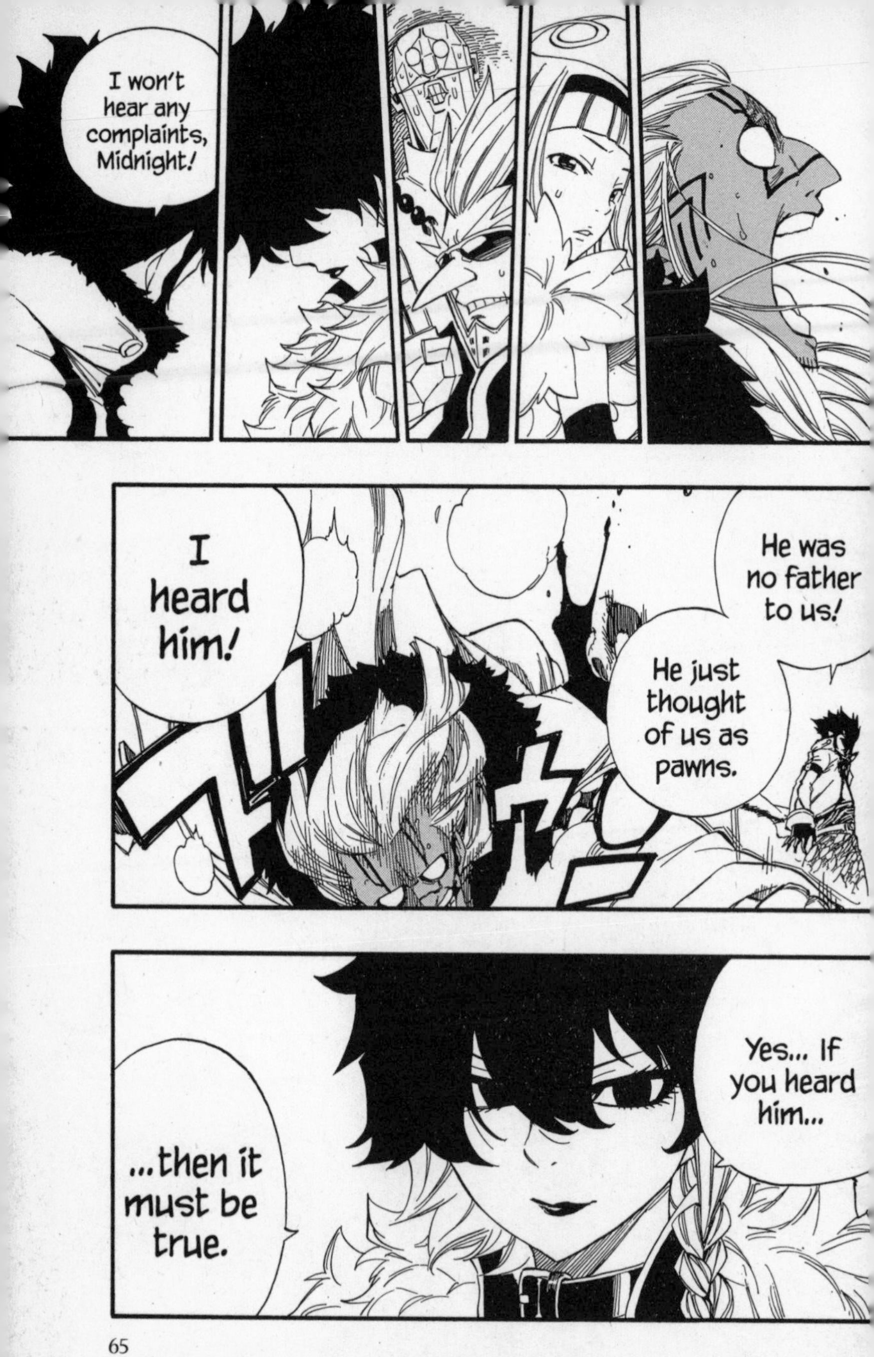
I won't hear any complaints, Midnight!
He was no father to us!
He just thought of us as pawns.
I heard him!
Yes... If you heard him...
...then it must be true.

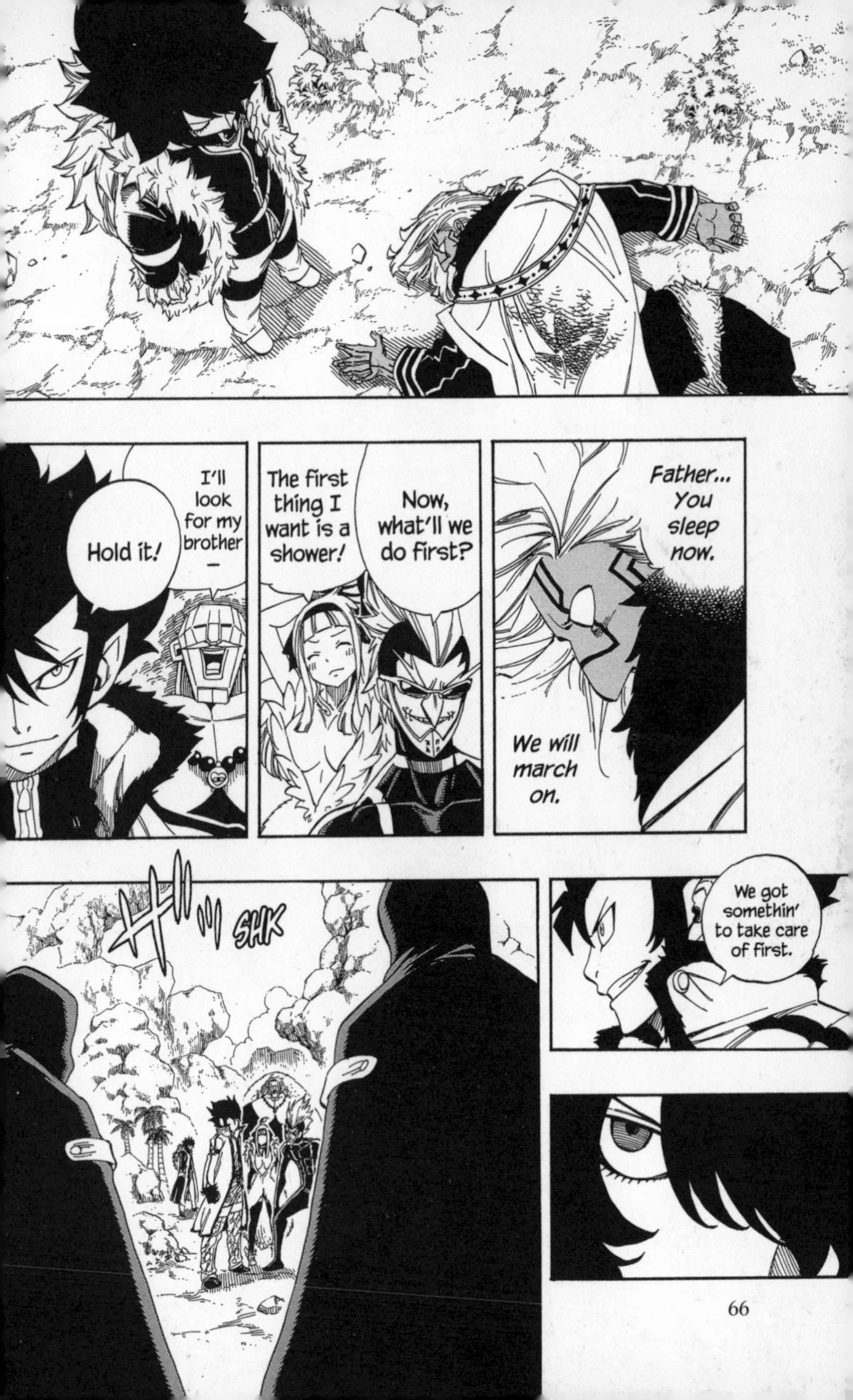
Father... You sleep now.
We will march on.
Now, what'll we do first?
The first thing I want is a shower!
I'll look for my brother —
Hold it!
We got somethin' to take care of first.
SHK

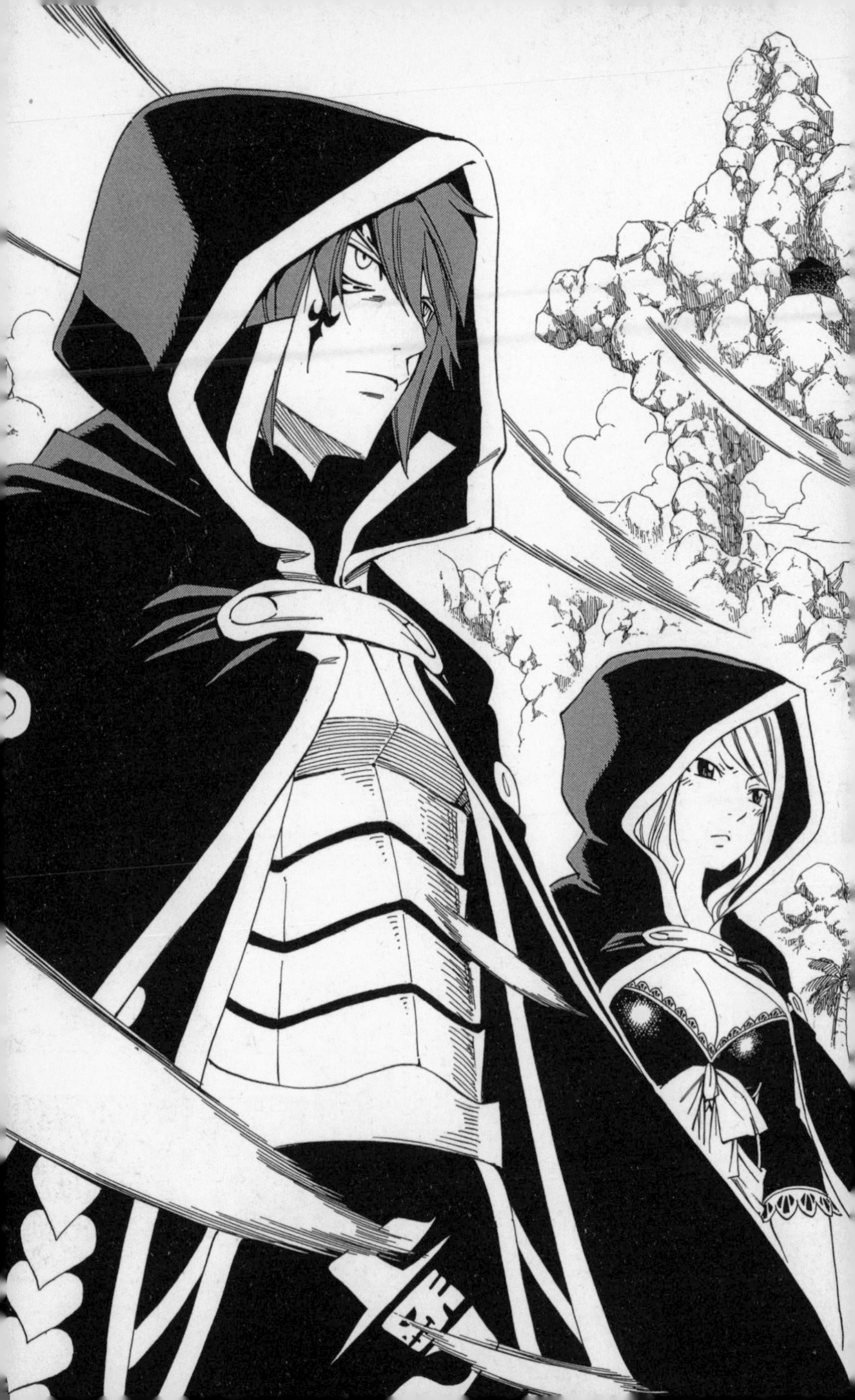

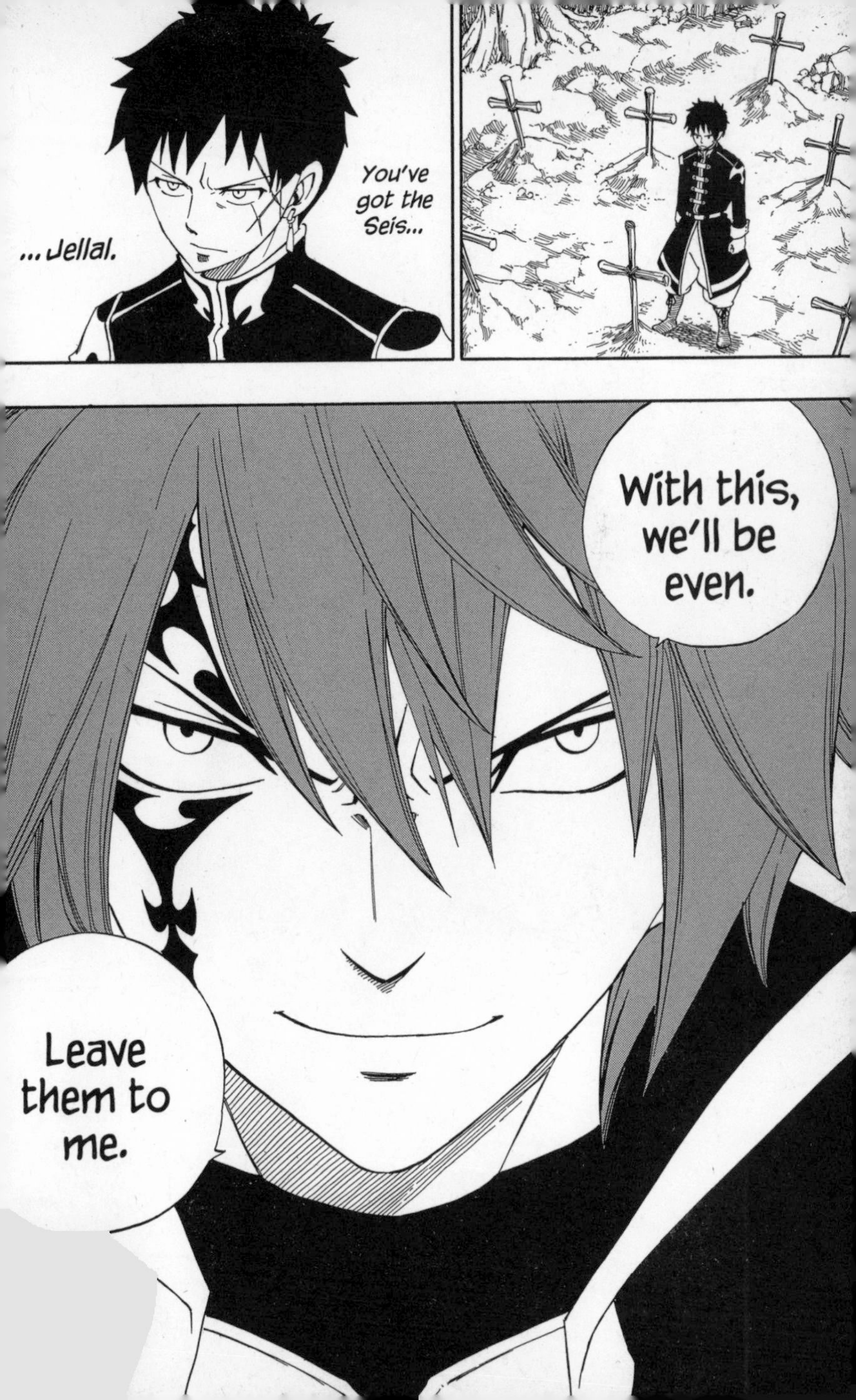
You've got the Seis...
...Jellal.
With this, we'll be even.
Leave them to me.

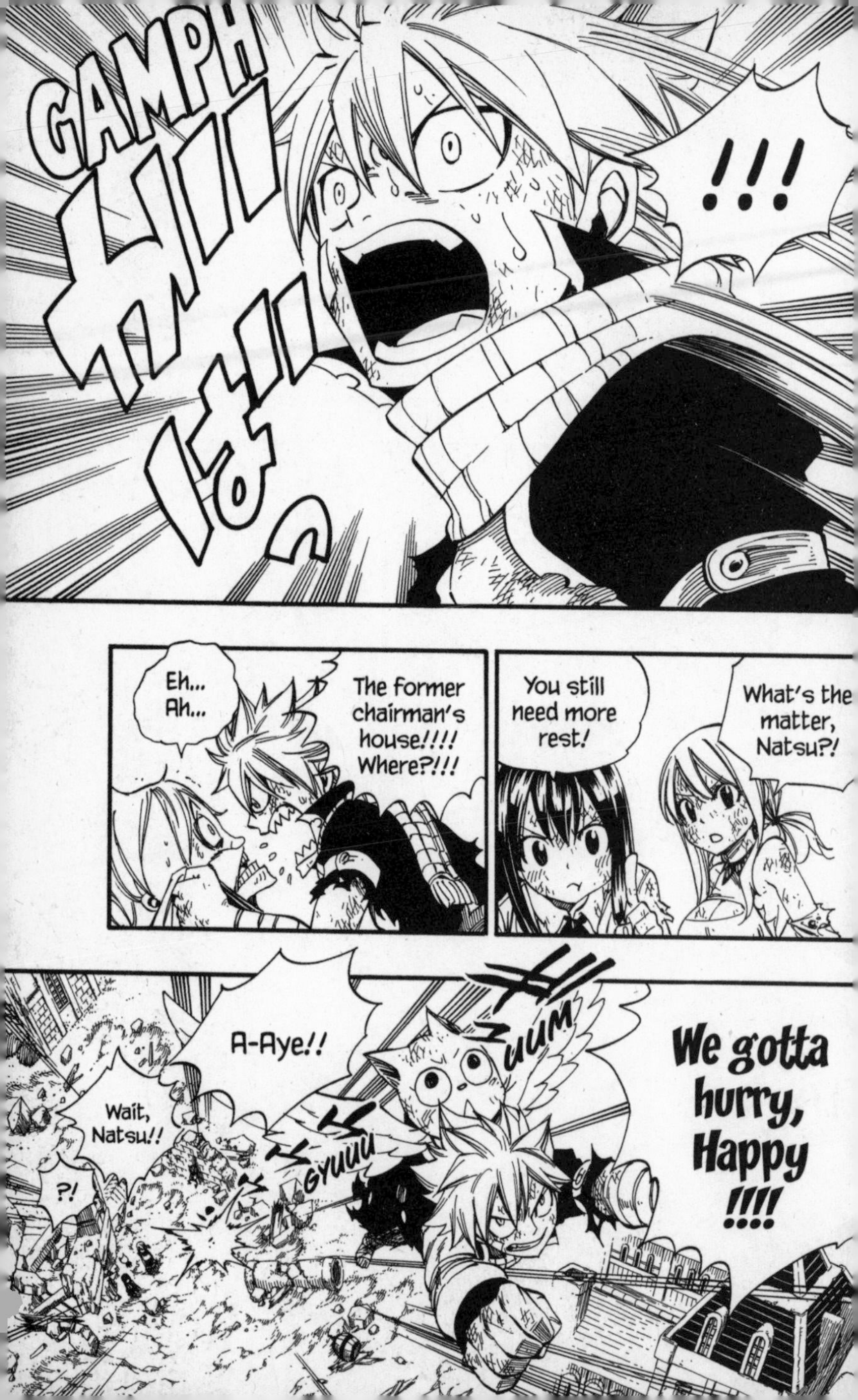
!!!
GAMPH
What's the matter, Natsu?!
You still need more rest!
The former chairman's house!!!! Where?!!!
Eh... Ah...
We gotta hurry, Happy!!!!
ZUUM
A-Aye!!
GYUUU
Wait, Natsu!!
?!

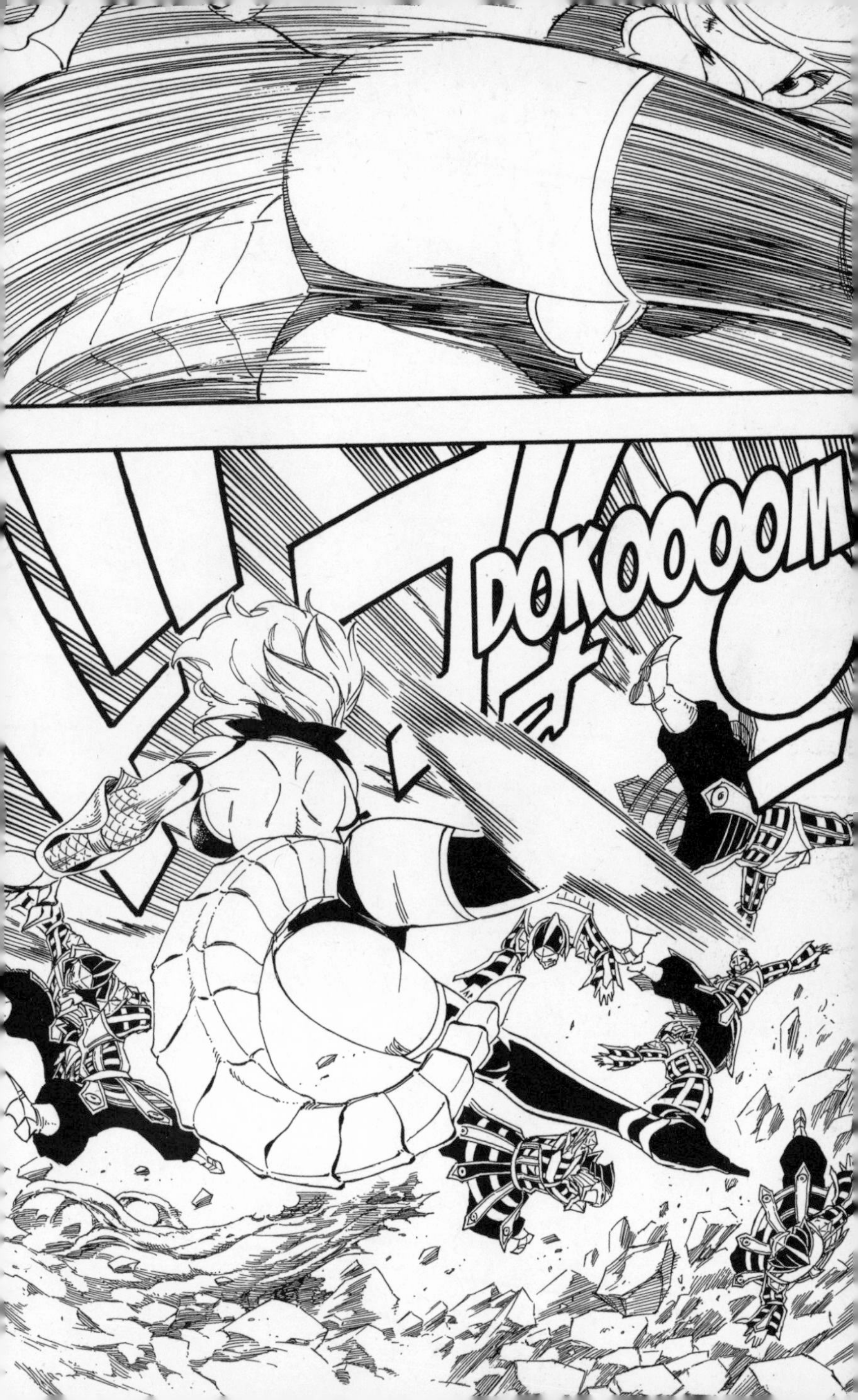
DOKOOOOM

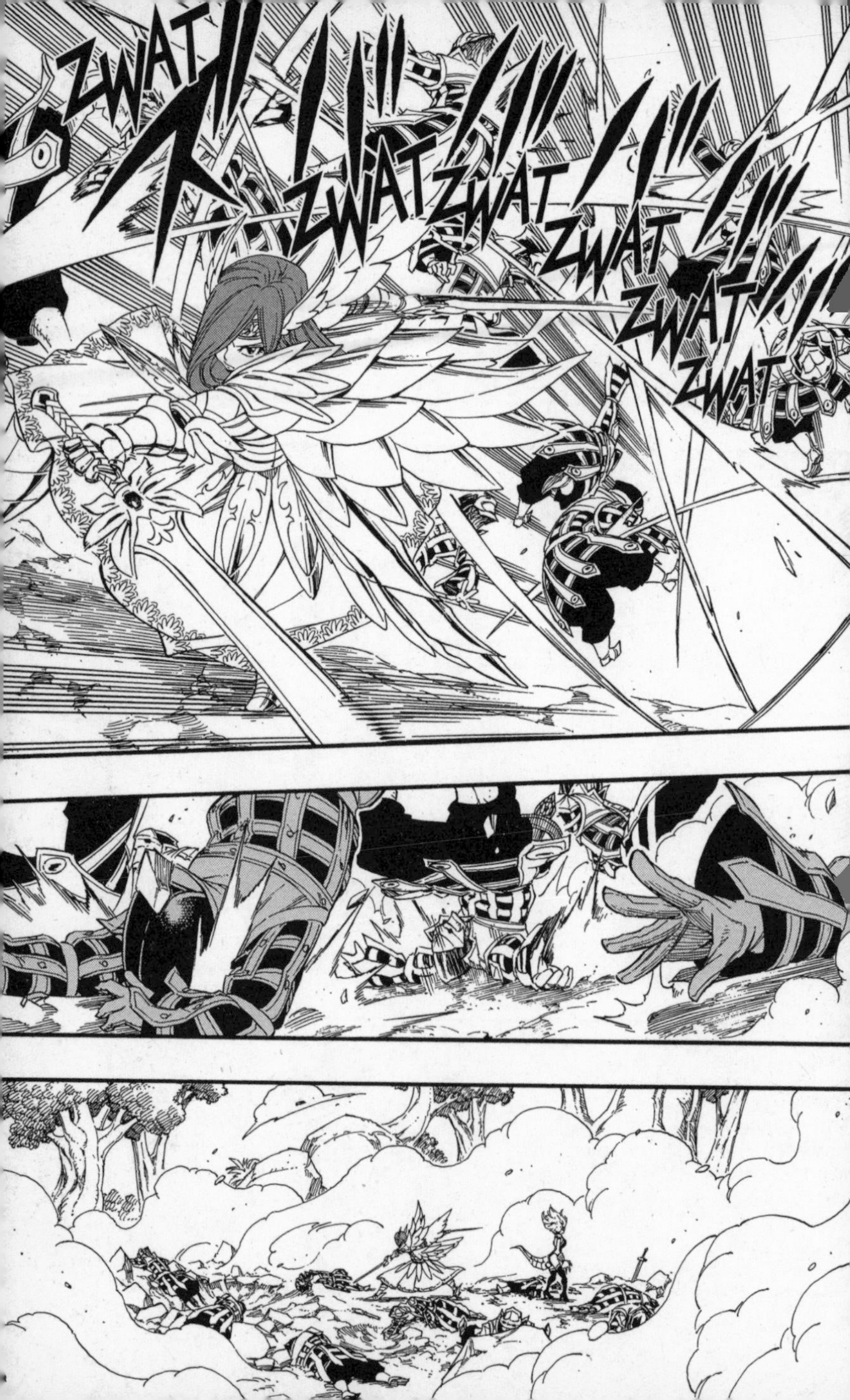
ZWAT!!
ZWAT!!
ZWAT!!
ZWAT!!
ZWAT!!
ZWAT

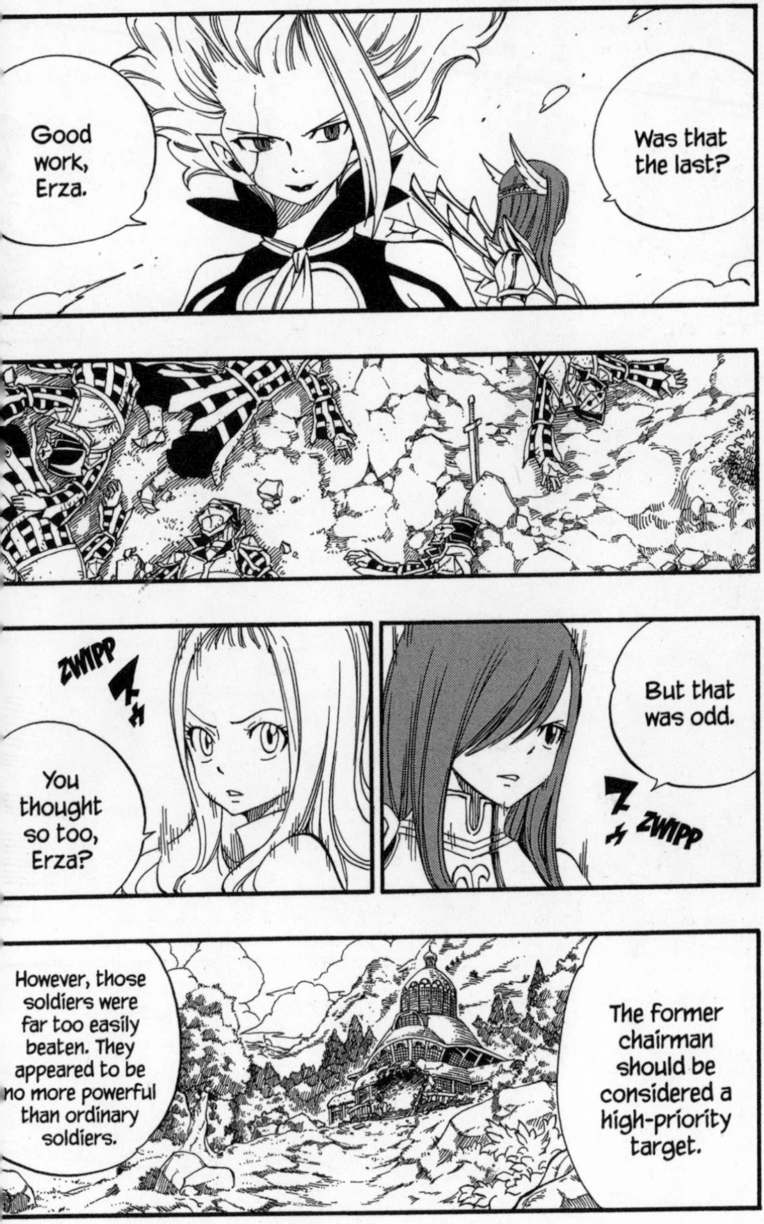
Was that the last?
Good work, Erza.
But that was odd.
ZWIPP
ZWIPP
You thought so too, Erza?
The former chairman should be considered a high-priority target.
However, those soldiers were far too easily beaten. They appeared to be no more powerful than ordinary soldiers.

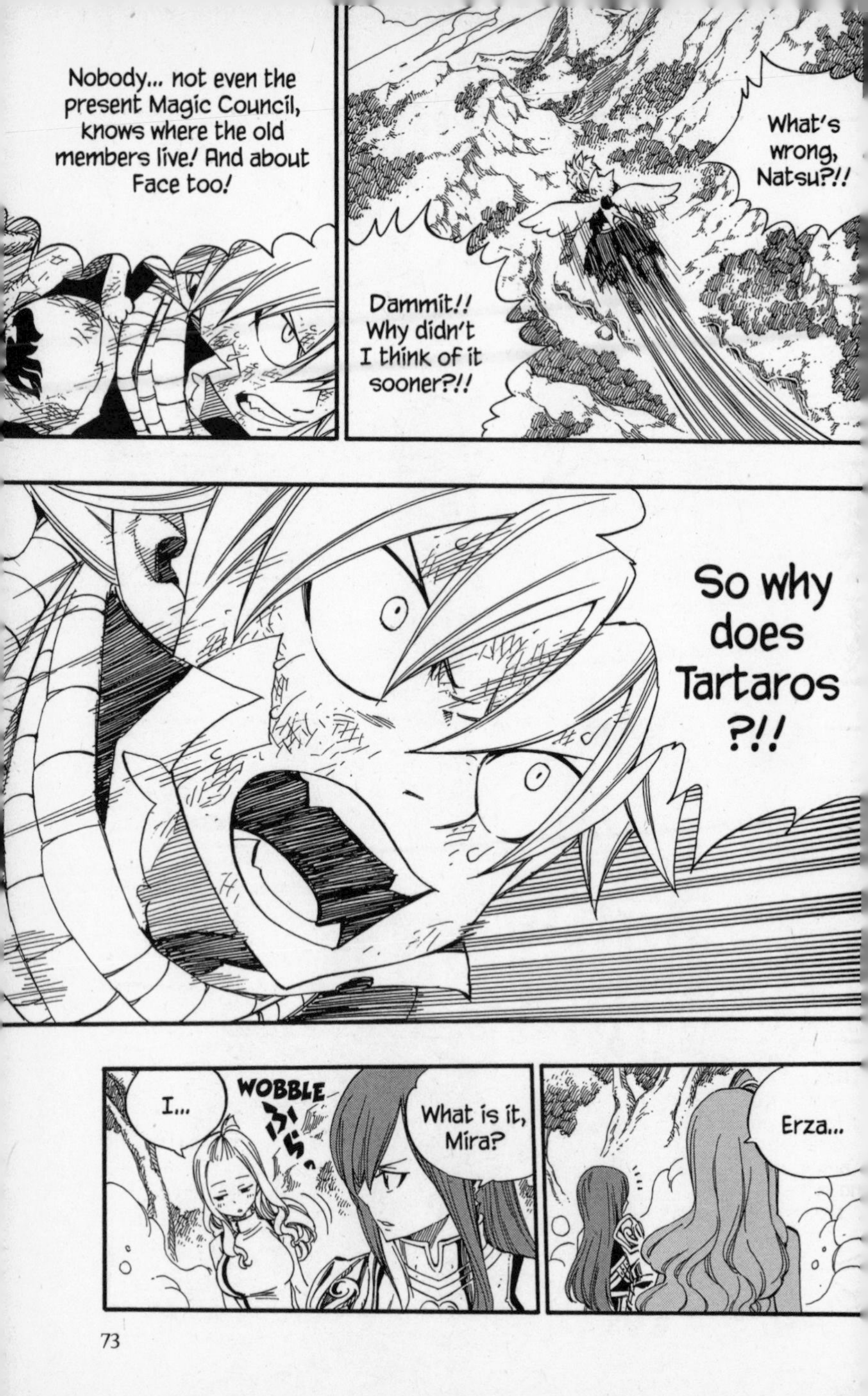
What's wrong, Natsu?!!
Dammit!! Why didn't I think of it sooner?!!
Nobody... not even the present Magic Council, knows where the old members live! And about Face too!
So why does Tartaros ?!!
Erza...
What is it, Mira?
WOBBLE
ふら
I...

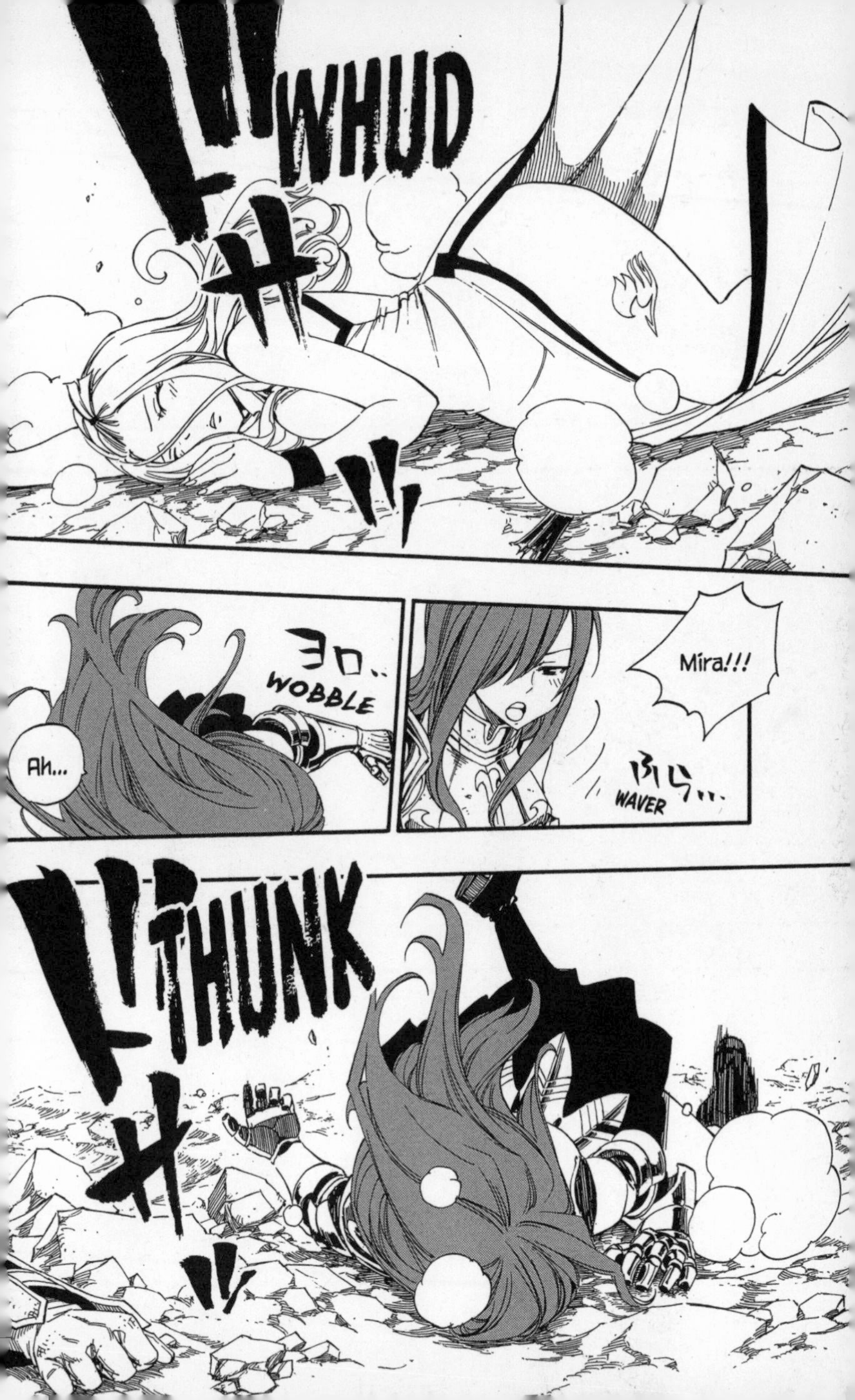
WHUD
Mira!!!
ふら‥
WAVER
ヨロ‥
WOBBLE
Ah...
THUNK

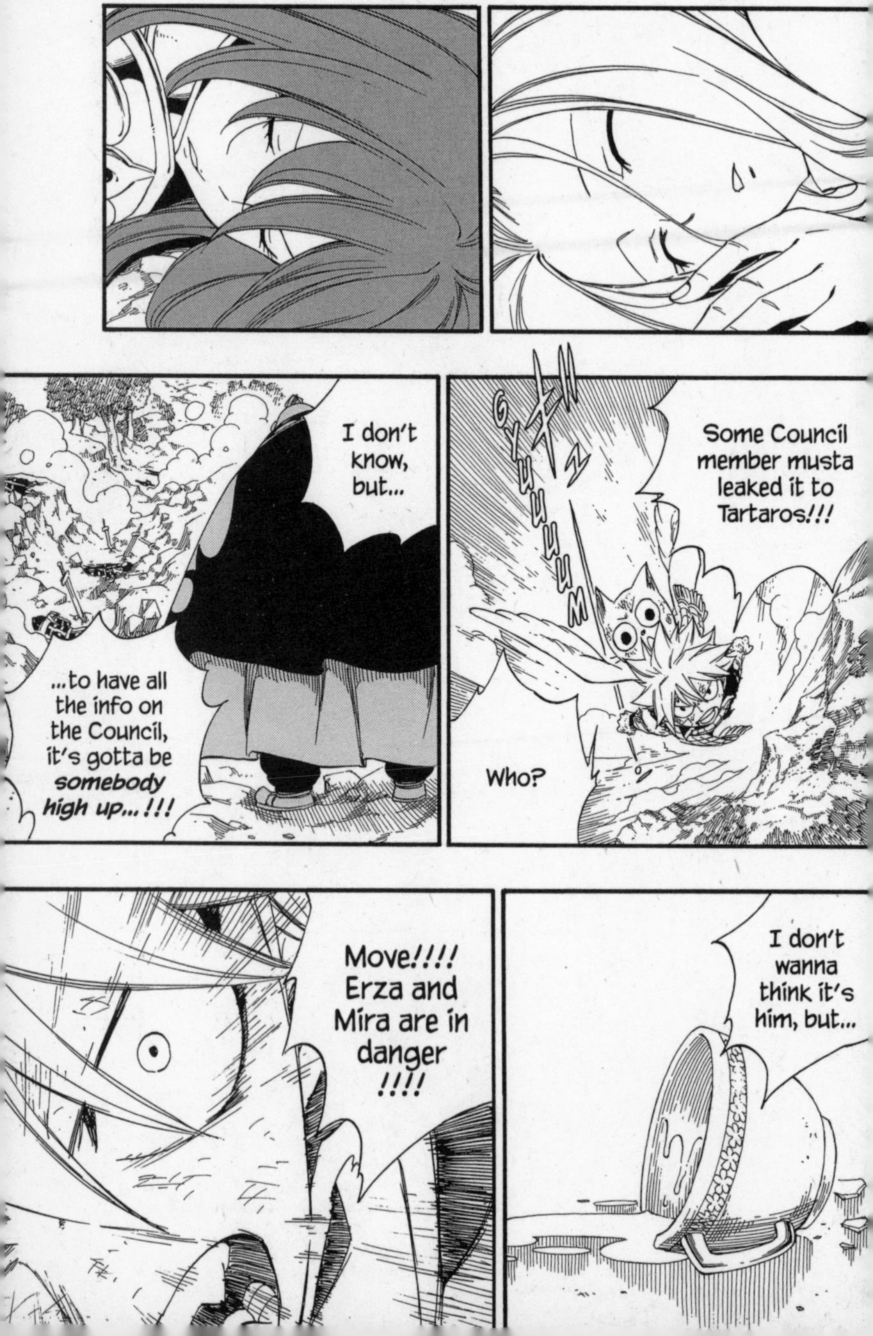
GYUUUUM
Some Council member musta leaked it to Tartaros!!!
Who?
I don't know, but...
...to have all the info on the Council, it's gotta be *somebody high up*...!!!
I don't wanna think it's him, but...
Move!!!! Erza and Mira are in danger!!!!

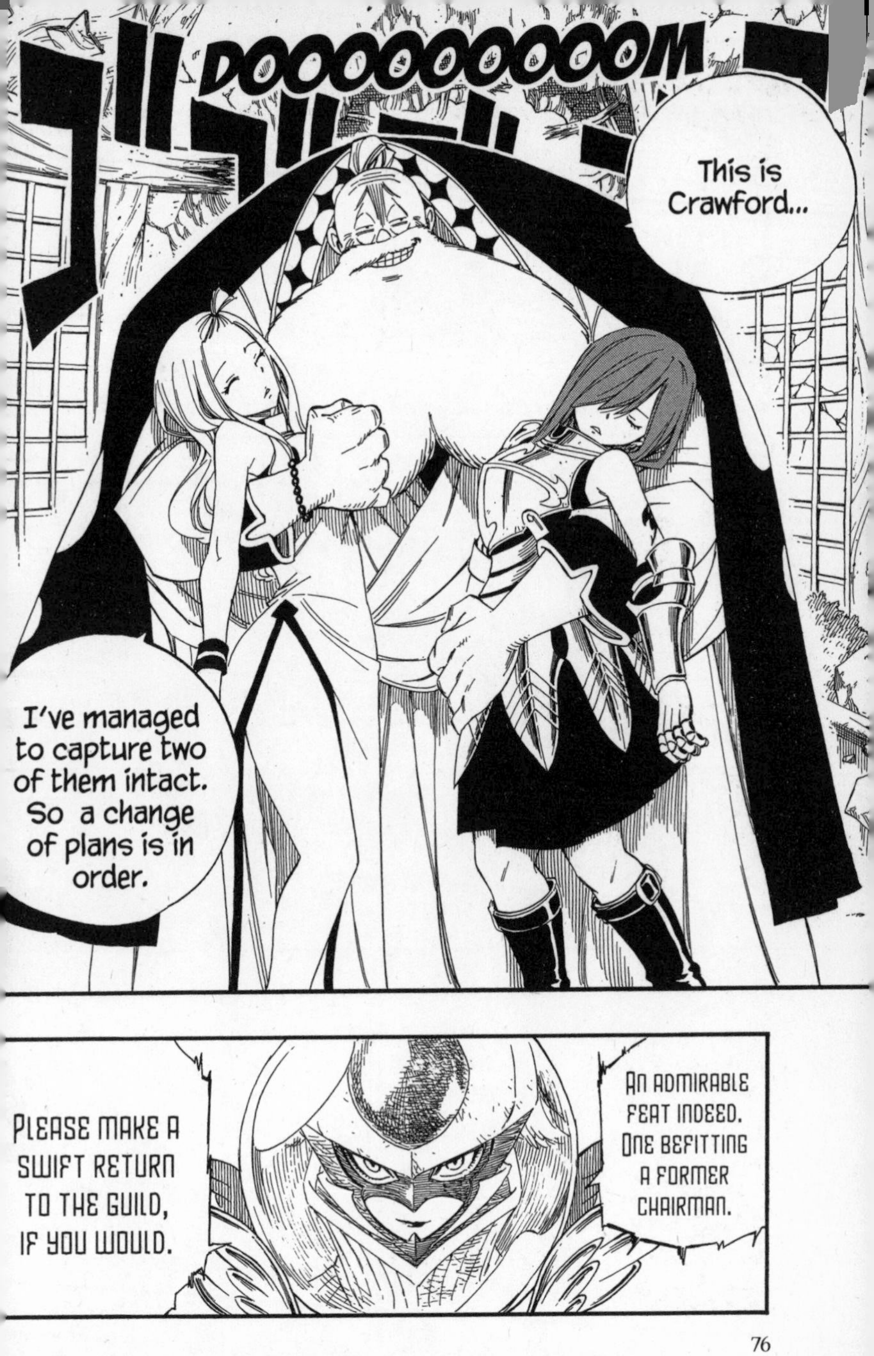
DOOOOOOOOM
This is Crawford...
I've managed to capture two of them intact. So a change of plans is in order.
An admirable feat indeed. One befitting a former chairman.
Please make a swift return to the guild, if you would.

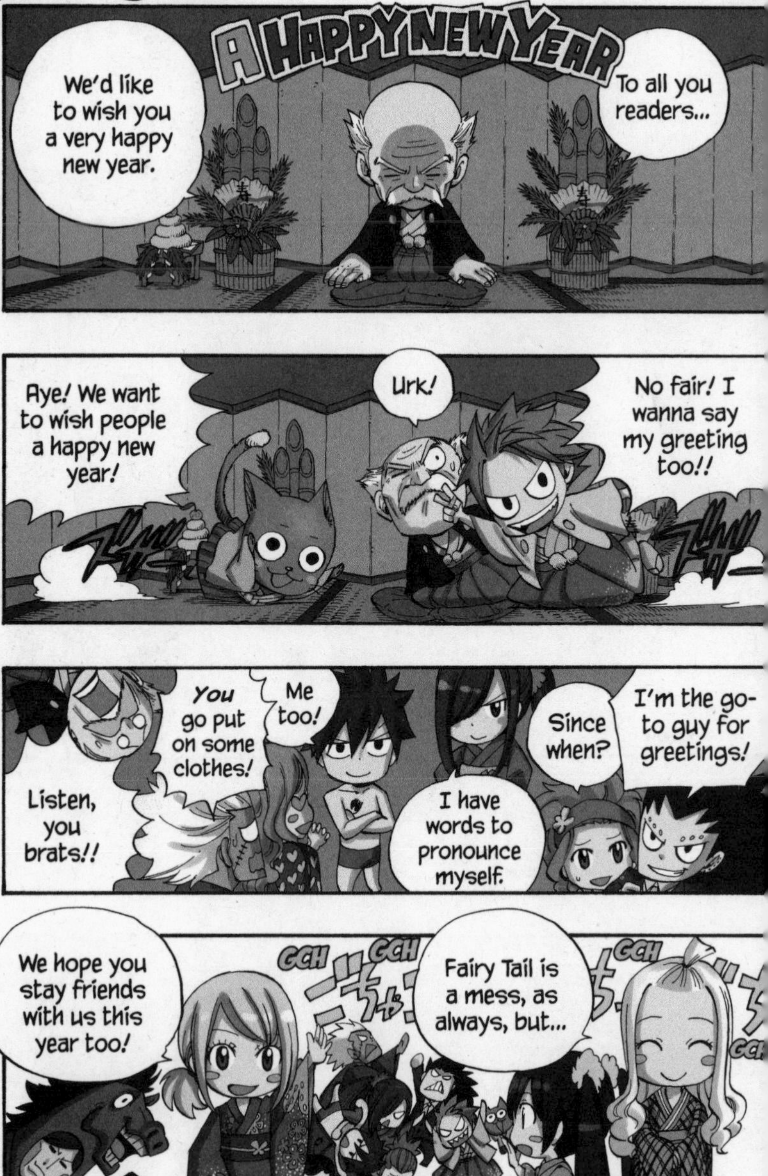
A HAPPY NEW YEAR
To all you readers...
We'd like to wish you a very happy new year.
No fair! I wanna say my greeting too!!
Urk!
Aye! We want to wish people a happy new year!
I'm the go-to guy for greetings!
Since when?
I have words to pronounce myself.
Me too!
You go put on some clothes!
Listen, you brats!!
GCH
GCH
GCH
Fairy Tail is a mess, as always, but...
GCH
We hope you stay friends with us this year too!

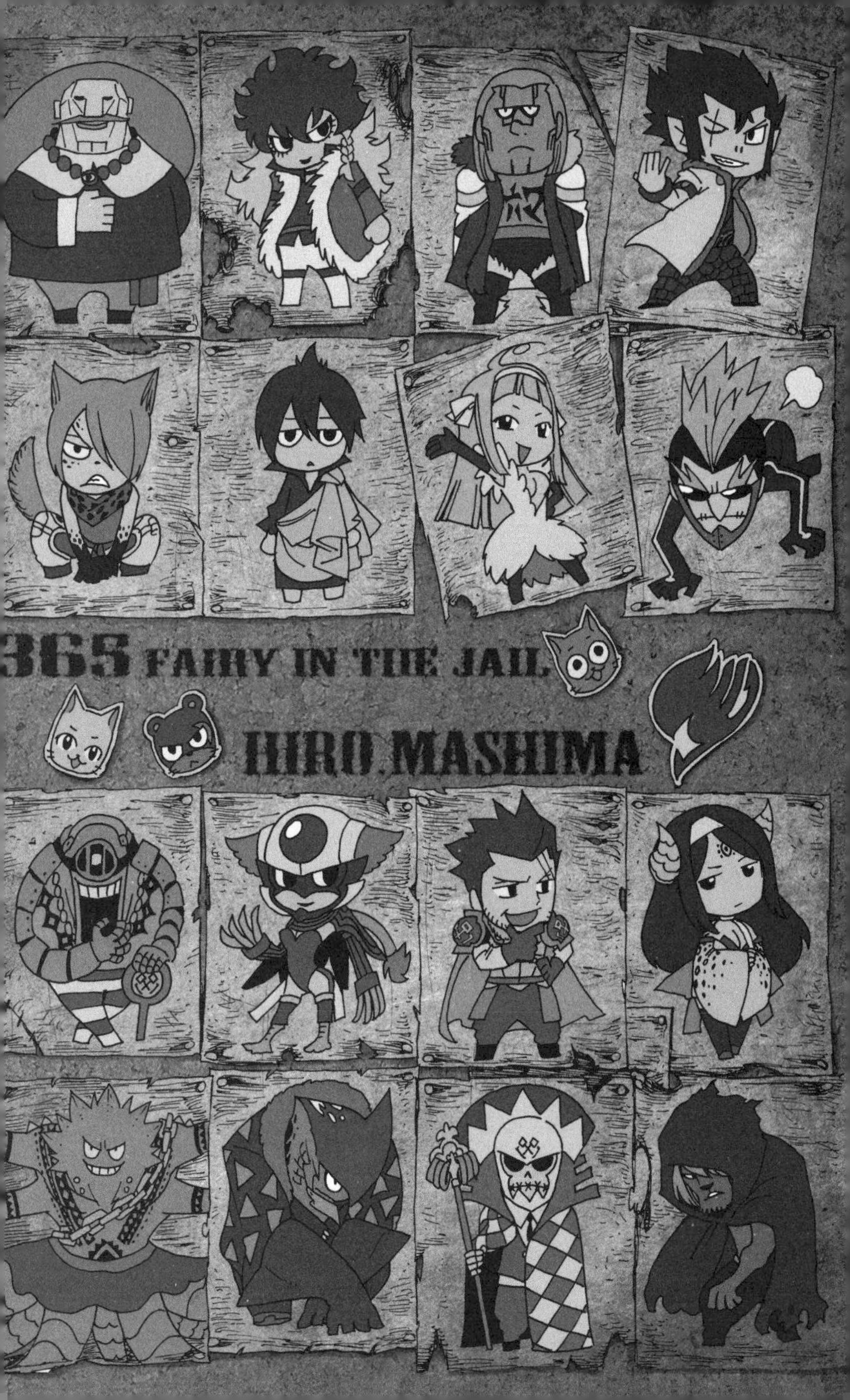
365 FAIRY IN THE JAIL
HIRO MASHIMA

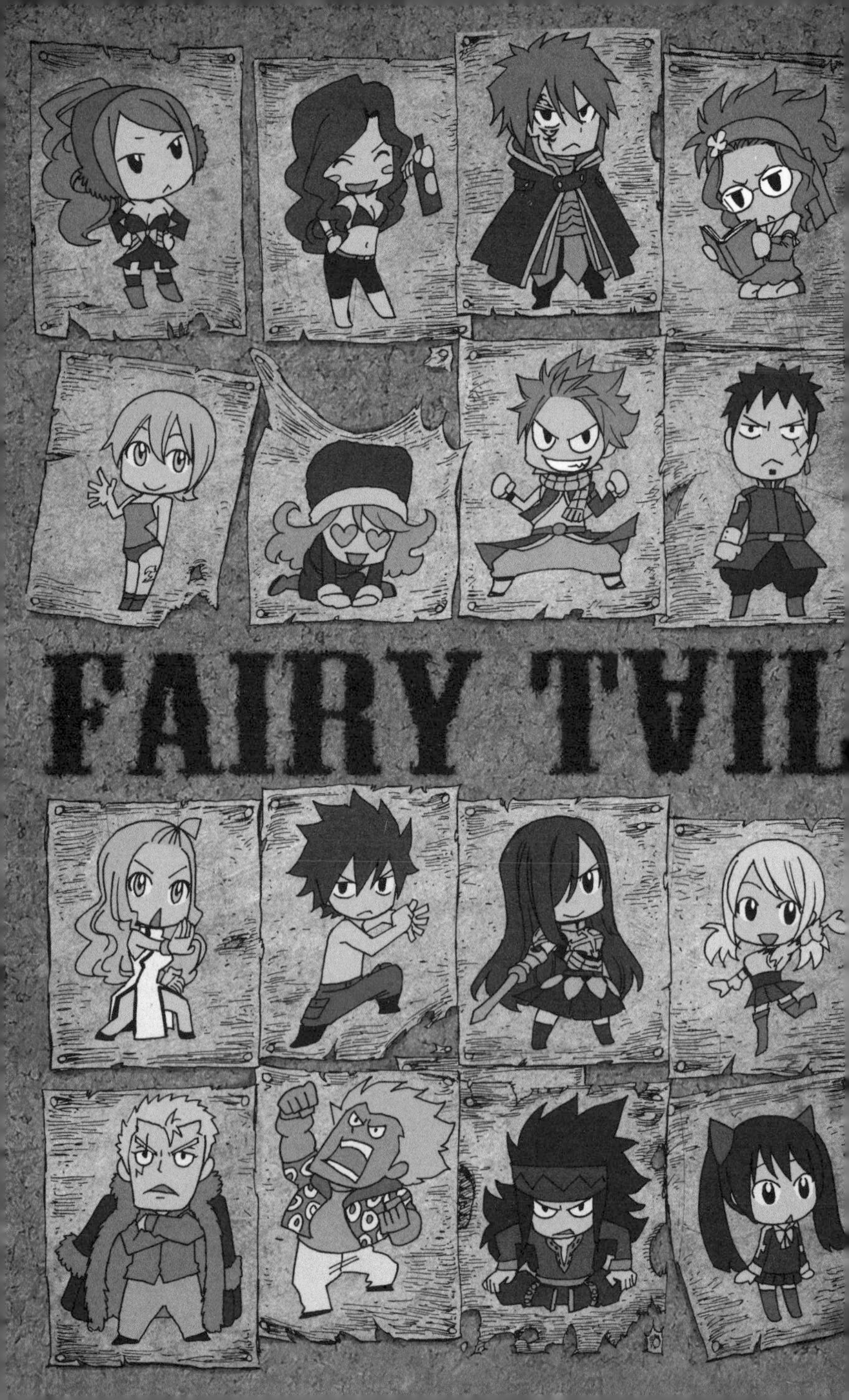
FAIRY TAIL

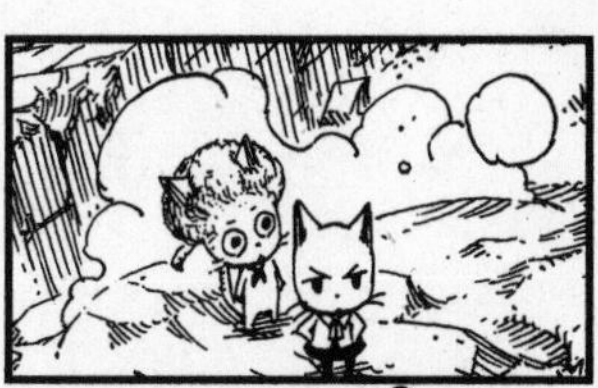

FAIRY TAIL

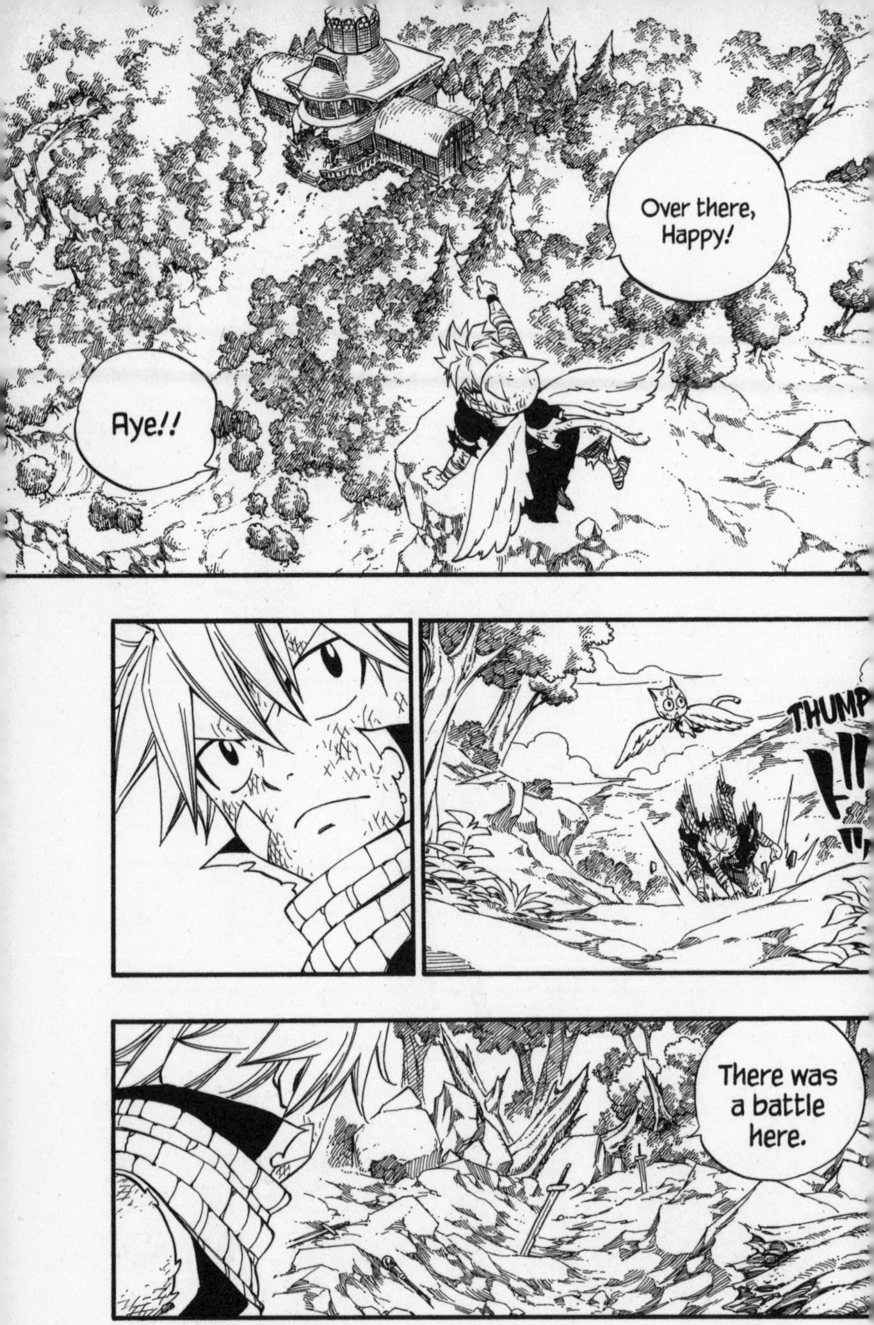
Over there, Happy!
Aye!!
THUMP
There was a battle here.

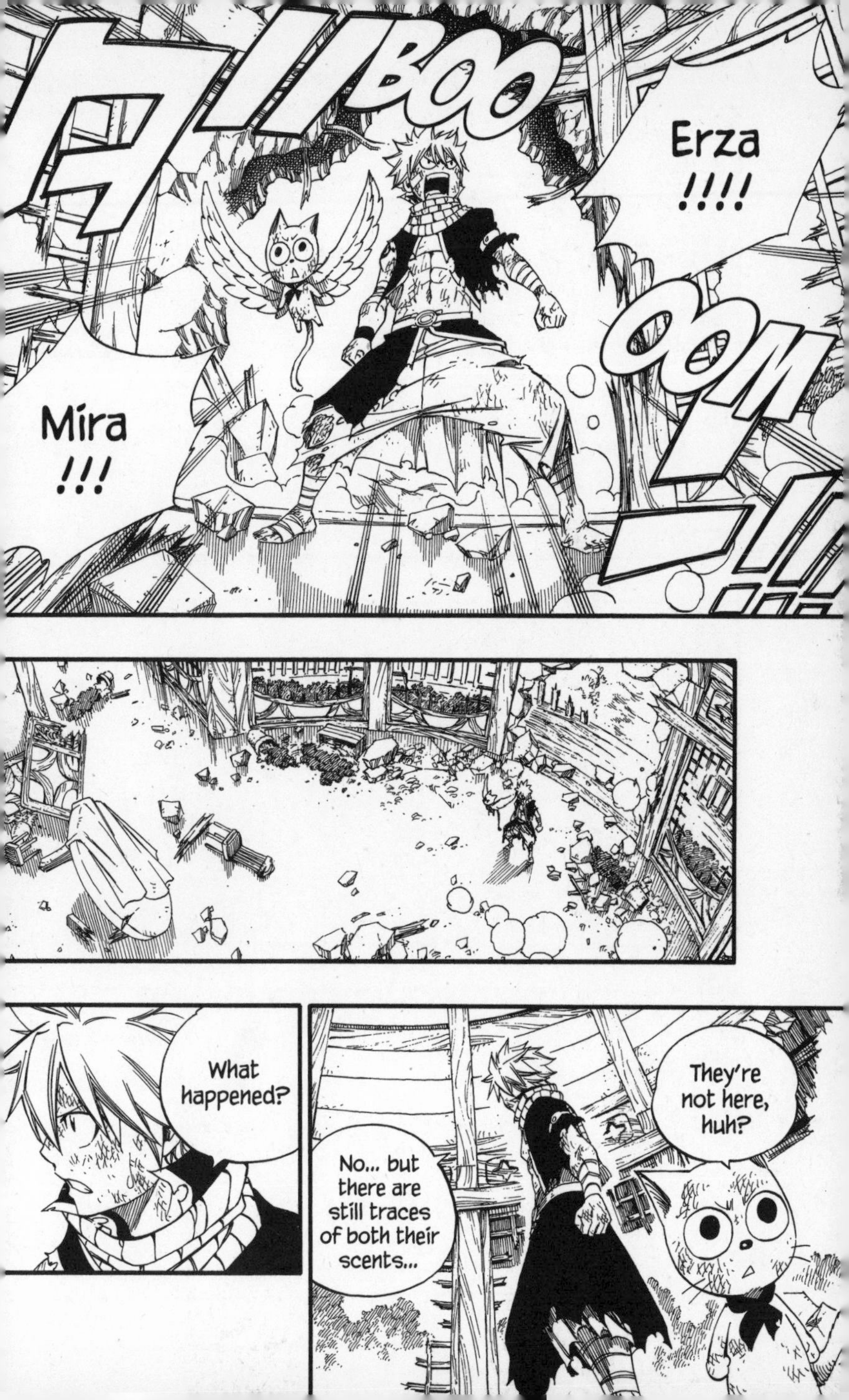
BOO
Erza !!!!
OOM
Mira !!!
They're not here, huh?
No... but there are still traces of both their scents...
What happened?

I... smell a strong odor of herbs.

That smell...

TUMP

TUMP

TUMP

SNIFF

SNIFF

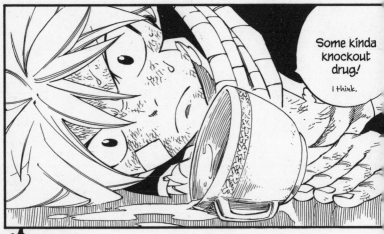

Some kinda knockout drug!

I think.

Da

mmi

iiit!!

GANNCH

TREMBLE

TREMBLE

TREMBLE

You don't think the guy put Erza and Mira to sleep, do you?

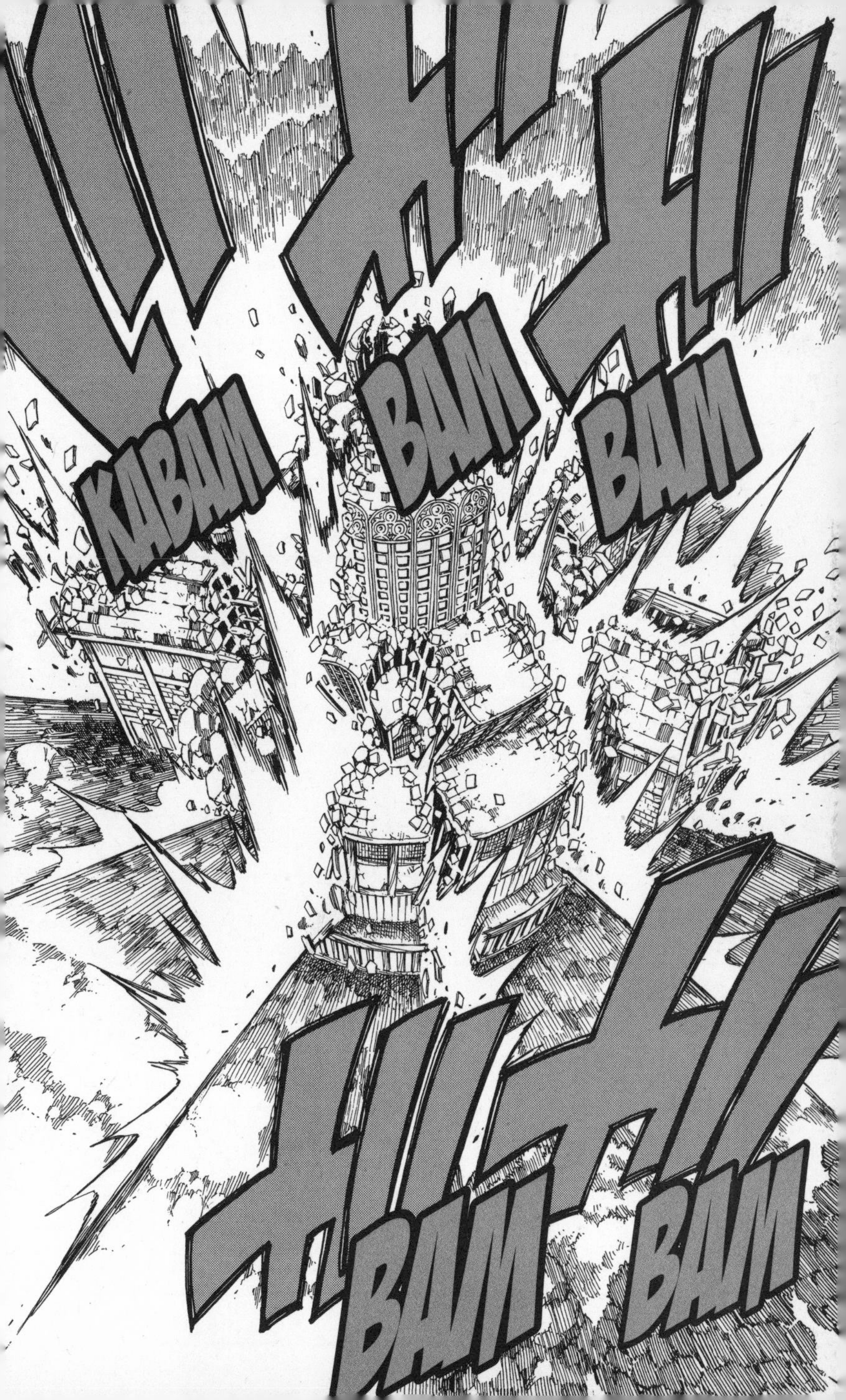
BAM
BAM
KABAM
BAM
BAM

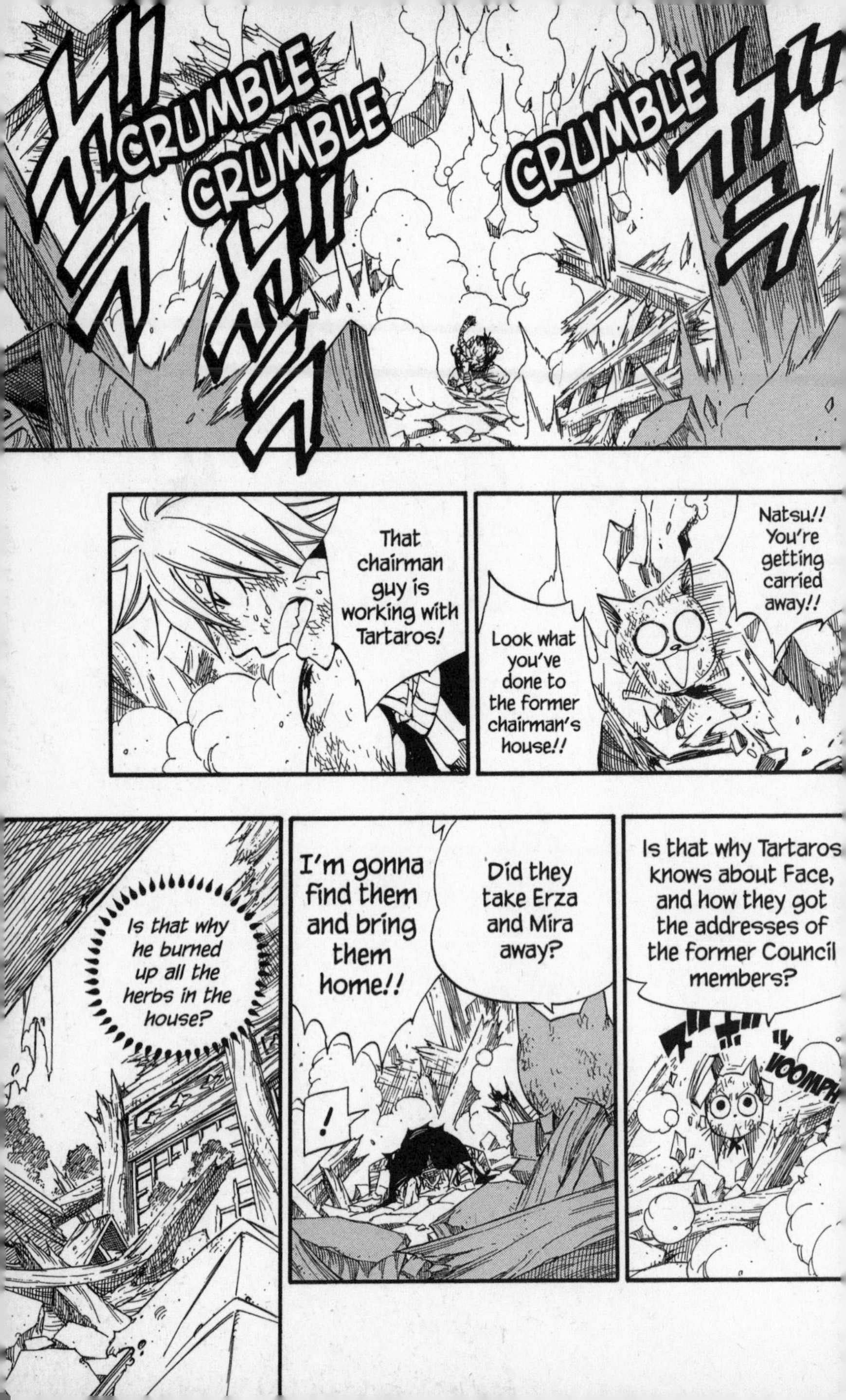
CRUMBLE
CRUMBLE
CRUMBLE
Natsu!! You're getting carried away!!
Look what you've done to the former chairman's house!!
That chairman guy is working with Tartaros!
Is that why Tartaros knows about Face, and how they got the addresses of the former Council members?
VOOMPH
Did they take Erza and Mira away?
I'm gonna find them and bring them home!!
!
Is that why he burned up all the herbs in the house?

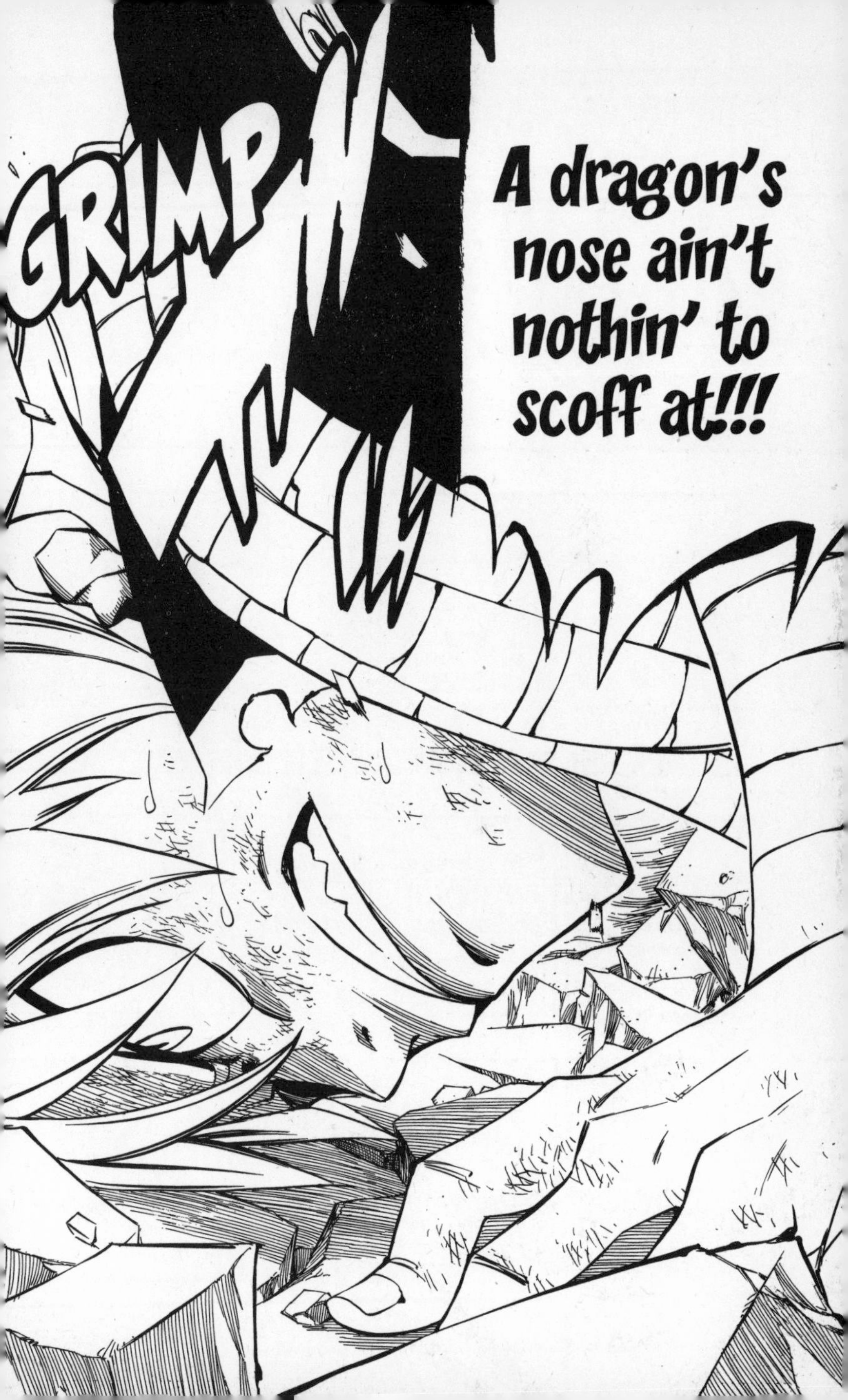
A dragon's nose ain't nothin' to scoff at!!!
GRIMP

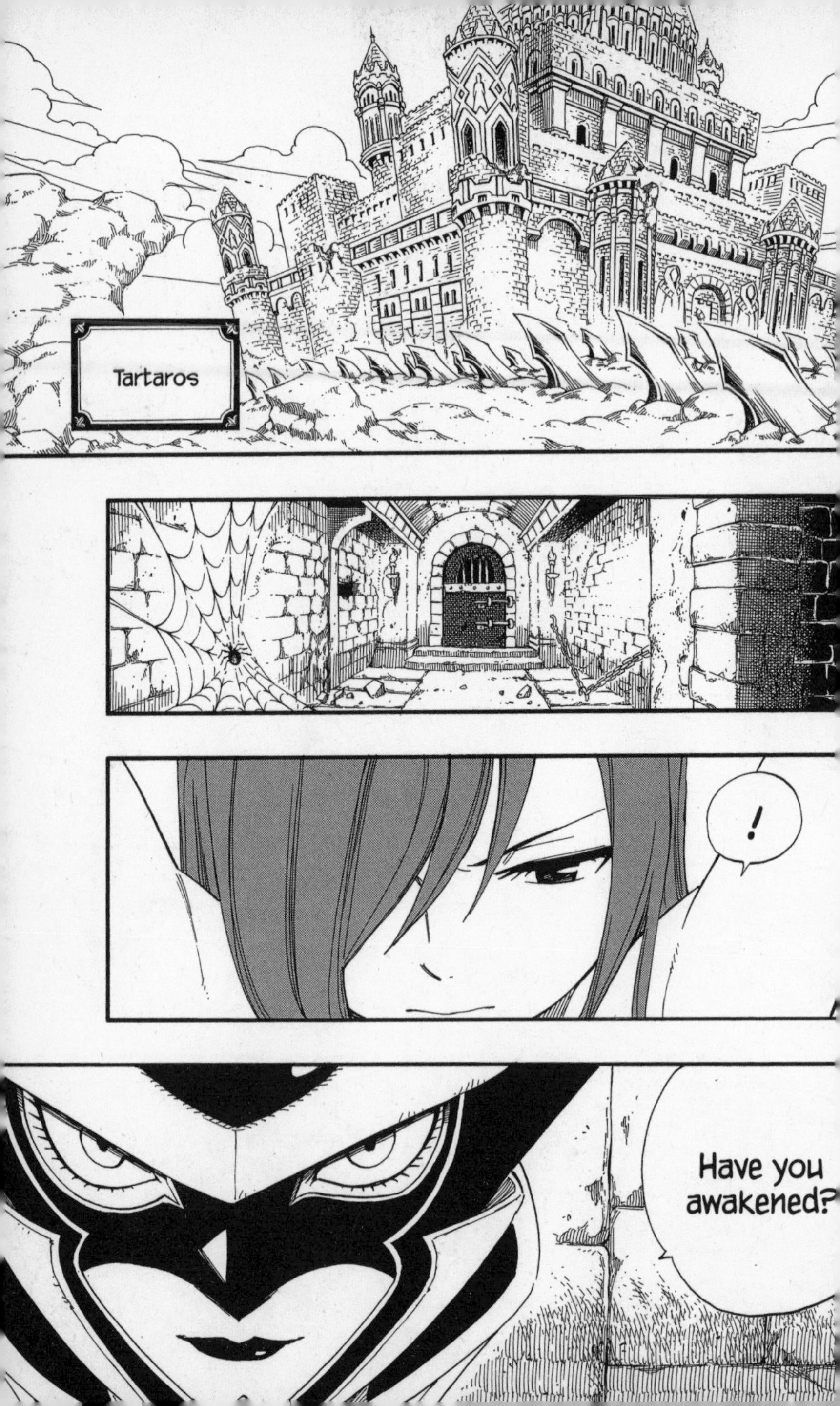
Tartaros
!
Have you awakened?

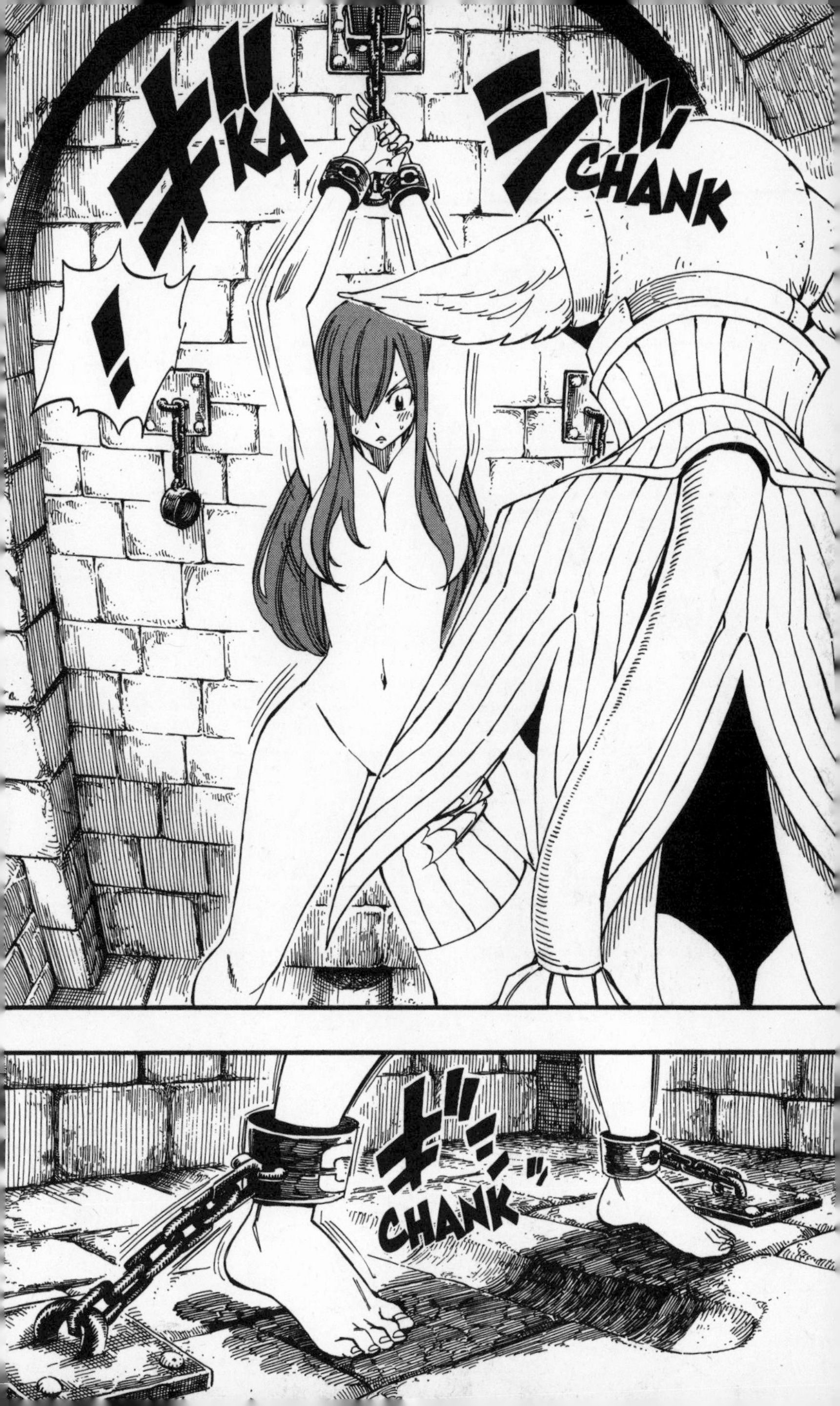
CHANK
KA
!
CHANK

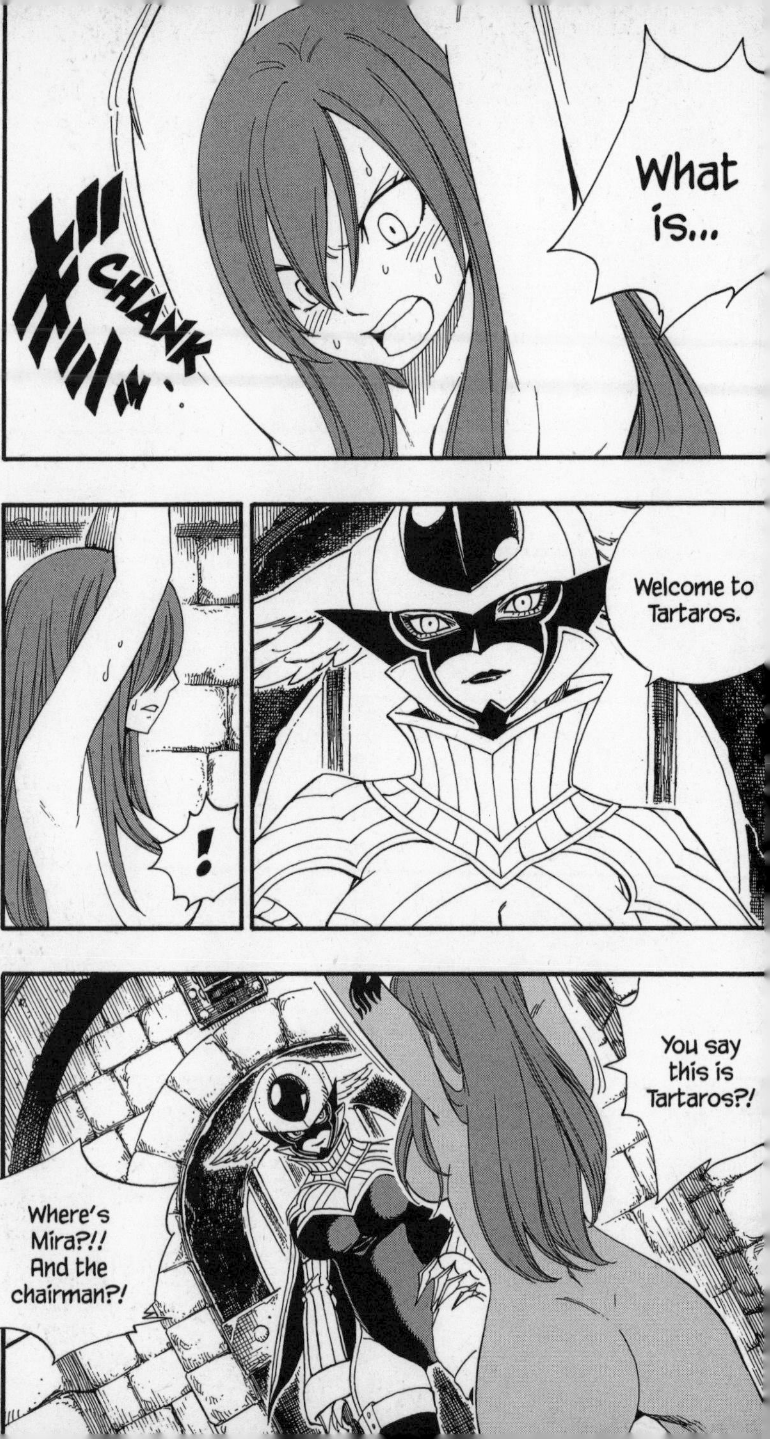

What is...
CHANK
Welcome to Tartaros.
!
You say this is Tartaros?!
Where's Mira?!! And the chairman?!

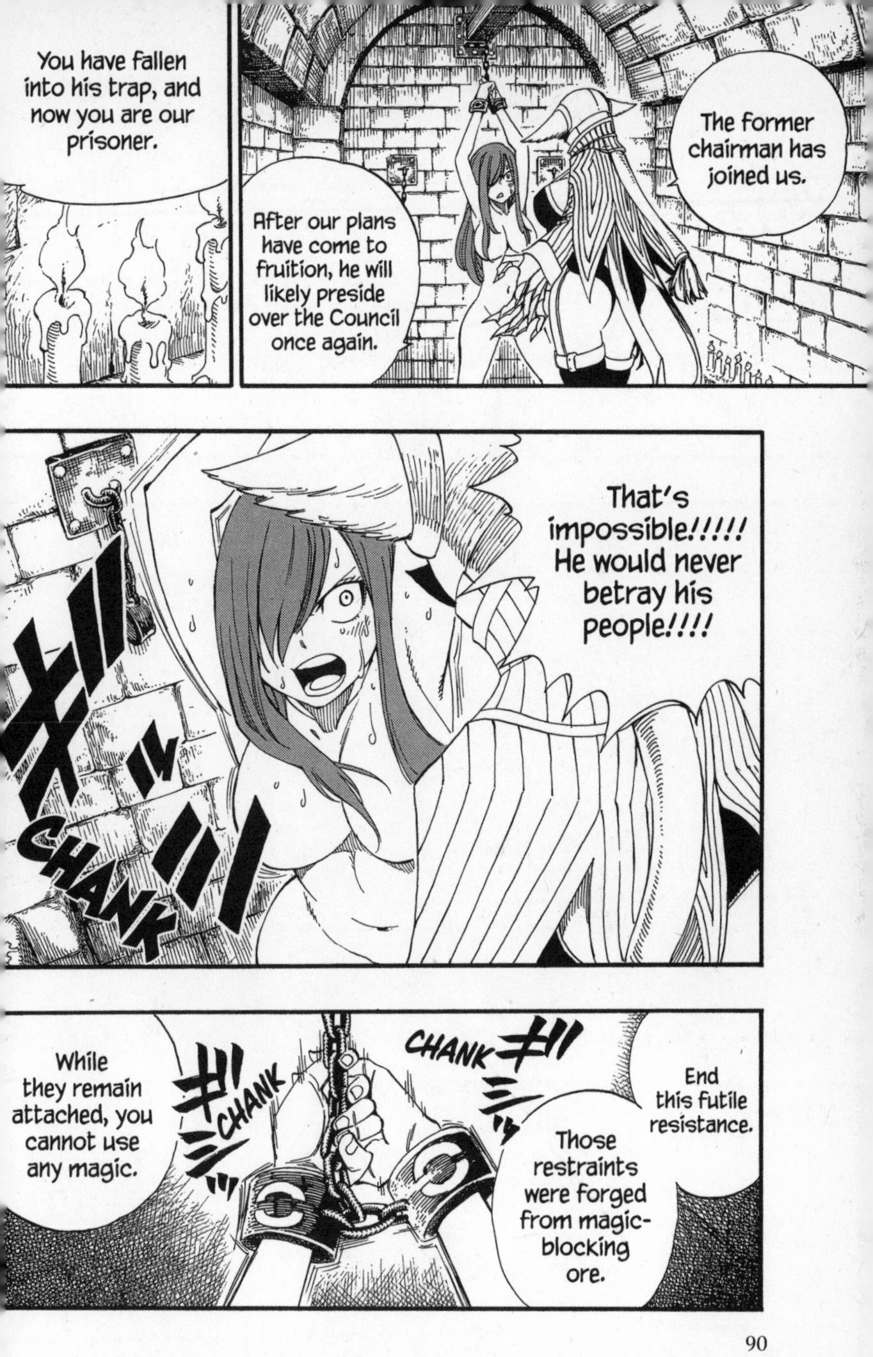
The former chairman has joined us.
After our plans have come to fruition, he will likely preside over the Council once again.
You have fallen into his trap, and now you are our prisoner.
That's impossible!!!!! He would never betray his people!!!!
CHANK
End this futile resistance.
Those restraints were forged from magic-blocking ore.
CHANK
CHANK
While they remain attached, you cannot use any magic.

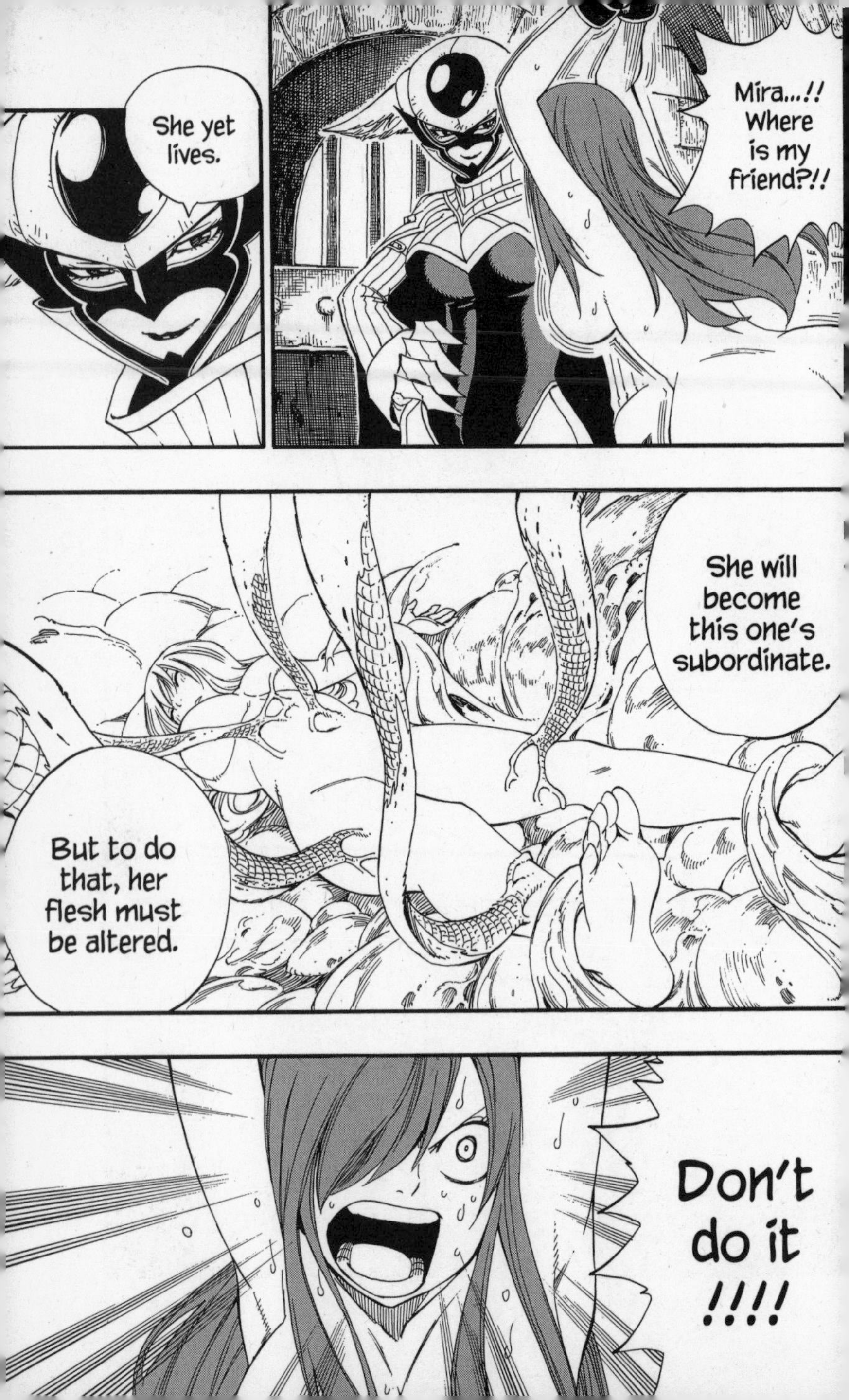
Mira...!! Where is my friend?!!
She yet lives.
She will become this one's subordinate.
But to do that, her flesh must be altered.
Don't do it !!!!

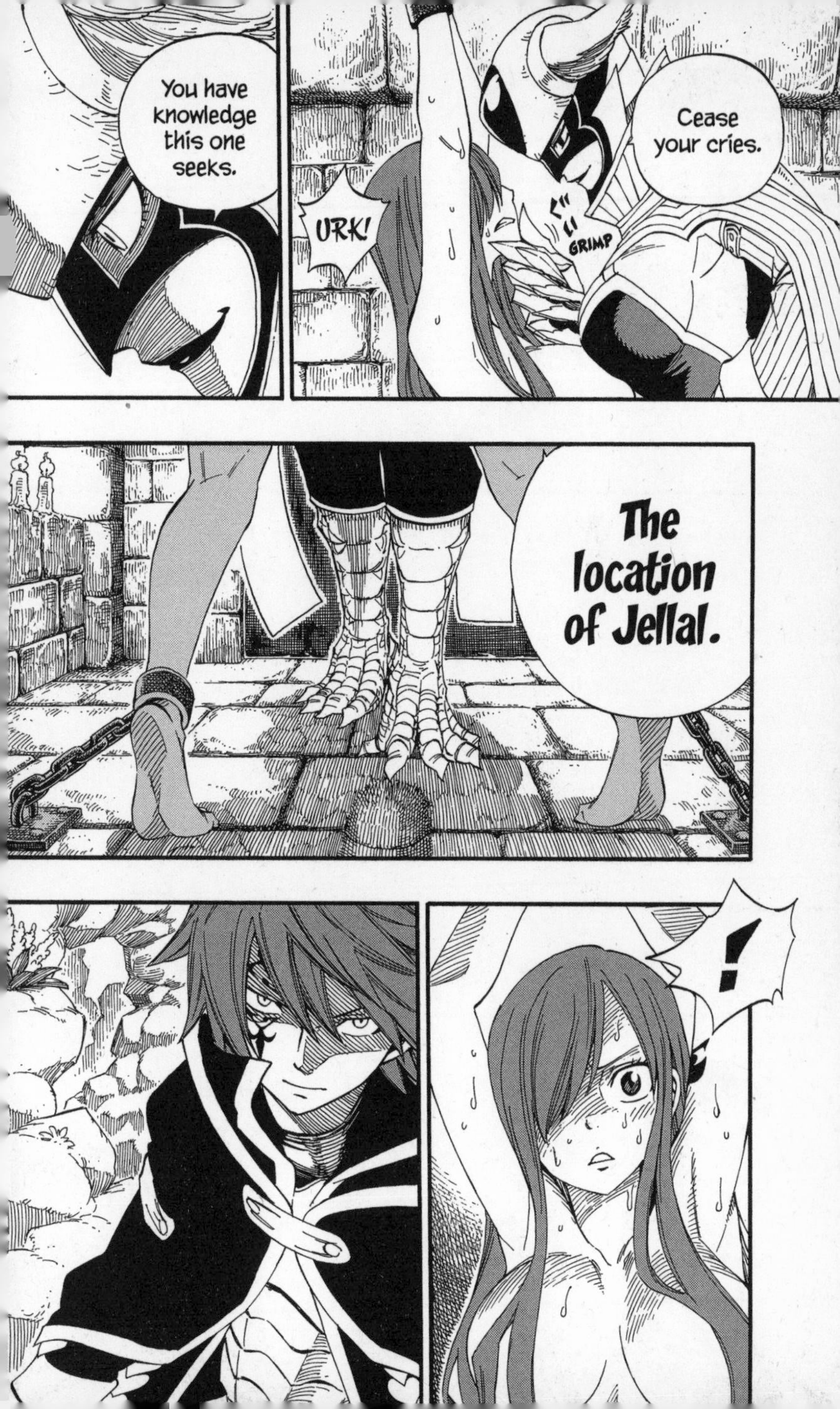
Cease your cries.
GRIMP
URK!
You have knowledge this one seeks.
The location of Jellal.
!

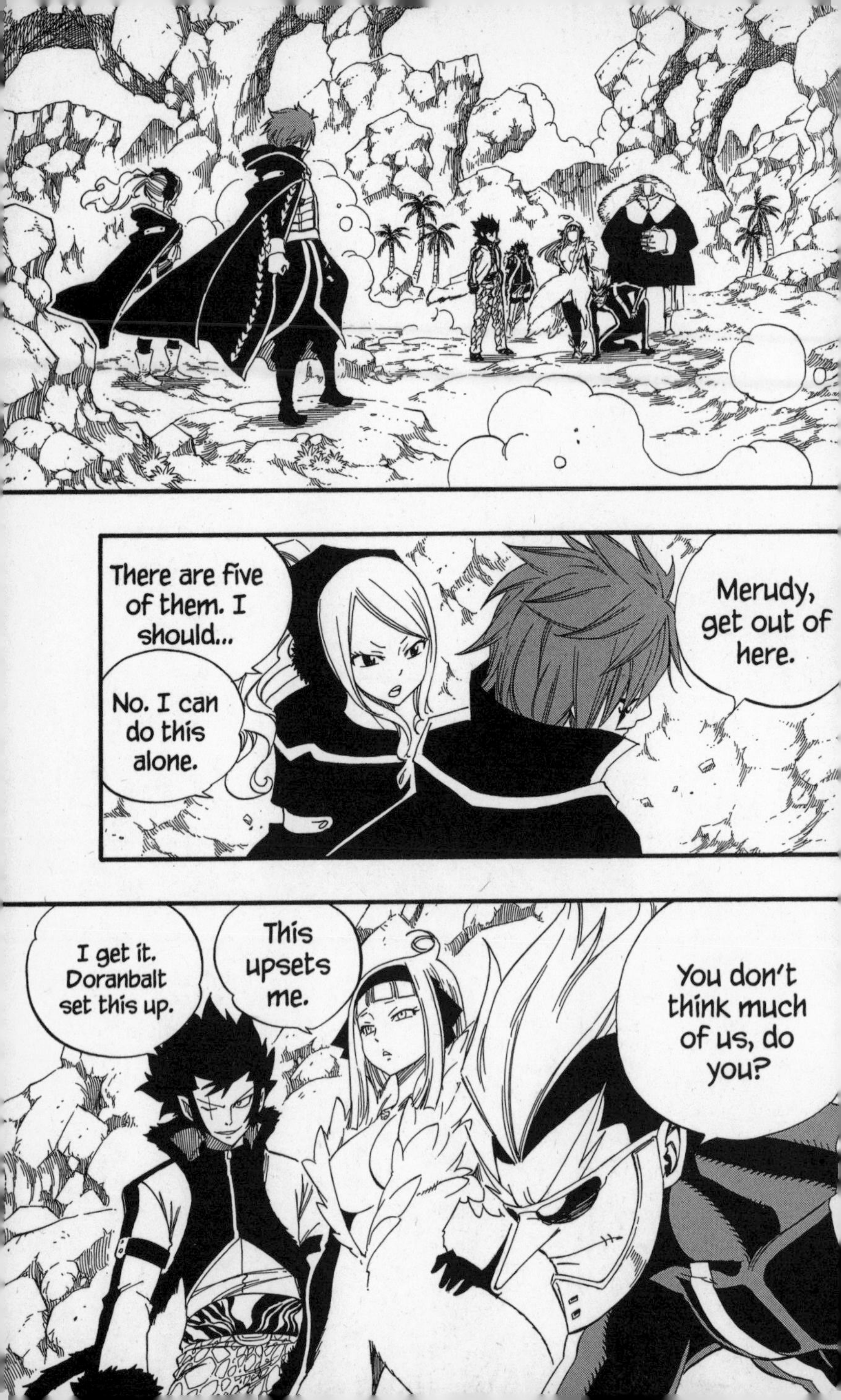
Merudy, get out of here.
There are five of them. I should...
No. I can do this alone.
You don't think much of us, do you?
This upsets me.
I get it. Doranbalt set this up.

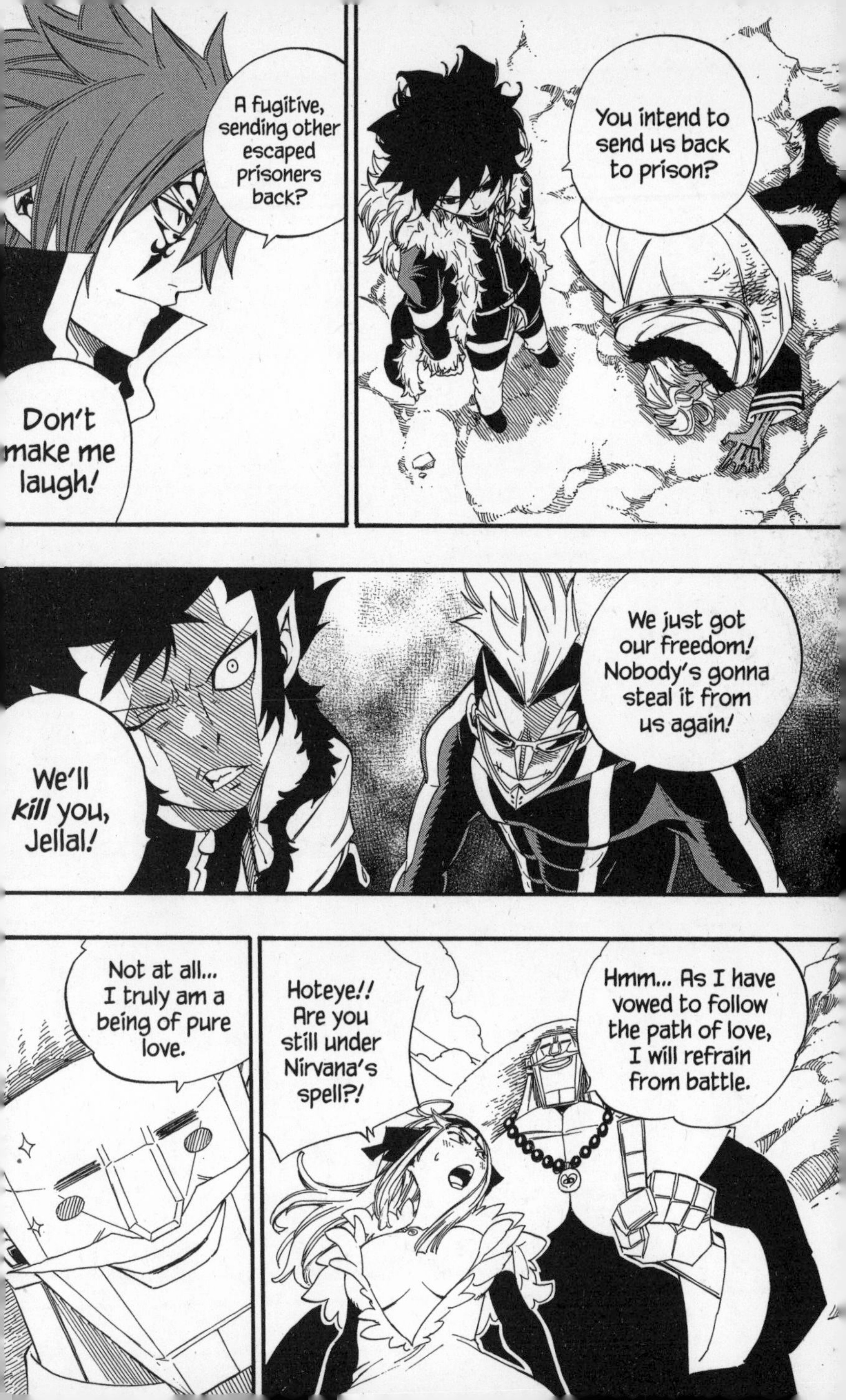
You intend to send us back to prison?
A fugitive, sending other escaped prisoners back?
Don't make me laugh!
We just got our freedom! Nobody's gonna steal it from us again!
We'll *kill* you, Jellal!
Hmm... As I have vowed to follow the path of love, I will refrain from battle.
Hoteye!! Are you still under Nirvana's spell?!
Not at all... I truly am a being of pure love.

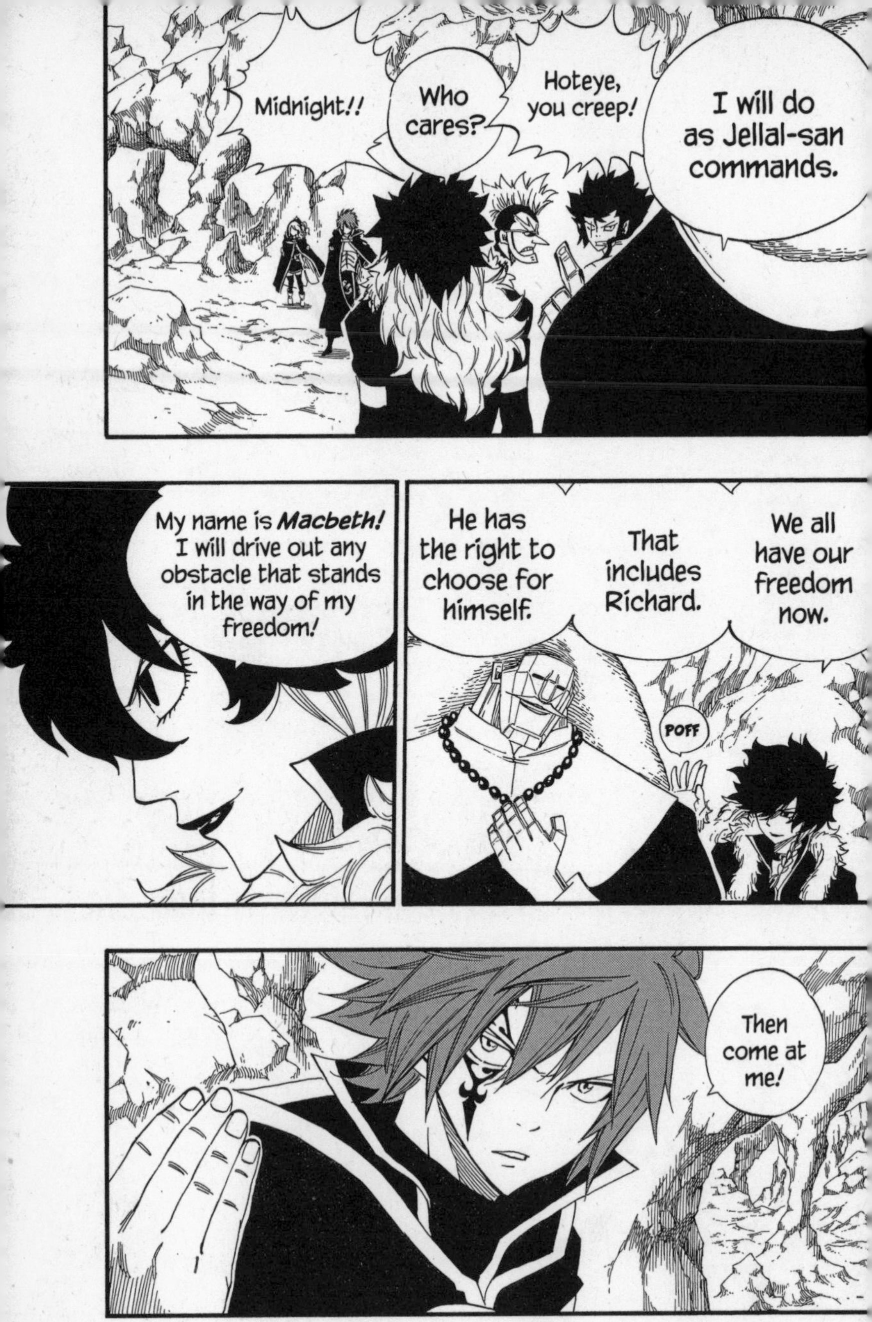
I will do as Jellal-san commands.
Hoteye, you creep!
Who cares?
Midnight!!
We all have our freedom now.
That includes Richard.
He has the right to choose for himself.
POFF
My name is *Macbeth!* I will drive out any obstacle that stands in the way of my freedom!
Then come at me!

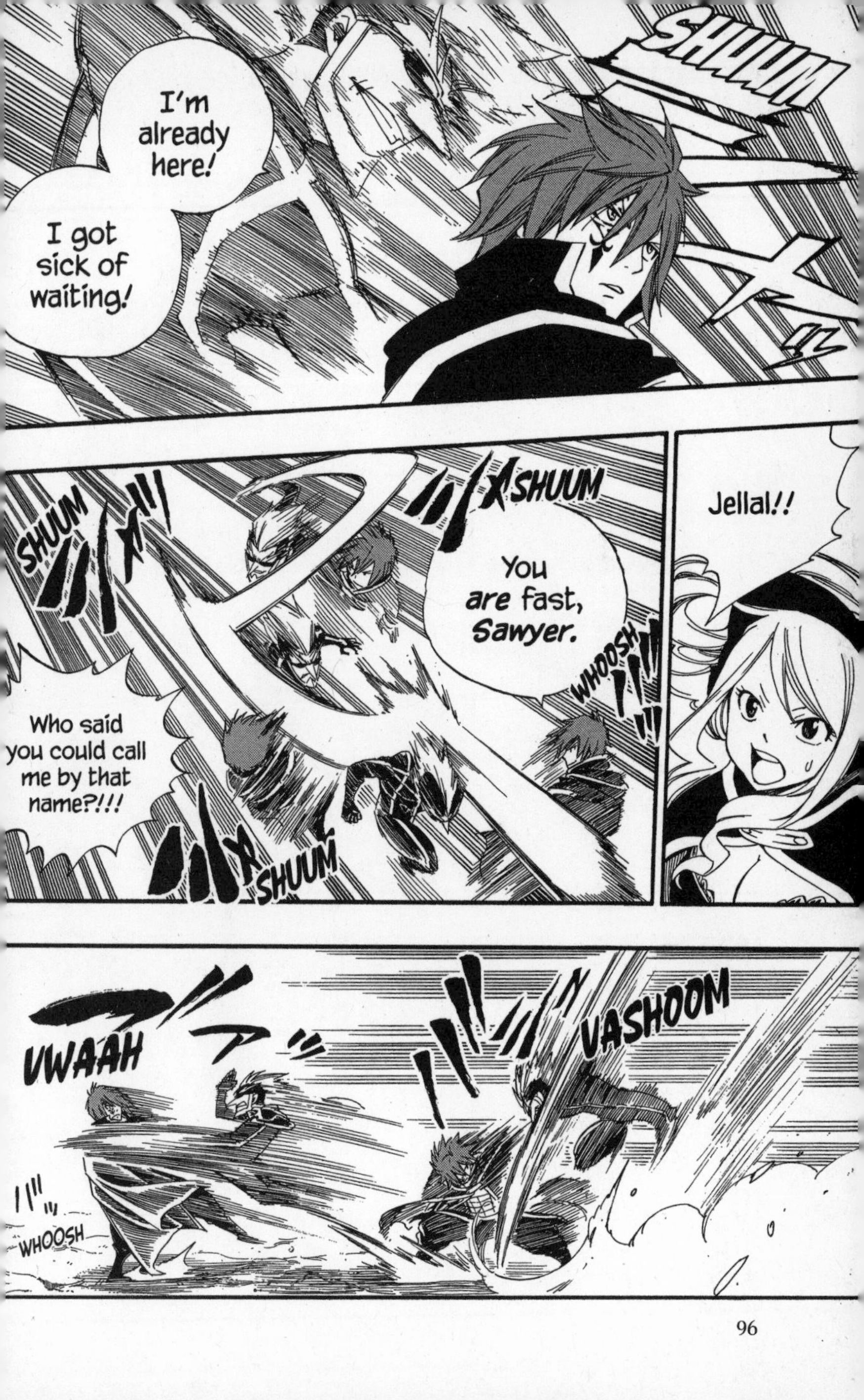
SHUUM
I'm already here!
I got sick of waiting!
Jellal!!
SHUUM
You are fast, Sawyer.
WHOOSH
SHUUM
Who said you could call me by that name?!!!
SHUUM
VASHOOM
UWAAH
WHOOSH

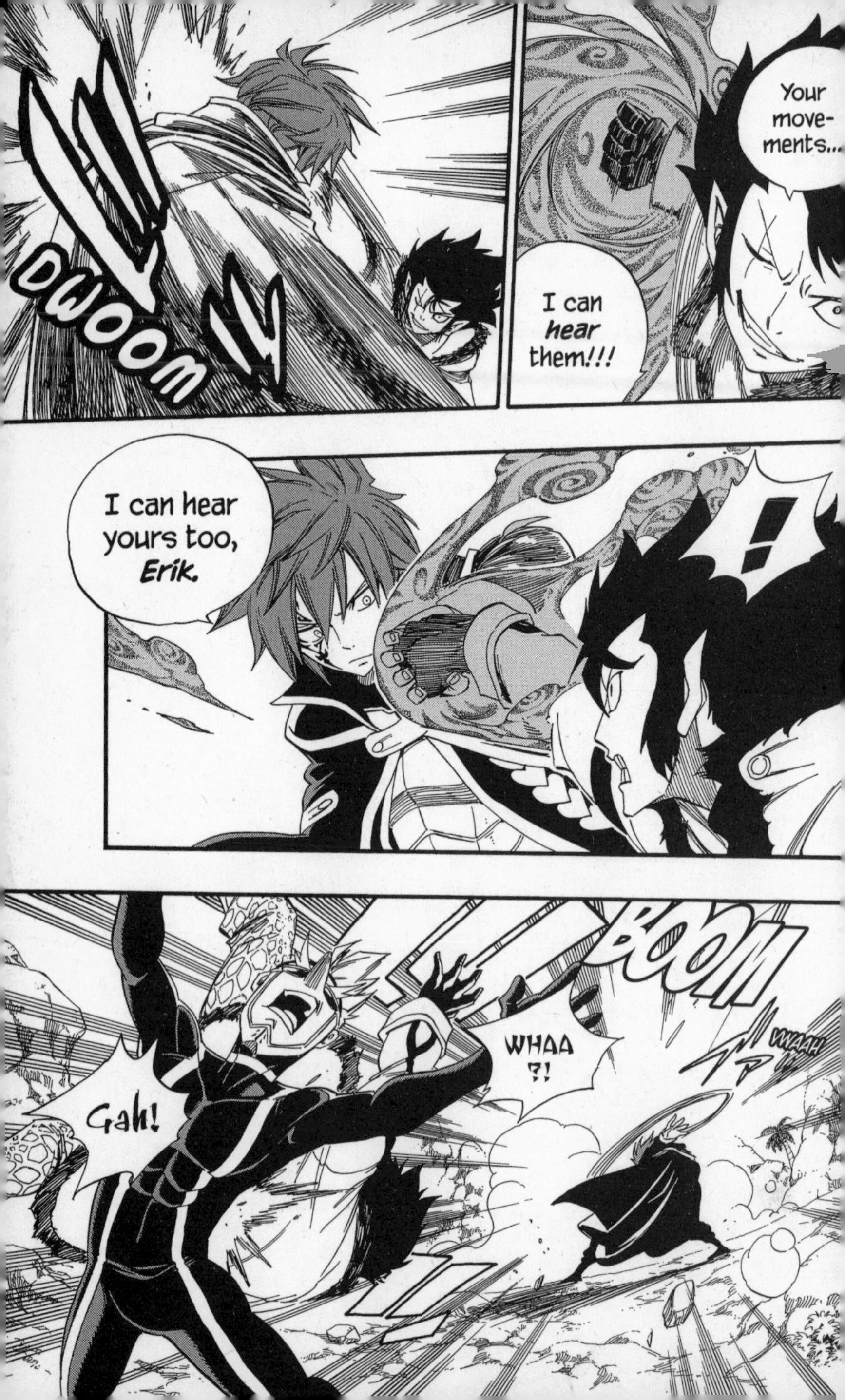
Your movements...
I can hear them!!!
DWOOM
!
I can hear yours too, Erik.
BOOM
VWAAH
WHAA ?!
Gah!

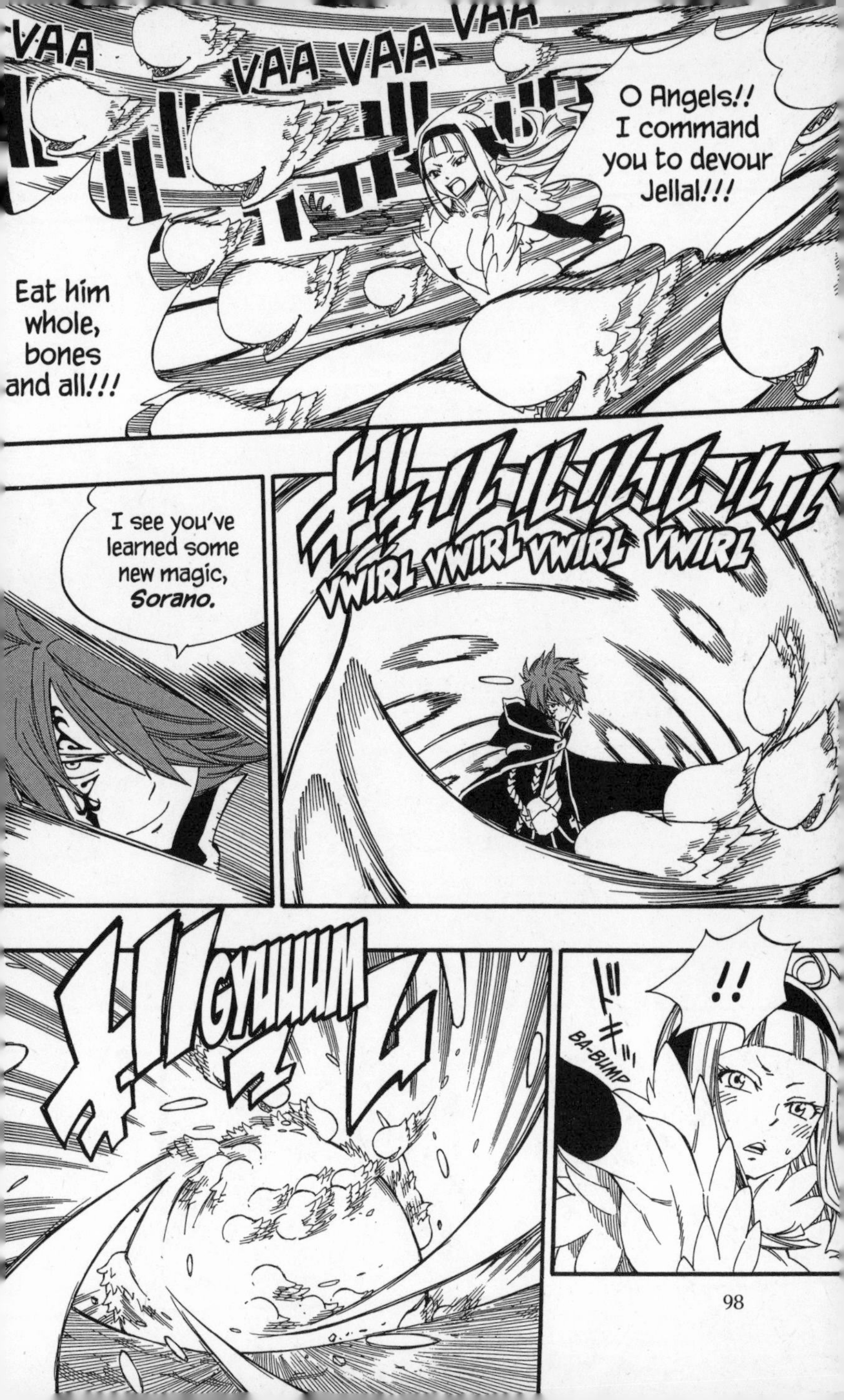
VAA VAA VAA VAA
O Angels!! I command you to devour Jellal!!!
Eat him whole, bones and all!!!
VWIRL VWIRL VWIRL VWIRL
I see you've learned some new magic, *Sorano.*
!!
BA-BUMP
GYUUUM

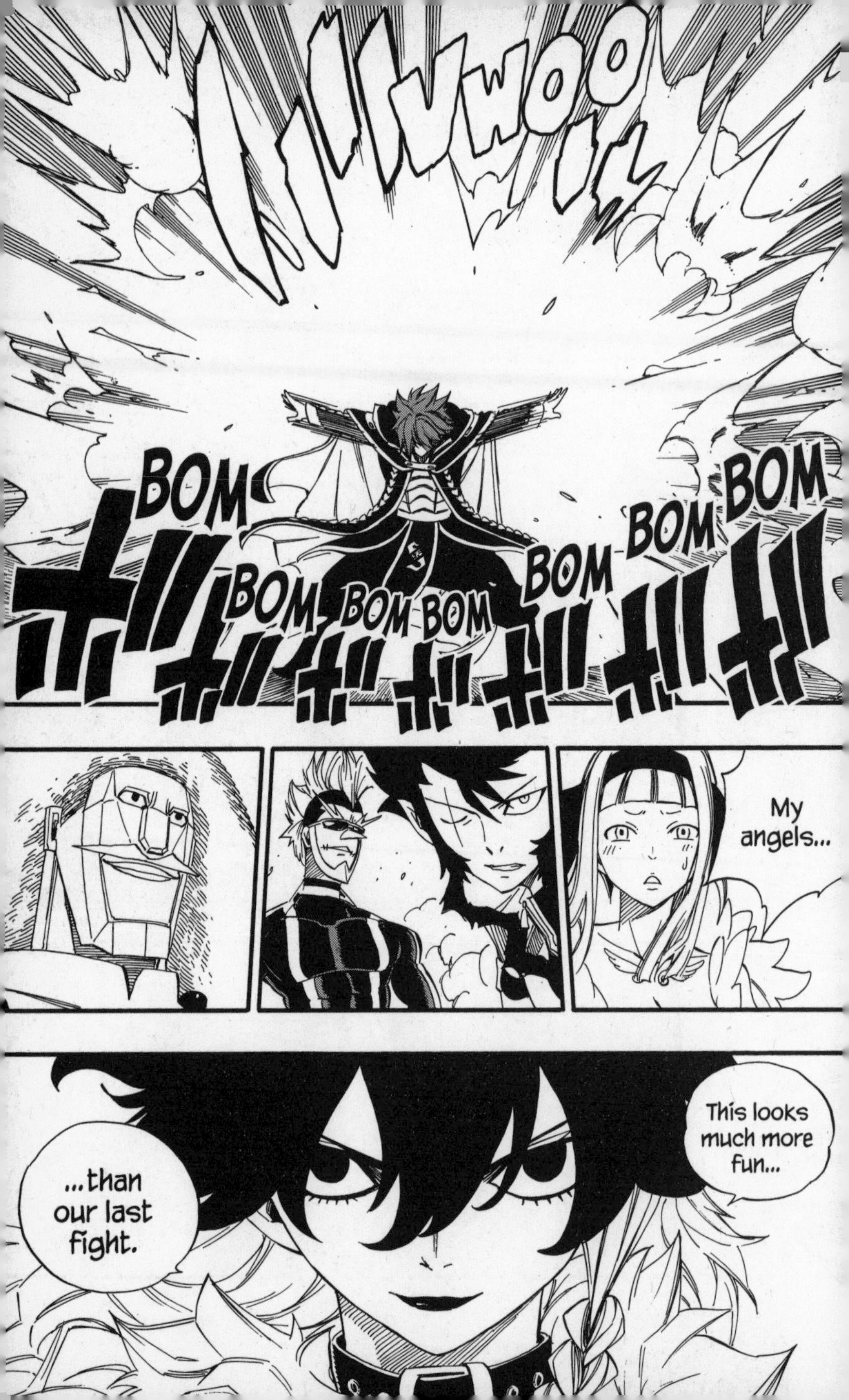

WOO
BOM BOM BOM BOM BOM BOM BOM
My angels...
This looks much more fun...
...than our last fight.

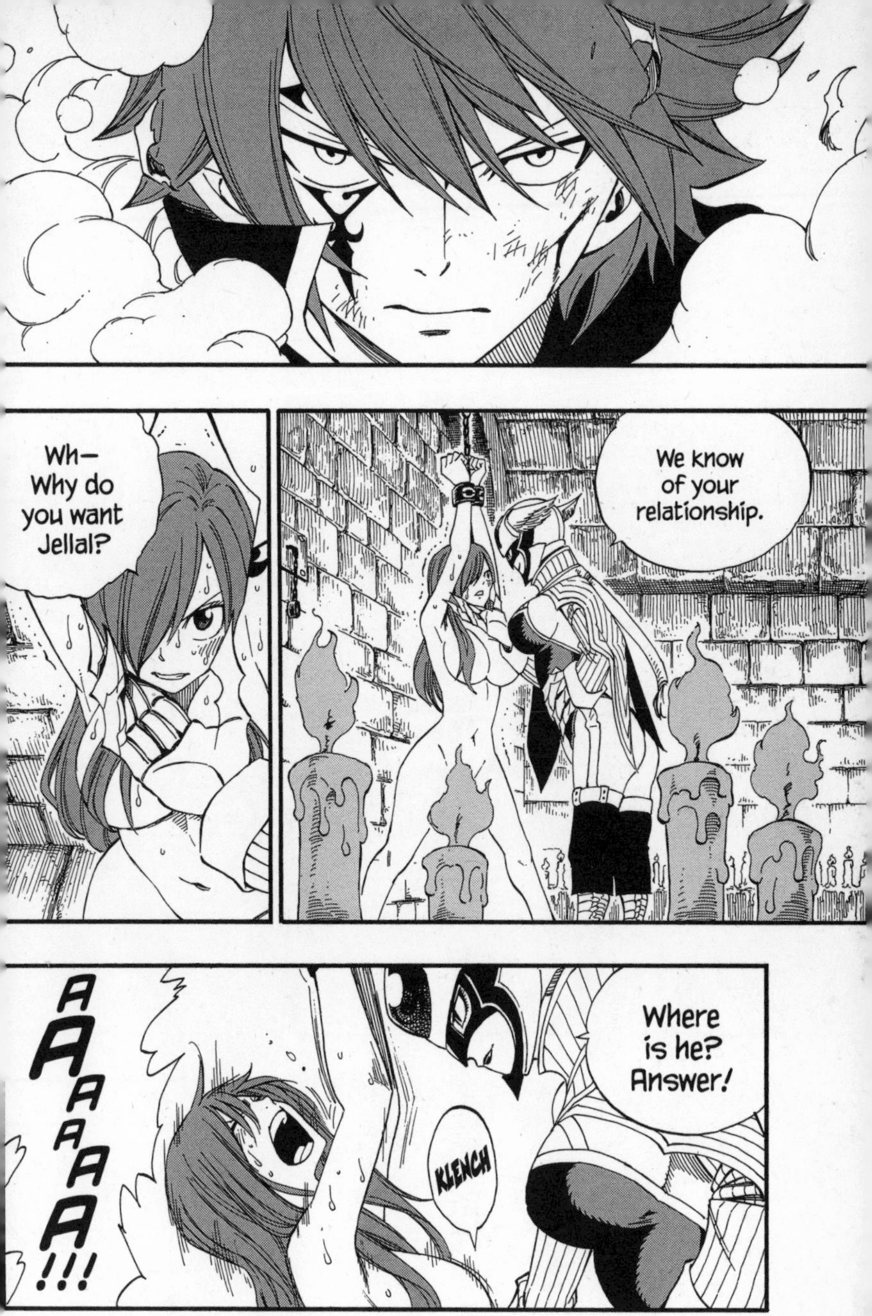
We know of your relationship.
Wh— Why do you want Jellal?
Where is he? Answer!
KLENCH
AAAAAAA!!!

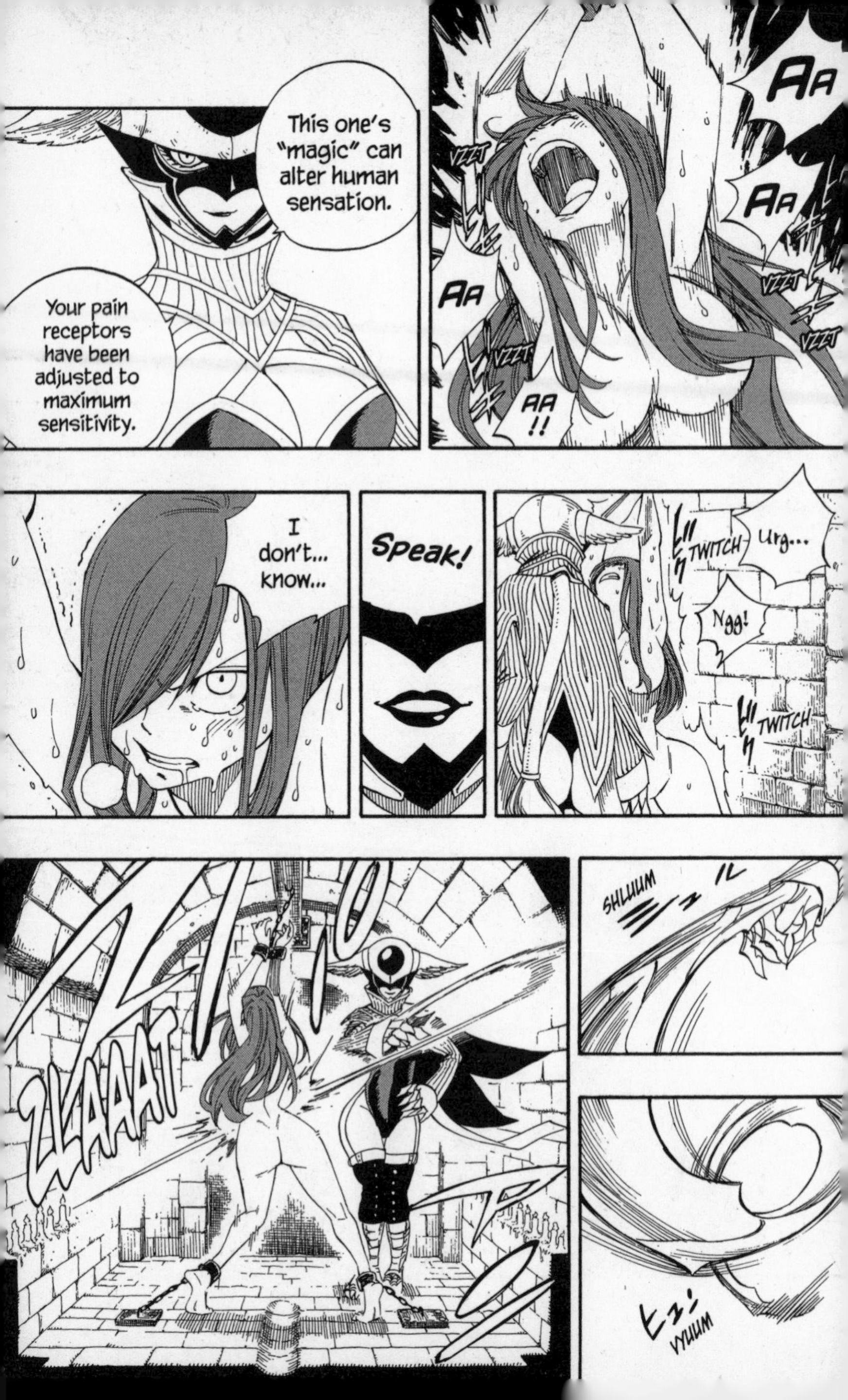

Aa
Aa
VZZT
VZZT
VZZT
VZZT
Aa
AA!!
This one's "magic" can alter human sensation.
Your pain receptors have been adjusted to maximum sensitivity.
TWITCH
Urg...
Ngg!
TWITCH
Speak!
I don't... know...
SHLUUM
VYUUM
ZLAAAT

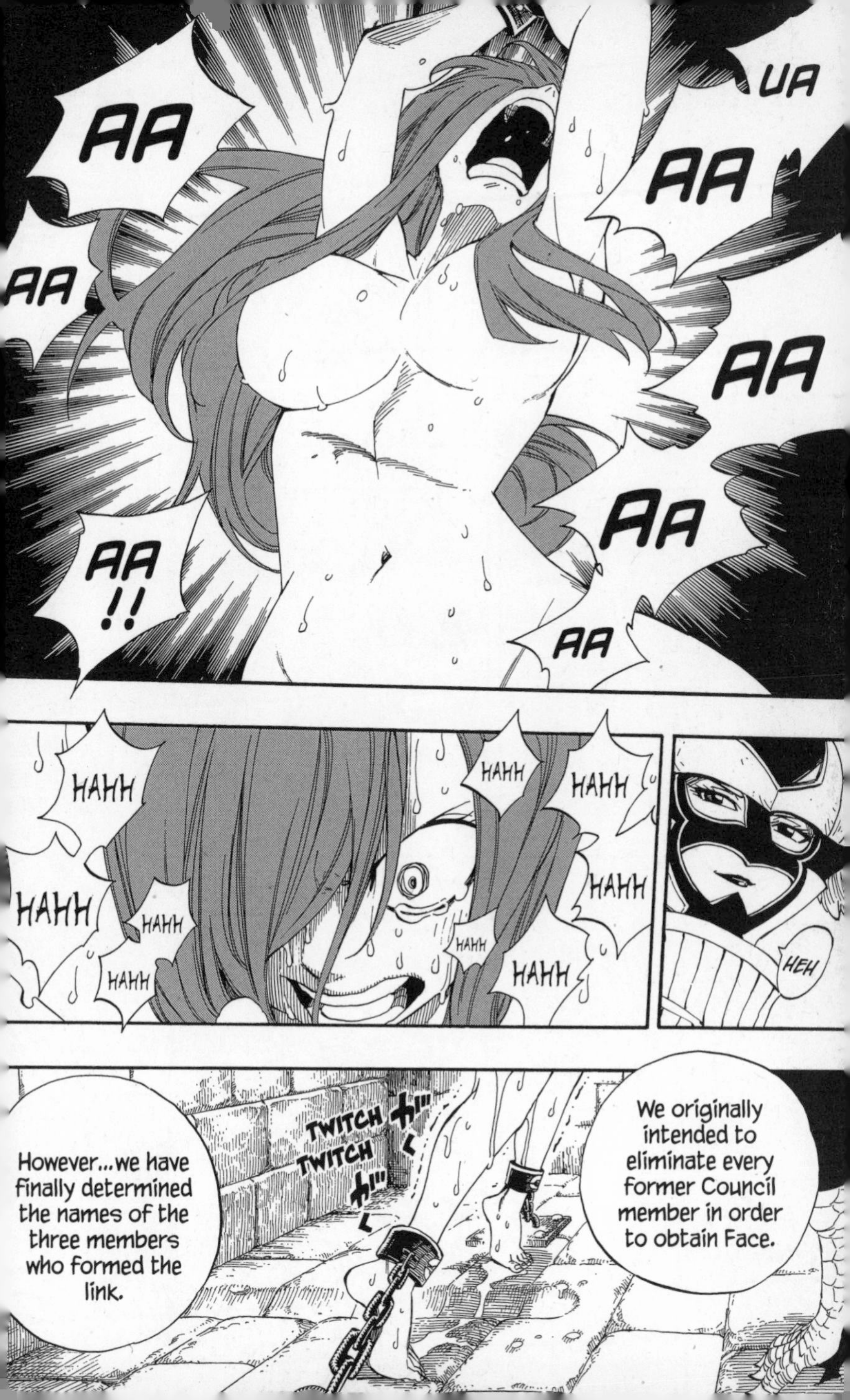

UA
AA
AA
AA
AA
AA
AA!!
AA
HEH
HAHH
HAHH
HAHH
HAHH
HAHH
HAHH
HAHH
HAHH
HAHH
We originally intended to eliminate every former Council member in order to obtain Face.
TWITCH
TWITCH
However...we have finally determined the names of the three members who formed the link.

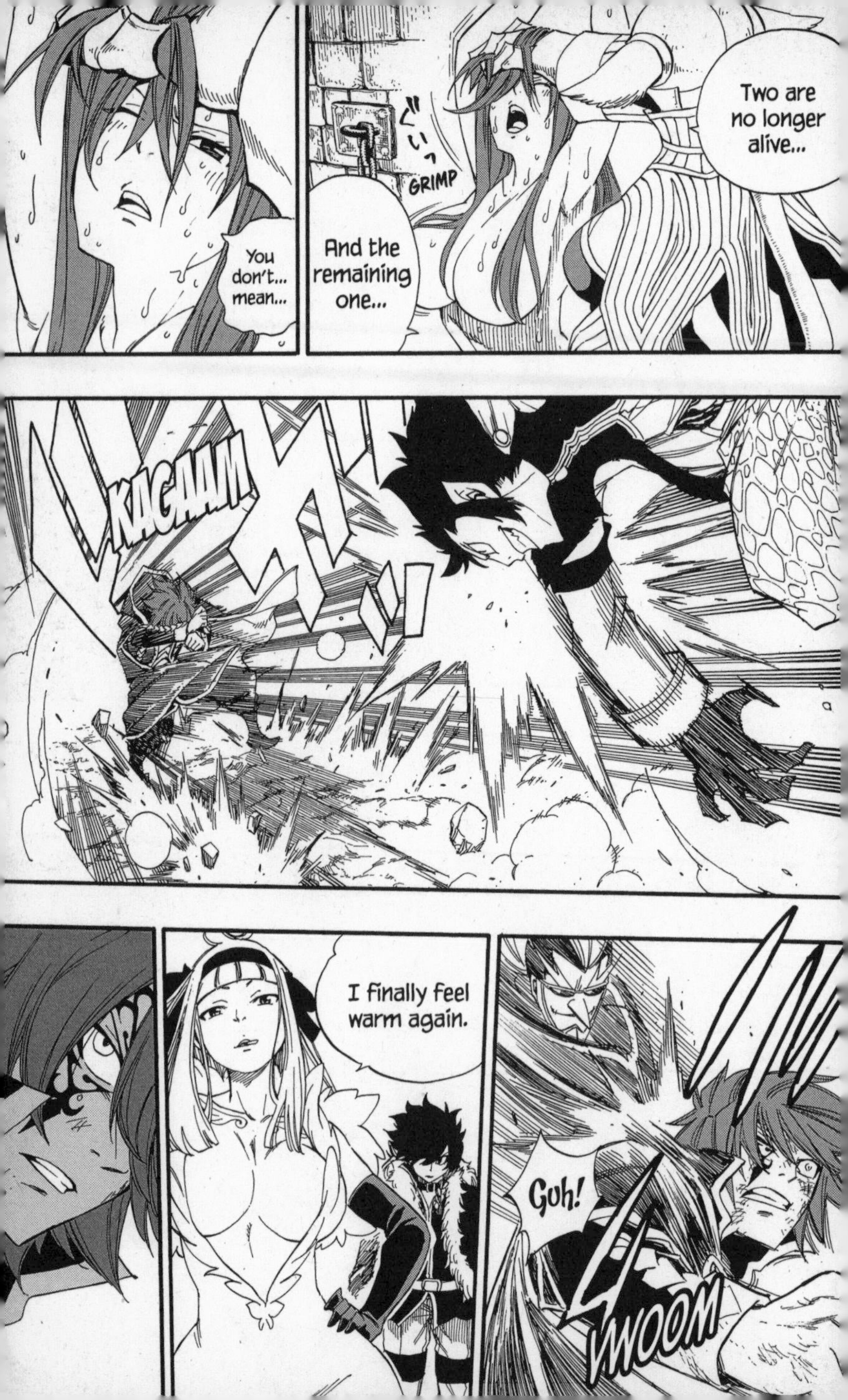
Two are no longer alive...
ぐいっ
GRIMP
And the remaining one...
You don't... mean...
KACAAM
Guh!
VWOOM
I finally feel warm again.

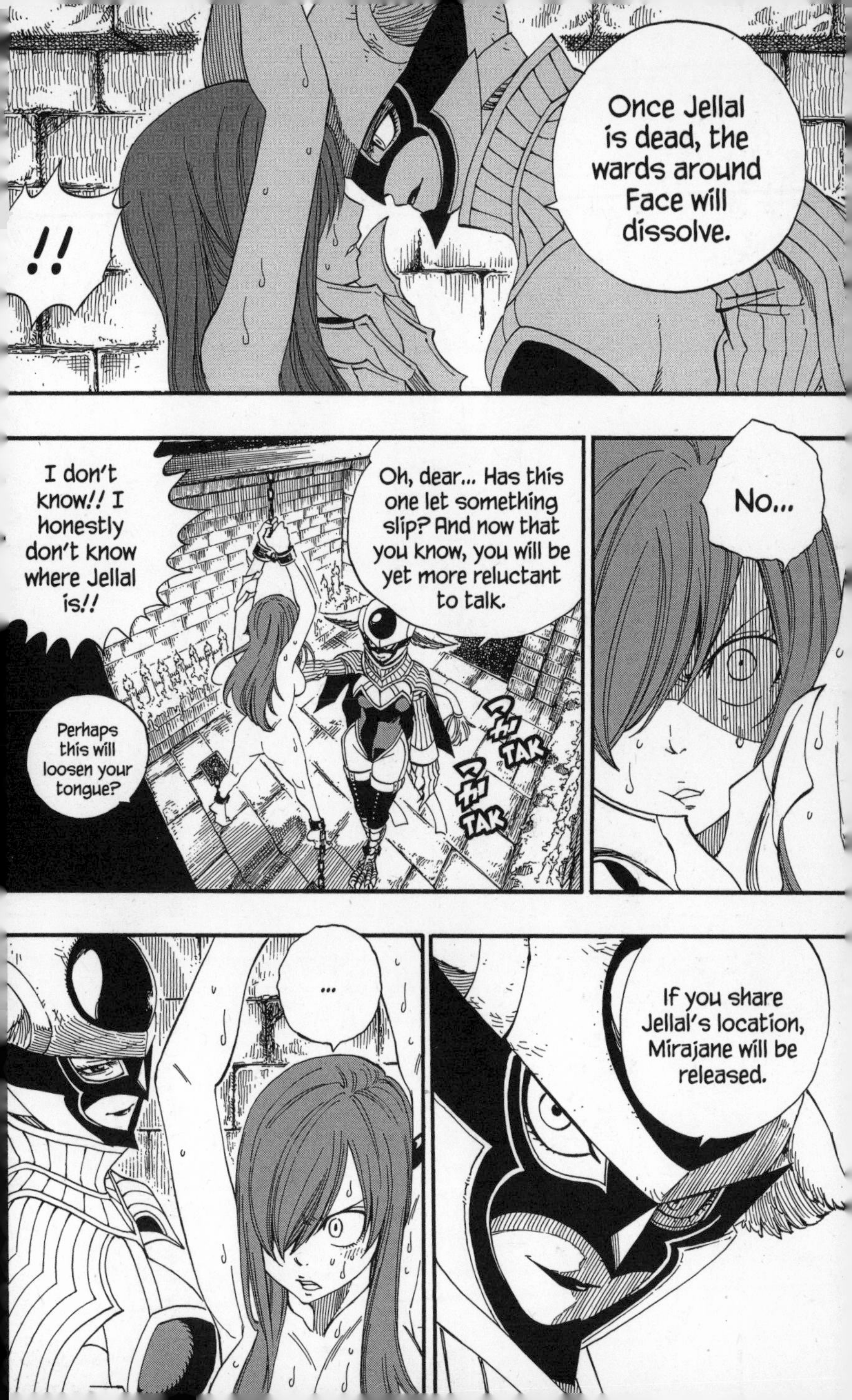
Once Jellal is dead, the wards around Face will dissolve.
!!
No...
Oh, dear... Has this one let something slip? And now that you know, you will be yet more reluctant to talk.
I don't know!! I honestly don't know where Jellal is!!
TAK
TAK
Perhaps this will loosen your tongue?
If you share Jellal's location, Mirajane will be released.
...

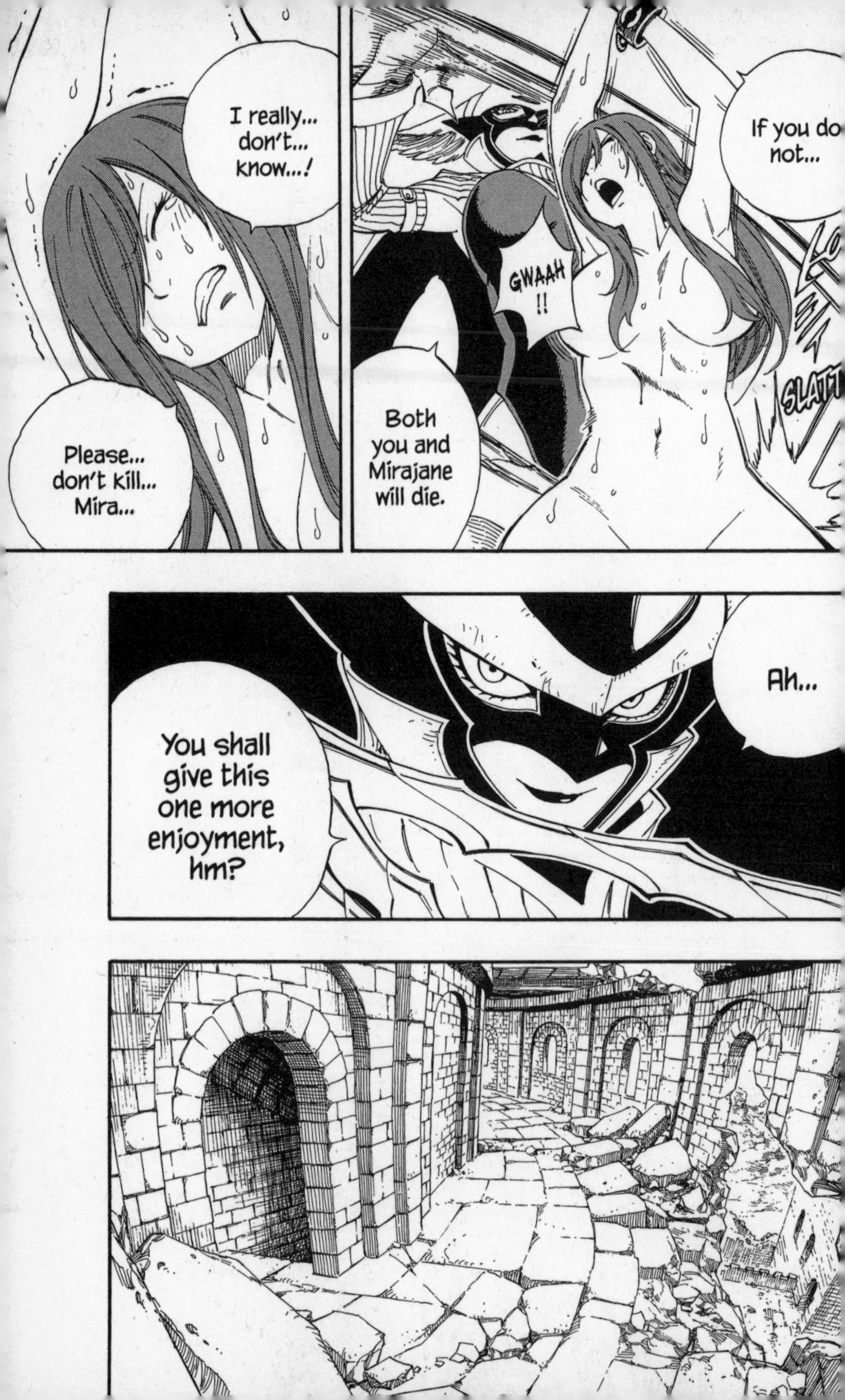
If you do not...
SLATT
GWAAH !!
Both you and Mirajane will die.
I really... don't... know...!
Please... don't kill... Mira...
Ah...
You shall give this one more enjoyment, hm?

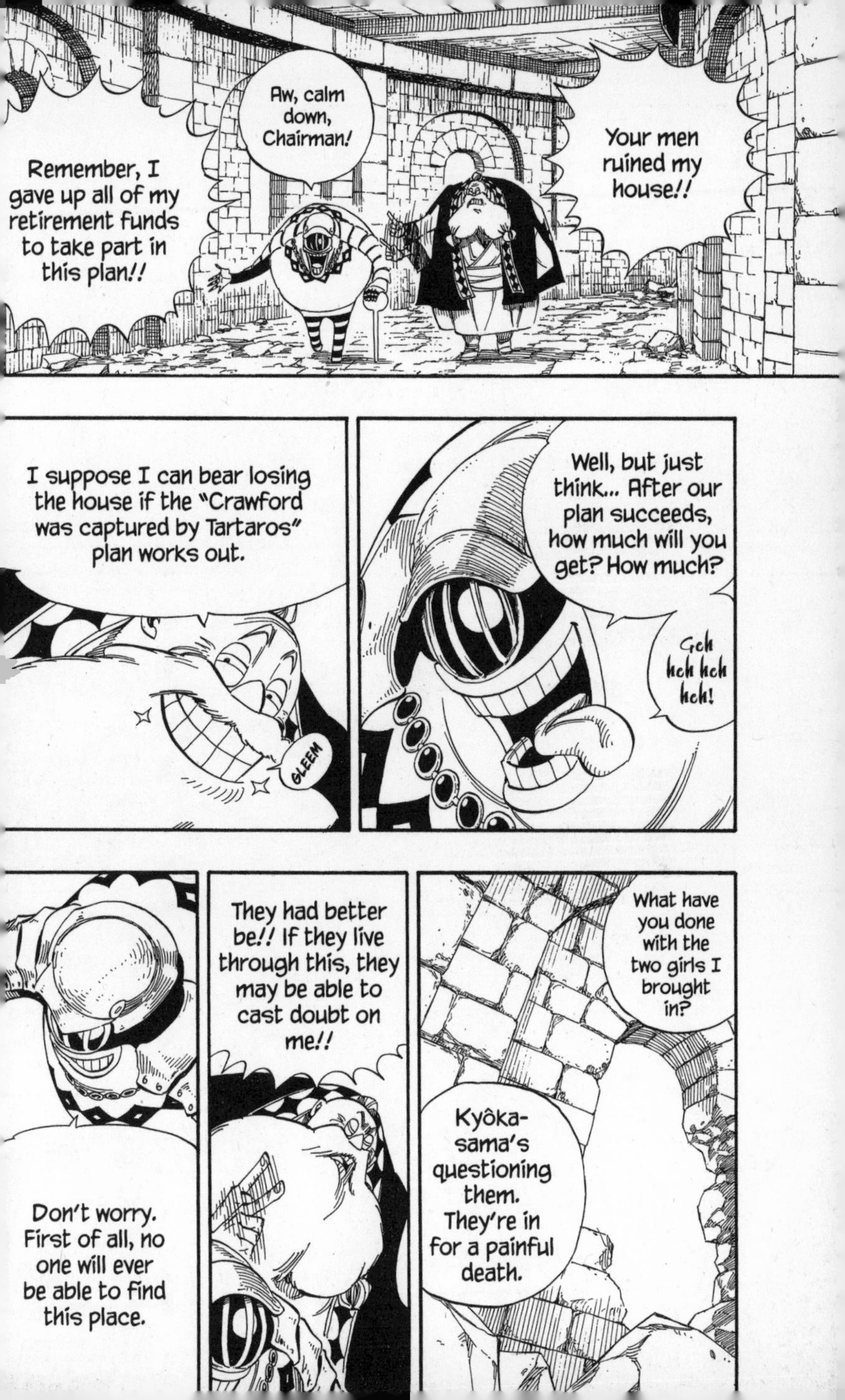
Your men ruined my house!!
Aw, calm down, Chairman!
Remember, I gave up all of my retirement funds to take part in this plan!!
Well, but just think... After our plan succeeds, how much will you get? How much?
Geh heh heh heh!
I suppose I can bear losing the house if the "Crawford was captured by Tartaros" plan works out.
GLEEM
What have you done with the two girls I brought in?
Kyôka-sama's questioning them. They're in for a painful death.
They had better be!! If they live through this, they may be able to cast doubt on me!!
Don't worry. First of all, no one will ever be able to find this place.

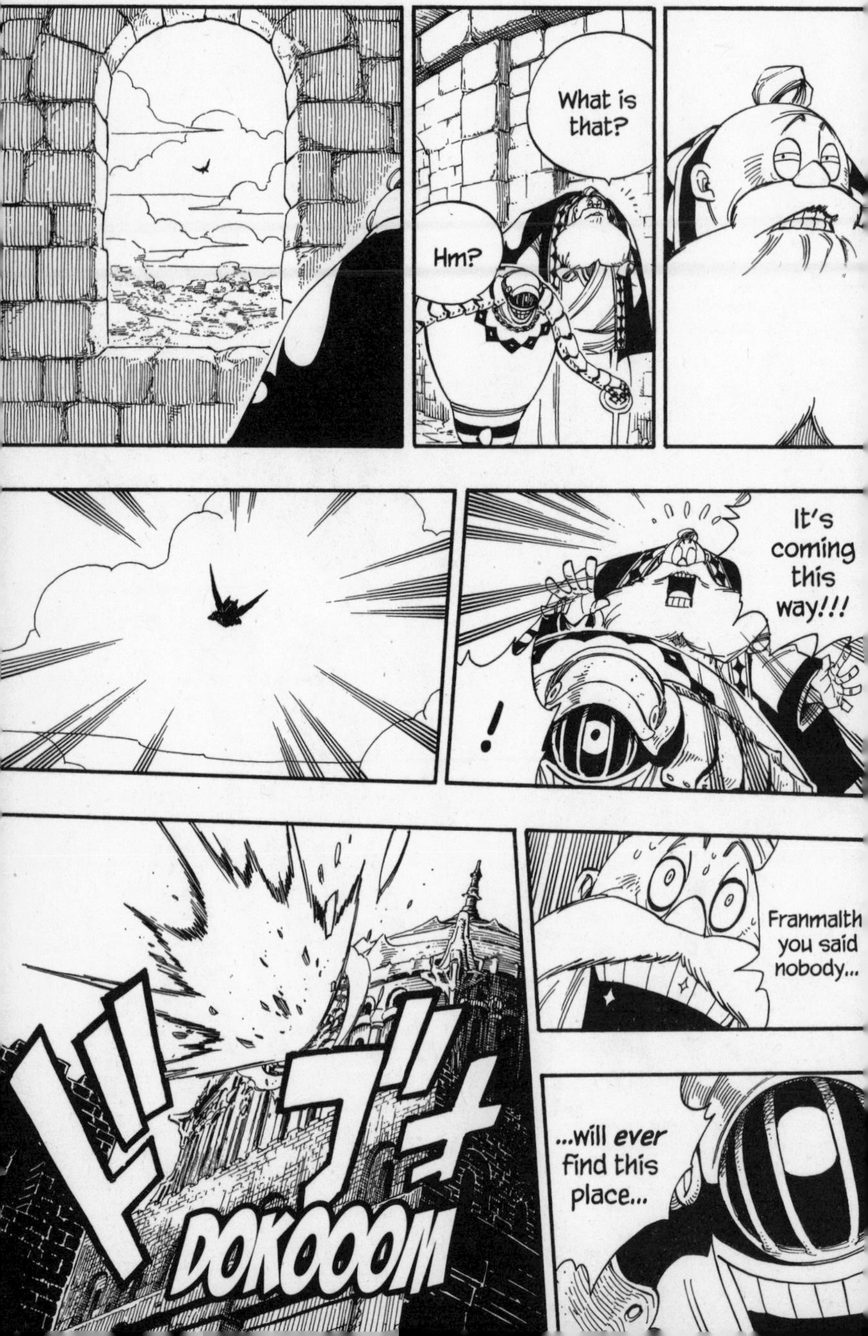
What is that?
Hm?
It's coming this way!!!
!
Franmalth you said nobody...
...will ever find this place...
DOKOOOM

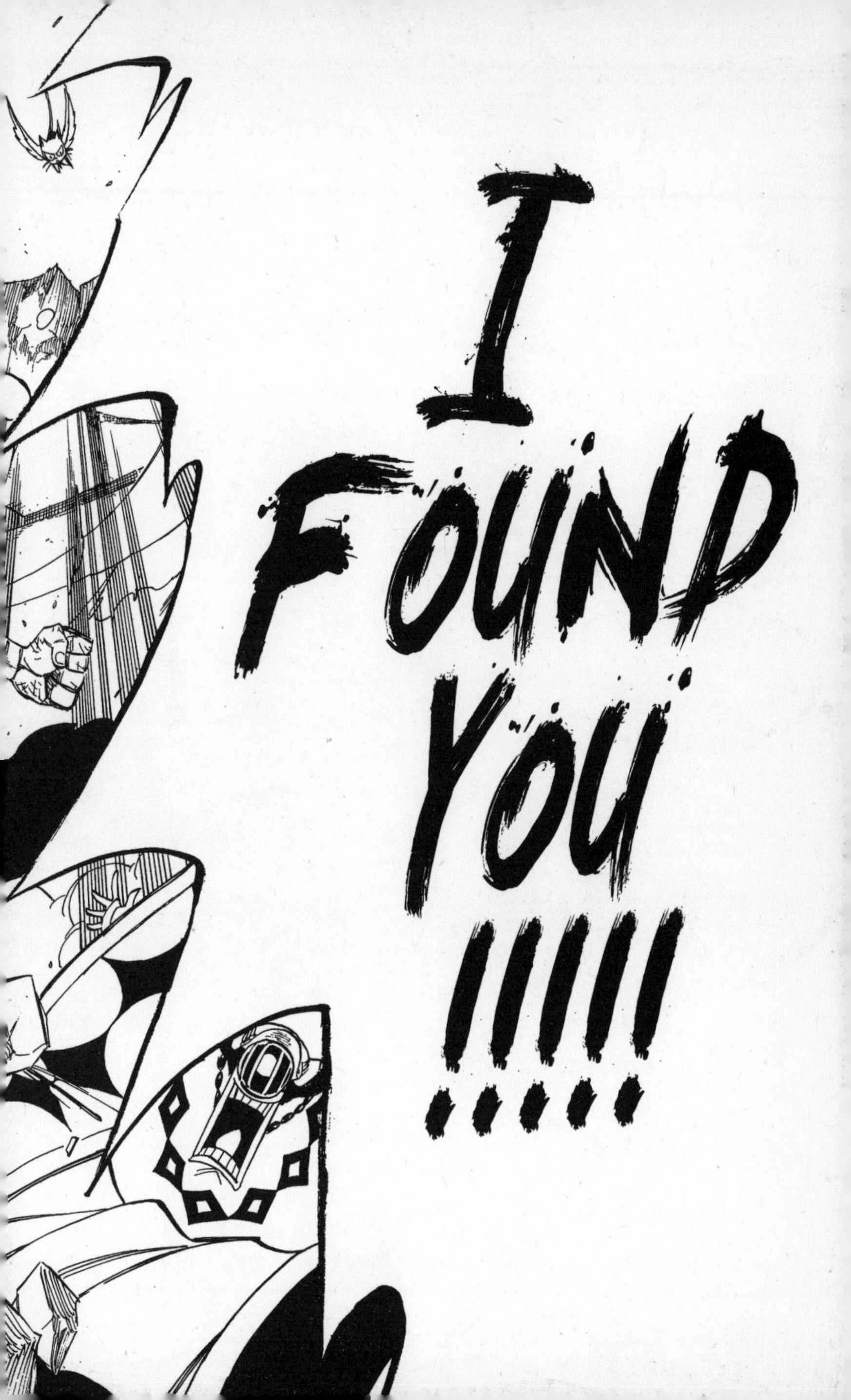
I FOUND YOU!!!!!

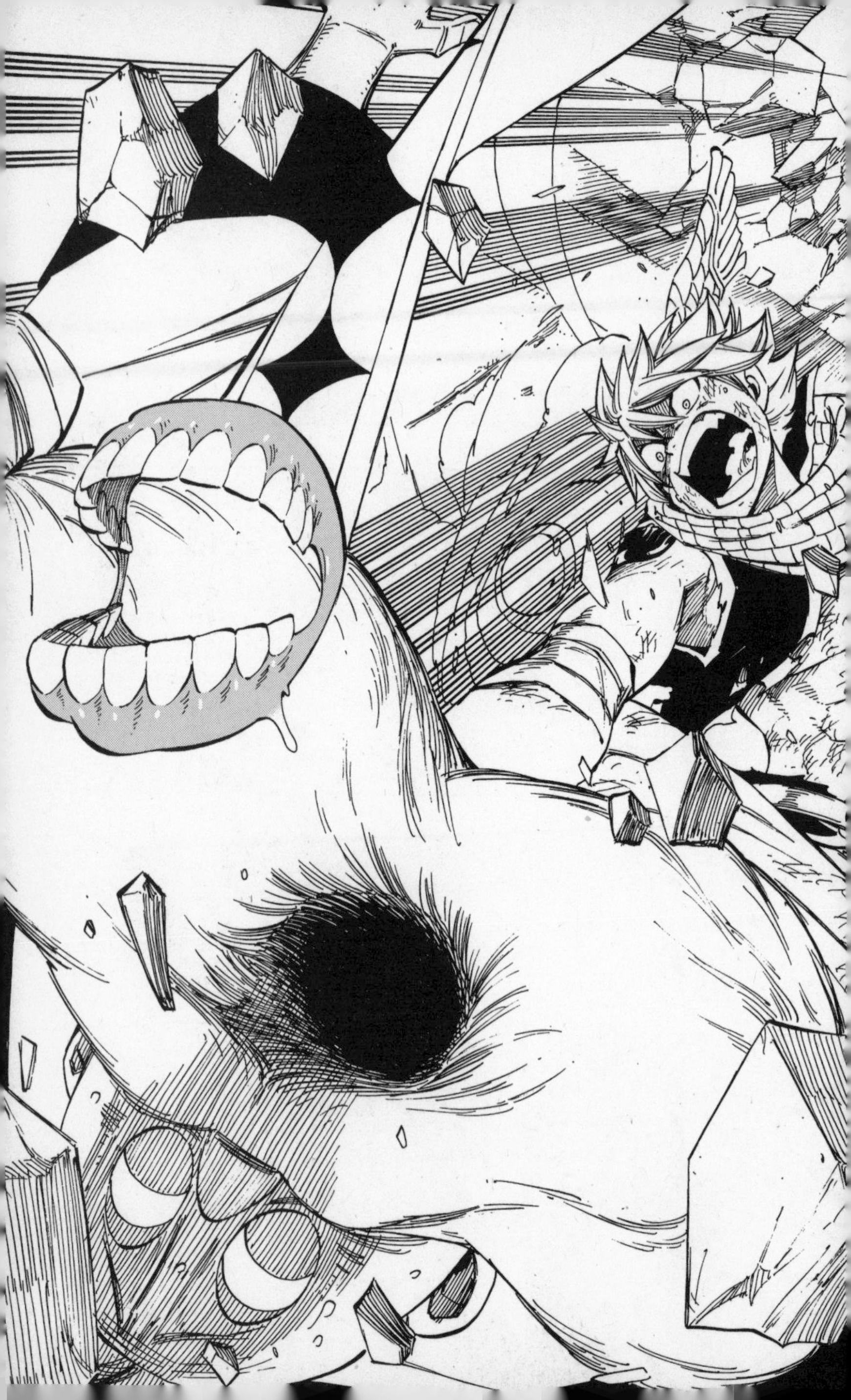

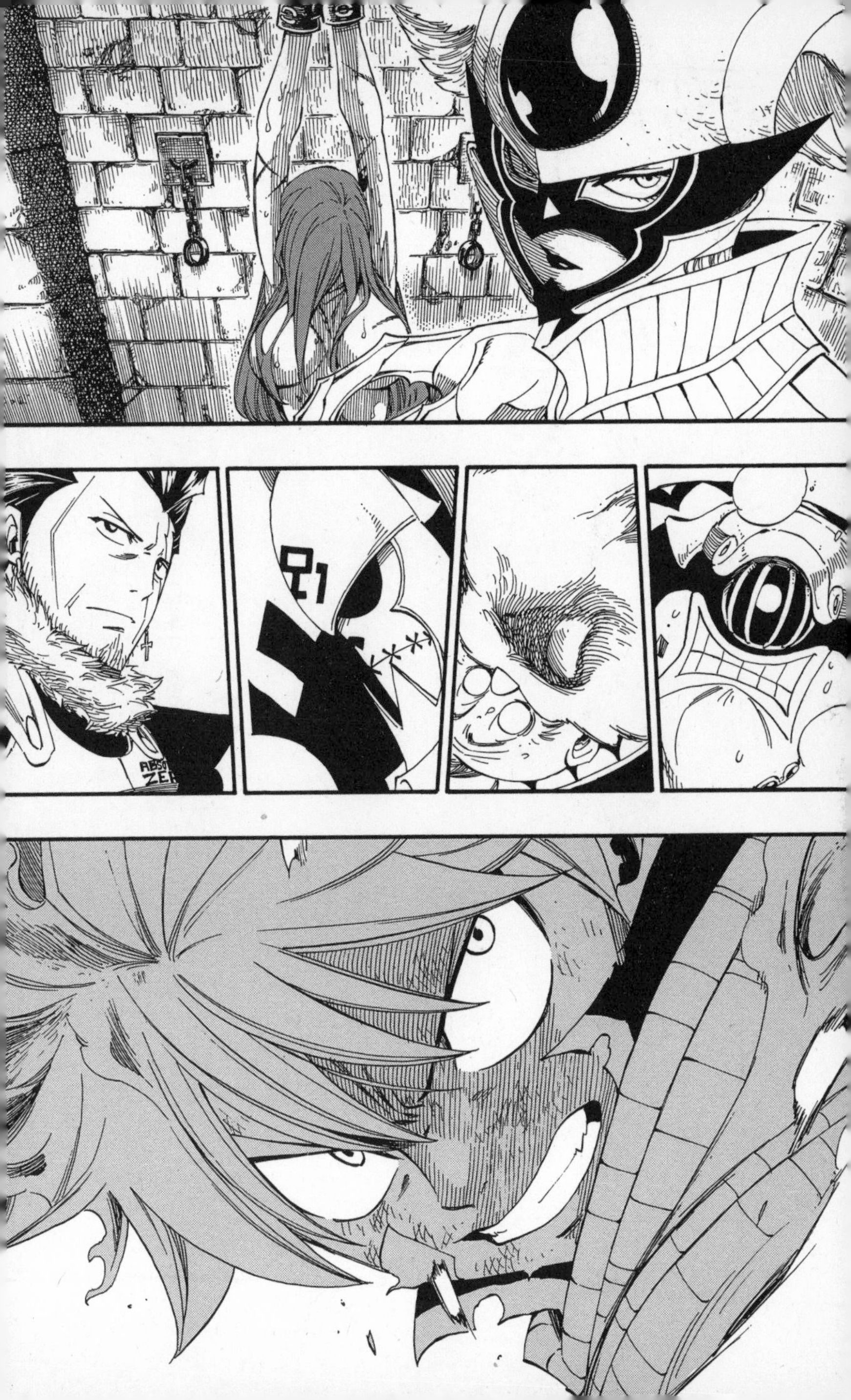
ABSO
ZER

FAIRY TAIL

Chapter 366: 1,000 Souls

MERMAID HEEL

Name: Kagura Mikazuchi **Age:** 23

Magic:

Gravity Magic, among others

Likes: **Dislikes:**

Her brother **Jellal**

Remarks

Like Erza, she came from Rosemary Village, but the child snatchers took her brother away. Ever since then, she's studied magic and the sword in order to find him again.

When she met Millianna, she learned about the death of her brother, and decided to dedicate her sword to a new goal: revenge against Jellal. But after encountering Erza in the Grand Magic Games, she has started to have doubts about her determination as well as her hatred of Jellal.

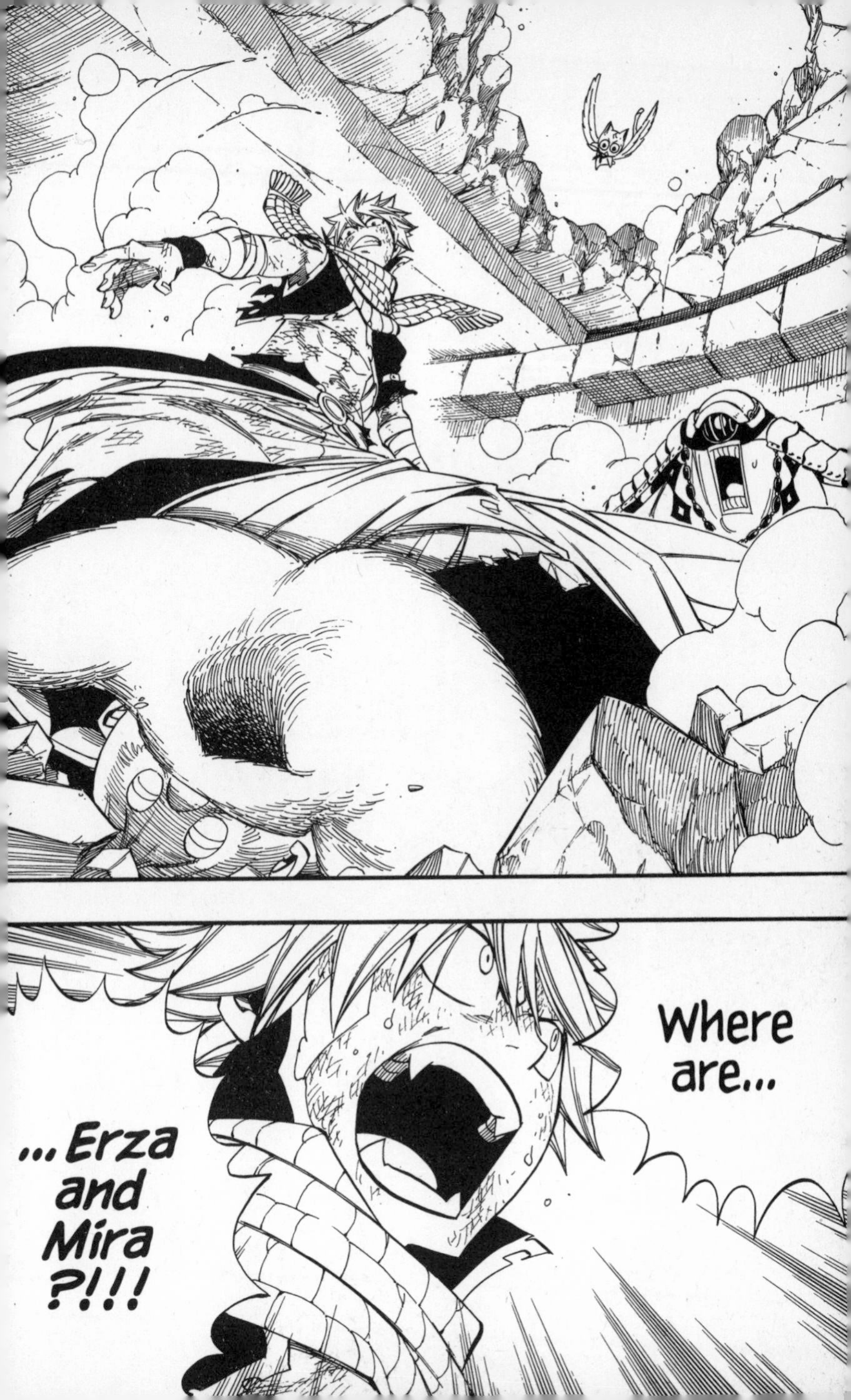
Where are...
...Erza and Mira?!!!

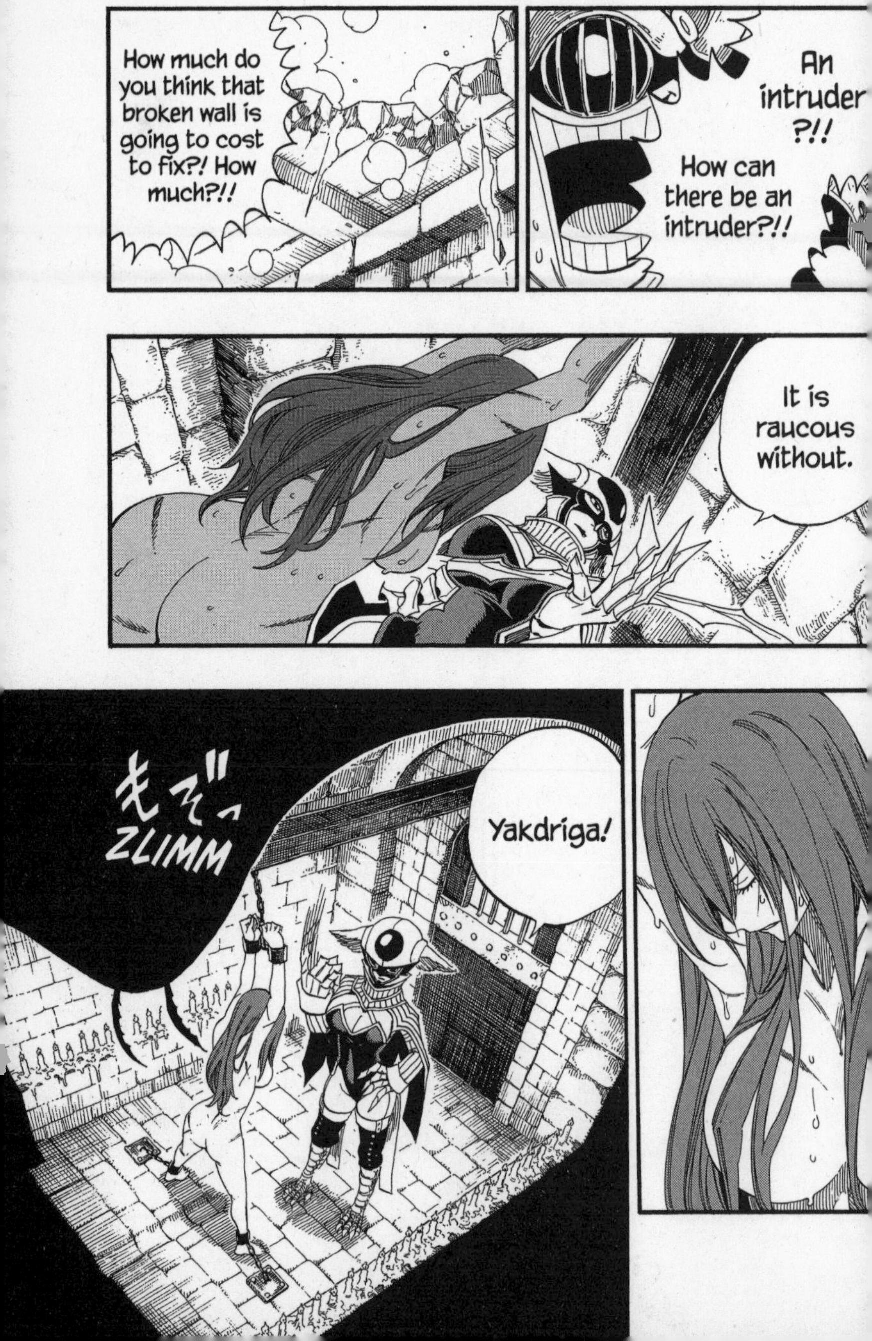
An intruder?!!
How can there be an intruder?!!
How much do you think that broken wall is going to cost to fix?! How much?!!
It is raucous without.
Yakdriga!
もぞ
ZLIMM

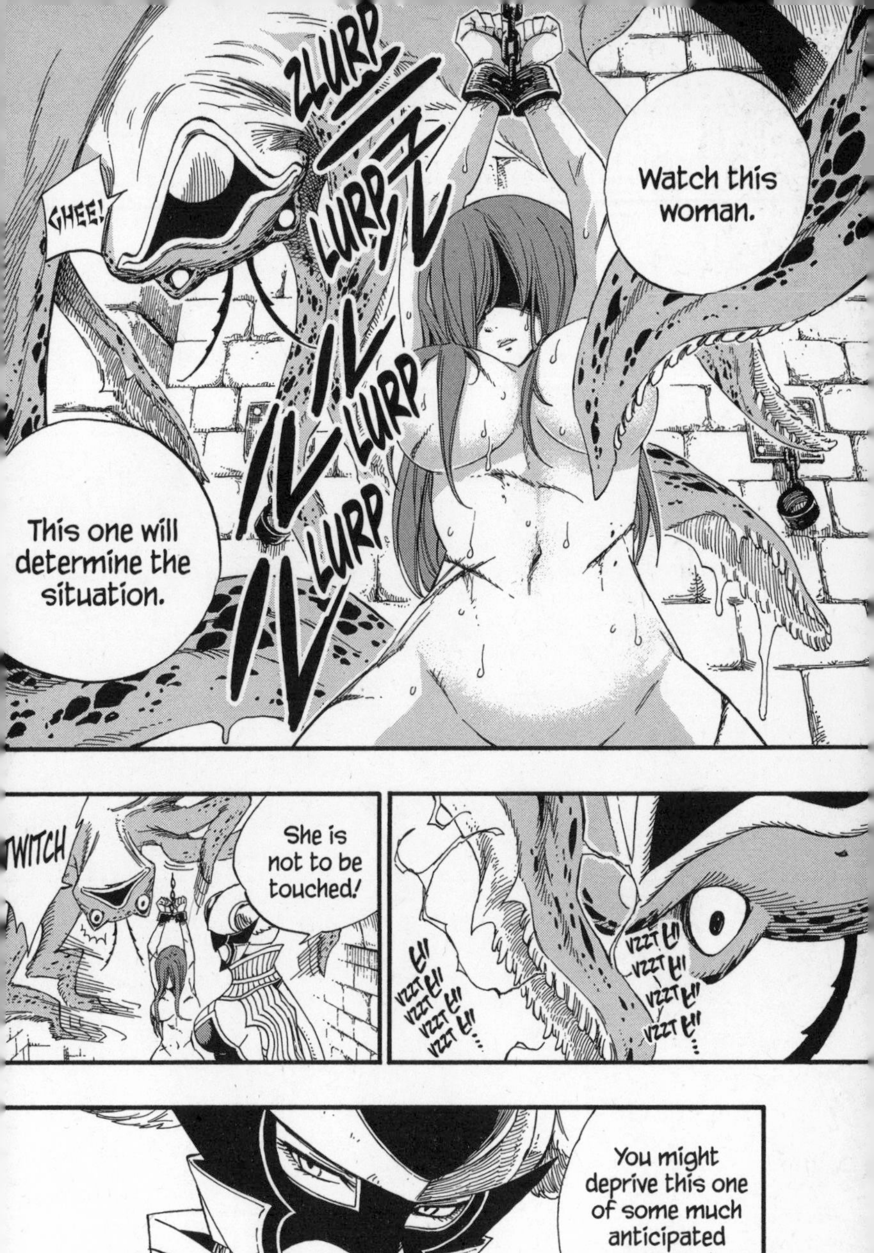
Watch this woman.
ZLURP
GHEE!
LURP
LURP
LURP
This one will determine the situation.
VZZT
VZZT
VZZT
VZZT
TWITCH
She is not to be touched!
VZZT
VZZT
VZZT
VZZT
You might deprive this one of some much anticipated enjoyment.

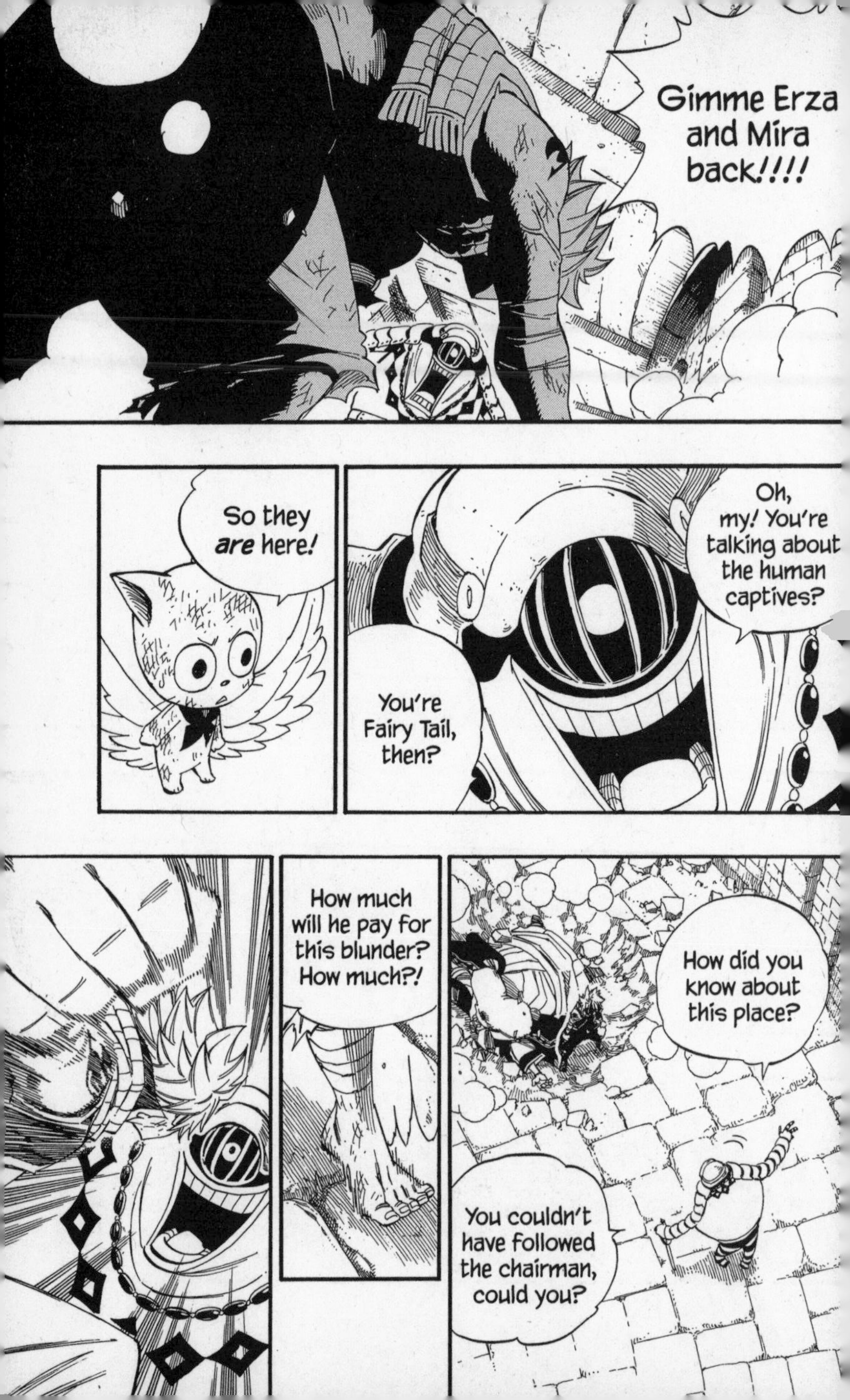
Gimme Erza and Mira back!!!!
Oh, my! You're talking about the human captives?
You're Fairy Tail, then?
So they *are* here!
How did you know about this place?
You couldn't have followed the chairman, could you?
How much will he pay for this blunder? How much?!

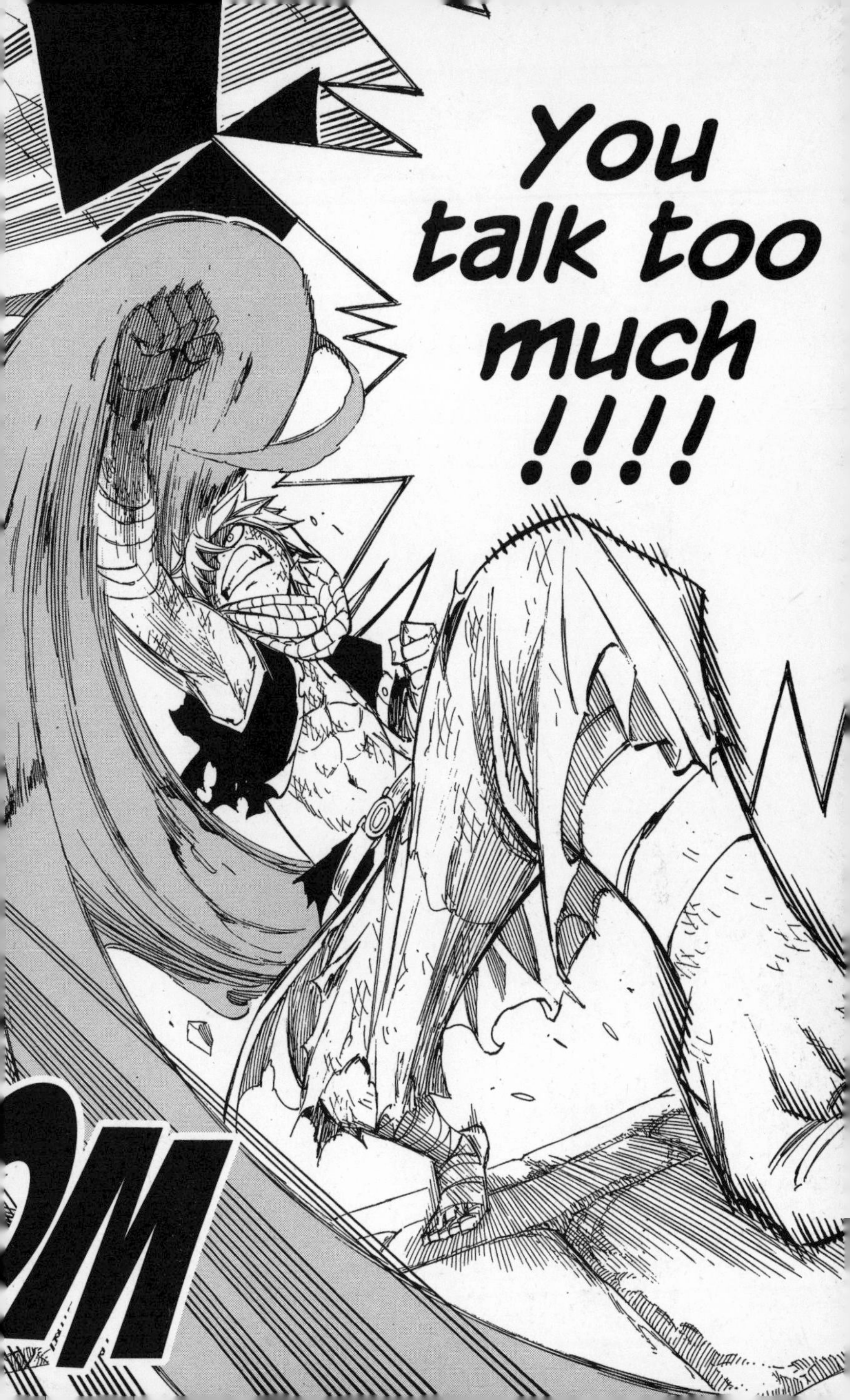
You talk too much!!!!

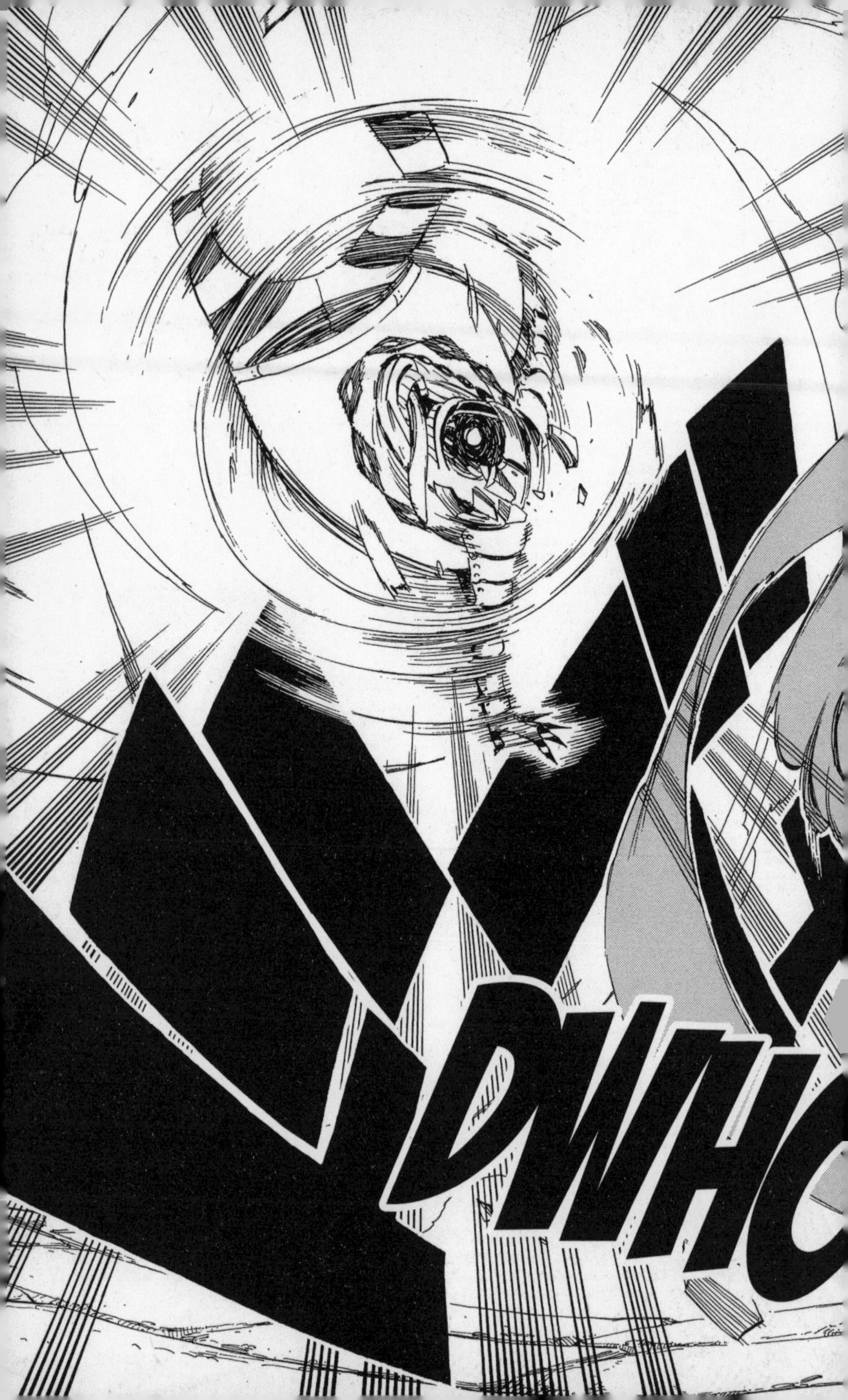

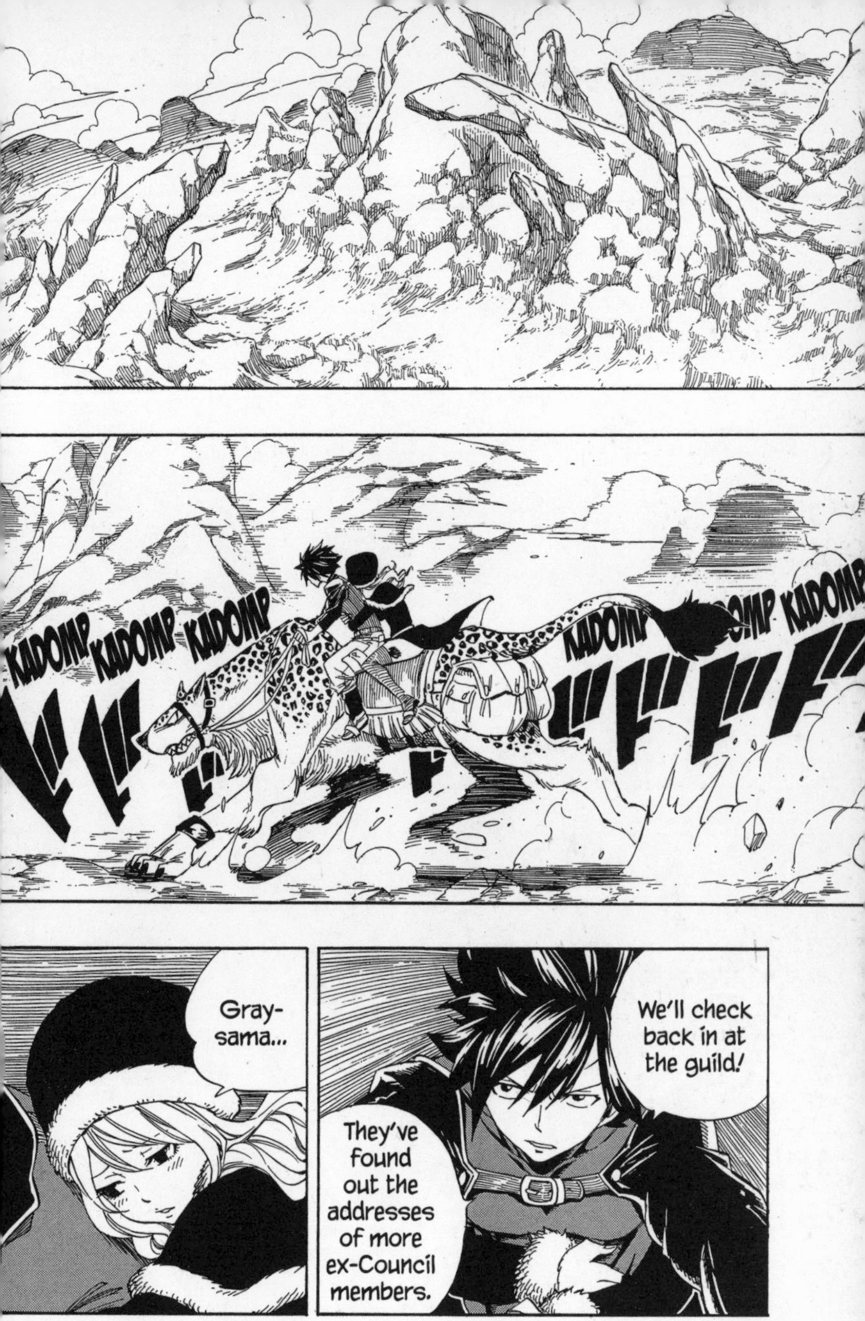
KADOMP KADOMP KADOMP
KADOMP KADOMP KADOMP
We'll check back in at the guild!
They've found out the addresses of more ex-Council members.
Gray-sama...

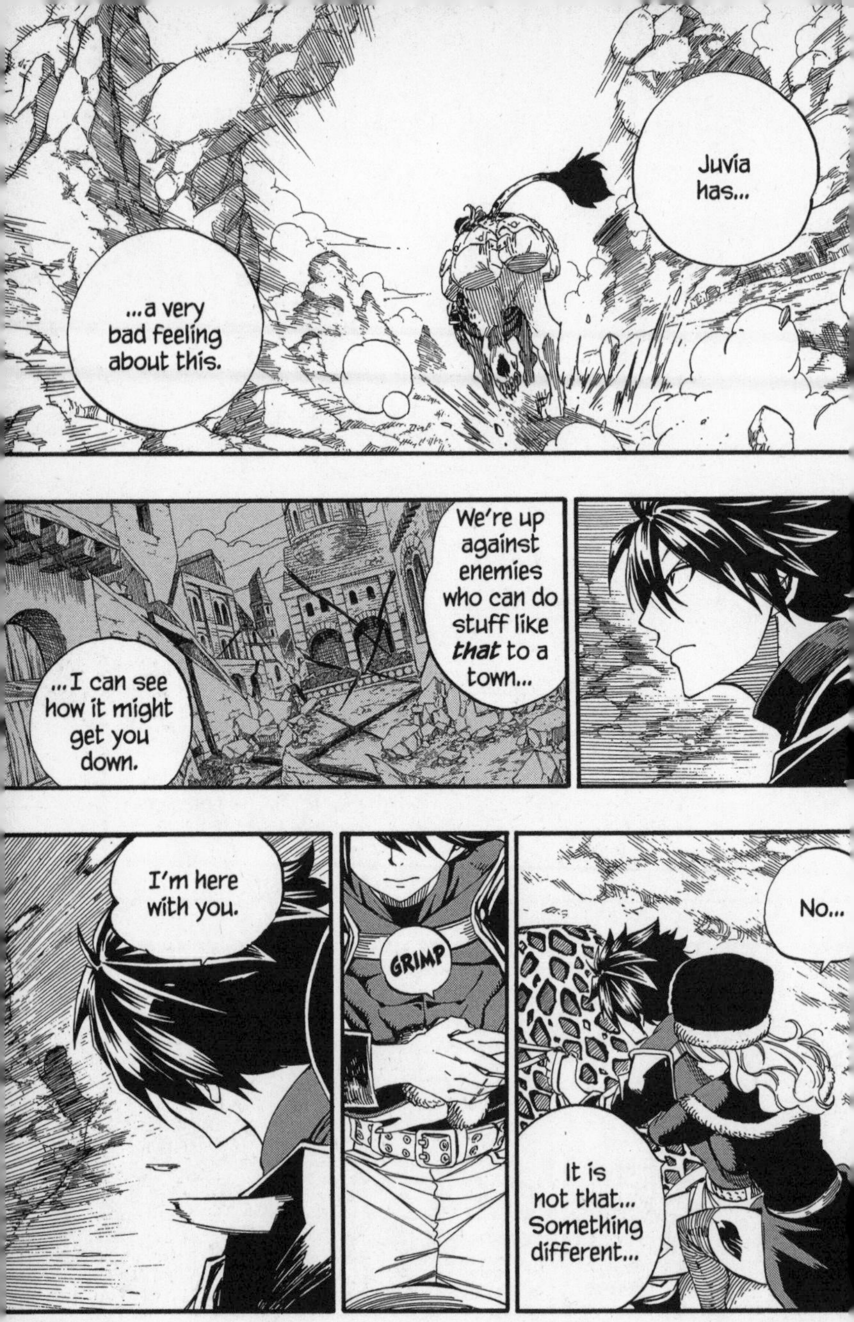
Juvia has...
...a very bad feeling about this.
We're up against enemies who can do stuff like *that* to a town...
...I can see how it might get you down.
No...
It is not that... Something different...
GRIMP
I'm here with you.

Fairy Tail will win, just like always.

You can count on it!

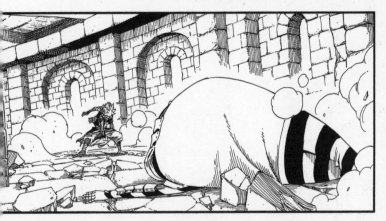

You dared to hit me?!

How much will you pay in punishment? How much?!

KACHAANNG

ZWIPP

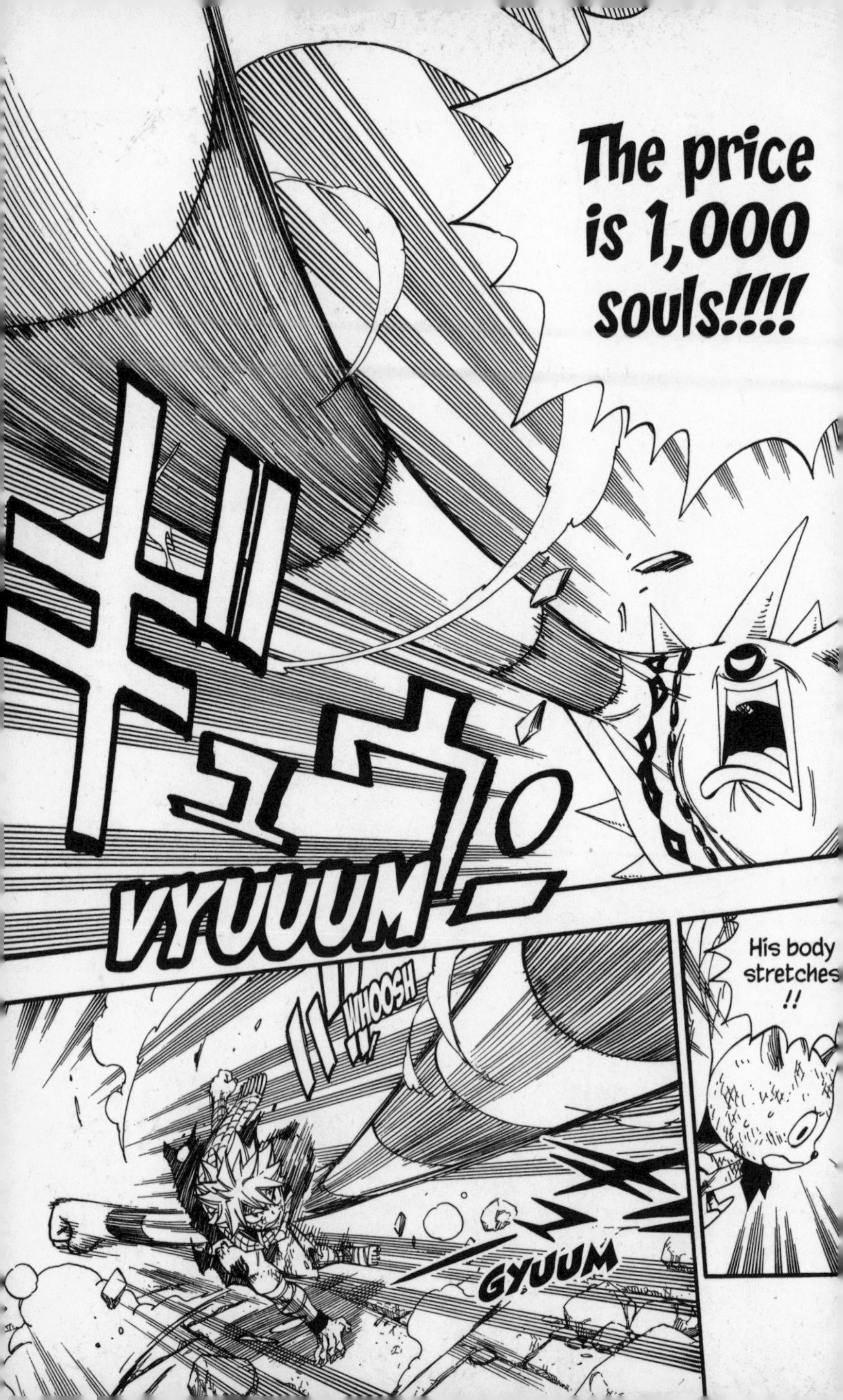
The price is 1,000 souls!!!!
VYUUUM
His body stretches !!
WHOOSH
GYUUM

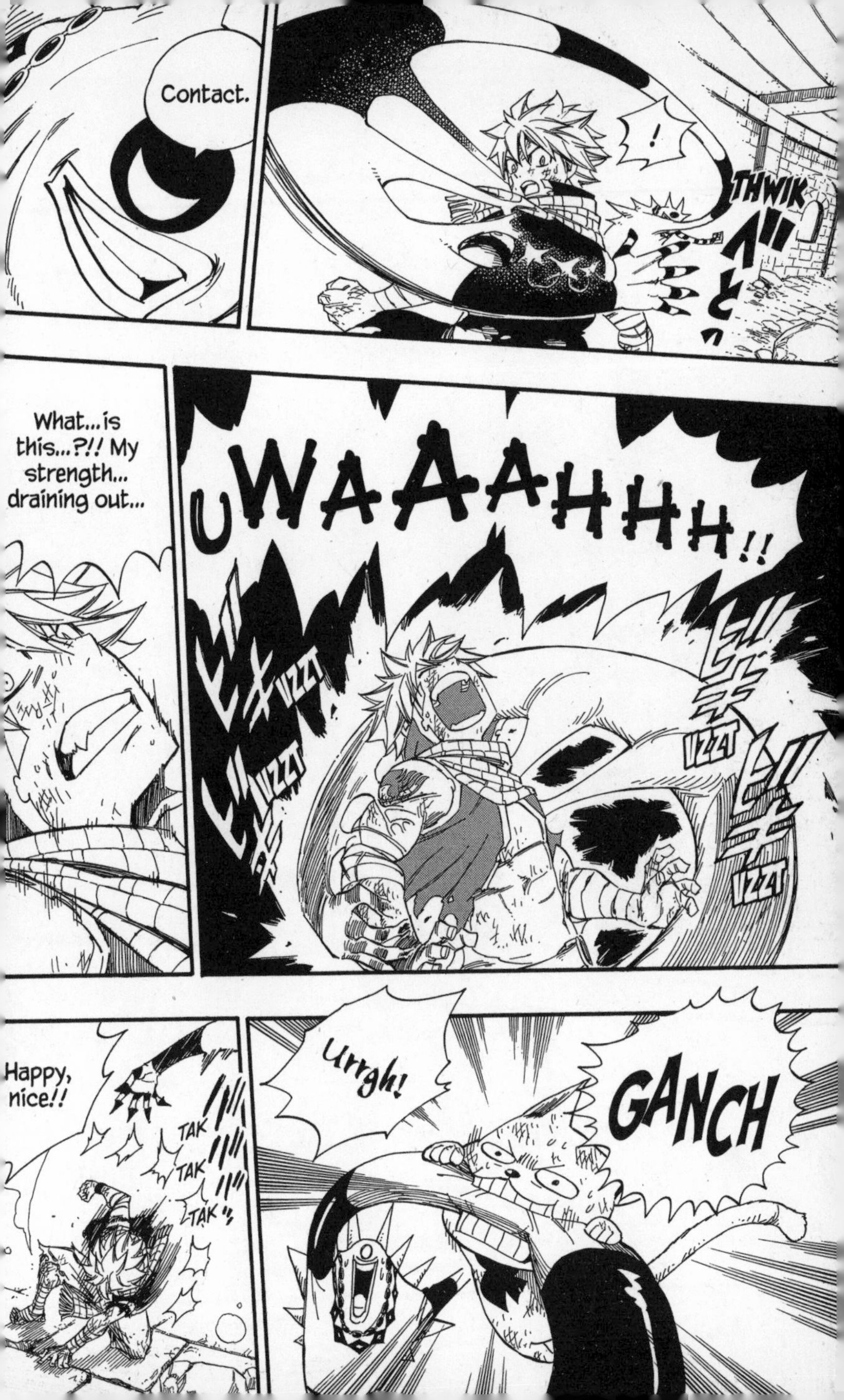
!
THWIK
Contact.
UWAAAHHHH!!
VZZT
VZZT
VZZT
VZZT
What...is this...?!! My strength... draining out...
Urrgh!
GANCH
Happy, nice!!
TAK
TAK
TAK

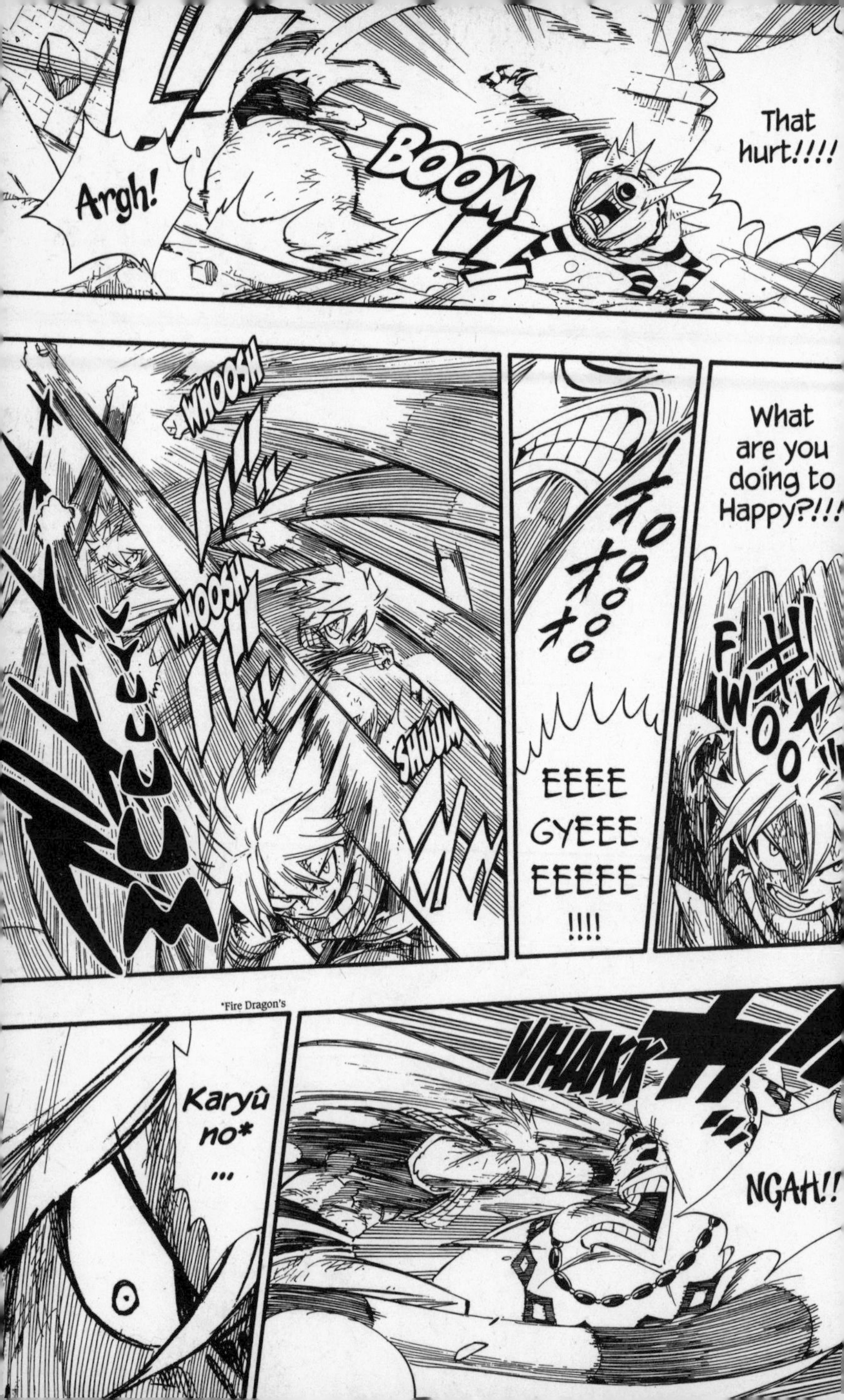
That hurt!!!!
BOOM
Argh!
What are you doing to Happy?!!!
FWOOO!!
EEEE GYEEE EEEEE !!!!
WHOOSH
WHOOSH
SHUUM
WHAKK
NGAH!!
Karyû no* ...

*Fire Dragon's

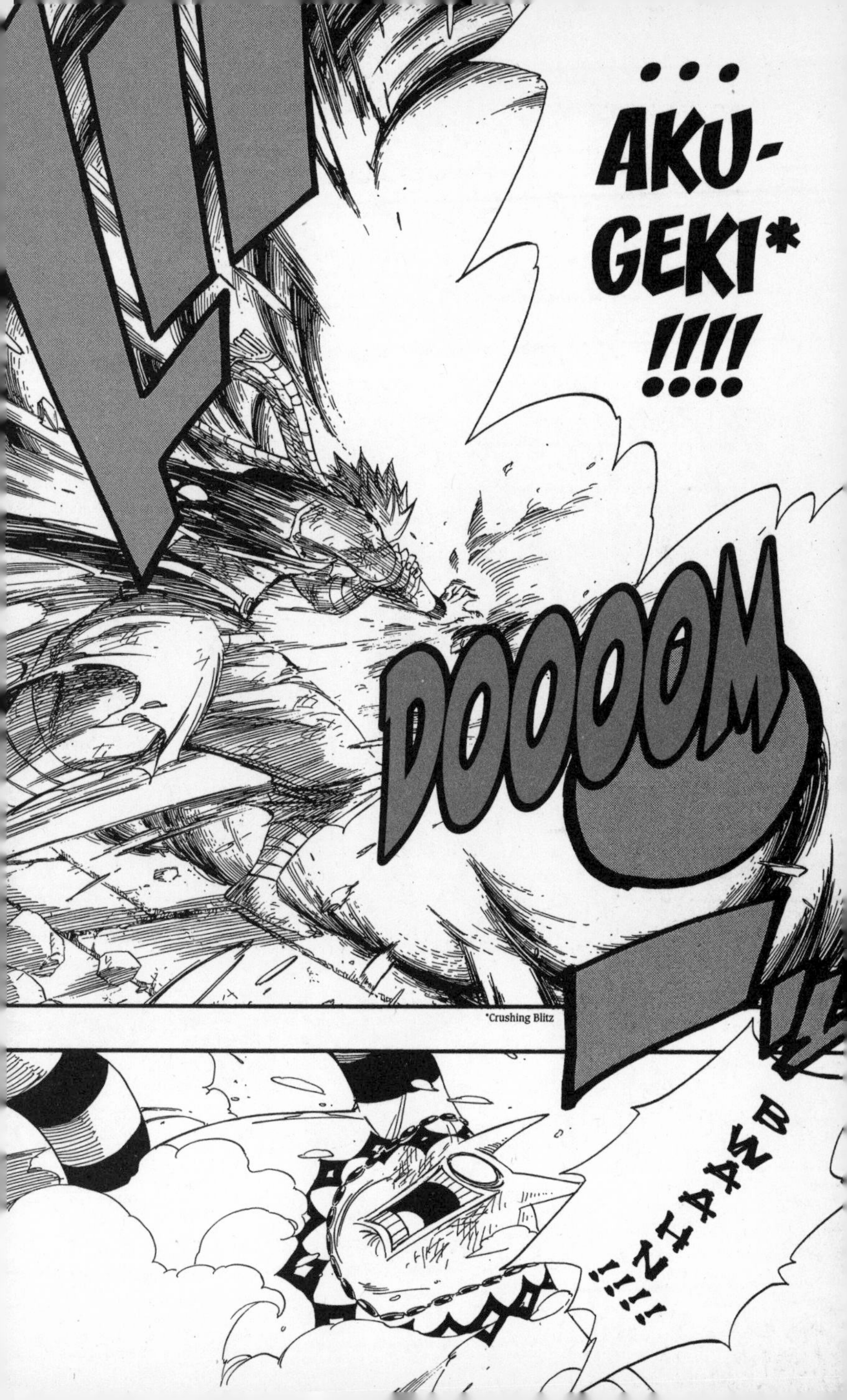
...AKU-GEKI*!!!!
DOOOOM
*Crushing Blitz
BWAHN!!!!

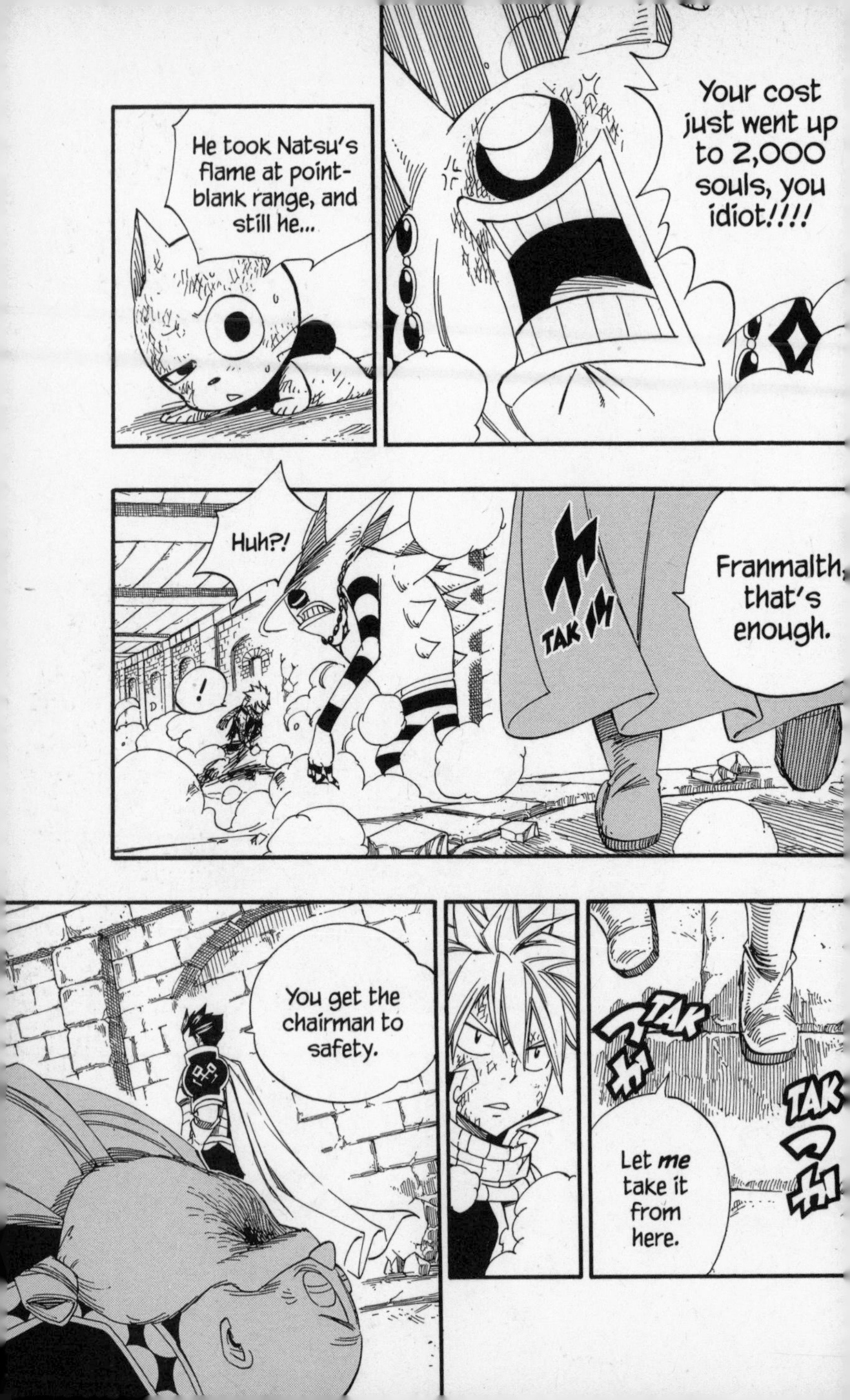
Your cost just went up to 2,000 souls, you idiot!!!!
He took Natsu's flame at point-blank range, and still he...
Franmalth, that's enough.
TAK
Huh?!
!
TAK
TAK
Let *me* take it from here.
You get the chairman to safety.

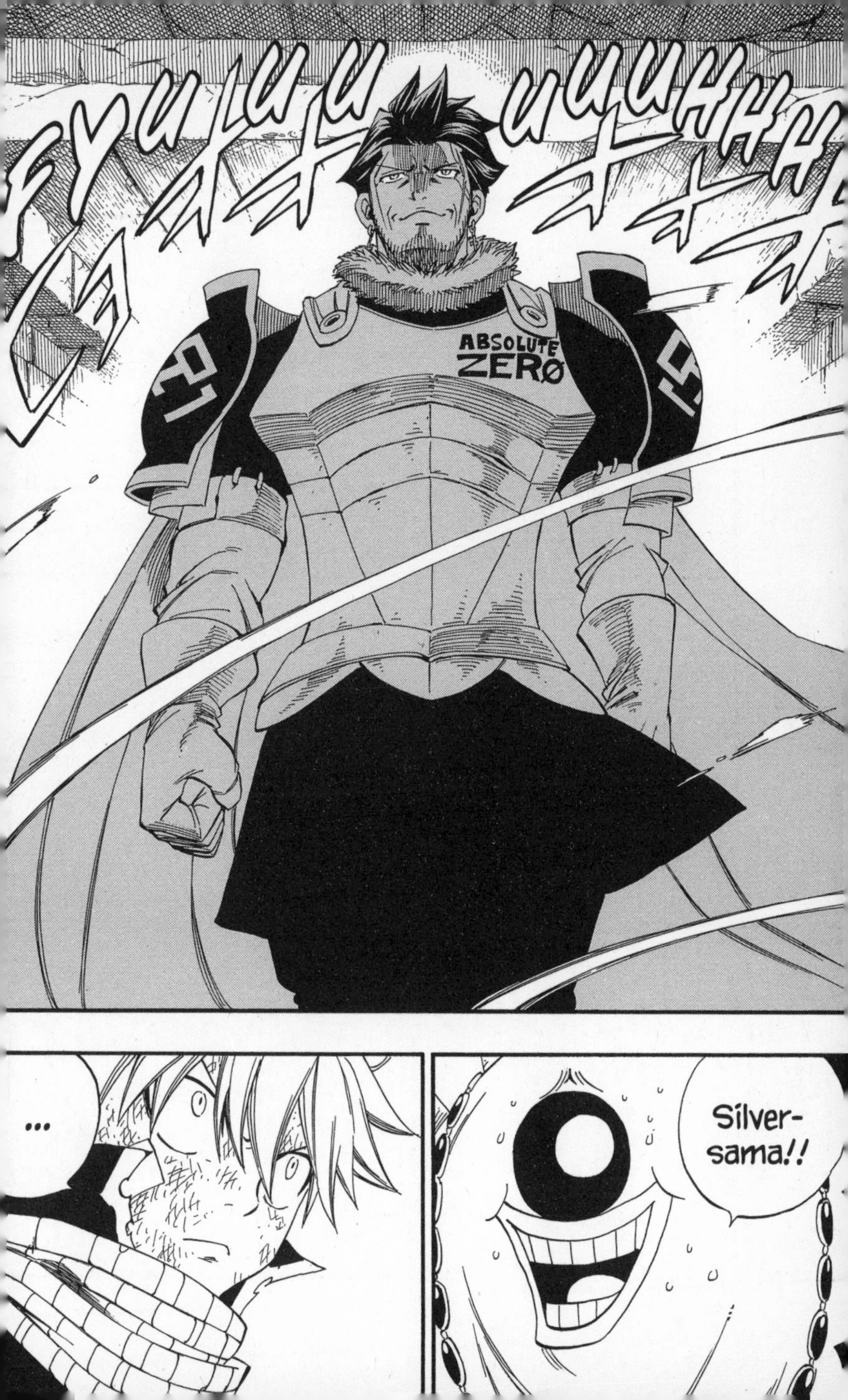
FYUUUU
UUUHH
ABSOLUTE ZERØ
21
21
Silver-sama!!
...

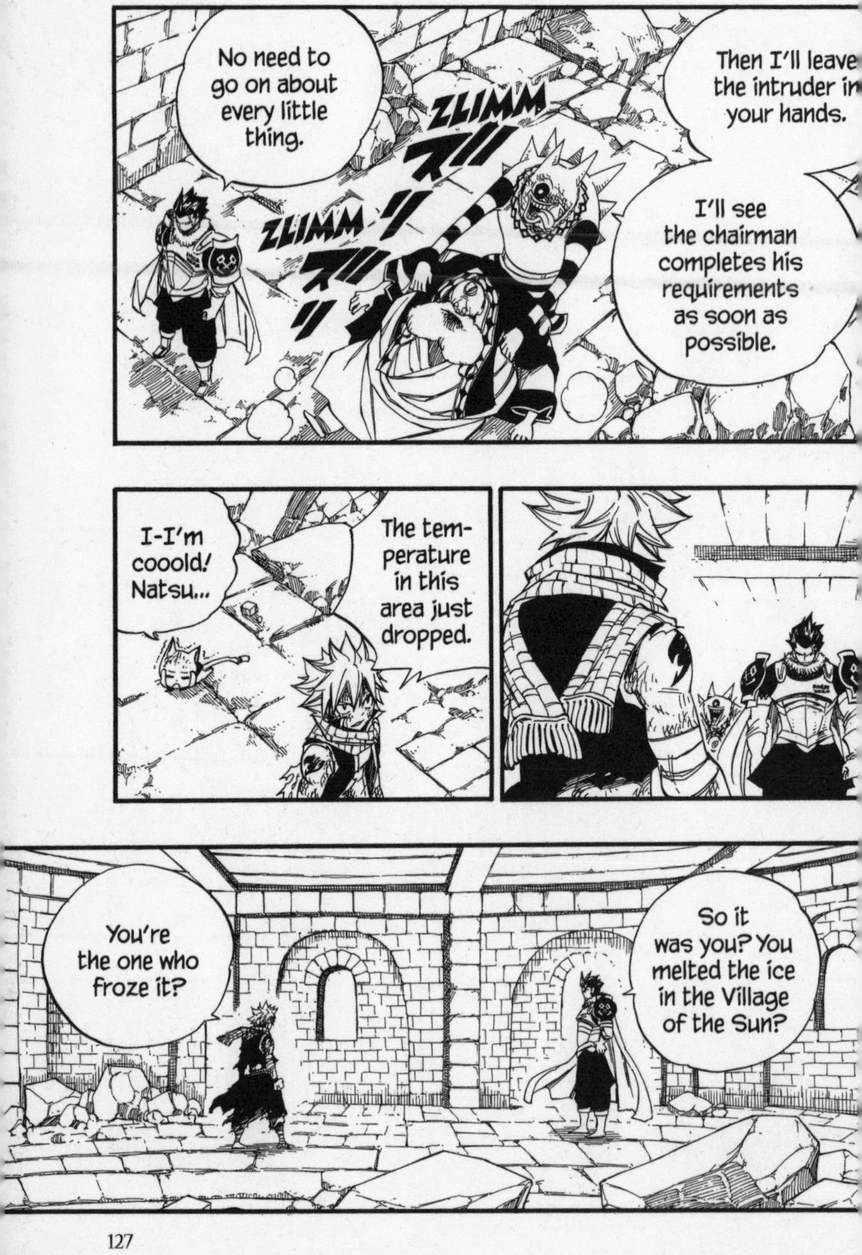
Then I'll leave the intruder in your hands.
I'll see the chairman completes his requirements as soon as possible.
No need to go on about every little thing.
ZLIMM
ZLIMM
The tem-perature in this area just dropped.
I-I'm cooold! Natsu...
So it was you? You melted the ice in the Village of the Sun?
You're the one who froze it?

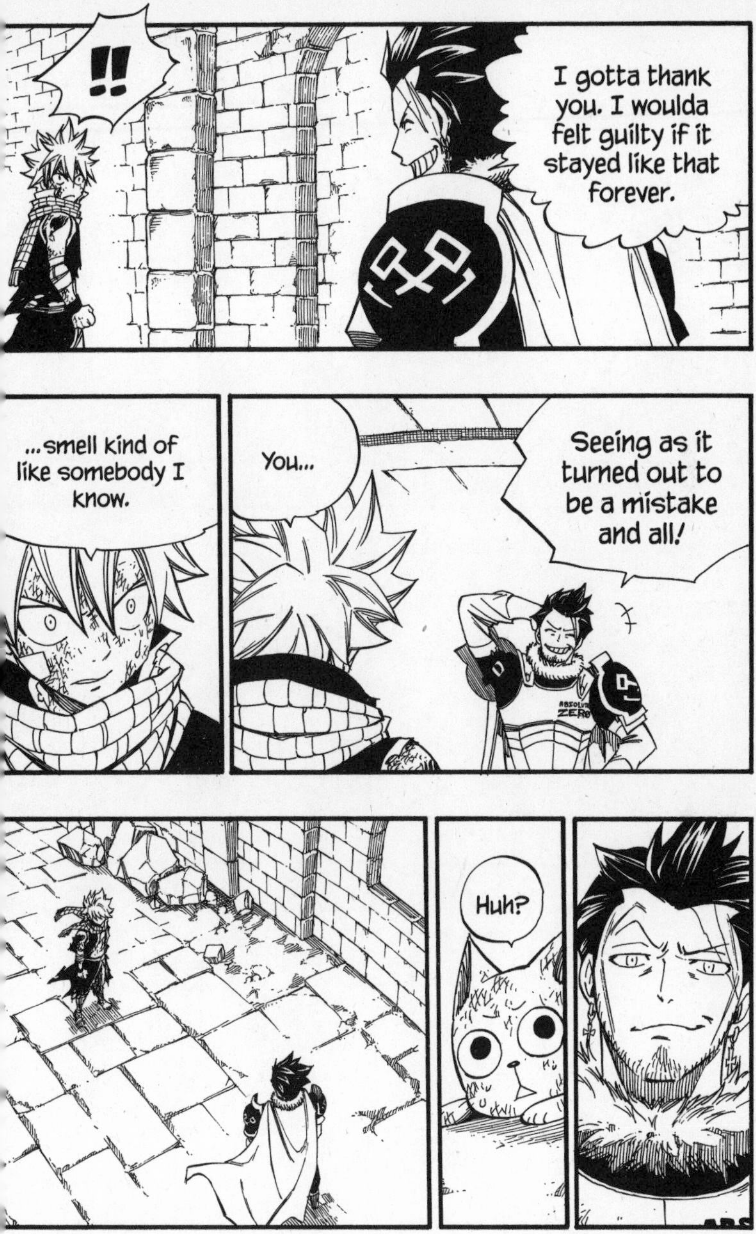
I gotta thank you. I woulda felt guilty if it stayed like that forever.
!!
Seeing as it turned out to be a mistake and all!
You...
...smell kind of like somebody I know.
Huh?

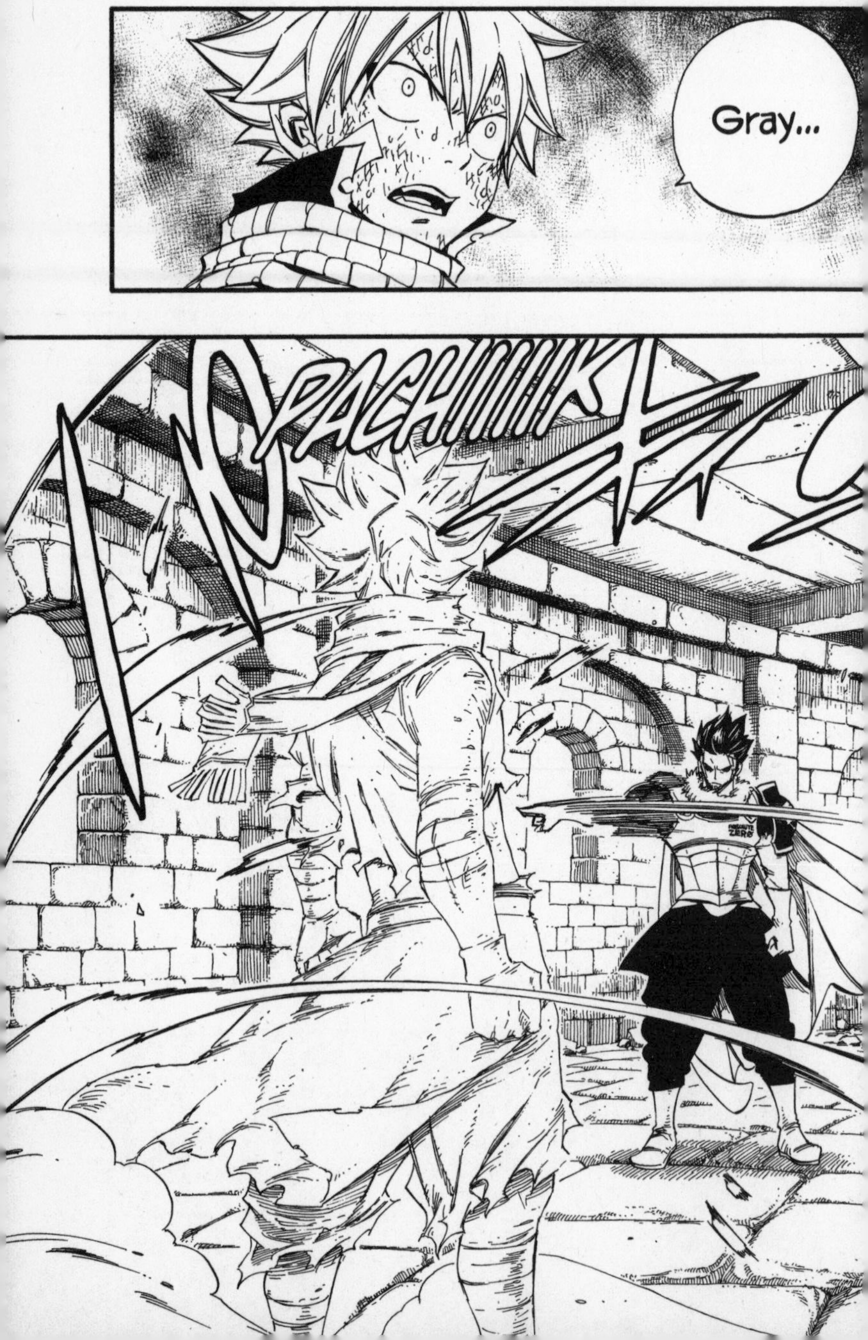
Gray...
PACHIIIIIK

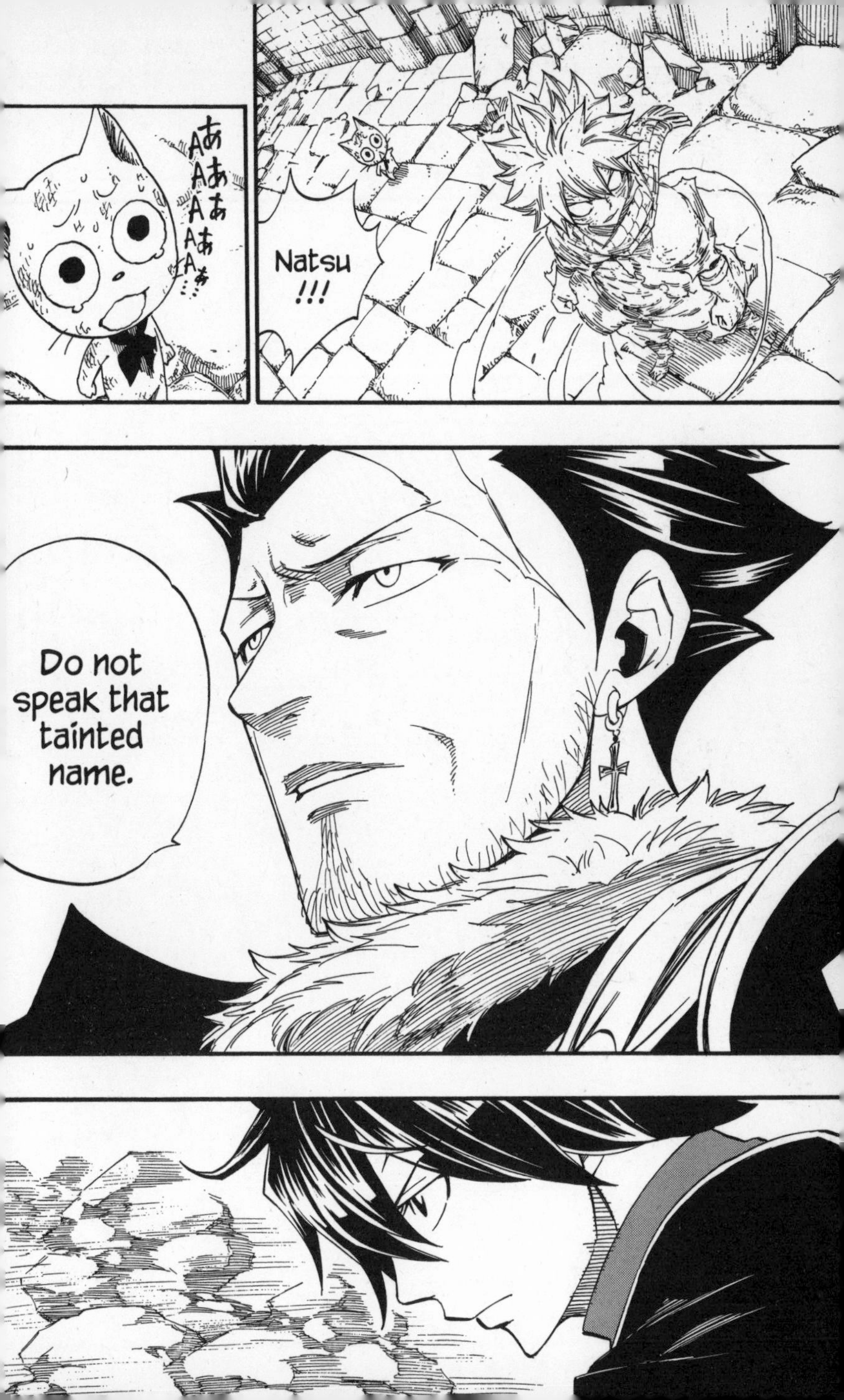
Natsu !!!
AAAAA...
Do not speak that tainted name.

FAIRY TAIL

Chapter 367: Jellal vs. Oración Seis

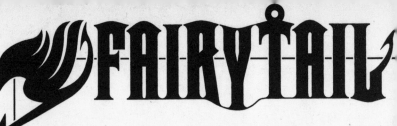

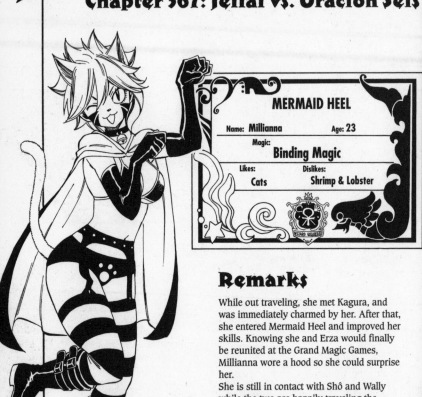

MERMAID HEEL

Name: Millianna **Age:** 23

Magic: Binding Magic

Likes: Cats

Dislikes: Shrimp & Lobster

Remarks

While out traveling, she met Kagura, and was immediately charmed by her. After that, she entered Mermaid Heel and improved her skills. Knowing she and Erza would finally be reunited at the Grand Magic Games, Millianna wore a hood so she could surprise her.

She is still in contact with Shô and Wally while the two are happily traveling the world. Her favorite saying is, "Are you all pumped up?"

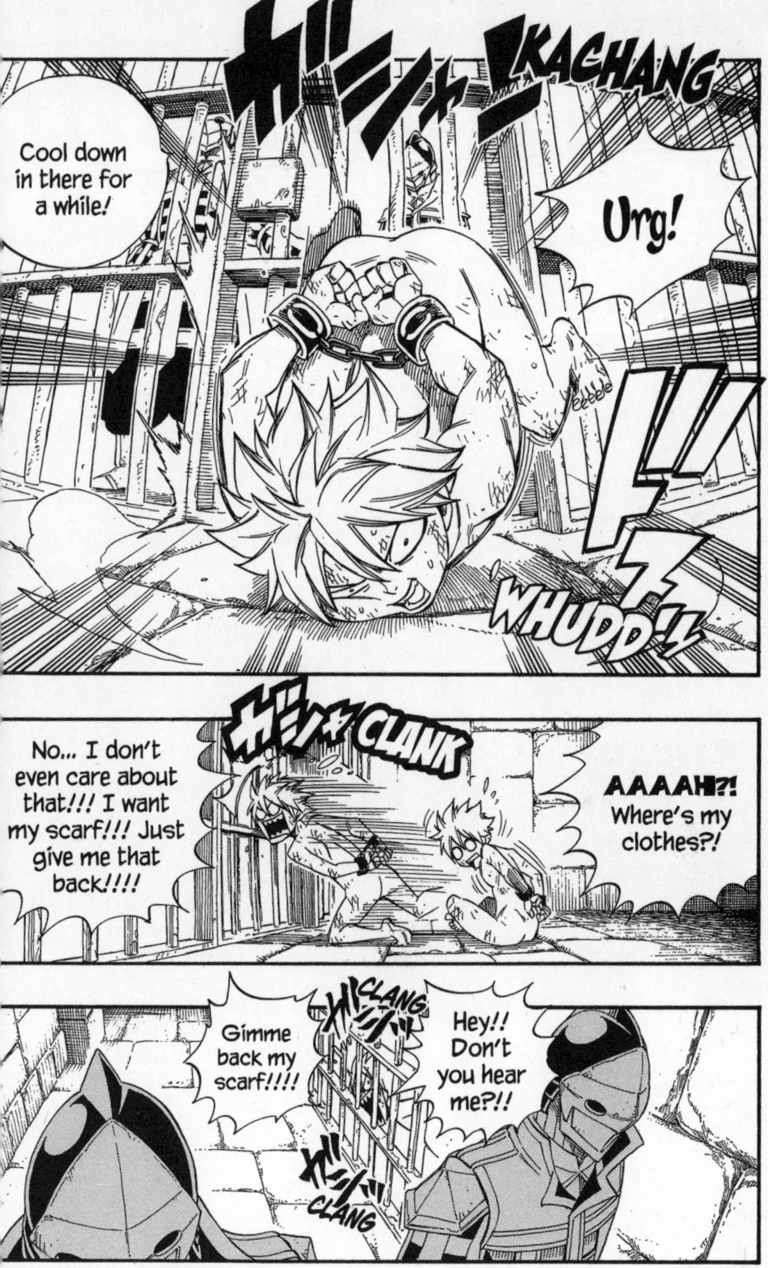
KACHANG
Cool down in there for a while!
Urg!
WHUDD!!
CLANK
AAAAH?! Where's my clothes?!
No... I don't even care about that!!! I want my scarf!!! Just give me that back!!!!
CLANG
Hey!! Don't you hear me?!!
Gimme back my scarf!!!!
CLANG

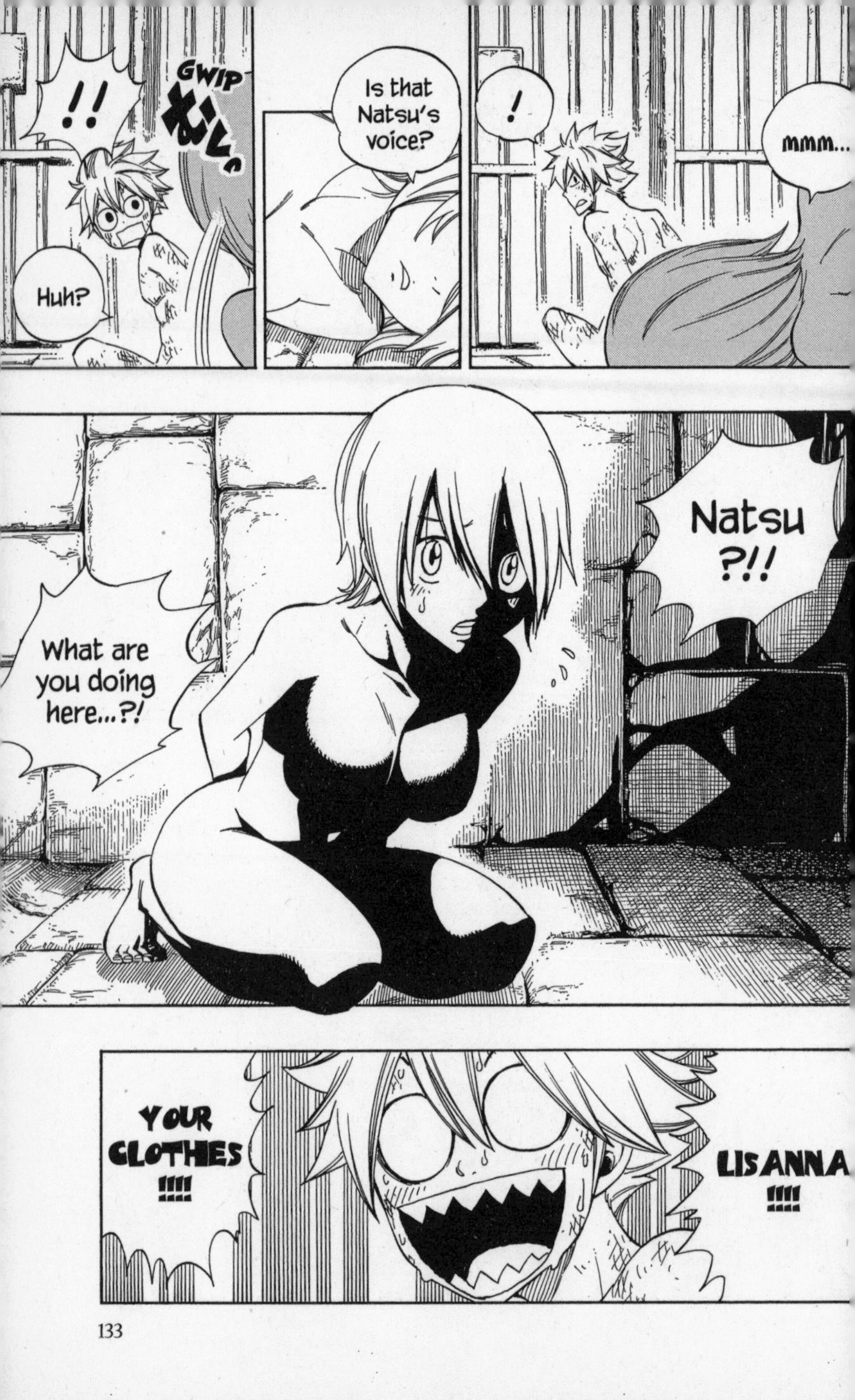
mmm...
!
Is that Natsu's voice?
!!
GWIP
Huh?
Natsu ?!!
What are you doing here...?!
LISANNA !!!!
YOUR CLOTHES !!!!

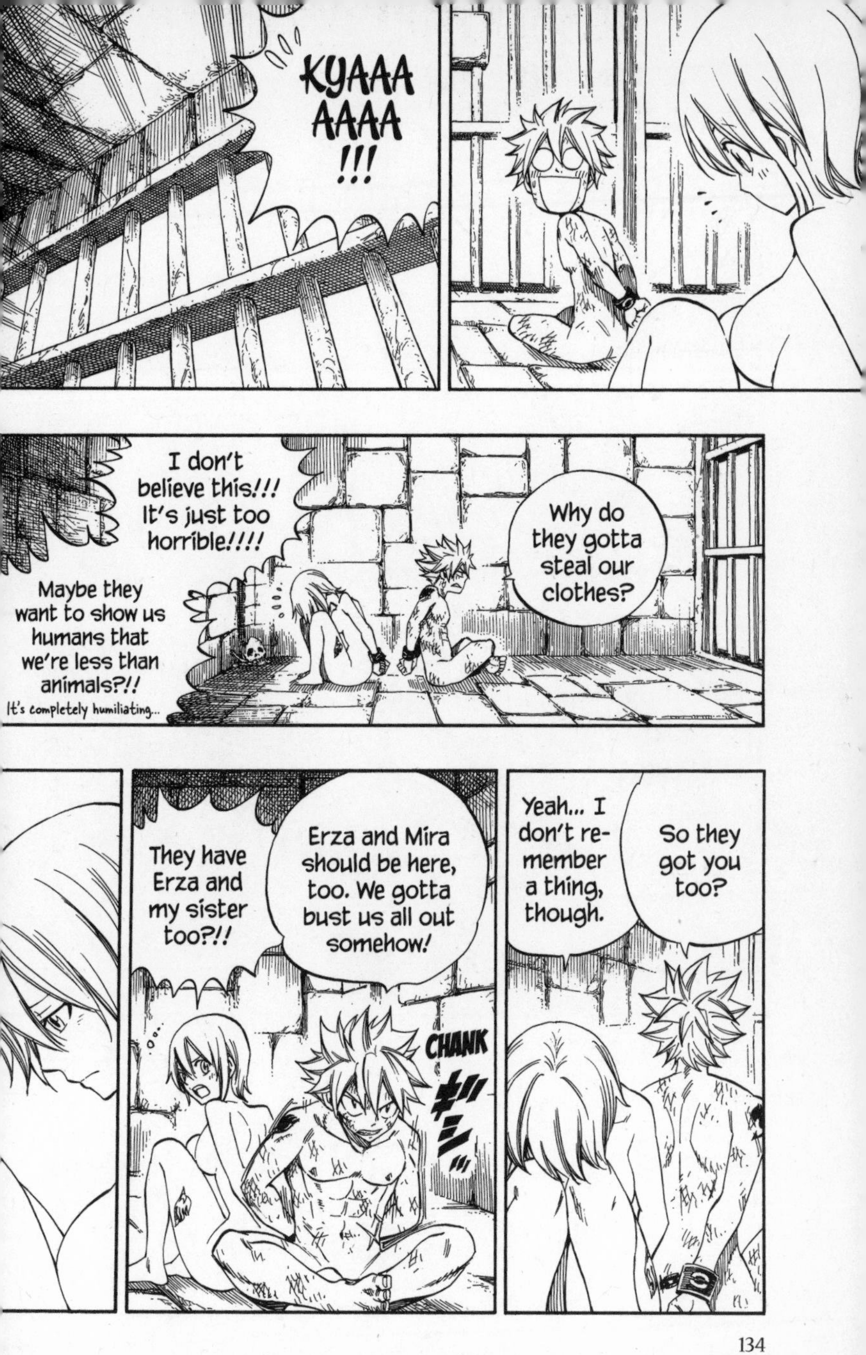
KYAAA AAAA !!!
Why do they gotta steal our clothes?
I don't believe this!!! It's just too horrible!!!!
Maybe they want to show us humans that we're less than animals?!!
It's completely humiliating...
So they got you too?
Yeah... I don't re-member a thing, though.
Erza and Mira should be here, too. We gotta bust us all out somehow!
They have Erza and my sister too?!!
CHANK

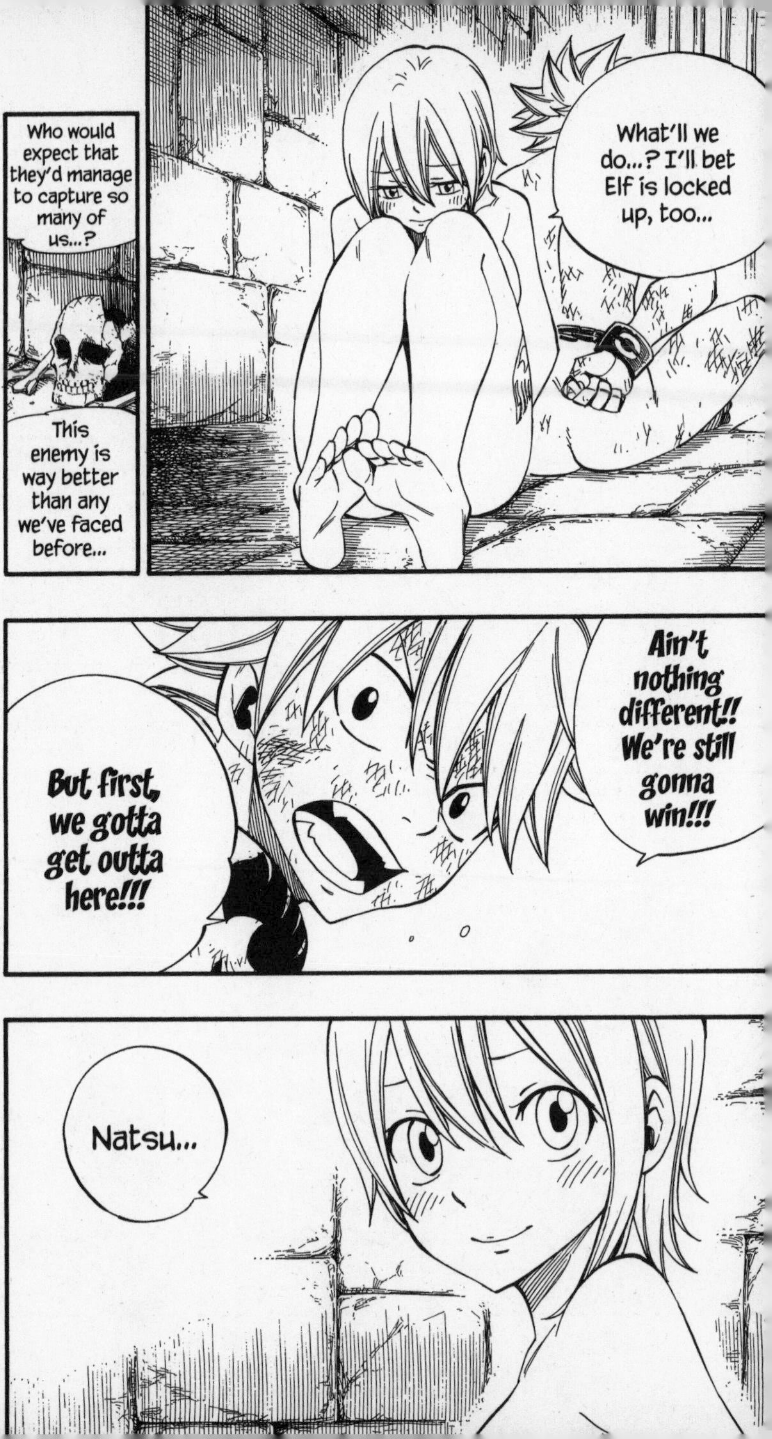
What'll we do...? I'll bet Elf is locked up, too...
Who would expect that they'd manage to capture so many of us...?
This enemy is way better than any we've faced before...
Ain't nothing different!! We're still gonna win!!!
But first, we gotta get outta here!!!
Natsu...

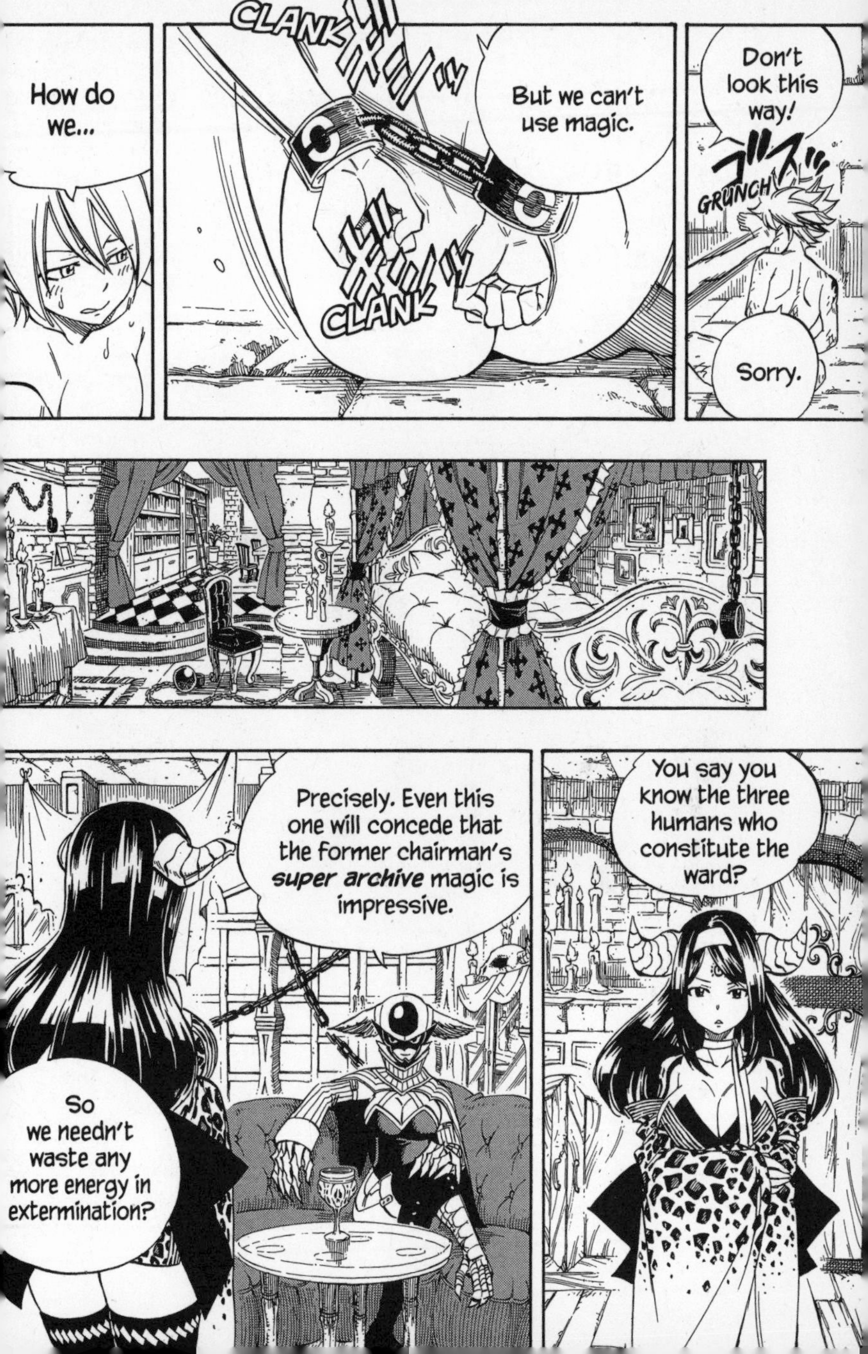
Don't look this way!
GRUNCH
Sorry.
CLANK
But we can't use magic.
CLANK
How do we...
You say you know the three humans who constitute the ward?
Precisely. Even this one will concede that the former chairman's *super archive* magic is impressive.
So we needn't waste any more energy in extermination?

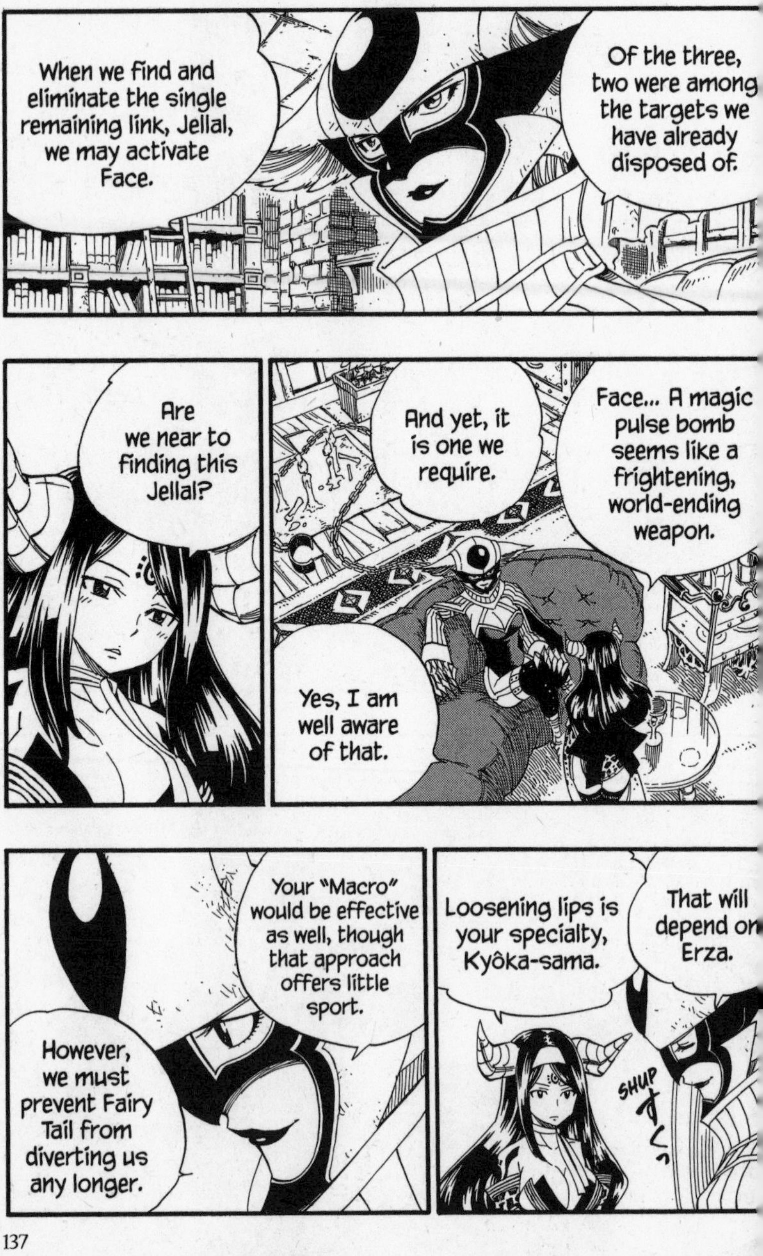

Of the three, two were among the targets we have already disposed of.
When we find and eliminate the single remaining link, Jellal, we may activate Face.
Face... A magic pulse bomb seems like a frightening, world-ending weapon.
And yet, it is one we require.
Yes, I am well aware of that.
Are we near to finding this Jellal?
That will depend on Erza.
Loosening lips is your specialty, Kyôka-sama.
SHUP
Your "Macro" would be effective as well, though that approach offers little sport.
However, we must prevent Fairy Tail from diverting us any longer.

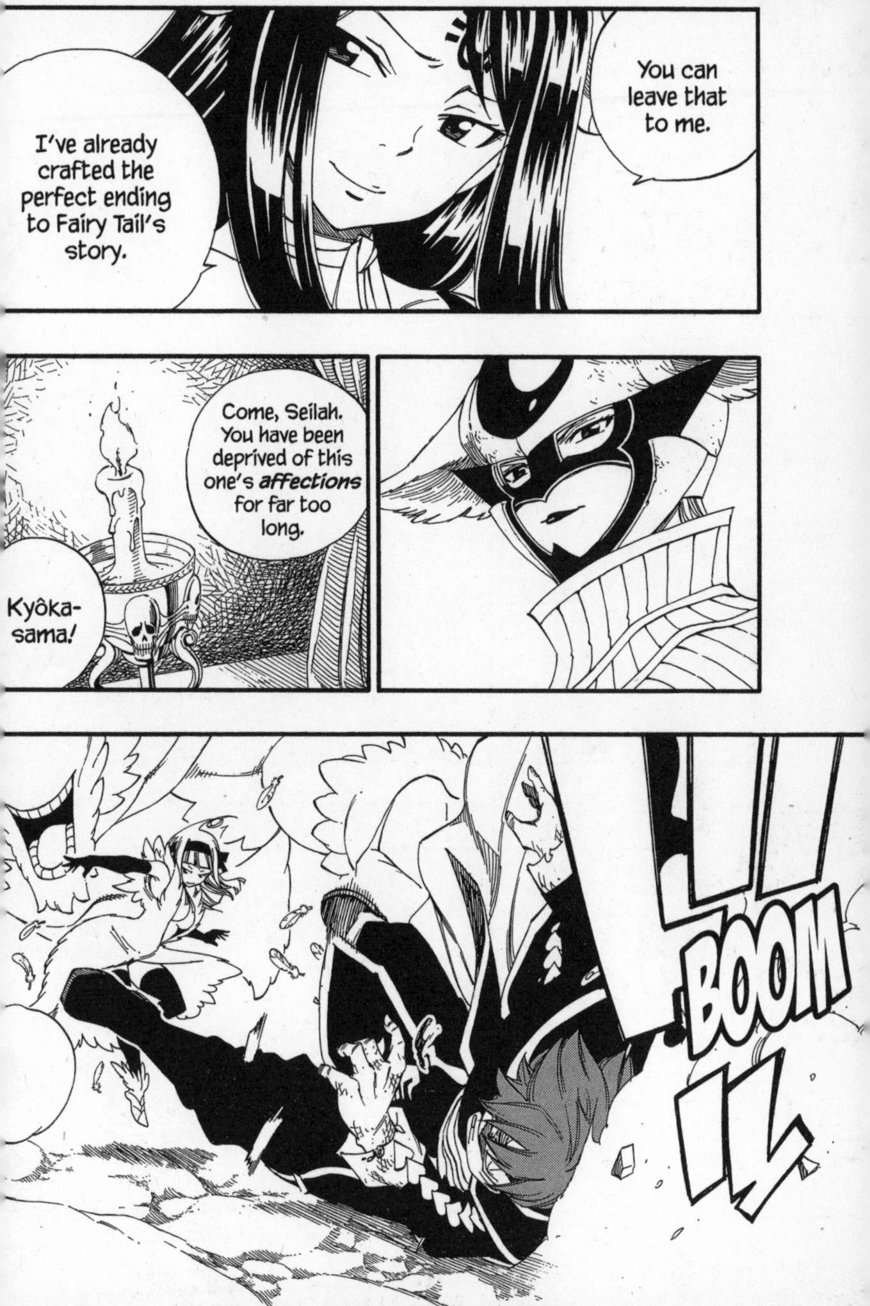
You can leave that to me.
I've already crafted the perfect ending to Fairy Tail's story.
Come, Seilah. You have been deprived of this one's *affections* for far too long.
Kyôka-sama!
BOOM

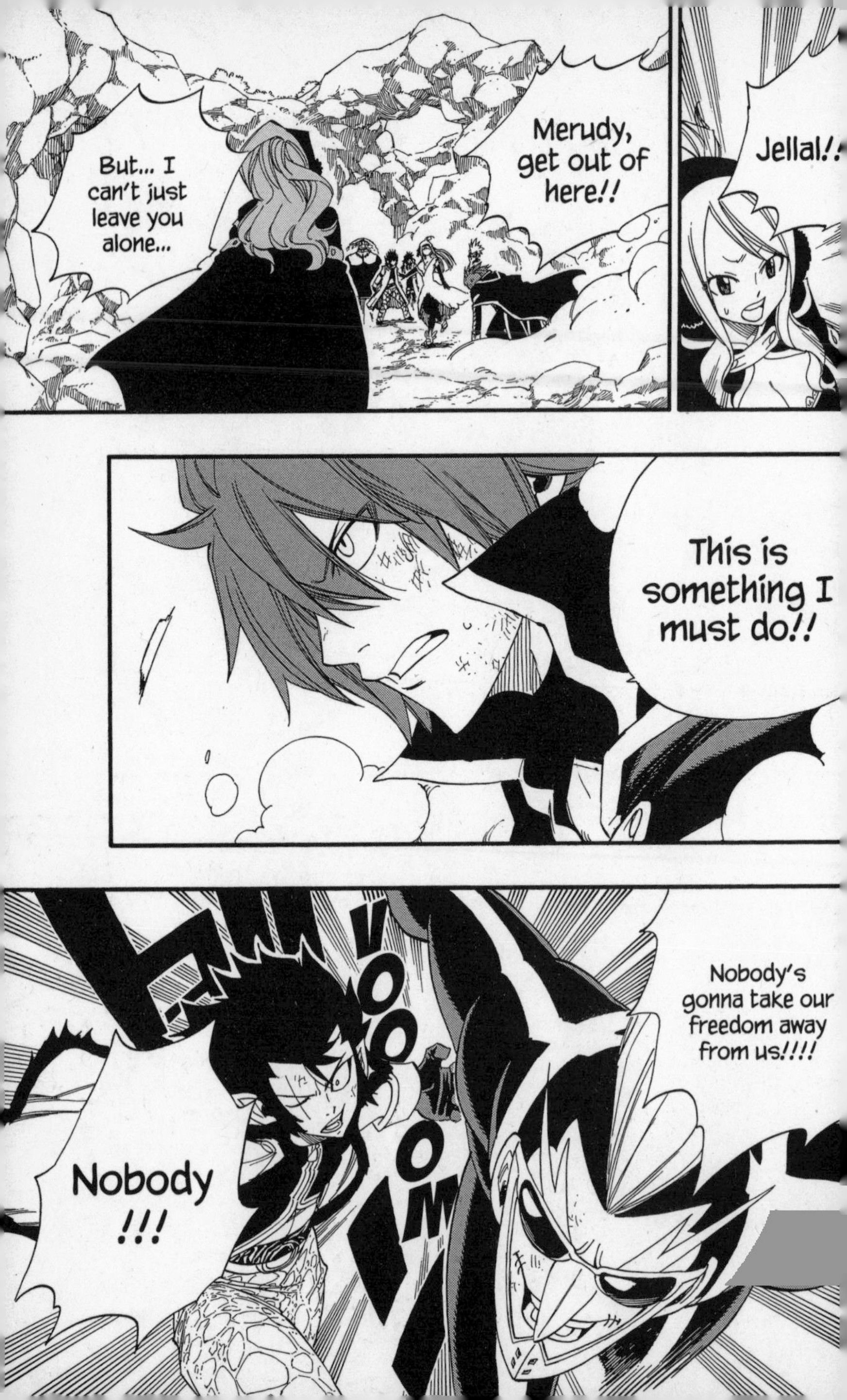
Jellal!!
Merudy, get out of here!!
But... I can't just leave you alone...
This is something I must do!!
Nobody's gonna take our freedom away from us!!!!
VOOOOM
Nobody !!!

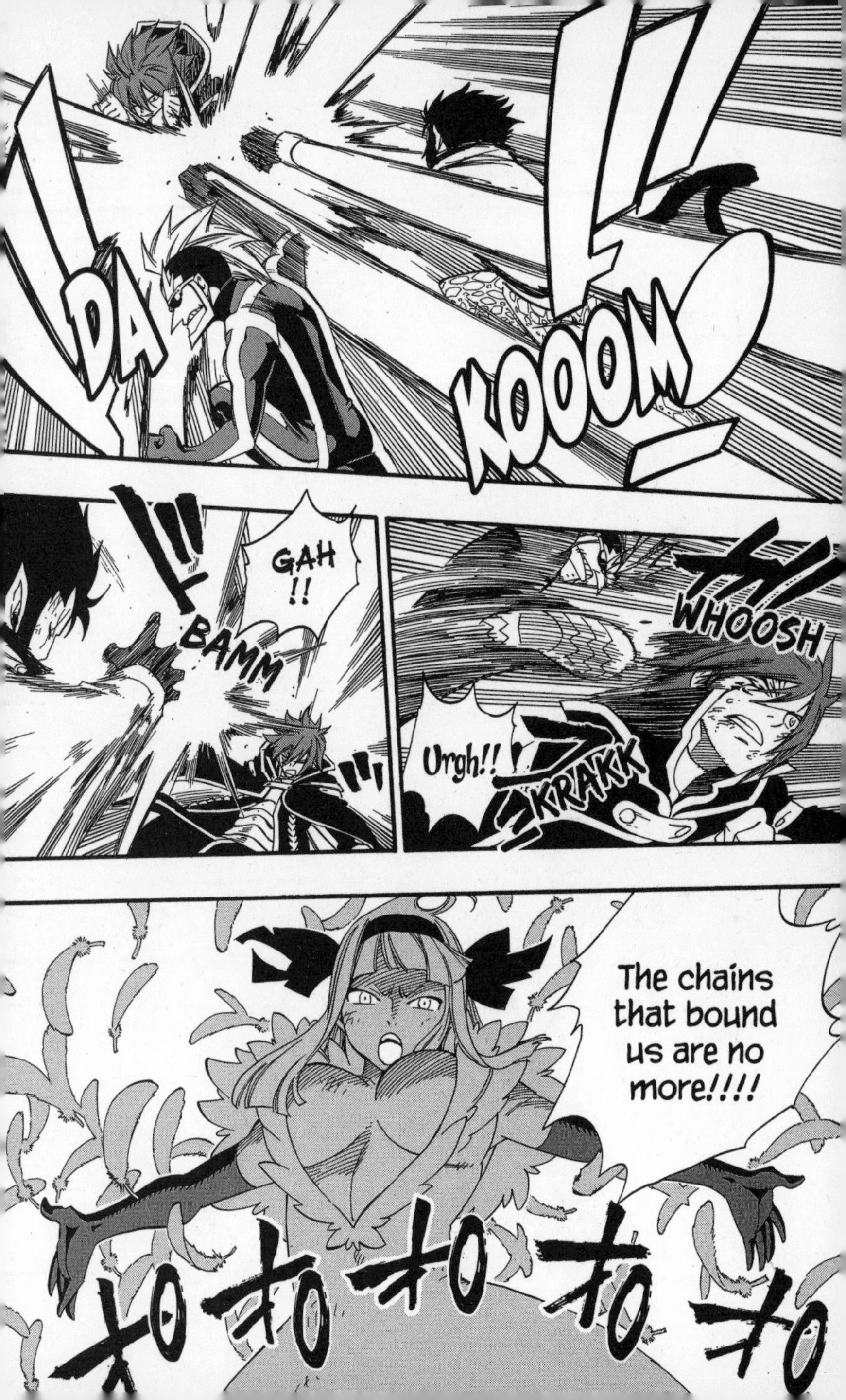
KOOOM
DA
WHOOSH
Urgh!!
KRAKK
GAH !!
BAMM
The chains that bound us are no more!!!!

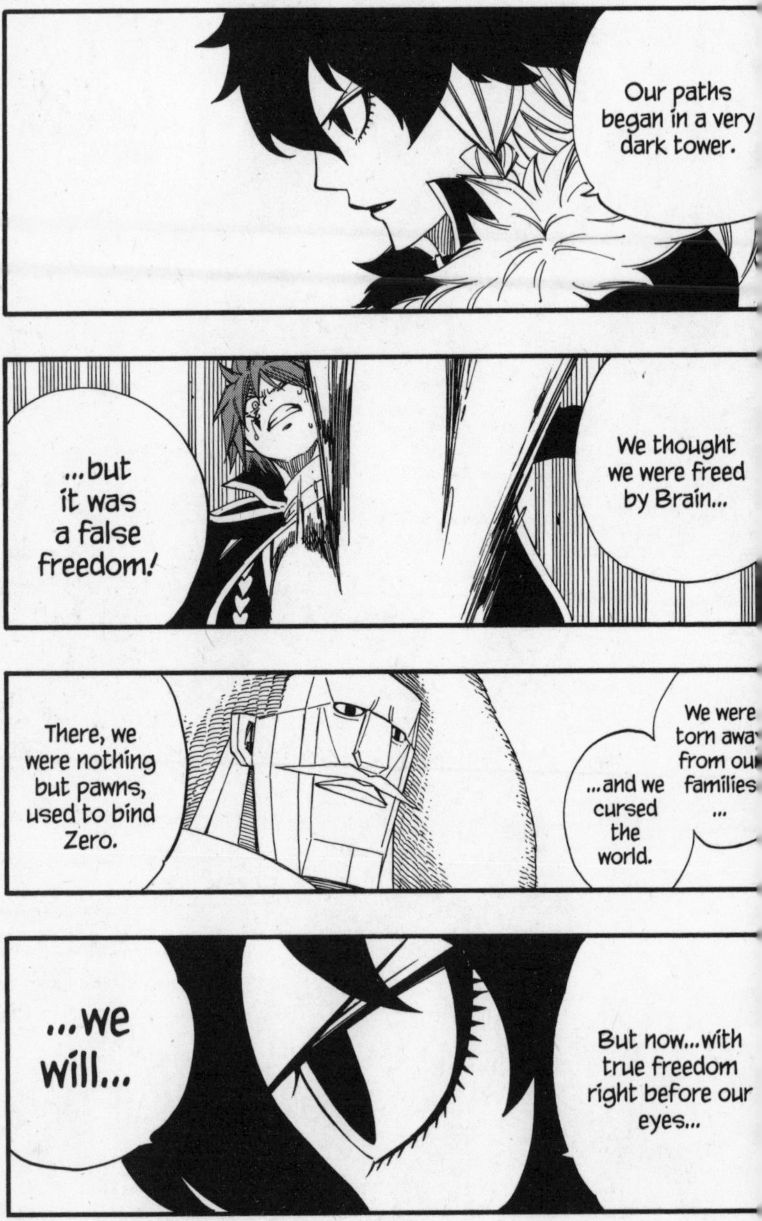

Our paths began in a very dark tower.
We thought we were freed by Brain...
...but it was a false freedom!
We were torn awa from ou families ...
...and we cursed the world.
There, we were nothing but pawns, used to bind Zero.
But now...with true freedom right before our eyes...
...we will...

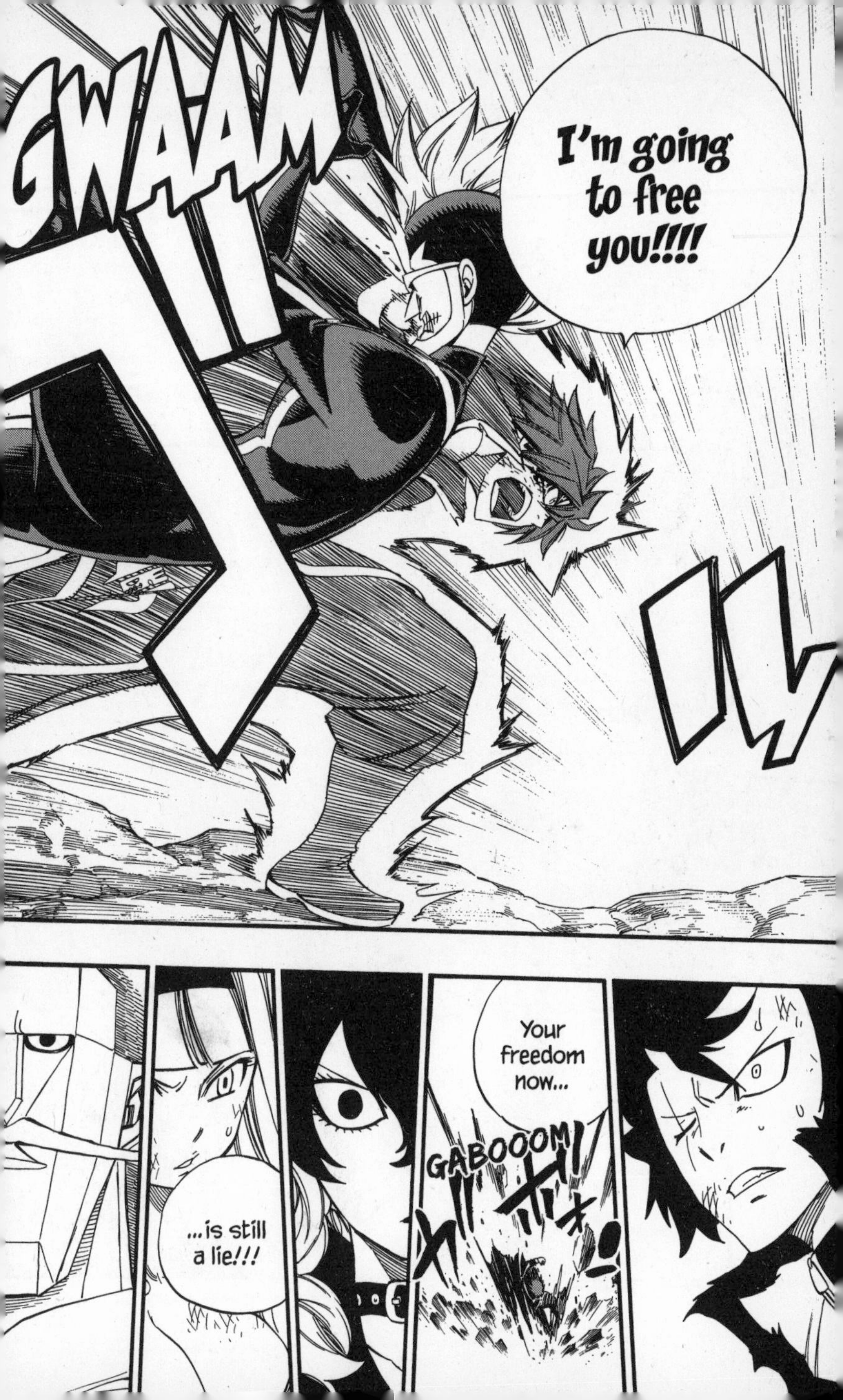
I'm going to free you!!!!
GWAAM
Your freedom now...
GABOOOM
...is still a lie!!!

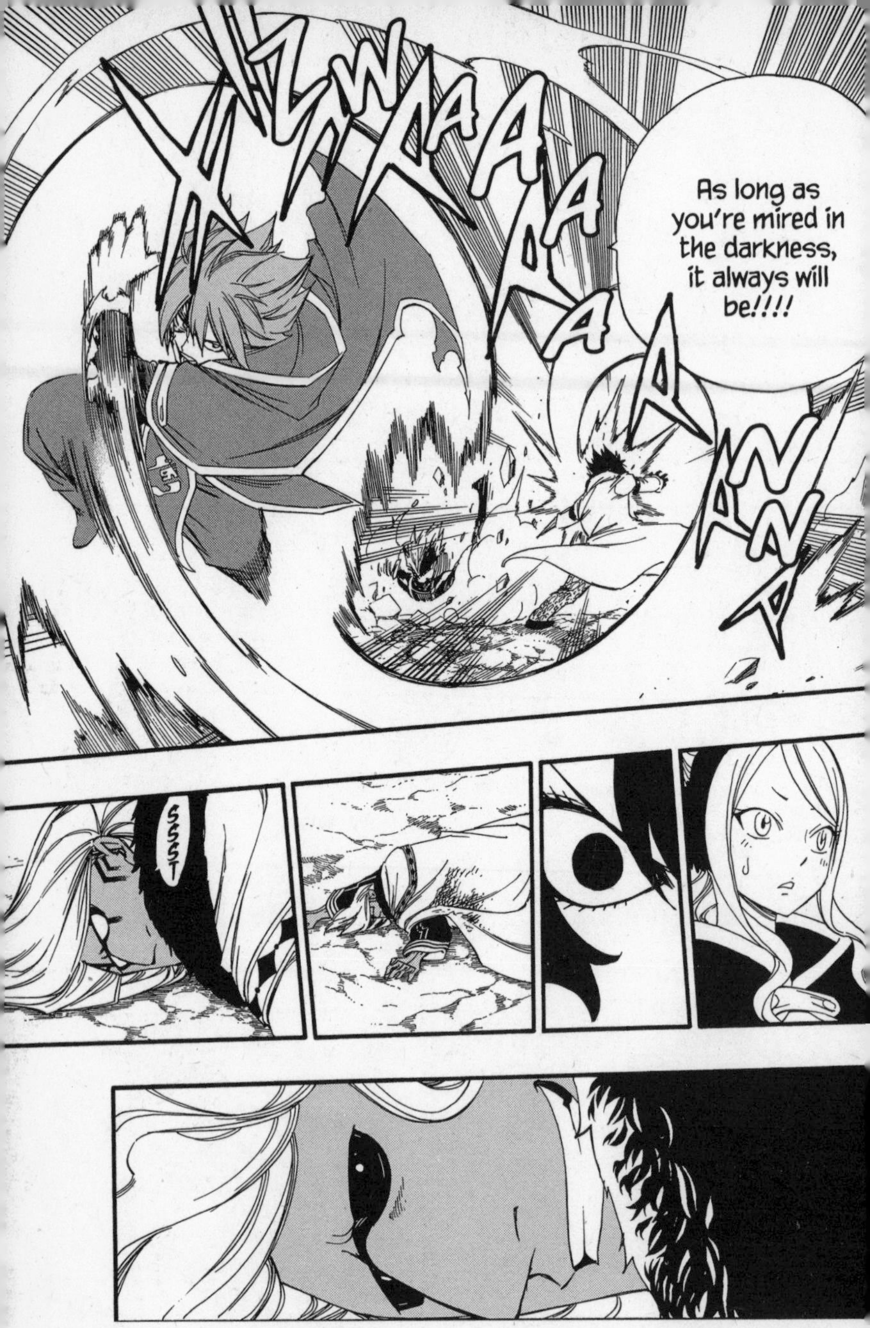
As long as you're mired in the darkness, it always will be!!!!
VWAAAAAAAAAAN
SSSST

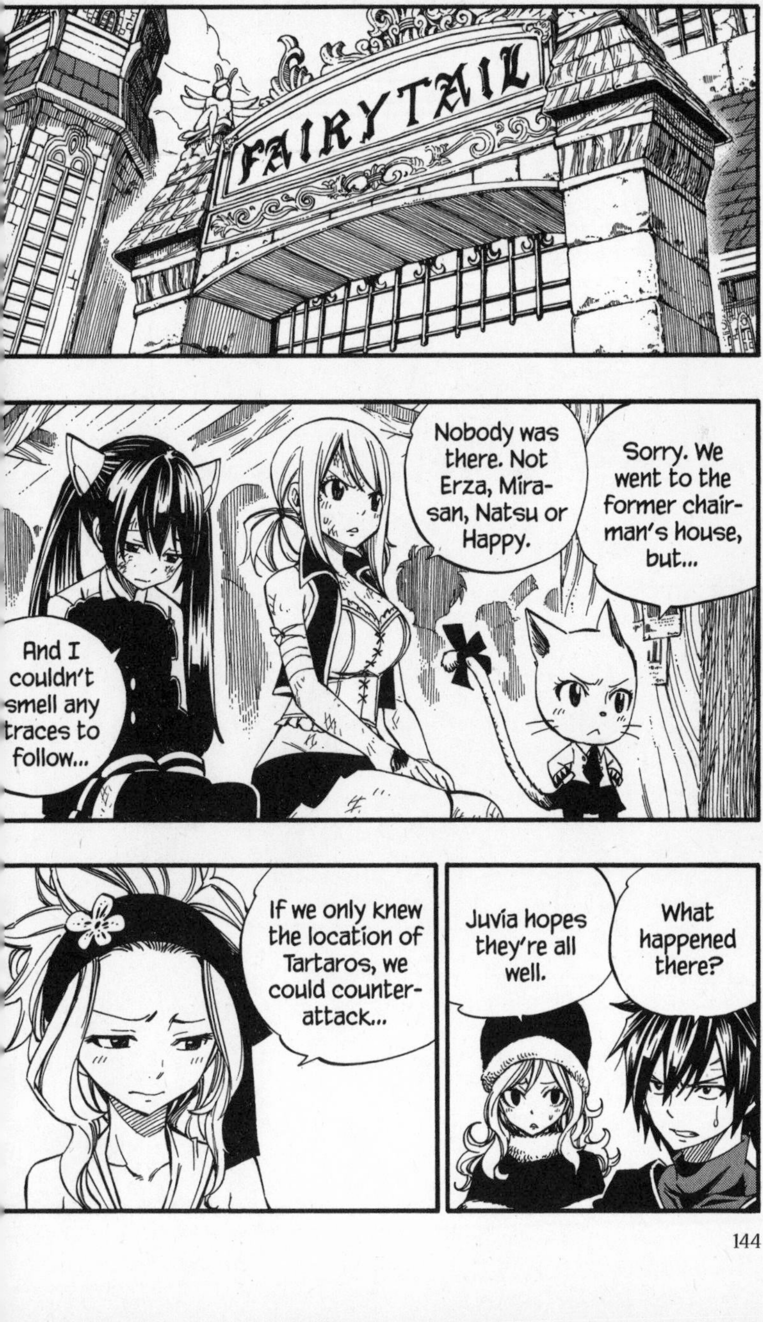
FAIRY TAIL
Sorry. We went to the former chairman's house, but...
Nobody was there. Not Erza, Mira-san, Natsu or Happy.
And I couldn't smell any traces to follow...
What happened there?
Juvia hopes they're all well.
If we only knew the location of Tartaros, we could counter-attack...

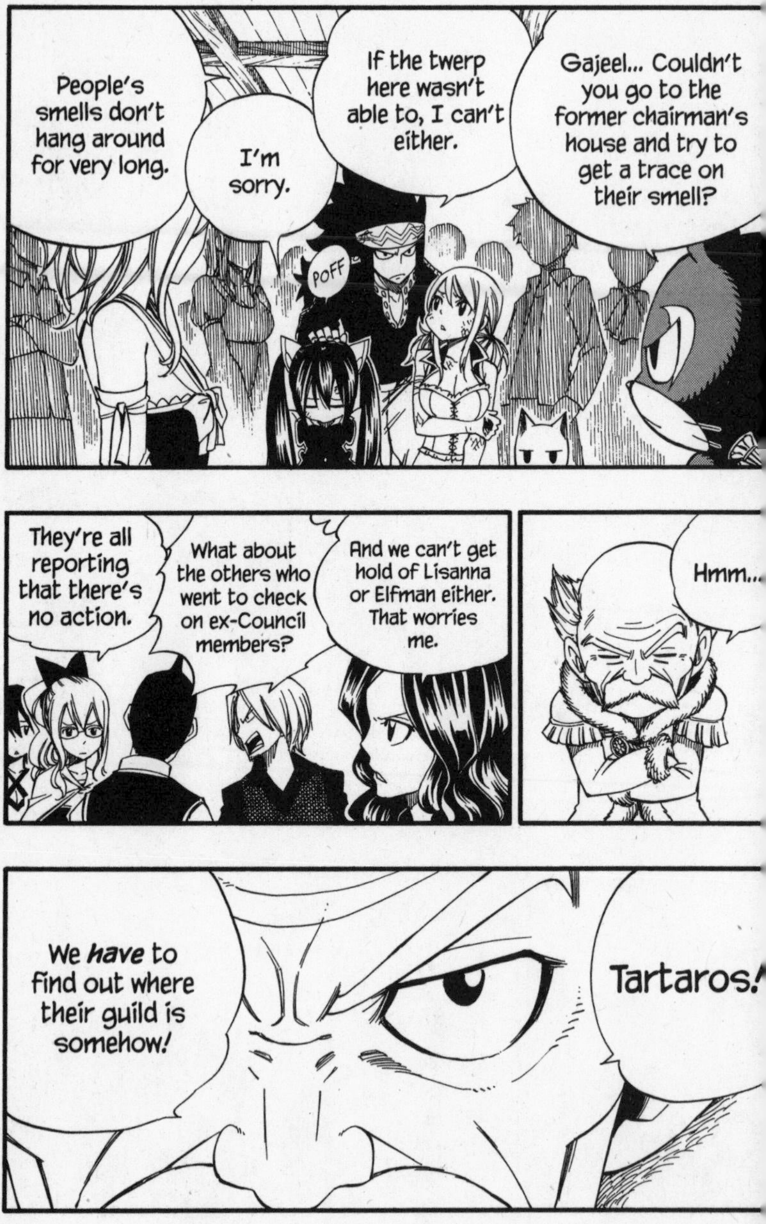
Gajeel... Couldn't you go to the former chairman's house and try to get a trace on their smell?
If the twerp here wasn't able to, I can't either.
I'm sorry.
POFF
People's smells don't hang around for very long.
Hmm...
And we can't get hold of Lisanna or Elfman either. That worries me.
What about the others who went to check on ex-Council members?
They're all reporting that there's no action.
Tartaros!
We *have* to find out where their guild is somehow!

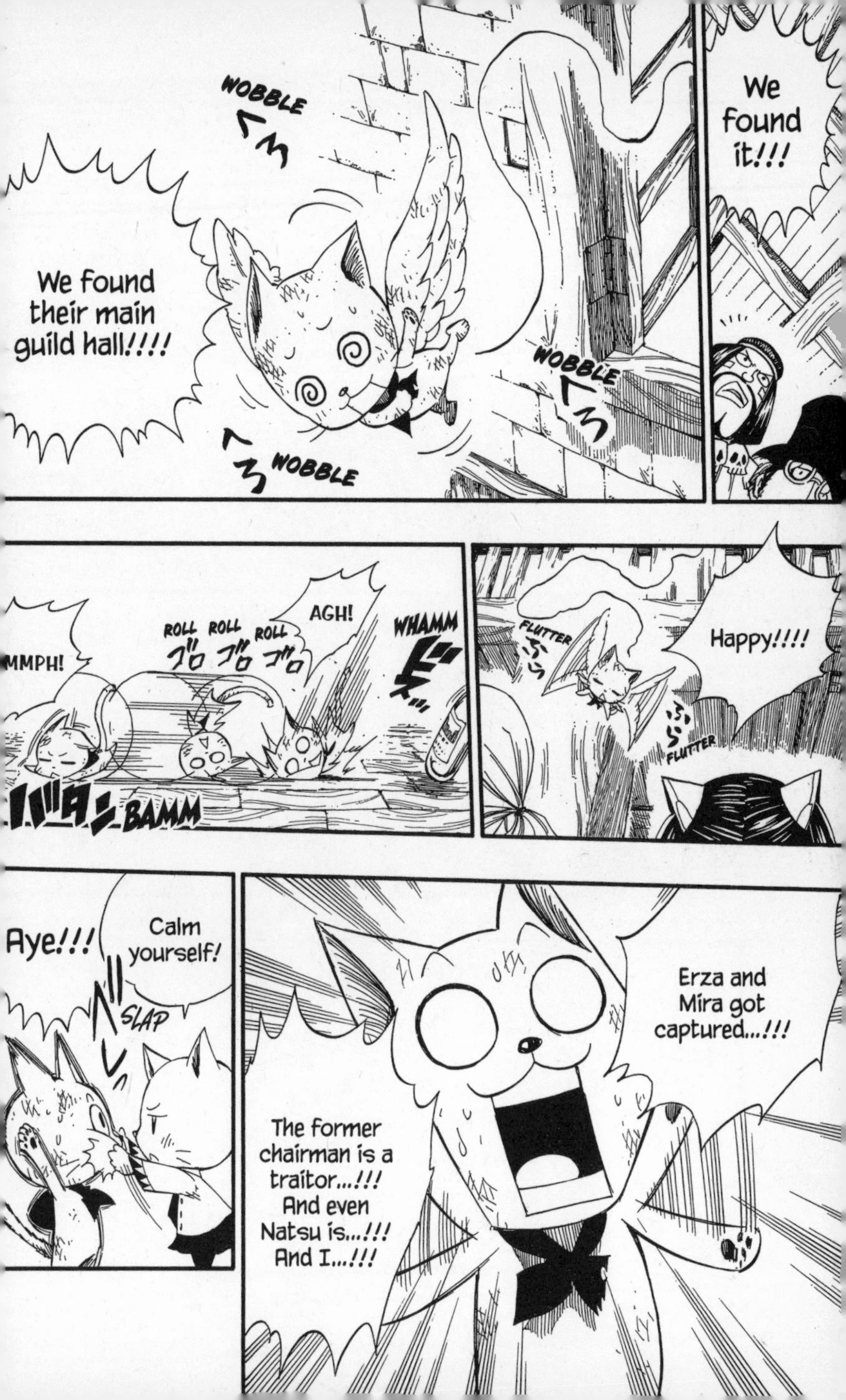
We found it!!!
WOBBLE
We found their main guild hall!!!!
WOBBLE
WOBBLE
Happy!!!!
FLUTTER
FLUTTER
WHAMM
AGH!
ROLL ROLL ROLL
MMPH!
BAMM
Erza and Mira got captured...!!!
The former chairman is a traitor...!!! And even Natsu is...!!! And I...!!!
Calm yourself!
Aye!!!
SLAP

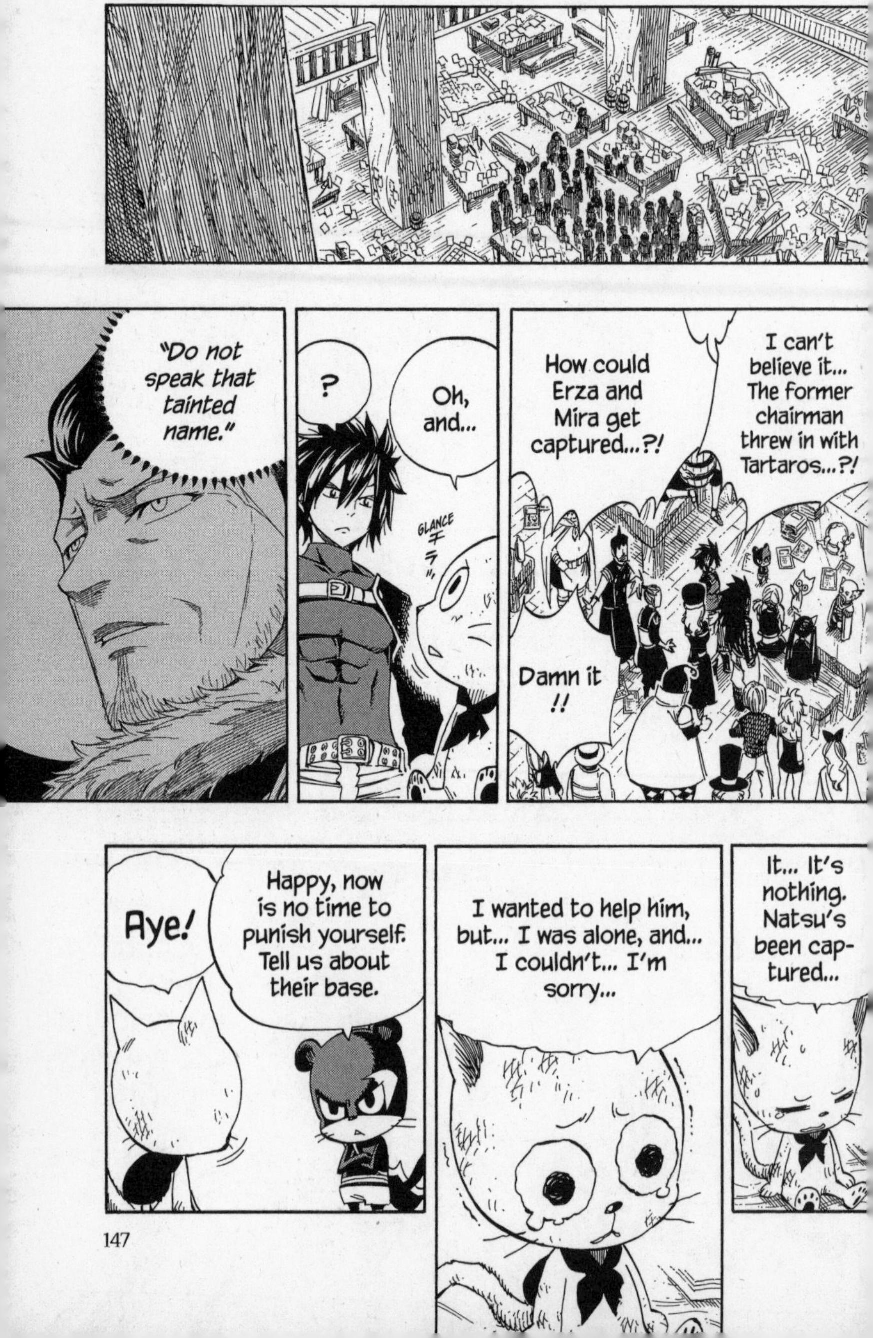
I can't believe it... The former chairman threw in with Tartaros...?!
How could Erza and Mira get captured...?!
Damn it !!
Oh, and...
?
GLANCE
"Do not speak that tainted name."
It... It's nothing. Natsu's been captured...
I wanted to help him, but... I was alone, and... I couldn't... I'm sorry...
Happy, now is no time to punish yourself. Tell us about their base.
Aye!

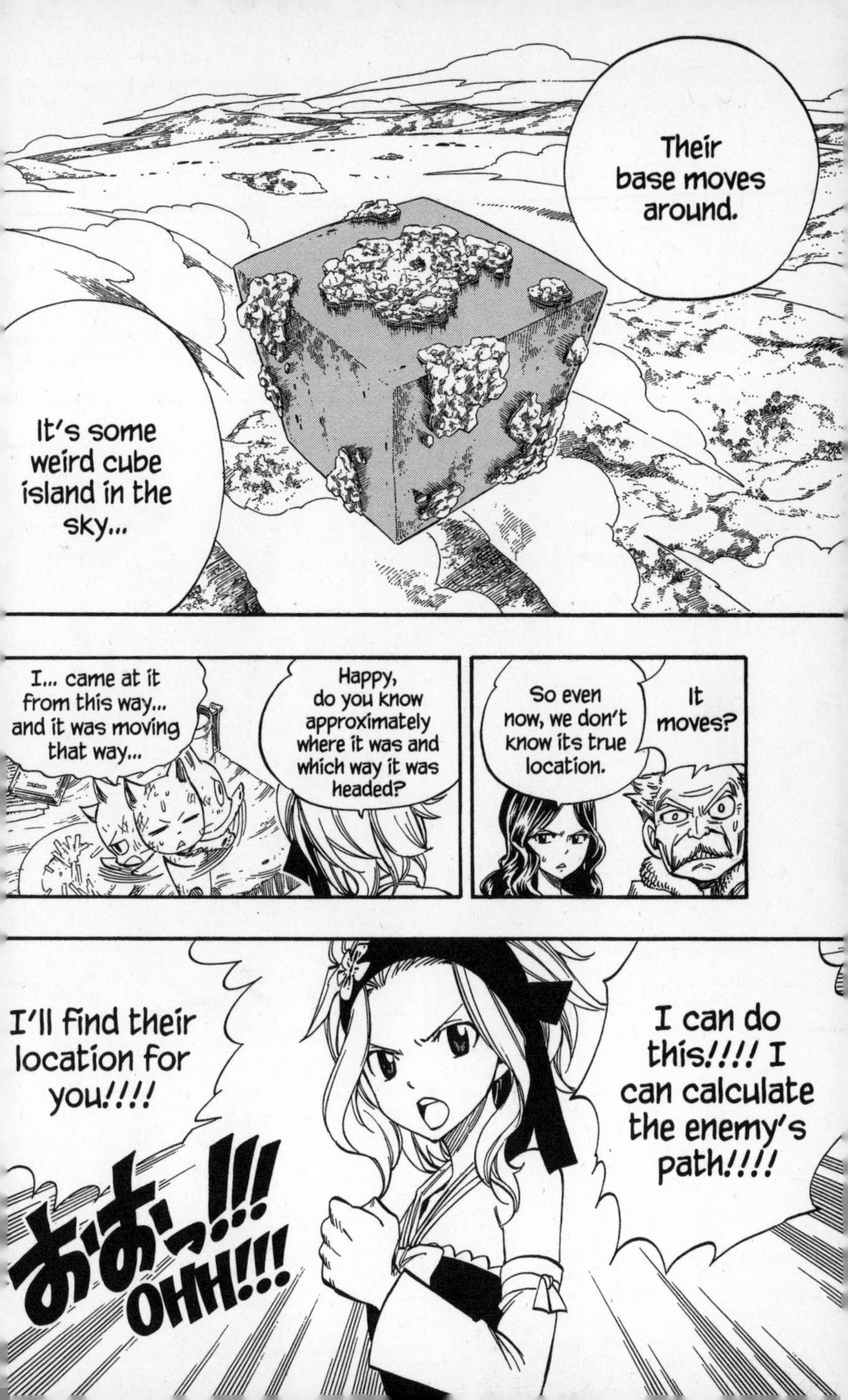
Their base moves around.
It's some weird cube island in the sky...
It moves?
So even now, we don't know its true location.
Happy, do you know approximately where it was and which way it was headed?
I... came at it from this way... and it was moving that way...
I can do this!!!! I can calculate the enemy's path!!!!
I'll find their location for you!!!!
おおっ!!!
OHH!!!

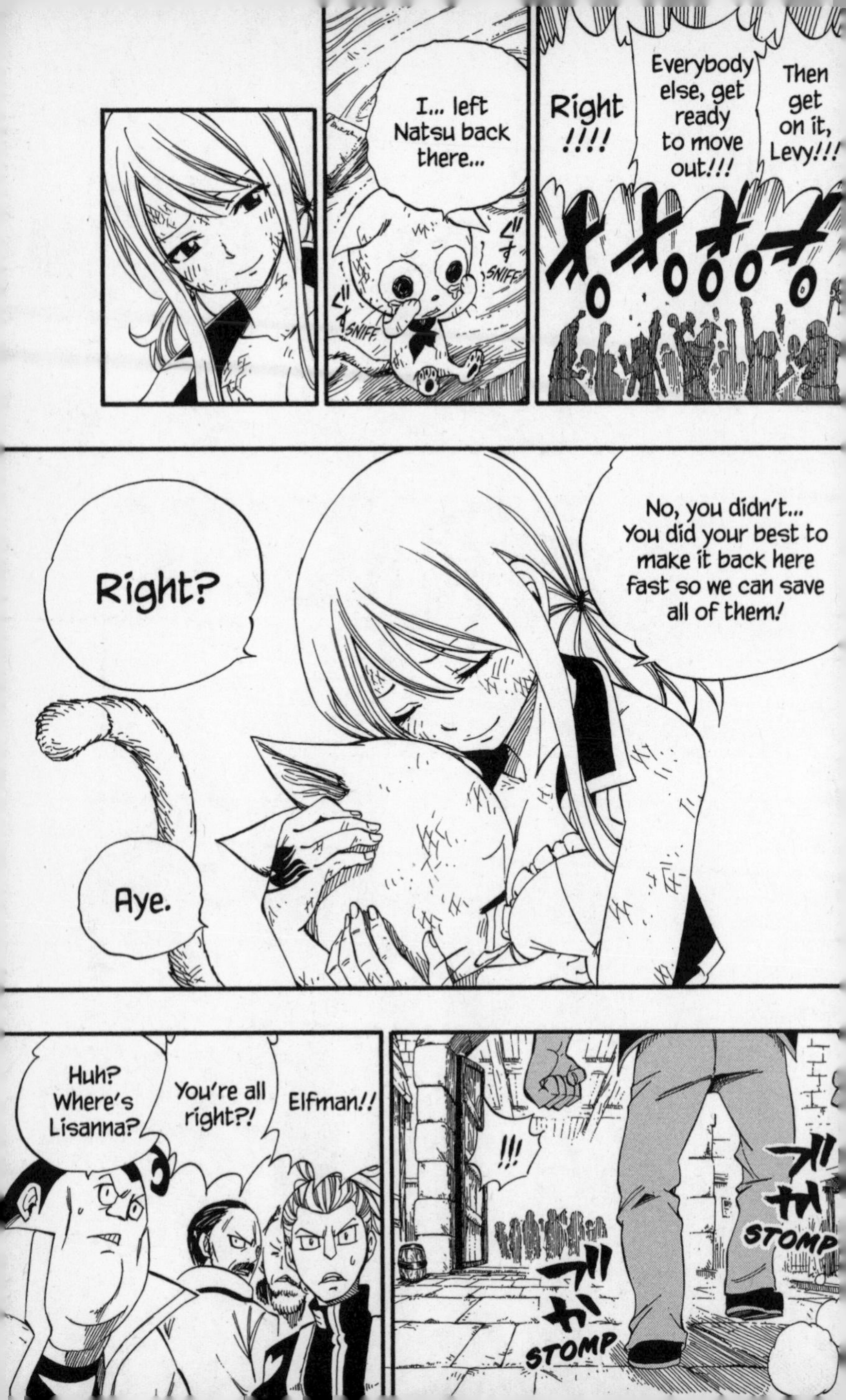

Then get on it, Levy!!!
Everybody else, get ready to move out!!!
Right!!!!
I... left Natsu back there...
ぐす
SNIFF
ぐす
SNIFF
No, you didn't... You did your best to make it back here fast so we can save all of them!
Right?
Aye.
!!!
ガッ
STOMP
ガッ
STOMP
Elfman!!
You're all right?!
Huh? Where's Lisanna?

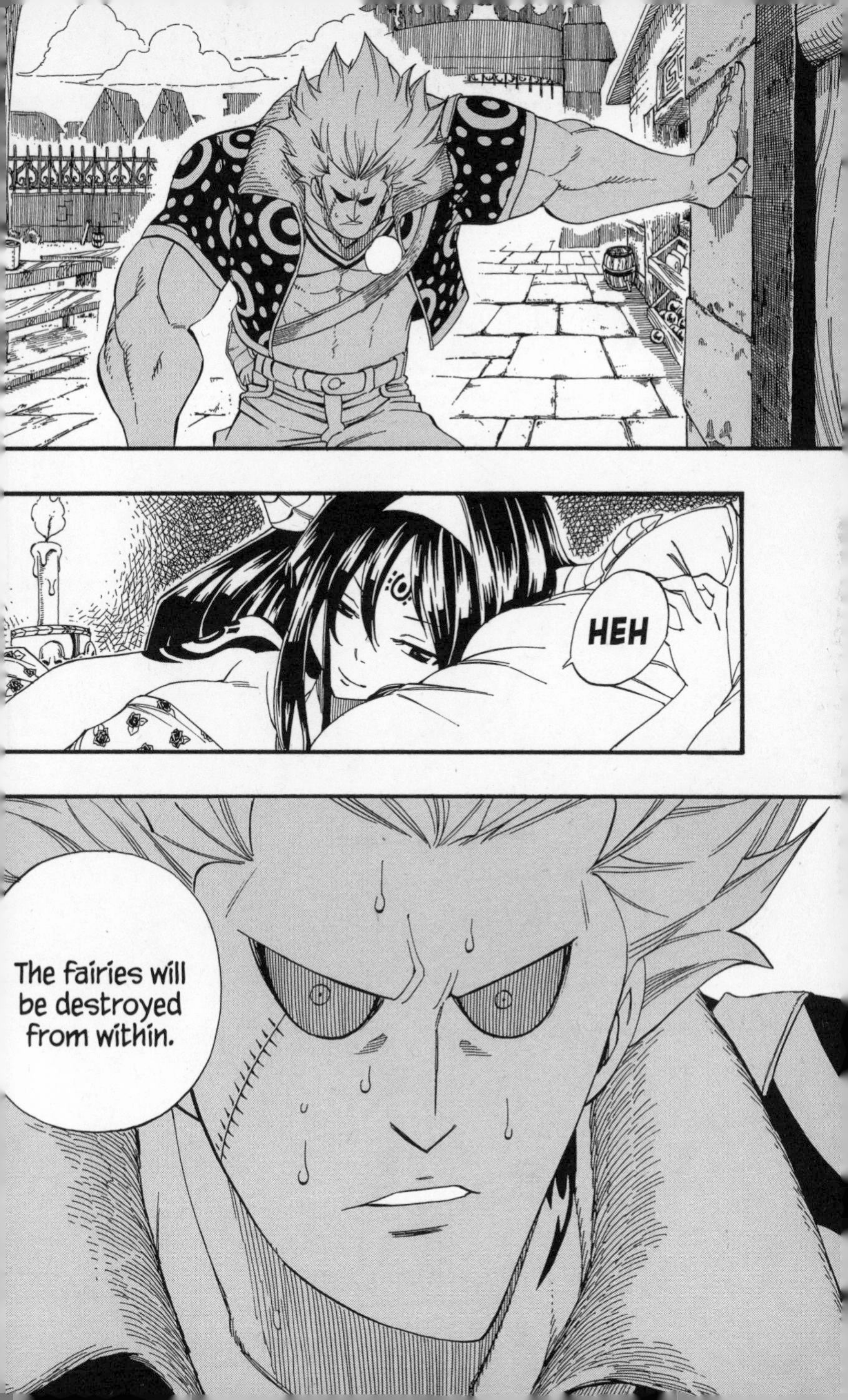
HEH
The fairies will be destroyed from within.

FAIRY TAIL

Chapter 368: The Third Ward

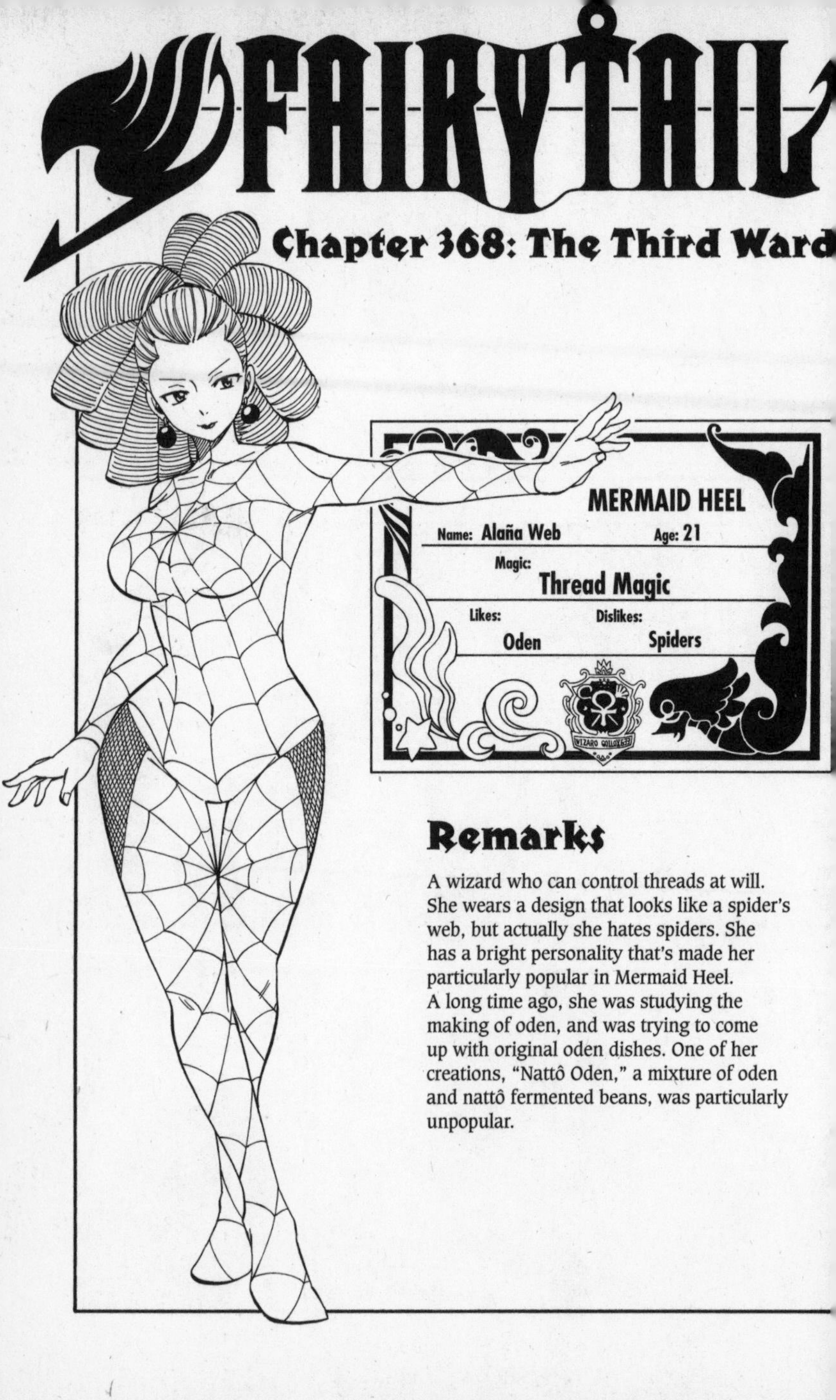

MERMAID HEEL

Name: Alaña Web **Age:** 21

Magic: Thread Magic

Likes: Oden **Dislikes:** Spiders

Remarks

A wizard who can control threads at will. She wears a design that looks like a spider's web, but actually she hates spiders. She has a bright personality that's made her particularly popular in Mermaid Heel.
A long time ago, she was studying the making of oden, and was trying to come up with original oden dishes. One of her creations, "Nattô Oden," a mixture of oden and nattô fermented beans, was particularly unpopular.

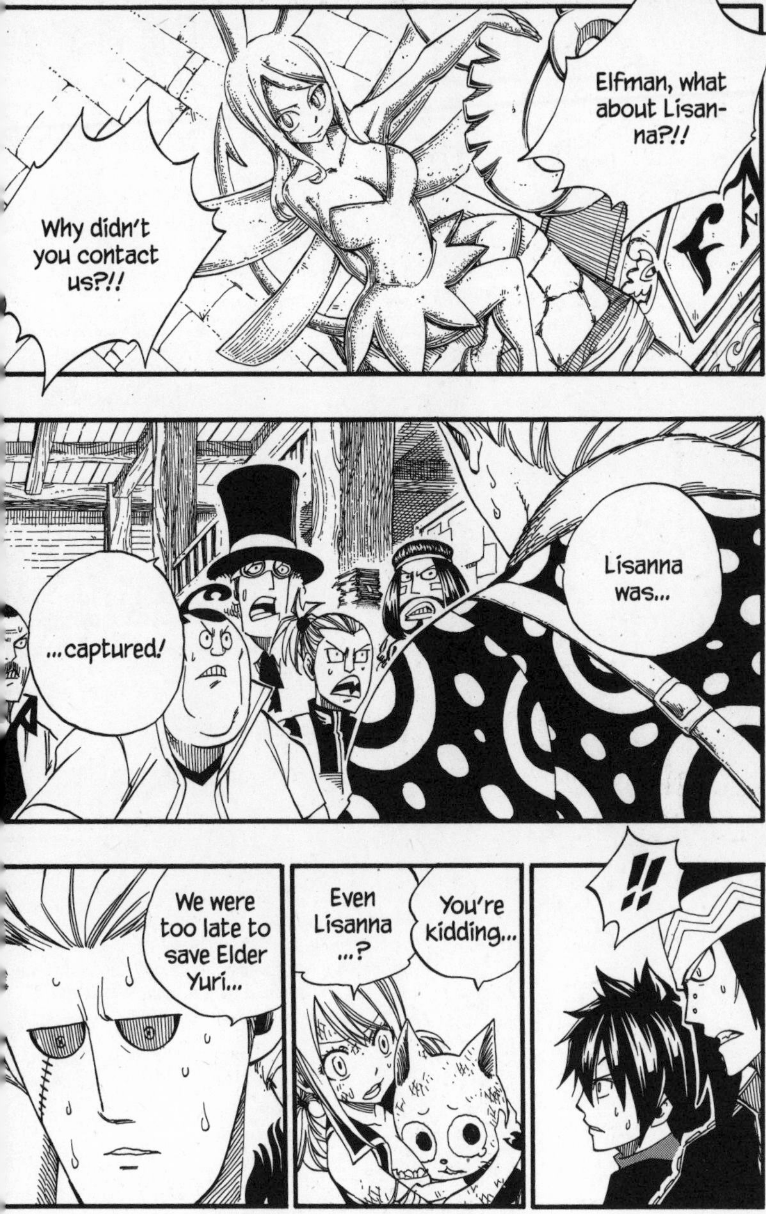
Elfman, what about Lisanna?!!
Why didn't you contact us?!!
Lisanna was...
...captured!
!!
You're kidding...
Even Lisanna ...?
We were too late to save Elder Yuri...

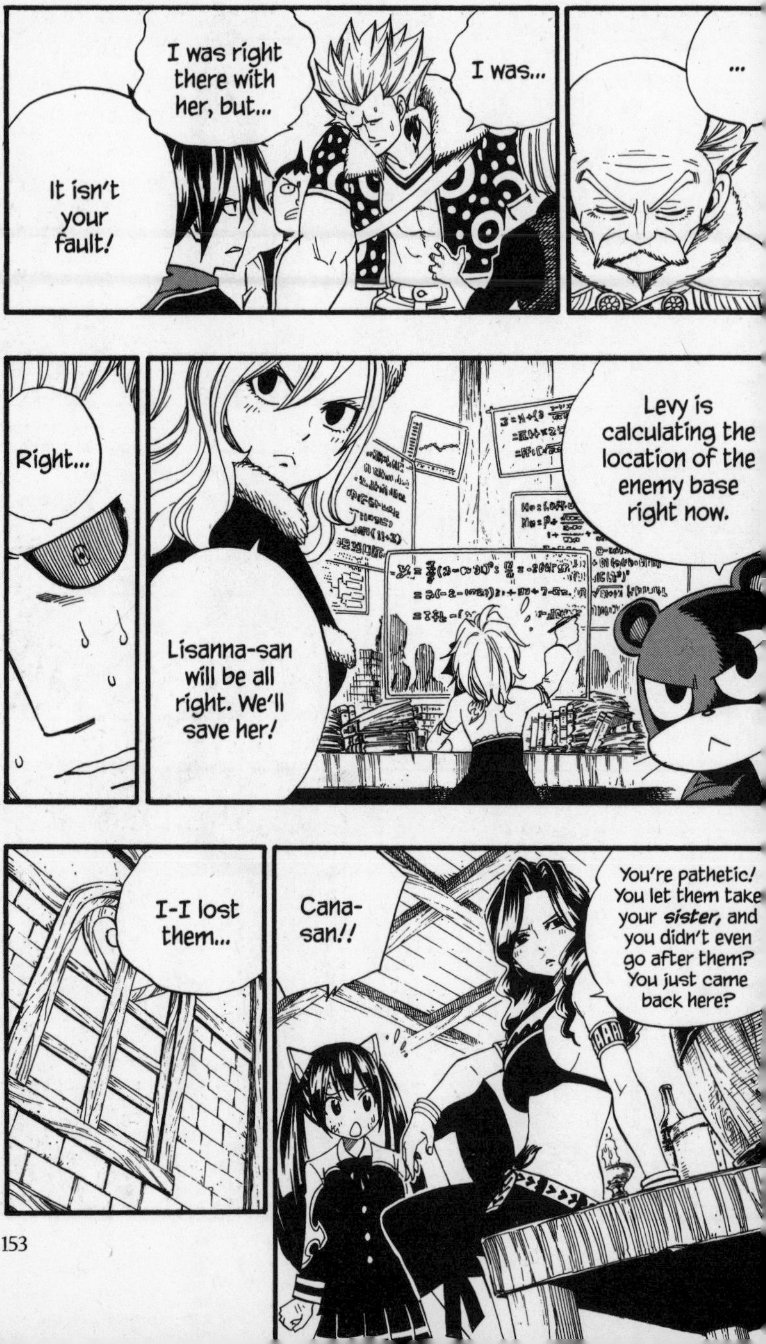
...
I was...
I was right there with her, but...
It isn't your fault!
Levy is calculating the location of the enemy base right now.
Lisanna-san will be all right. We'll save her!
Right...
You're pathetic! You let them take your *sister,* and you didn't even go after them? You just came back here?
Cana-san!!
I-I lost them...

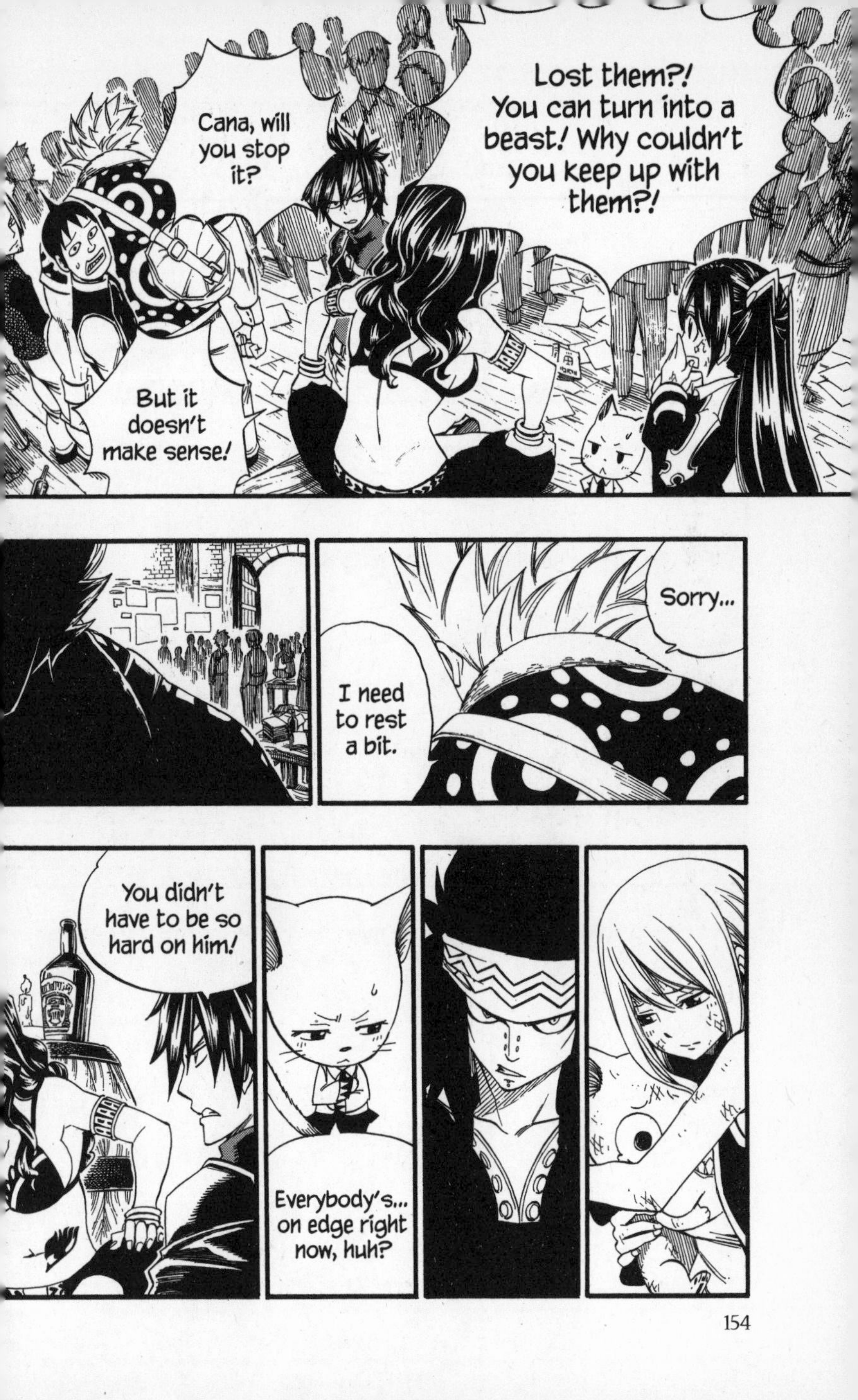
Lost them?! You can turn into a beast! Why couldn't you keep up with them?!
Cana, will you stop it?
But it doesn't make sense!
Sorry...
I need to rest a bit.
Everybody's... on edge right now, huh?
You didn't have to be so hard on him!

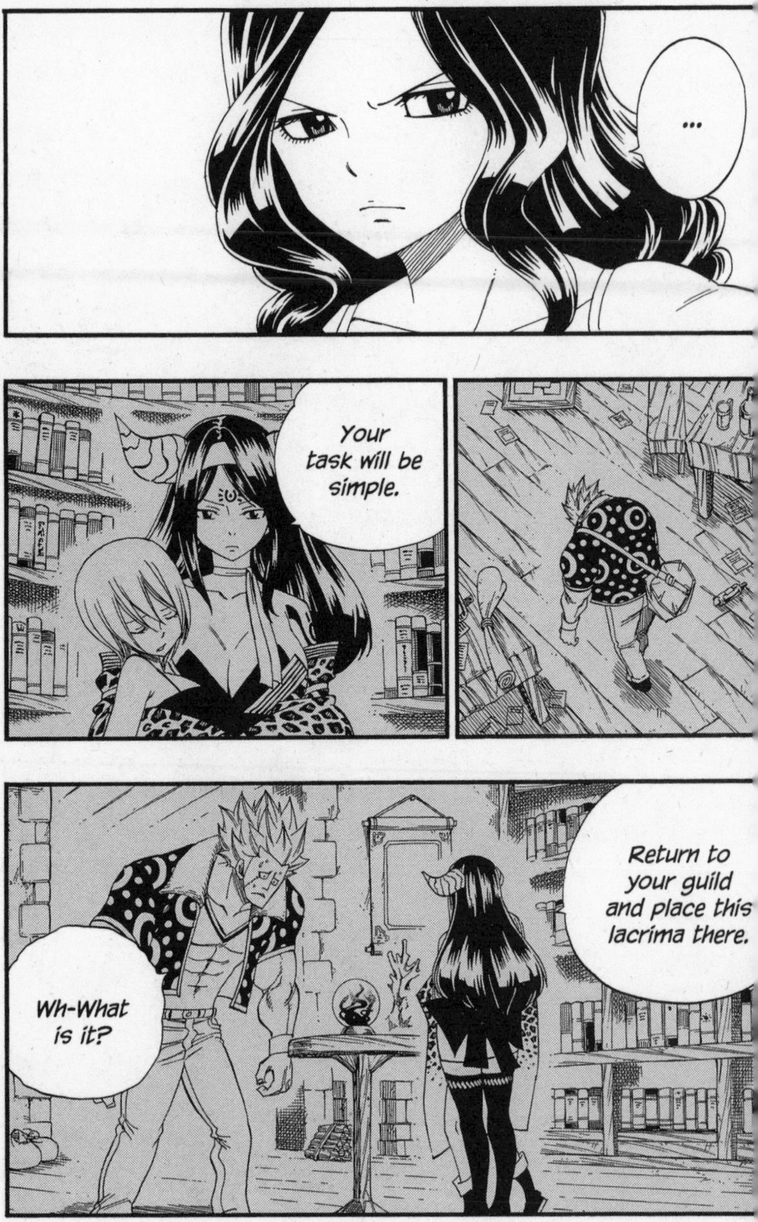
...
Your task will be simple.
Return to your guild and place this lacrima there.
Wh-What is it?

It emits highly concentrated ether.

It's approximately **500** times stronger than the Jupiter Cannon. ...It should wipe out the guild in an instant.

You **will** do it.

I can't do that...

That's awful...

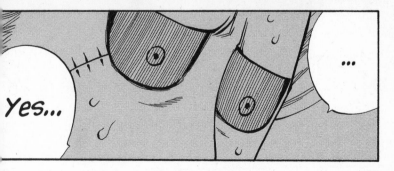

Yes...

...

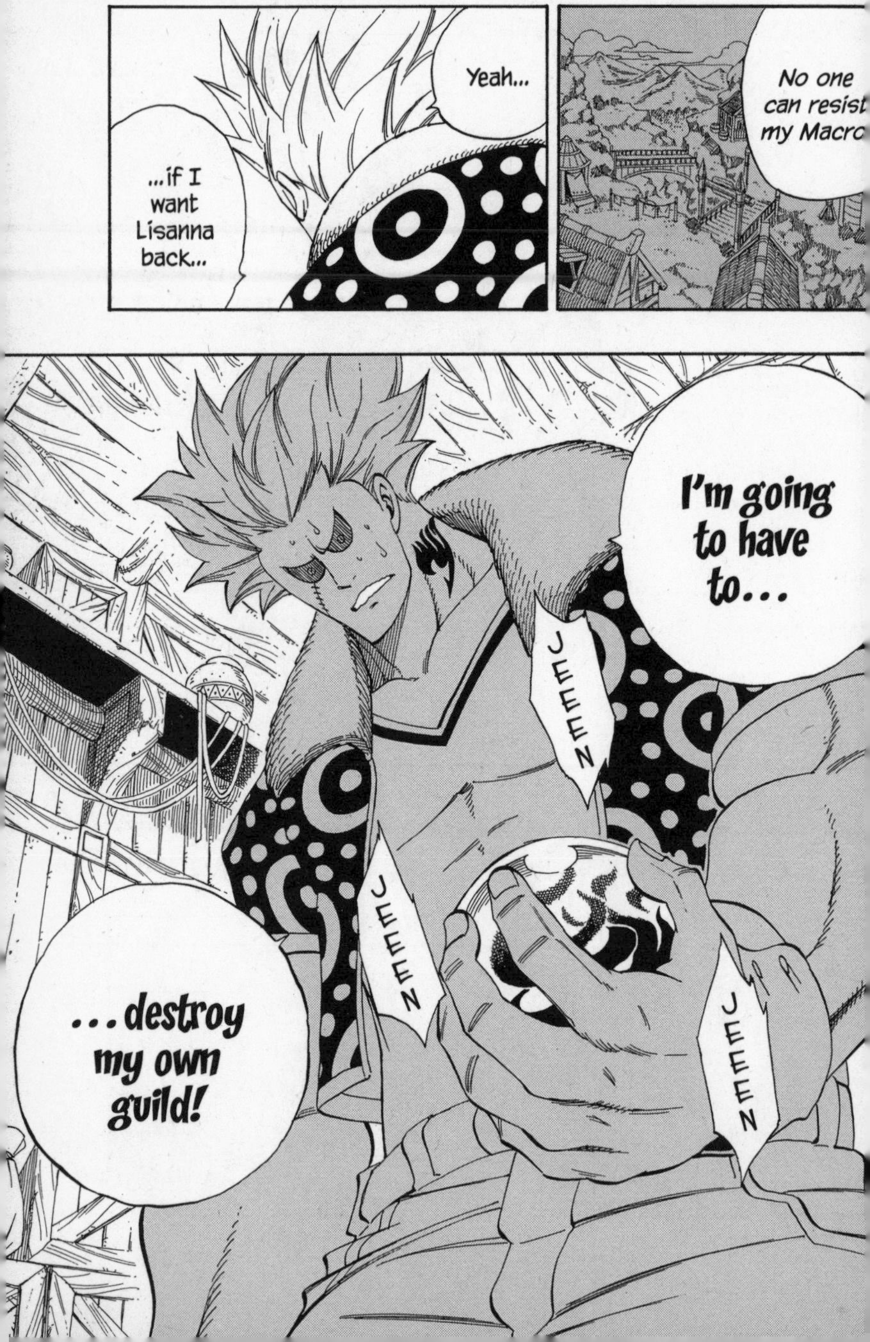
No one can resist my Macro
Yeah...
...if I want Lisanna back...
I'm going to have to...
JEEEN
JEEEN
JEEEN
...destroy my own guild!

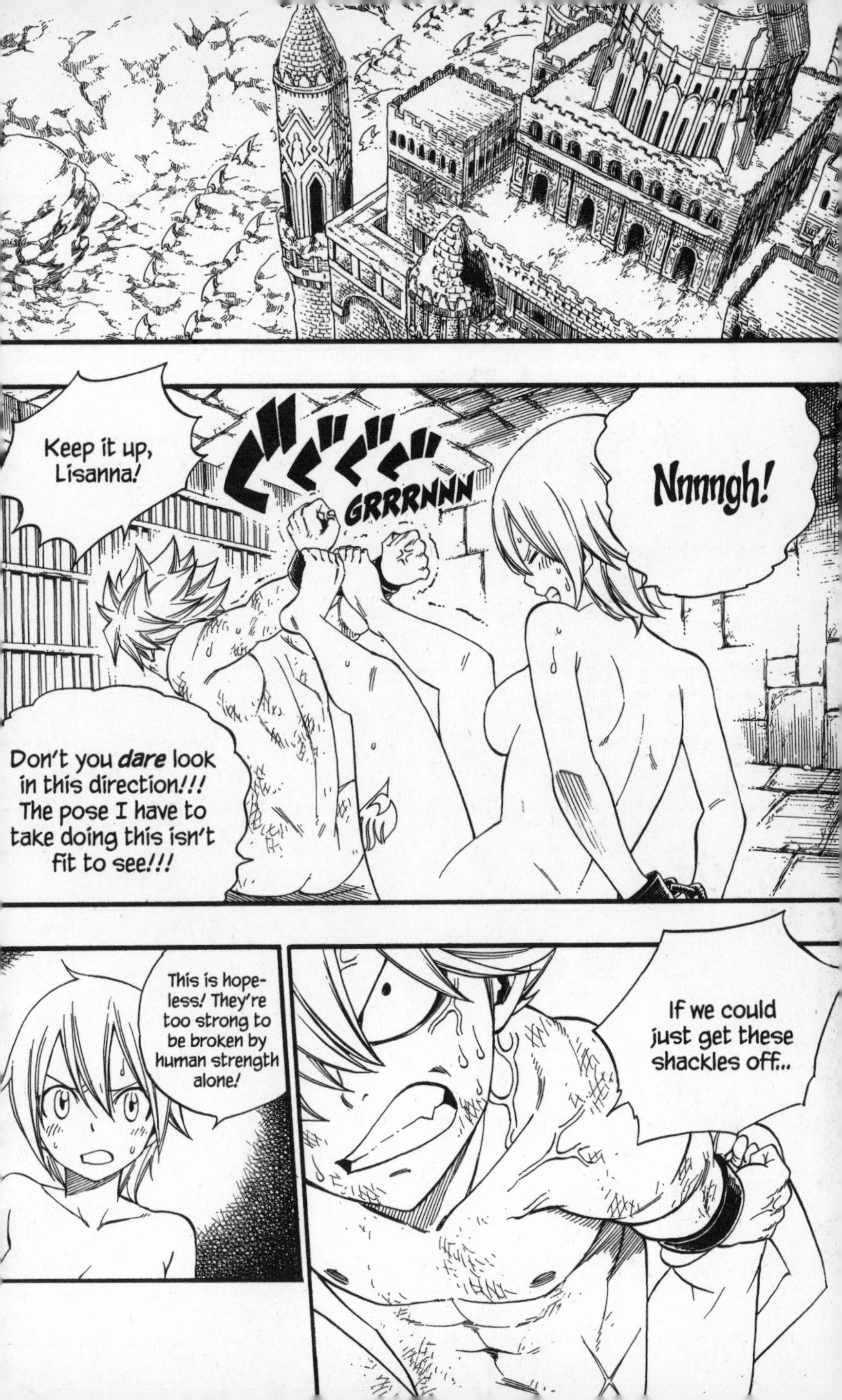
Nnnngh!
GRRRNNN
Keep it up, Lisanna!
Don't you *dare* look in this direction!!! The pose I have to take doing this isn't fit to see!!!
If we could just get these shackles off...
This is hopeless! They're too strong to be broken by human strength alone!

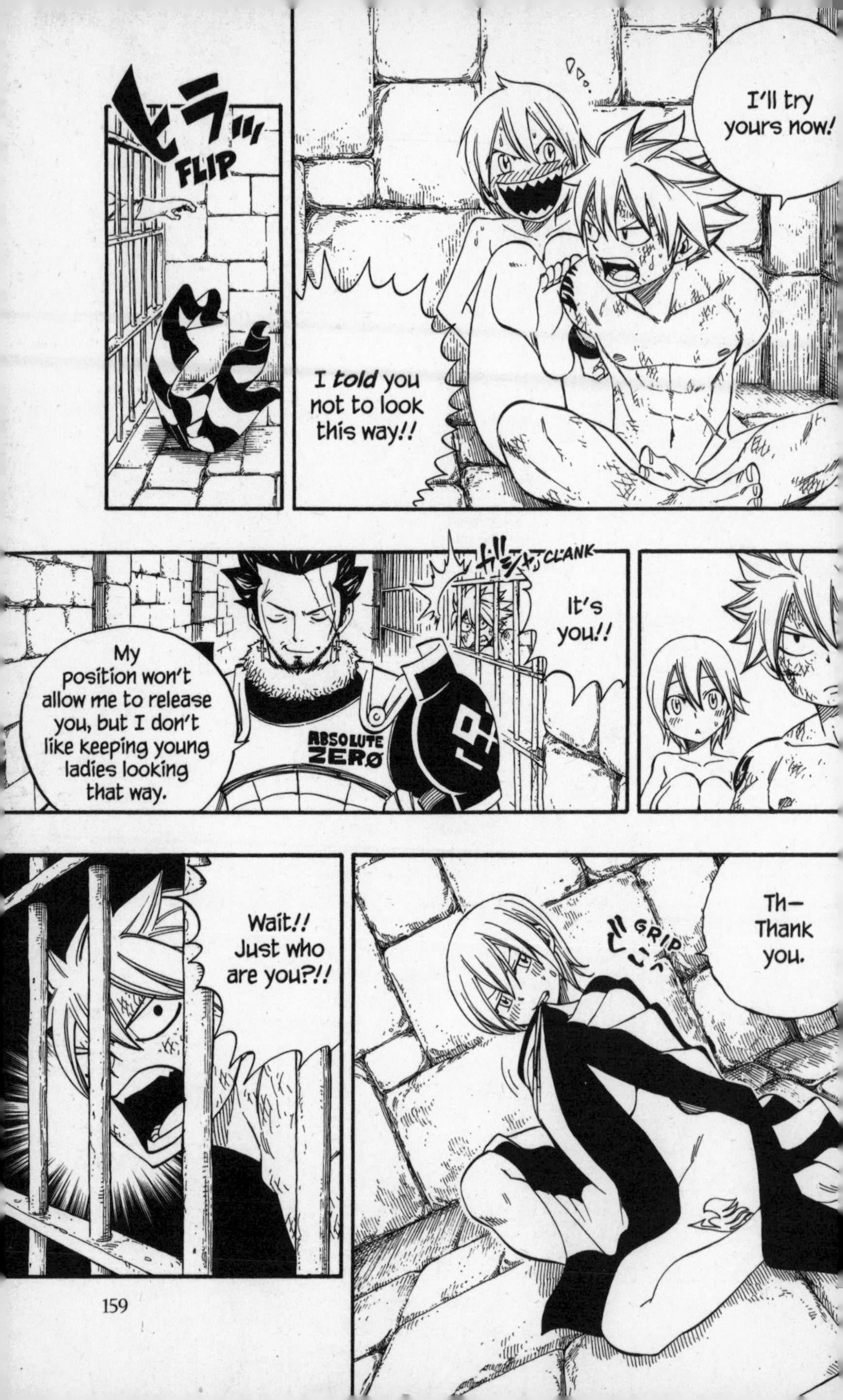

I'll try yours now!
I *told* you not to look this way!!
FLIP
CLANK
It's you!!
My position won't allow me to release you, but I don't like keeping young ladies looking that way.
ABSOLUTE ZERØ
GRIP
Th— Thank you.
Wait!! Just who are you?!!

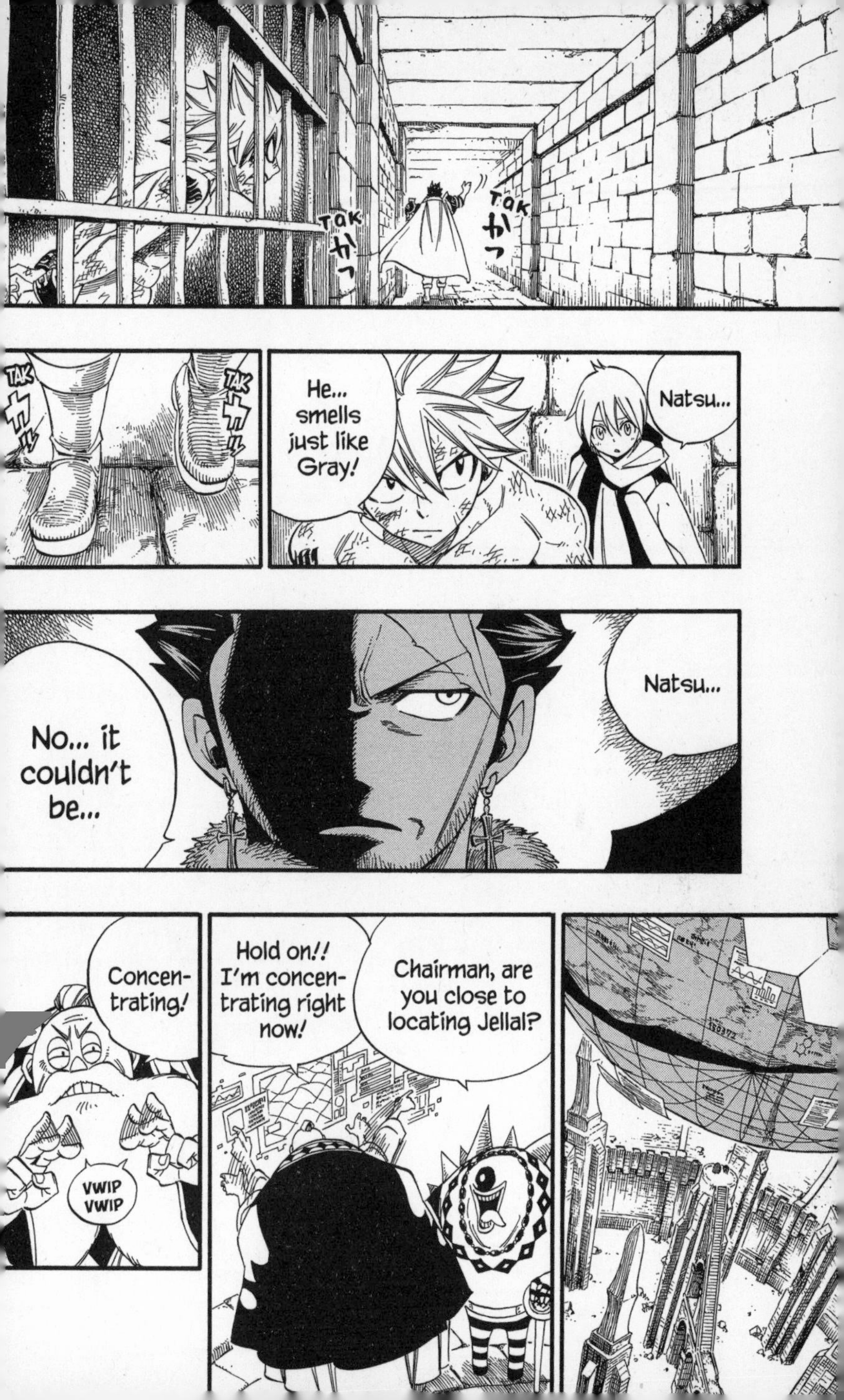
TAK
かっ
TAK
かっ
Natsu...
He... smells just like Gray!
TAK
TAK
Natsu...
No... it couldn't be...
Chairman, are you close to locating Jellal?
Hold on!! I'm concen-trating right now!
Concen-trating!
VWIP VWIP

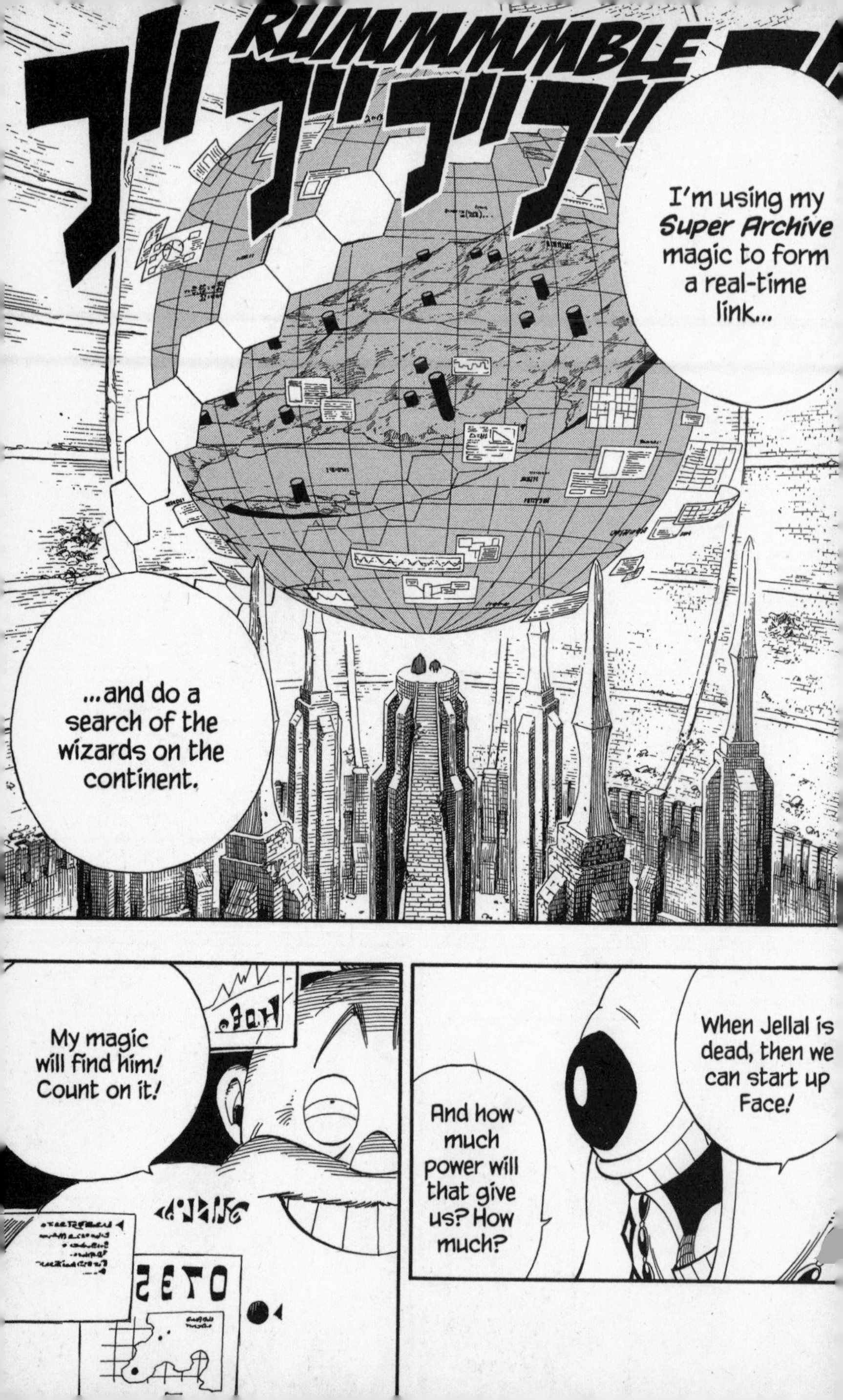
RUMMMMBLE
I'm using my *Super Archive* magic to form a real-time link...
...and do a search of the wizards on the continent.
When Jellal is dead, then we can start up Face!
And how much power will that give us? How much?
My magic will find him! Count on it!

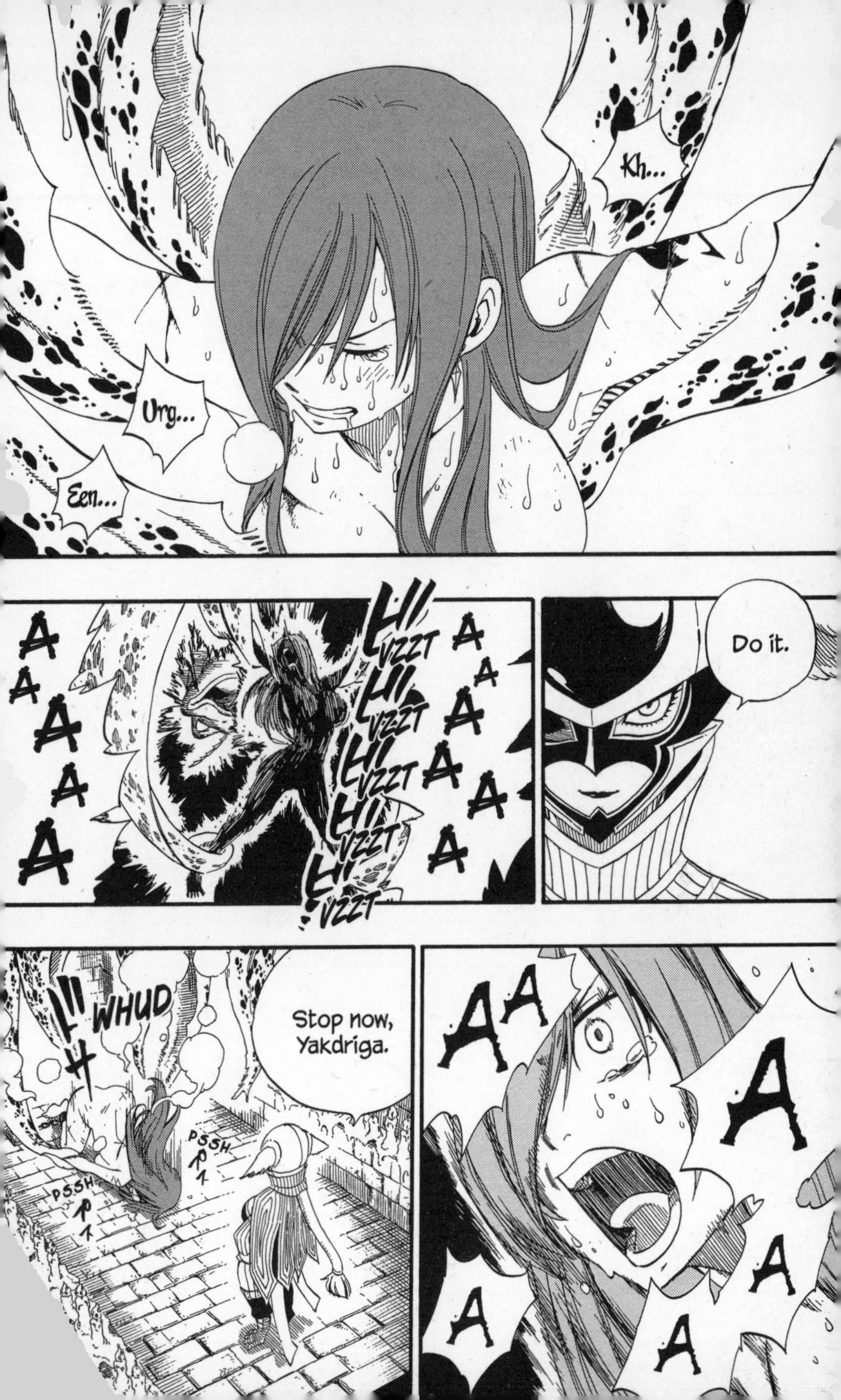
Kh...
Urg...
Een...
Do it.
AAAAAA
VZZT VZZT VZZT VZZT VZZT VZZT
AAAAAA
AAAAAA
Stop now, Yakdriga.
WHUD
PSSH
PSSH

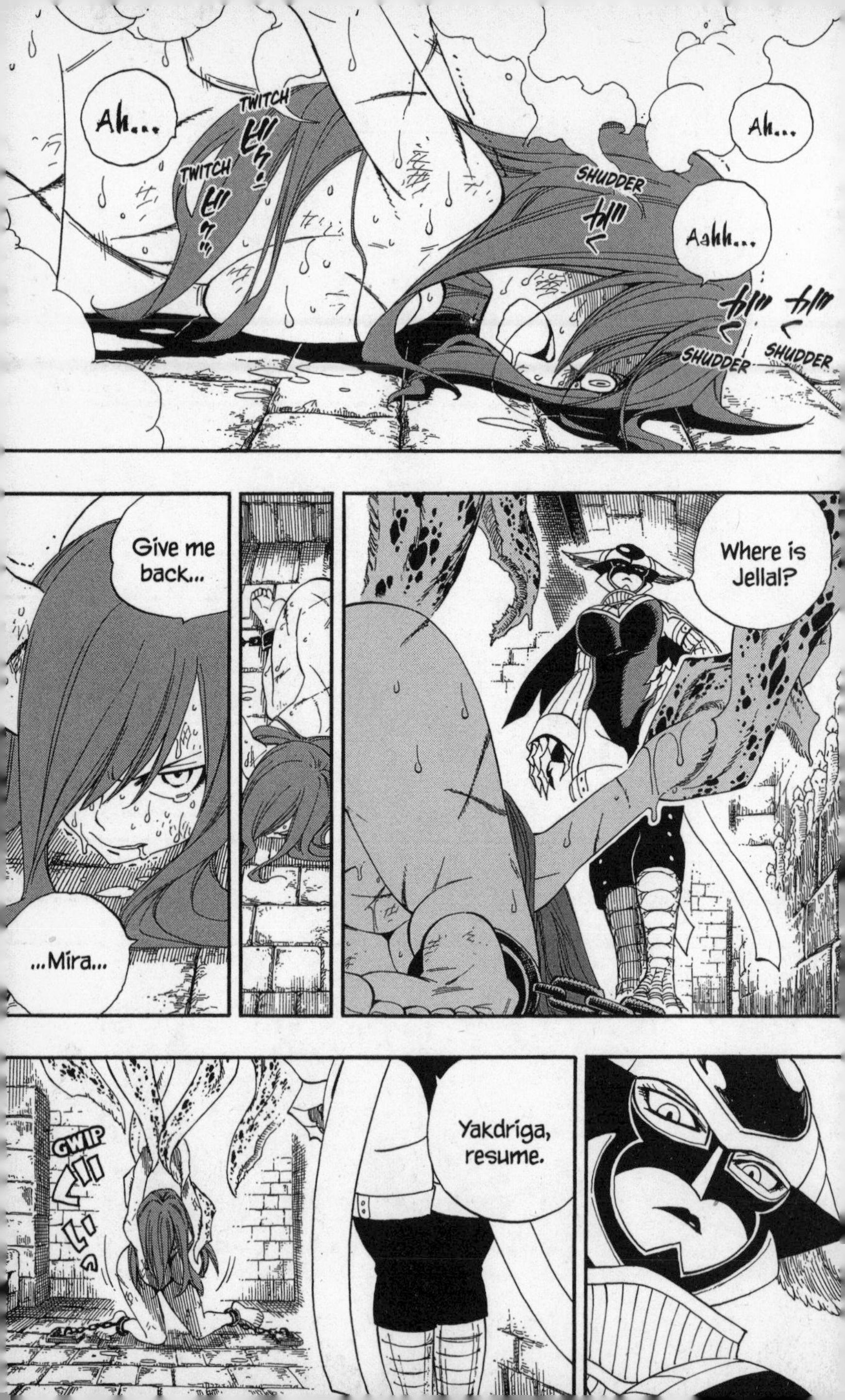
Ah...
SHUDDER
Aahh...
SHUDDER
SHUDDER
TWITCH
TWITCH
Ah...
Where is Jellal?
Give me back...
...Mira...
Yakdriga, resume.
GWIP

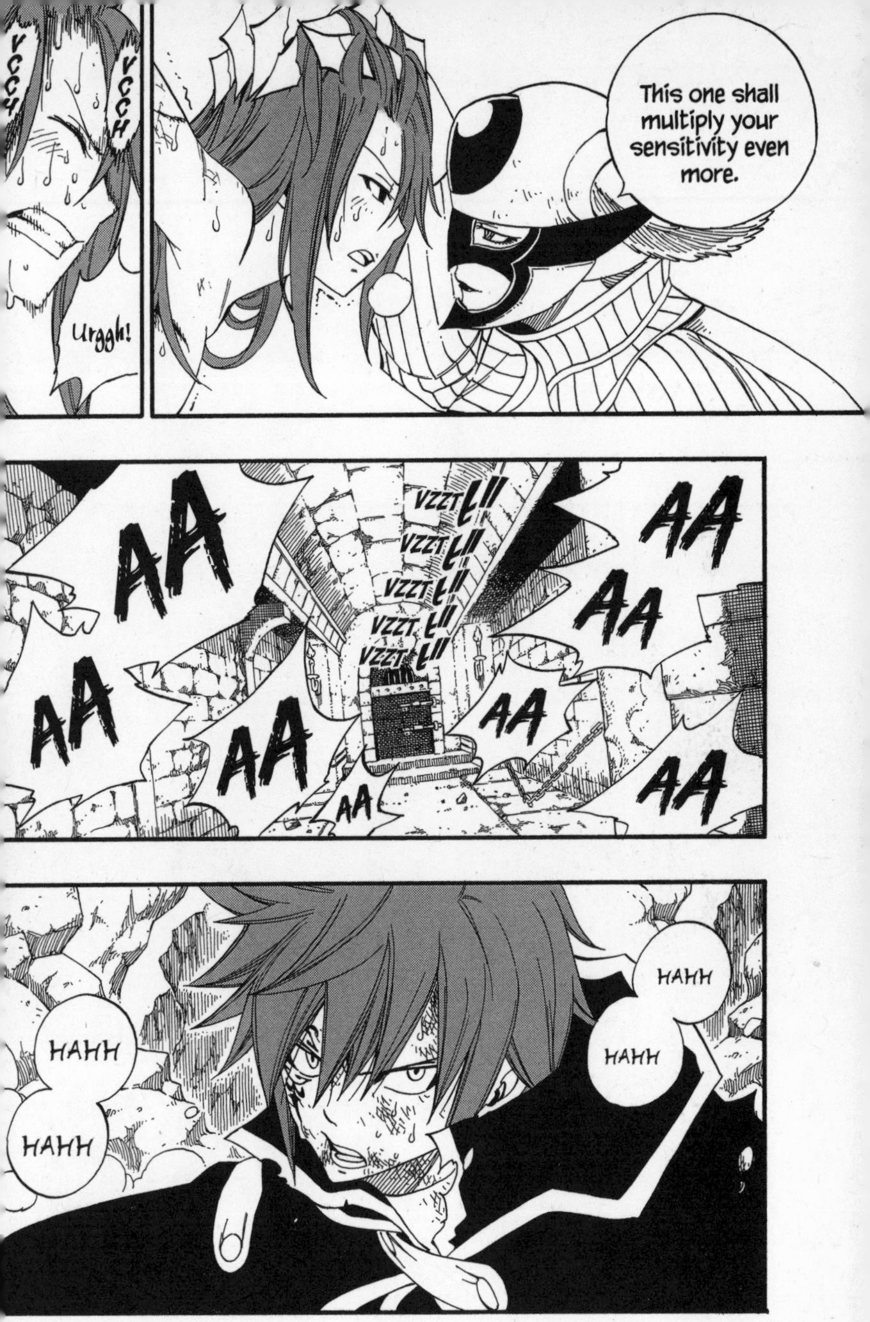
This one shall multiply your sensitivity even more.
VCCH
VCCH
Urggh!
AA
AA
VZZT
VZZT
VZZT
VZZT
VZZT
AA
AA
AA
AA
AA
AA
HAHH
HAHH
HAHH
HAHH

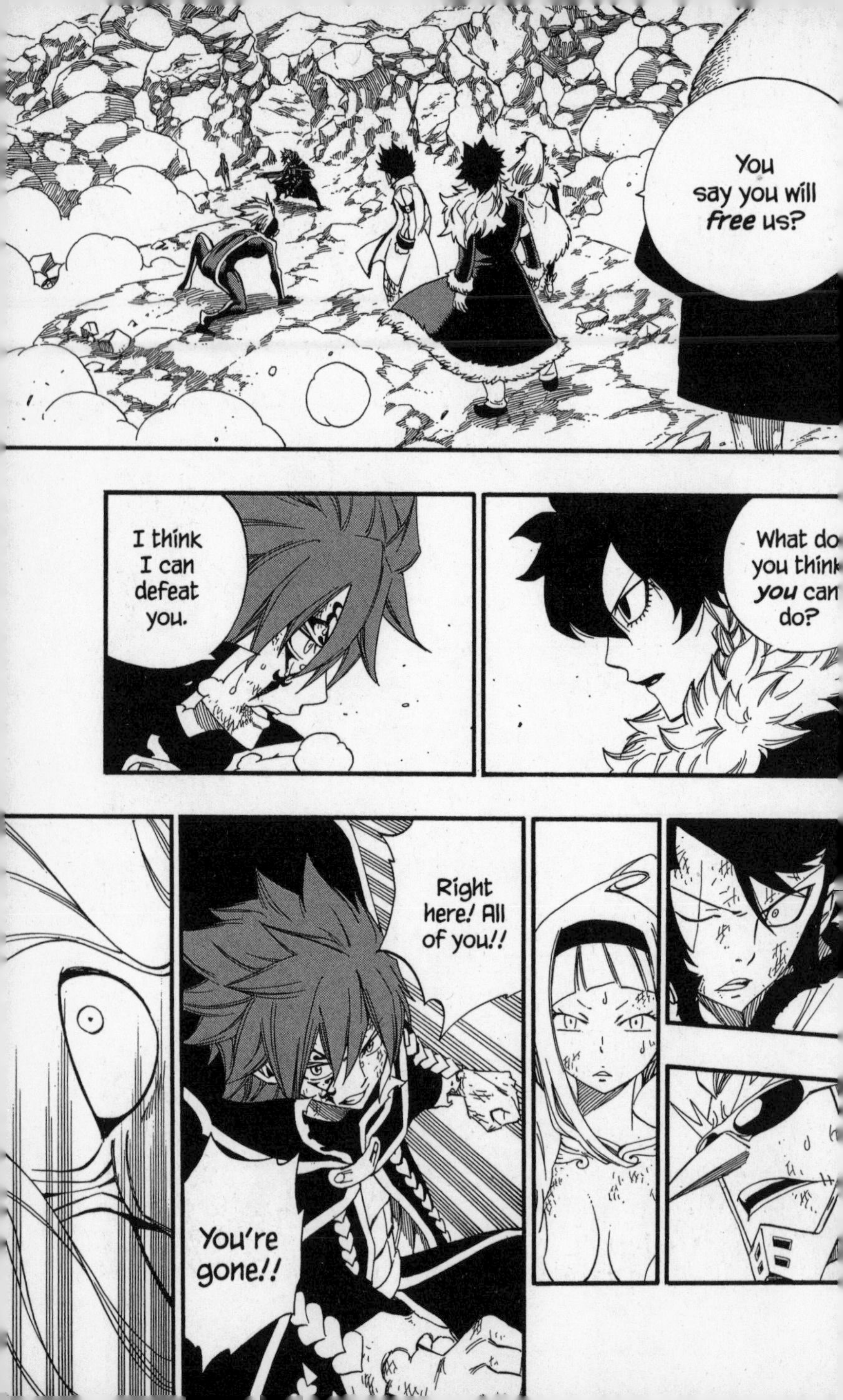

You say you will *free* us?
What do you think *you* can do?
I think I can defeat you.
Right here! All of you!!
You're gone!!

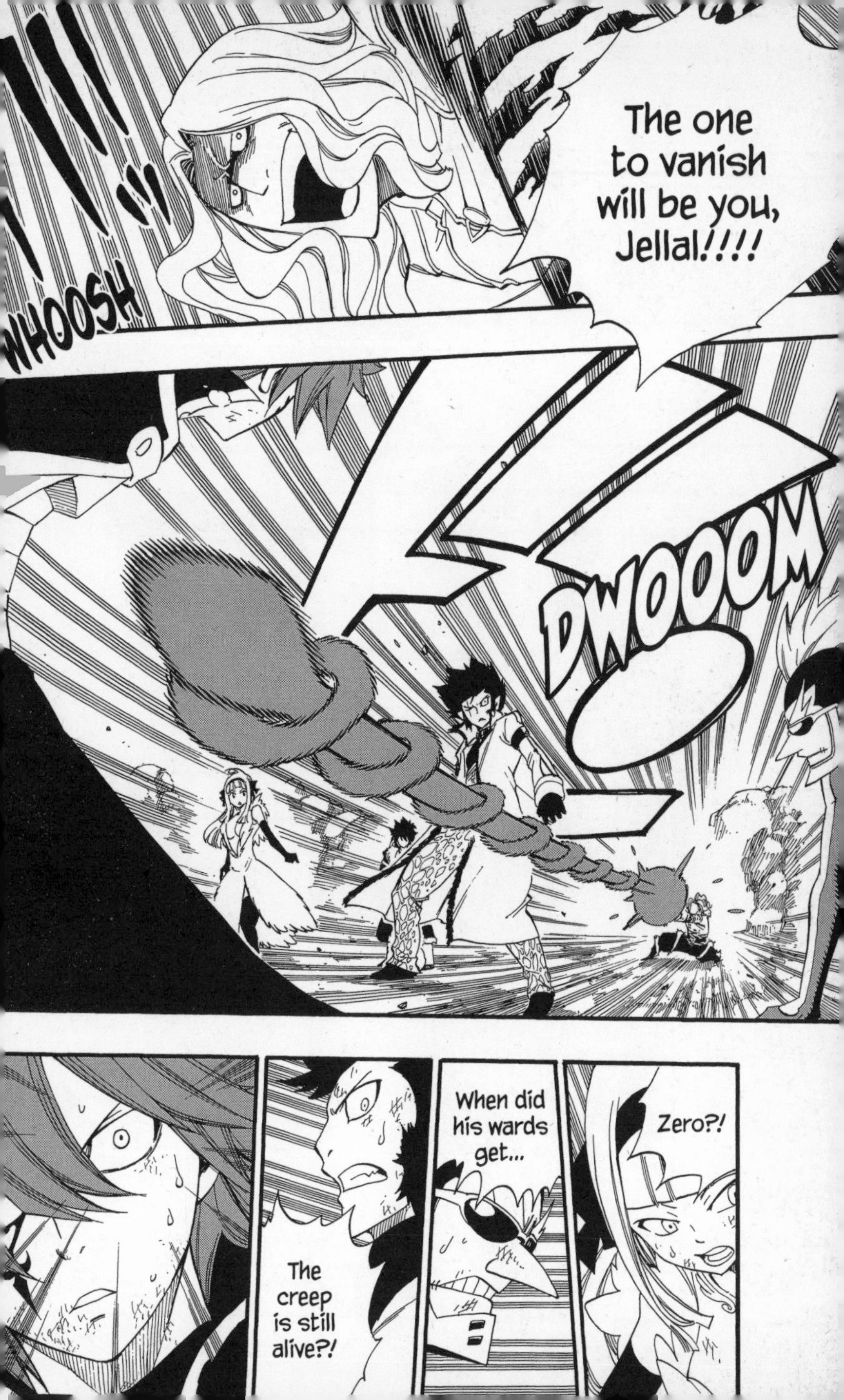
The one to vanish will be you, Jellal!!!!
WHOOSH
DWOOOM
Zero?!
When did his wards get...
The creep is still alive?!

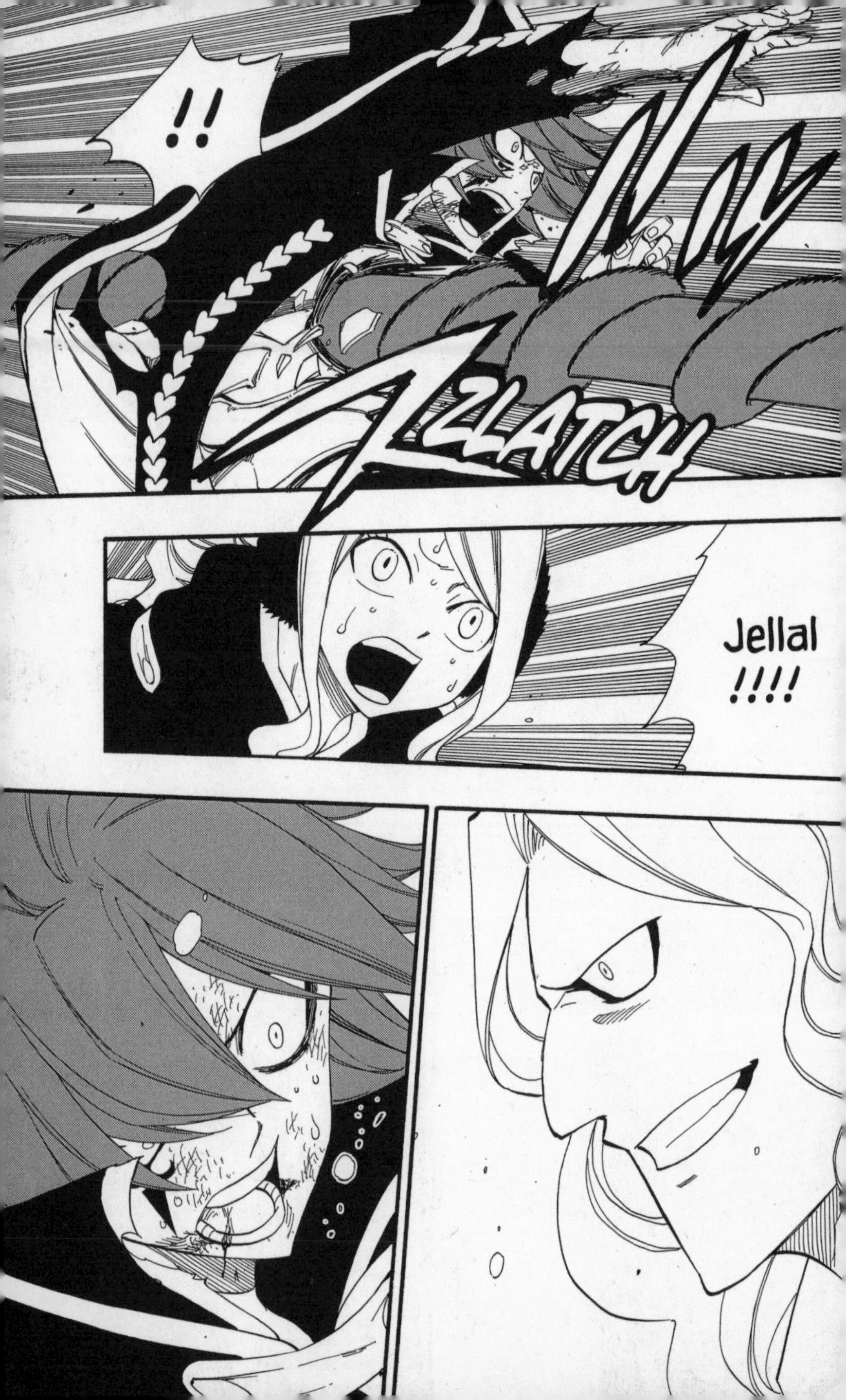

!!
Nay
ZZLATCH
Jellal
!!!!

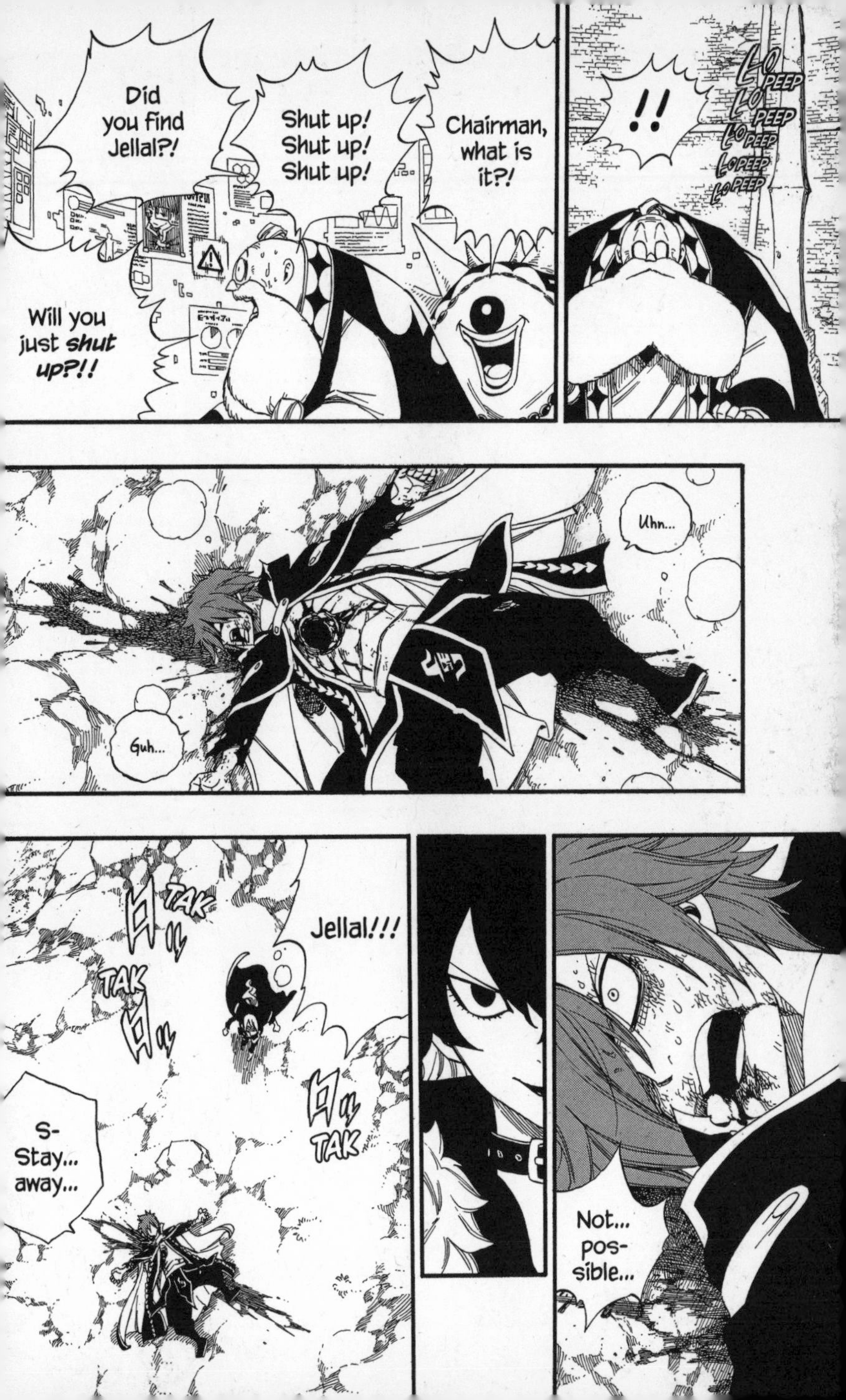

!!
PEEP
PEEP
PEEP
PEEP
PEEP
Chairman, what is it?!
Shut up! Shut up! Shut up!
Did you find Jellal?!
Will you just *shut up*?!!
Uhn...
Guh...
Not... pos-sible...
Jellal!!!
TAK
TAK
TAK
S-Stay... away...

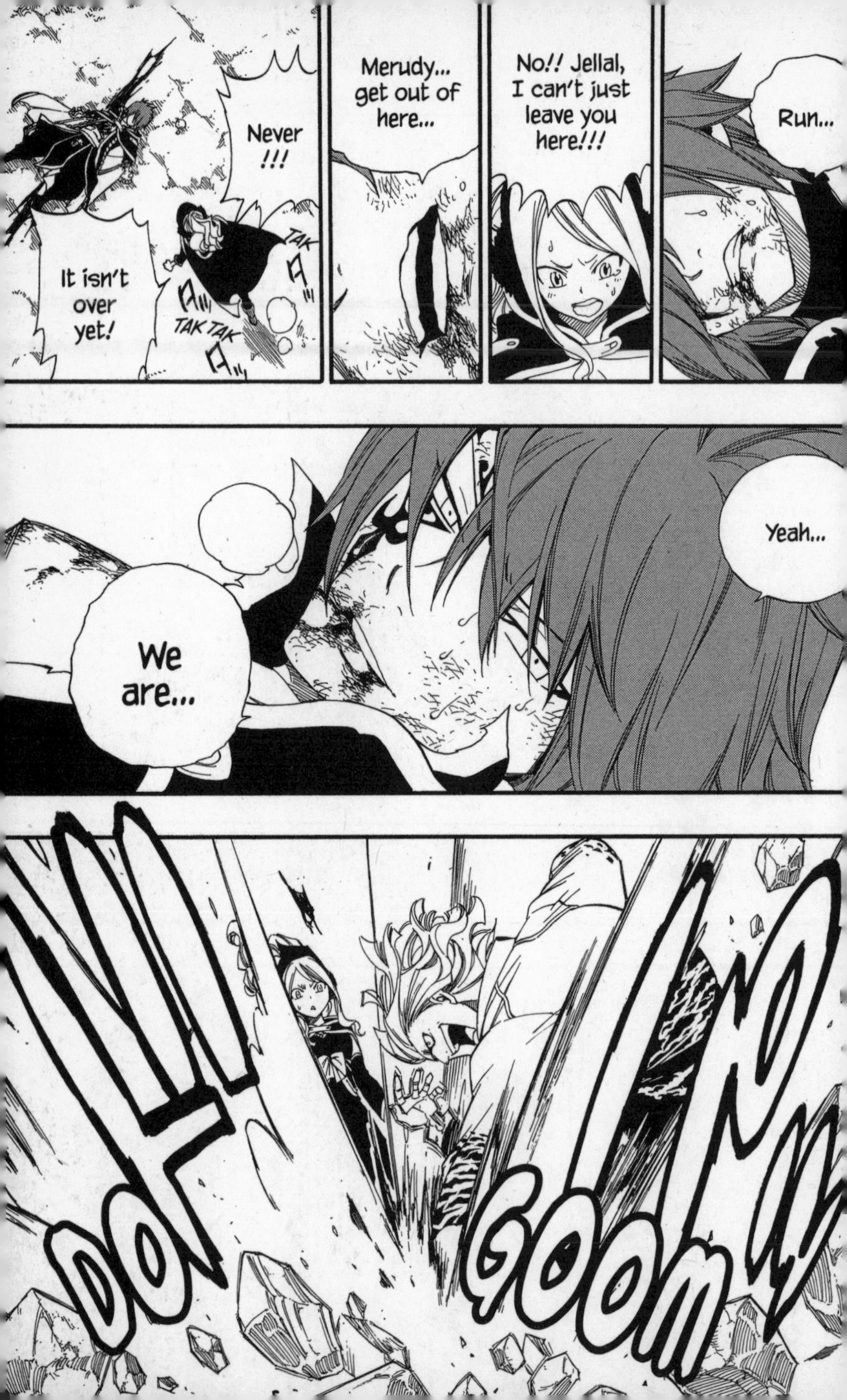

Run...
No!! Jellal, I can't just leave you here!!!
Merudy... get out of here...
Never!!!
TAK
TAK TAK
It isn't over yet!
Yeah...
We are...
DO GOOM!!

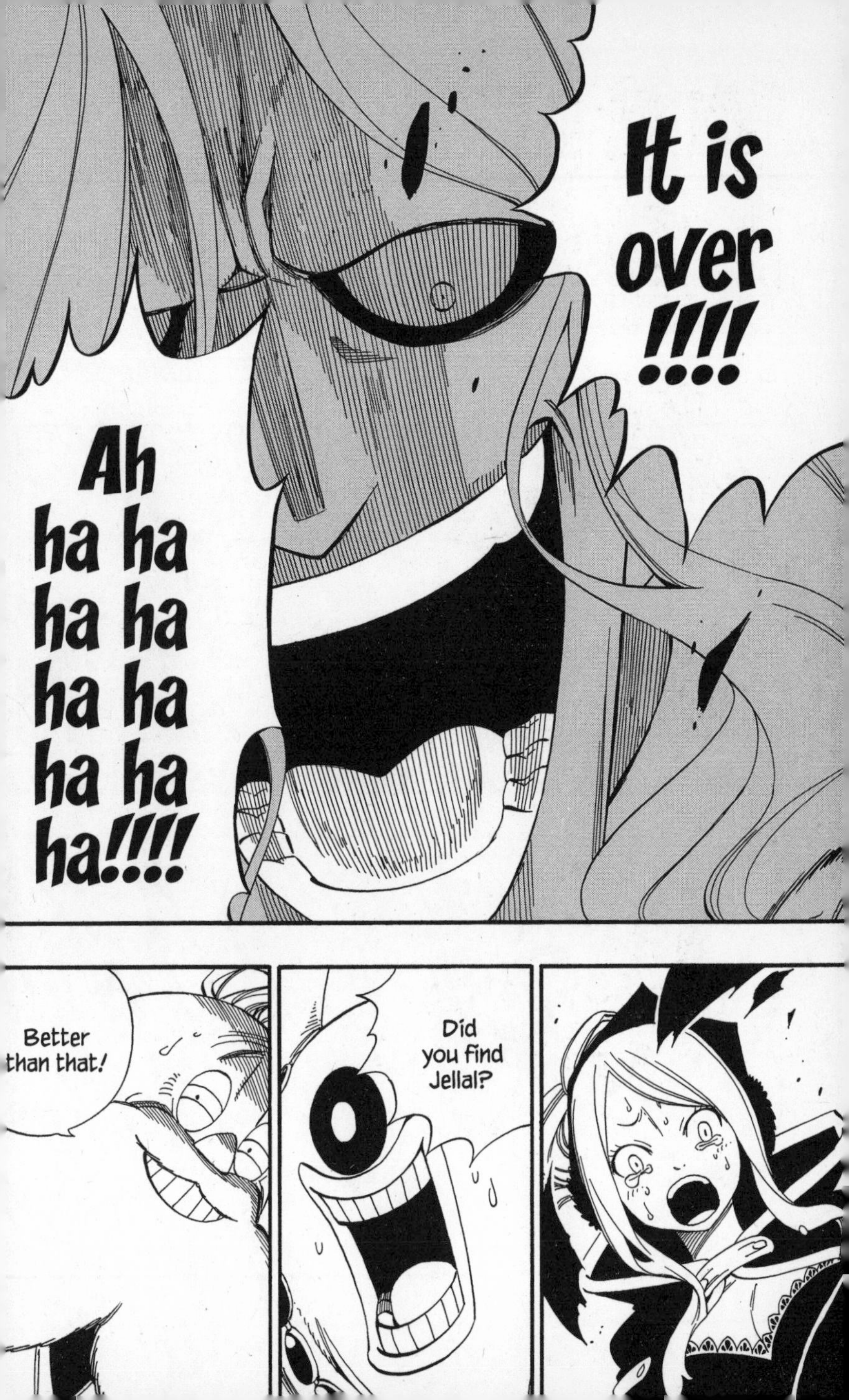
It is over!!!!
Ah ha ha ha ha ha ha ha ha ha ha!!!!
Did you find Jellal?
Better than that!

Chapter 369: Where Prayers Go

MERMAID HEEL

Name: Lislie Law   Age: 24

Magic:
Gravity Change

Likes: Dislikes:
Her guild   **High heels**

Remarks

A plus-size young woman. The rest of her guild sees her as a maternal figure because of her outward appearance and calm demeanor. Outside the guild too, some think she's the motherly type, but she's unmarried and has no children.
With her Gravity Change magic, she can turn herself into a slim girl with the proportions of a model, but she likes her plump body as it is.

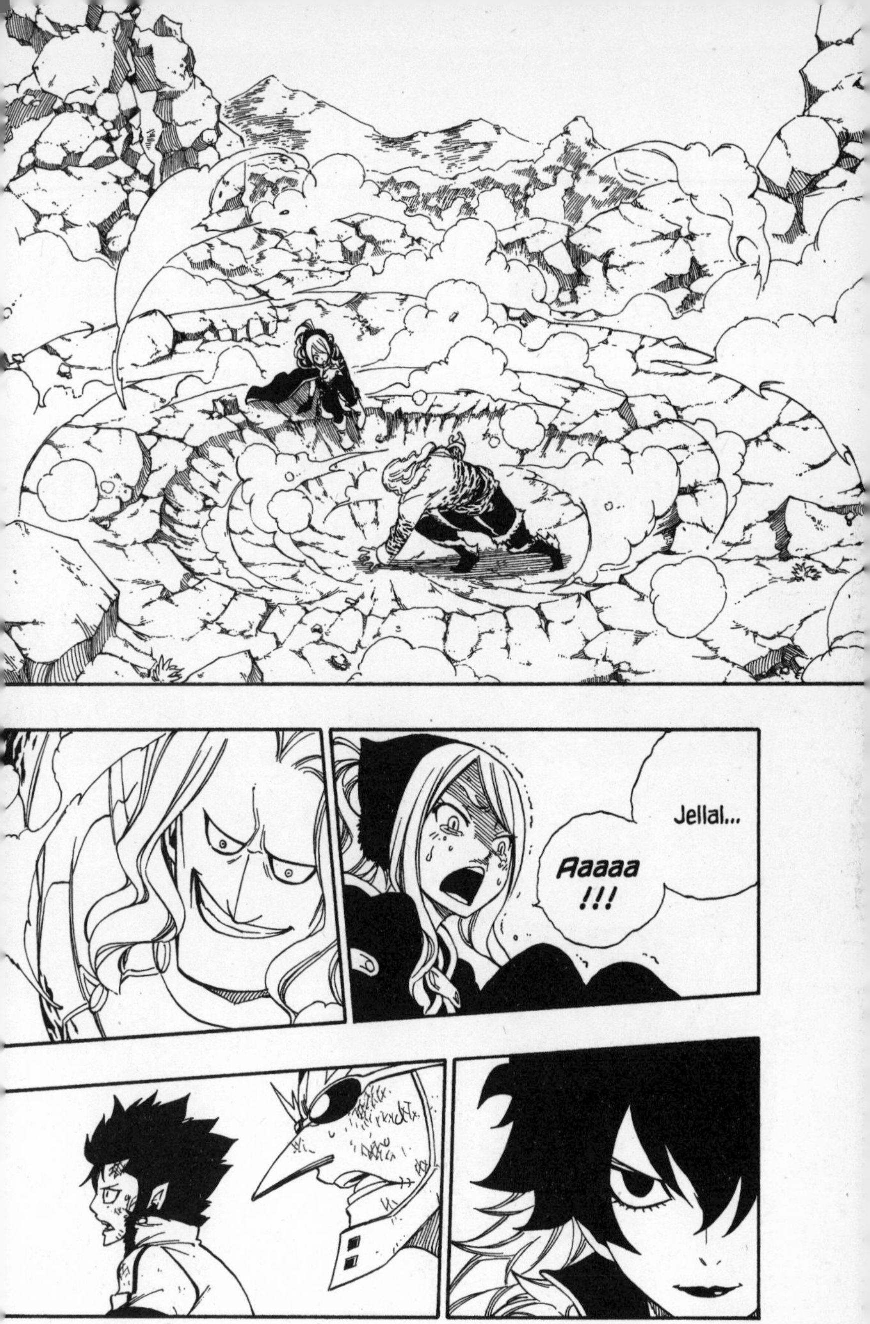
Jellal...
Aaaaa !!!

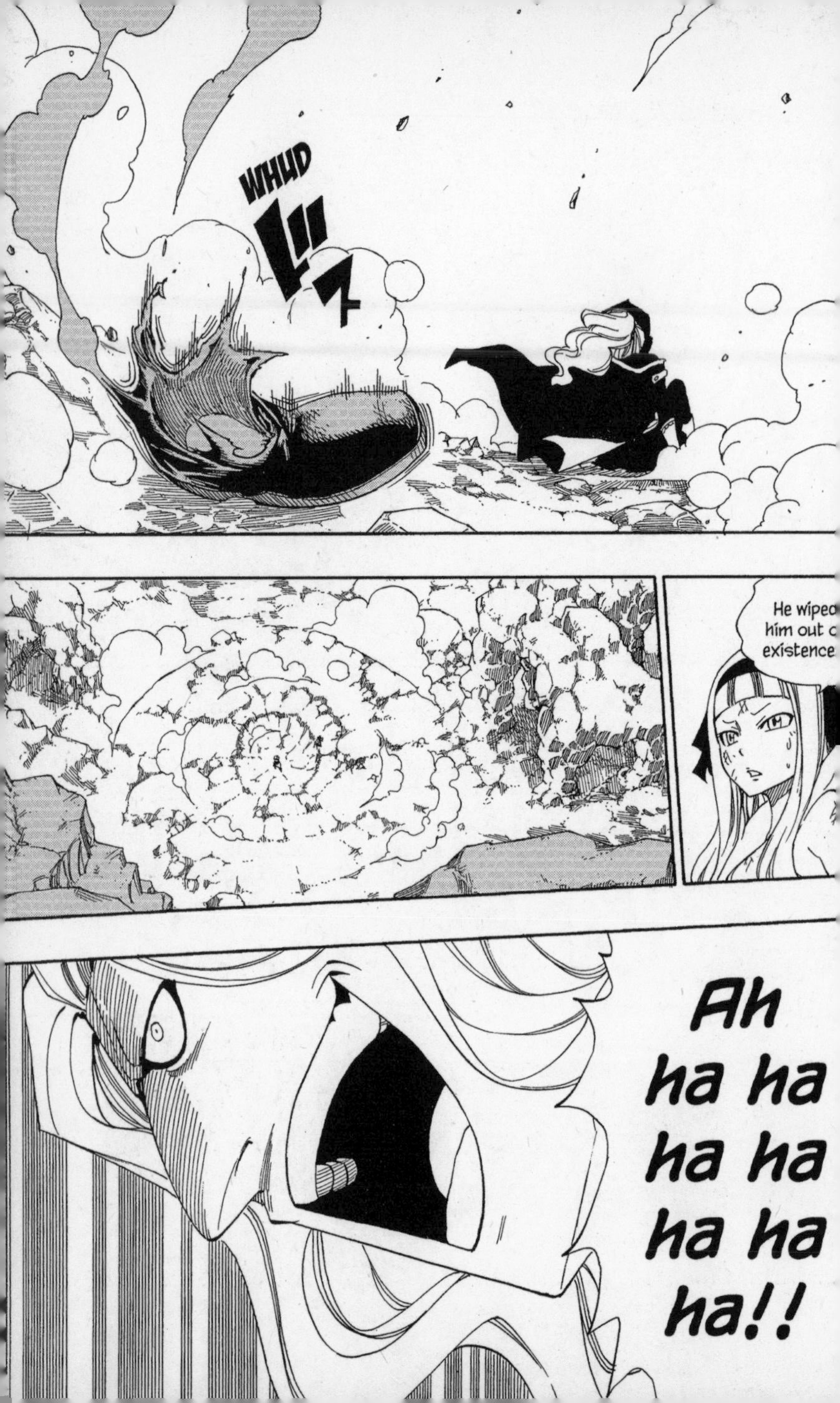
WHUD
He wiped him out o existence
Ah ha ha ha ha ha ha ha!!

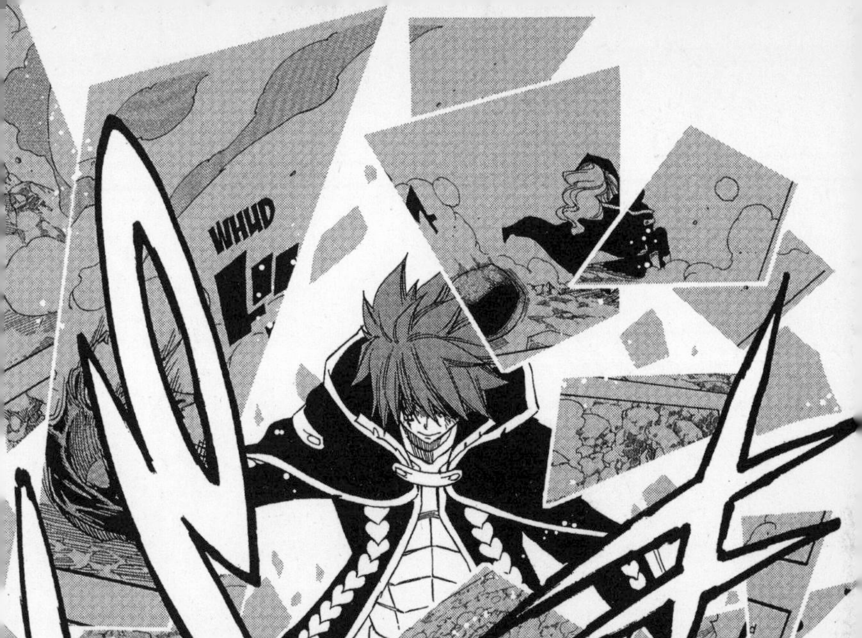
WHUD
CRAKK
ha ha ha

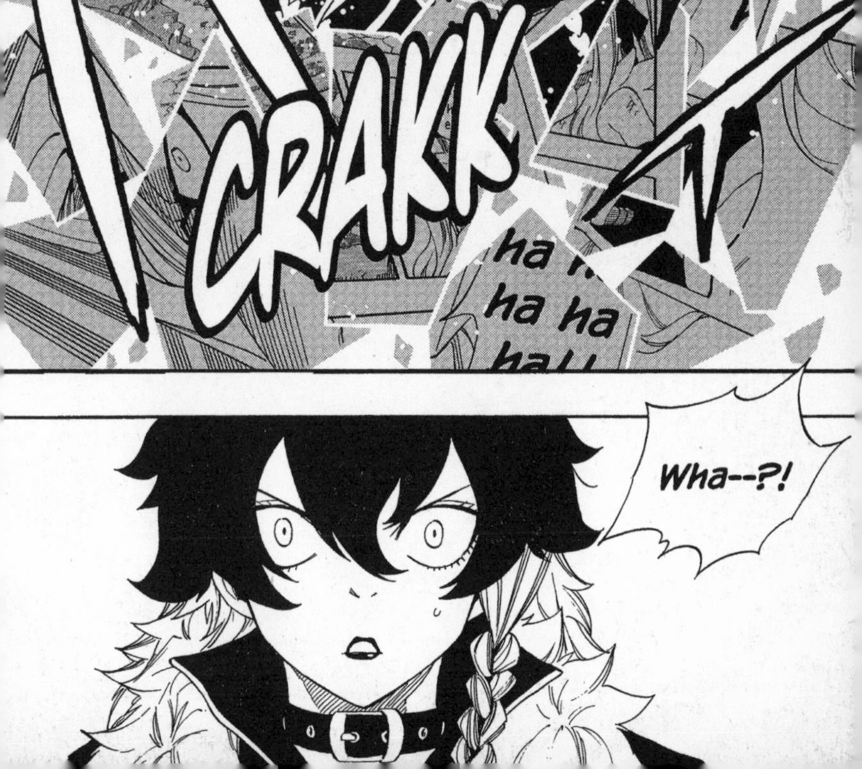
Wha--?!

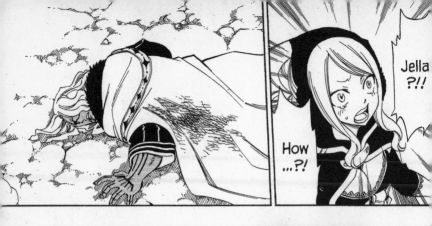

Jella?!!

How...?!

You saw through it...?!!

My nightmare...

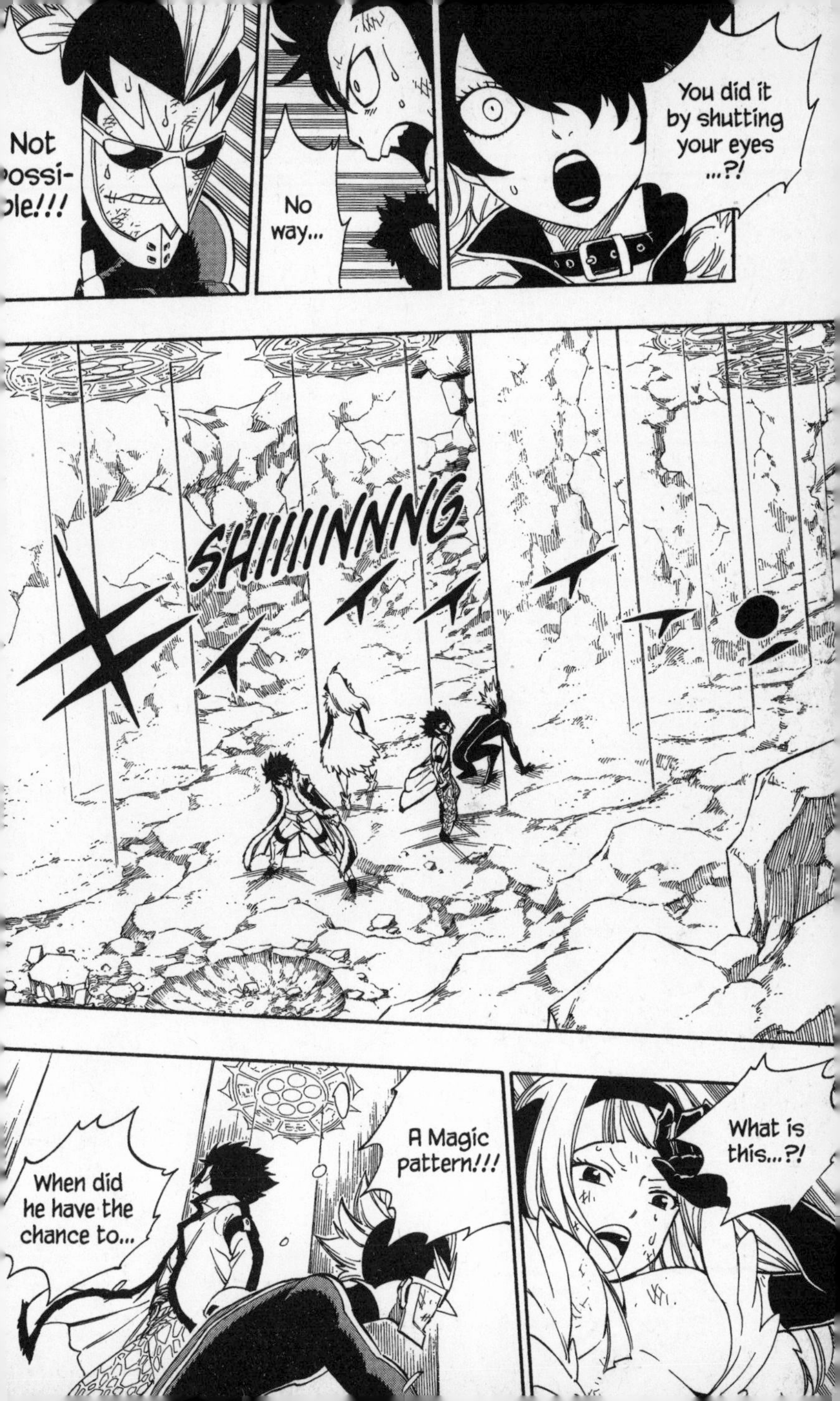

You did it by shutting your eyes ...?!
No way...
Not ossi- le!!!
SHIIIINNNG
What is this...?!
A Magic pattern!!!
When did he have the chance to...

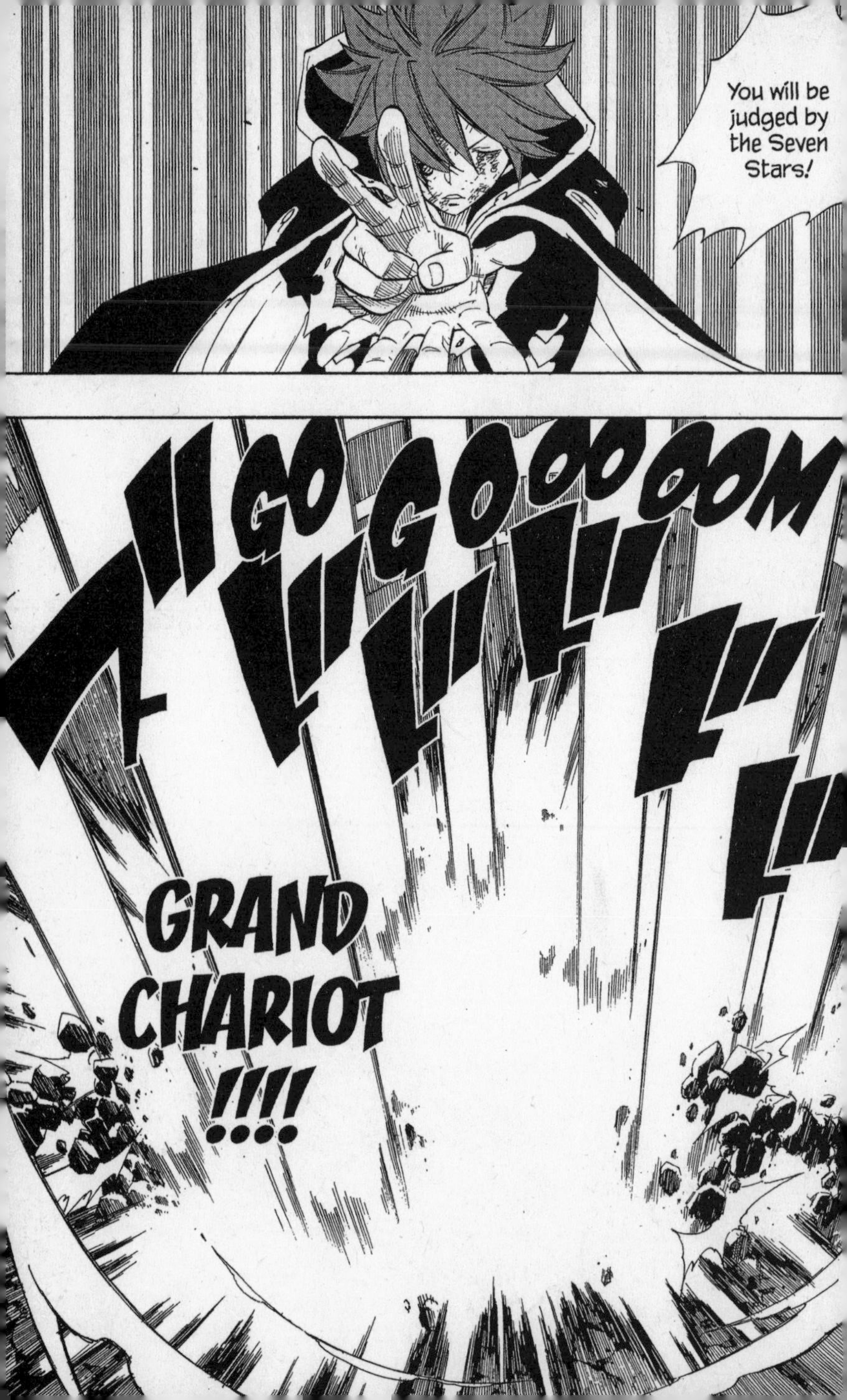
You will be judged by the Seven Stars!
ZGOGOOOOOM
GRAND CHARIOT!!!!

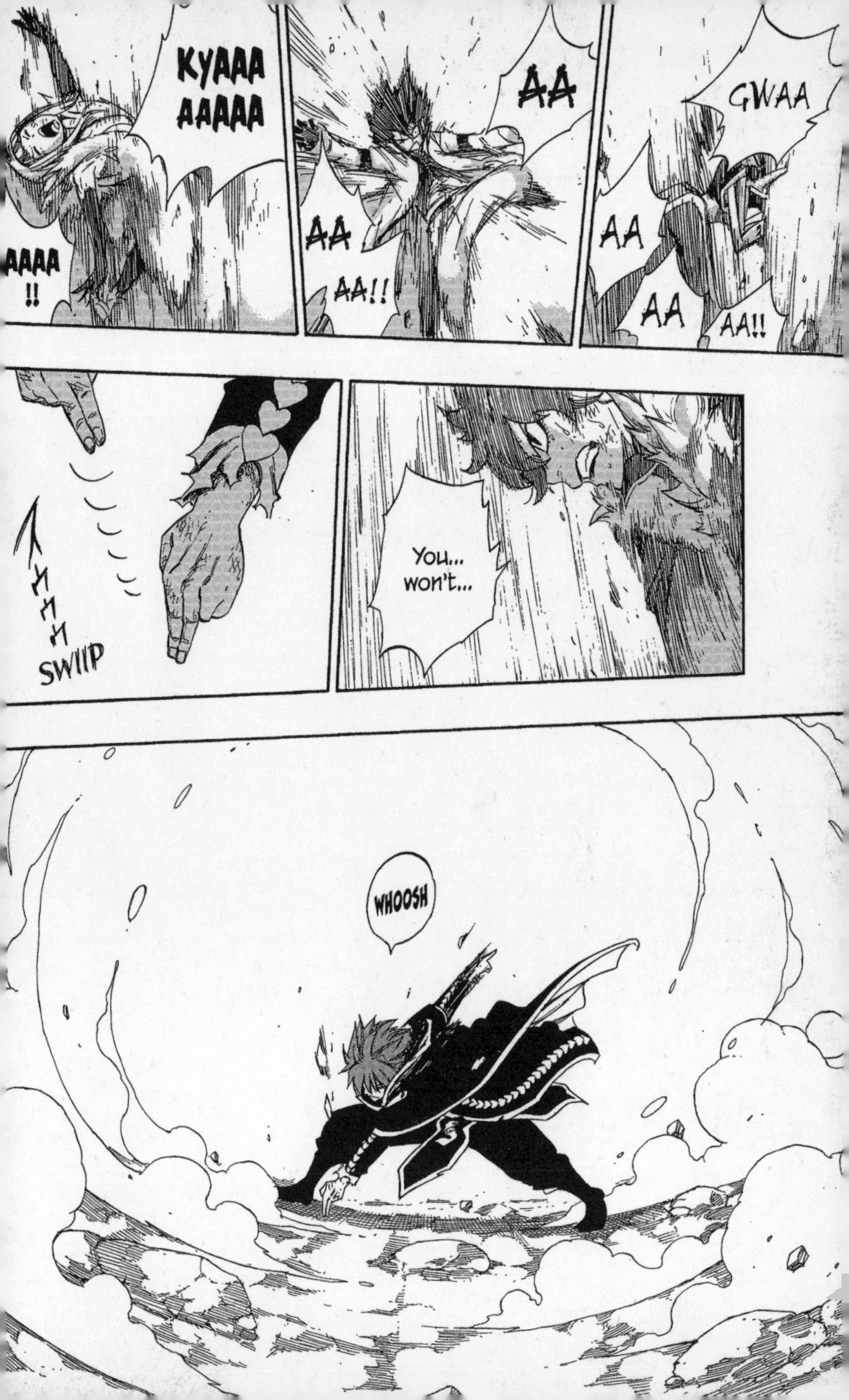
GWAA
AA
AA
AA!!
AA
AA
AA!!
KYAAA AAAAA
AAAA !!
You... won't...
SWIIP
WHOOSH

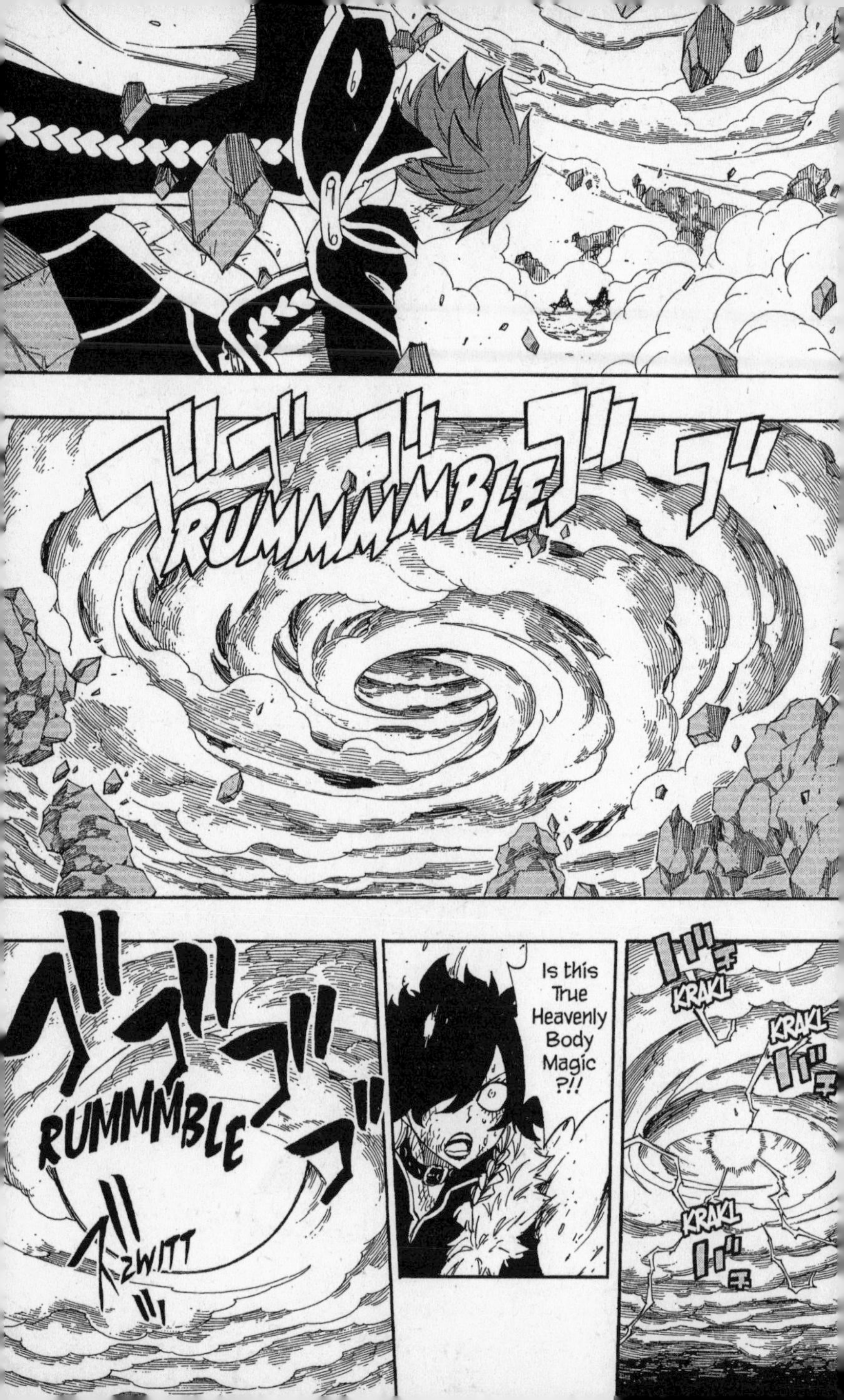
ゴゴゴゴゴ
RUMMMMBLE
KRAKL
KRAKL
KRAKL
Is this True Heavenly Body Magic ?!!
RUMMMBLE
ZWITT

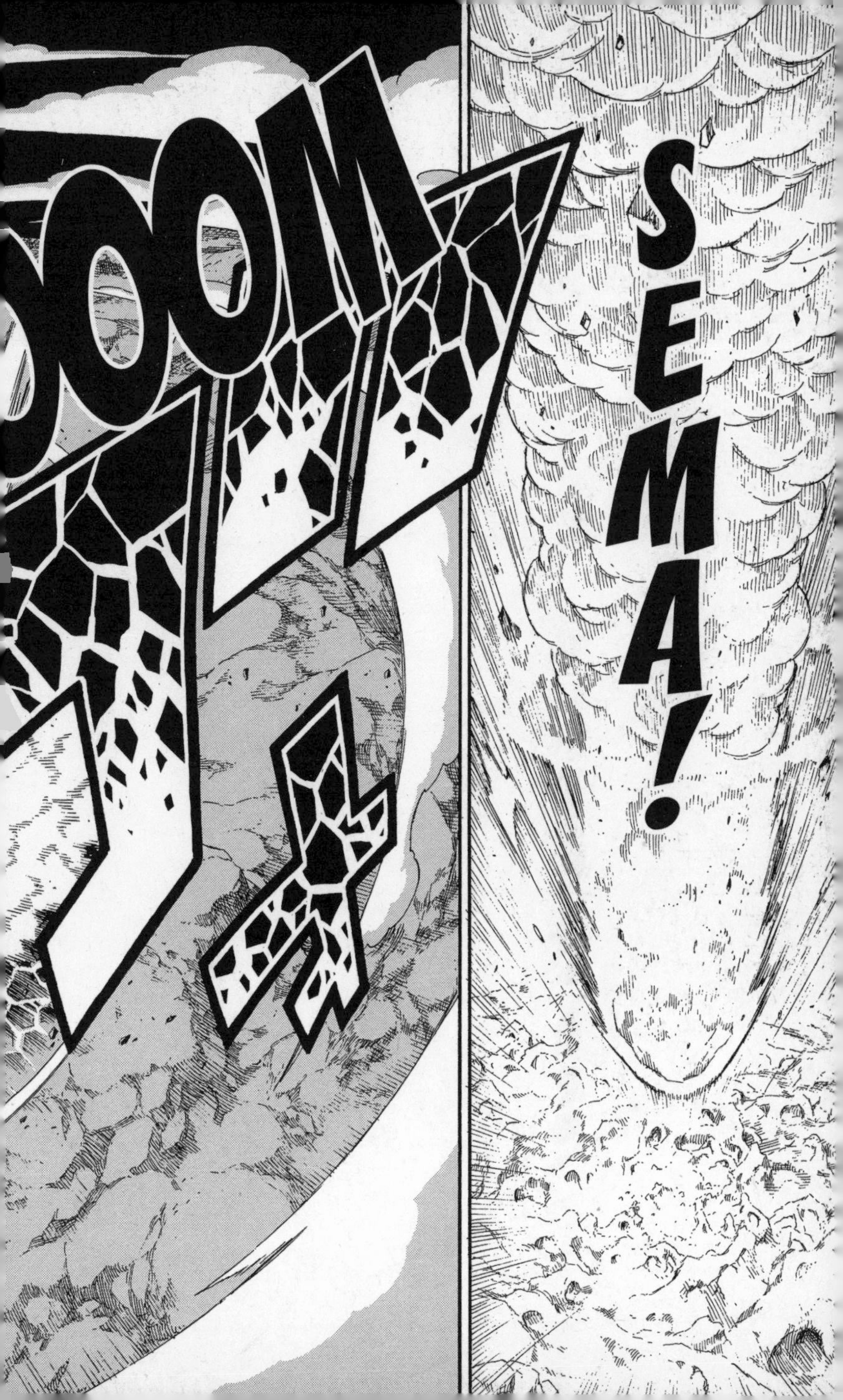
SEMA!
OOM

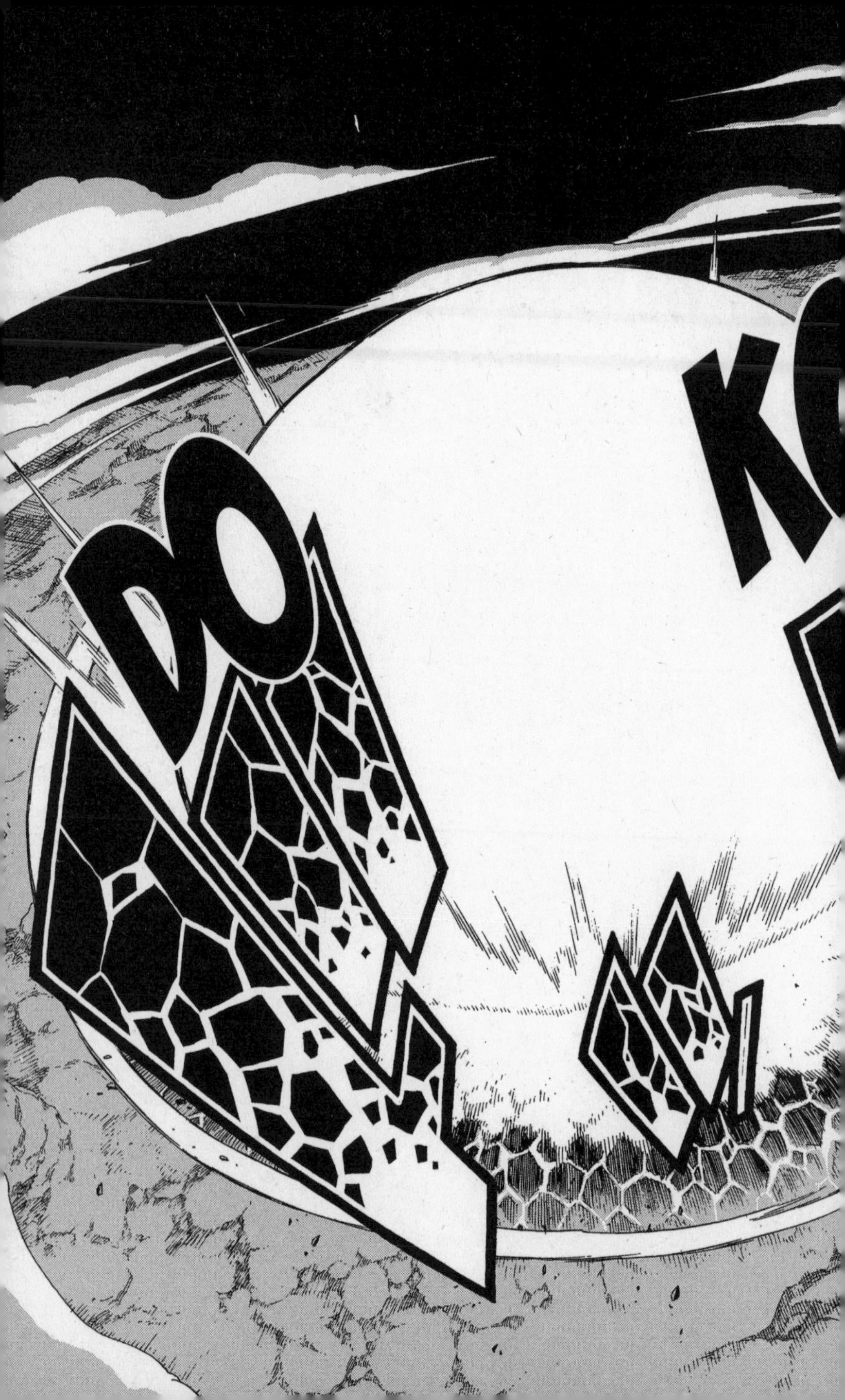
DO
K

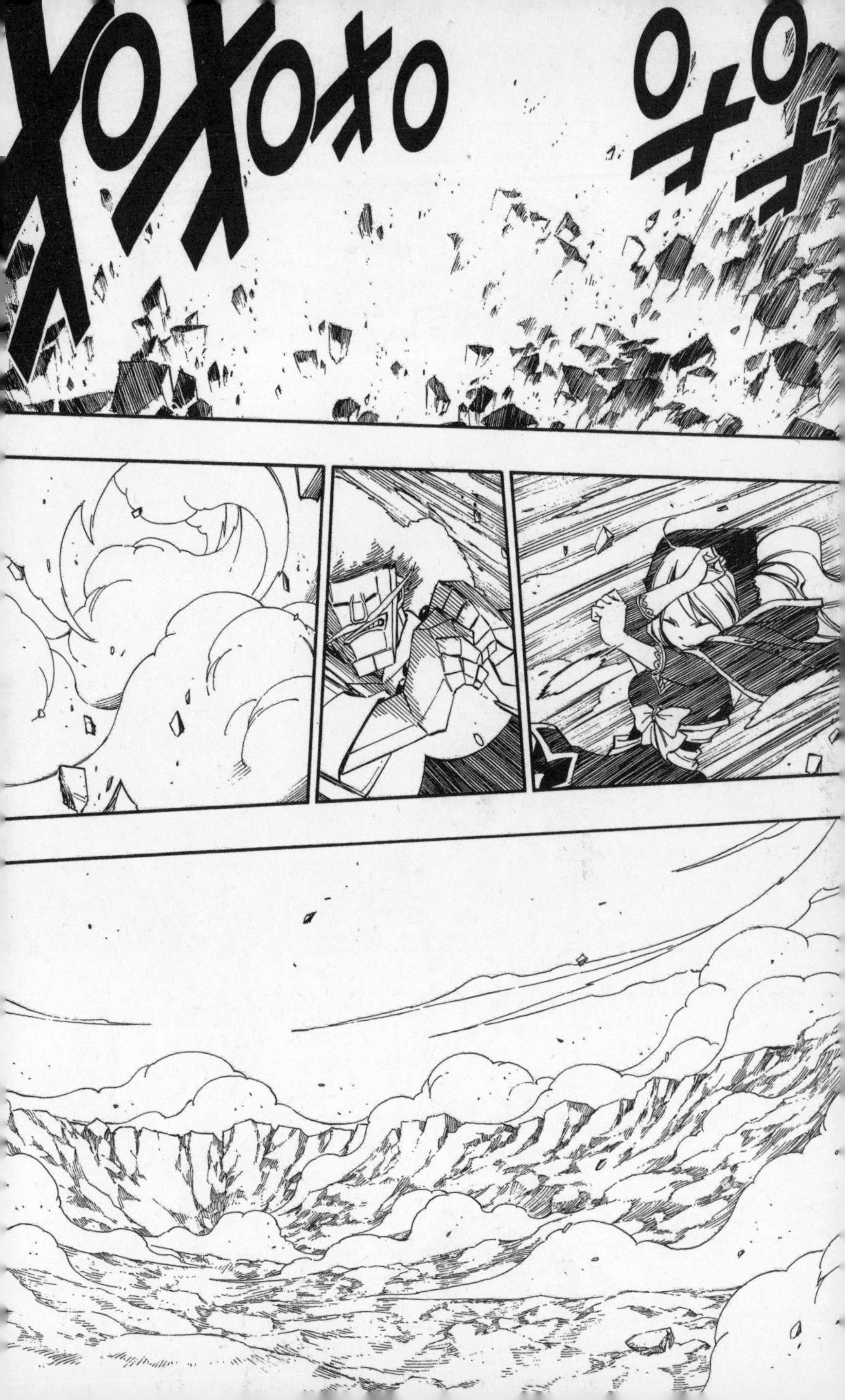

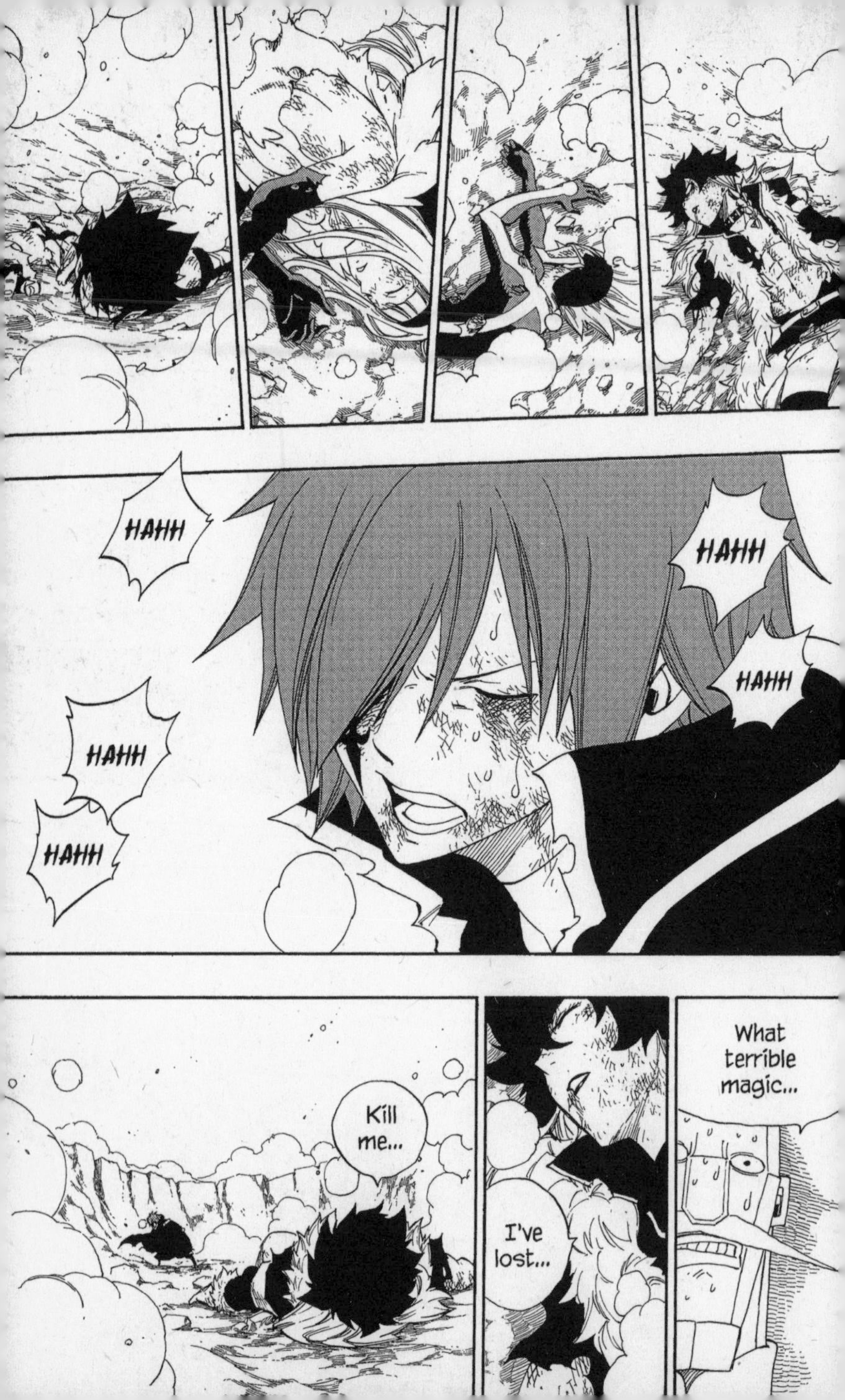
HAHH
HAHH
HAHH
HAHH
HAHH
What terrible magic...
I've lost...
Kill me...

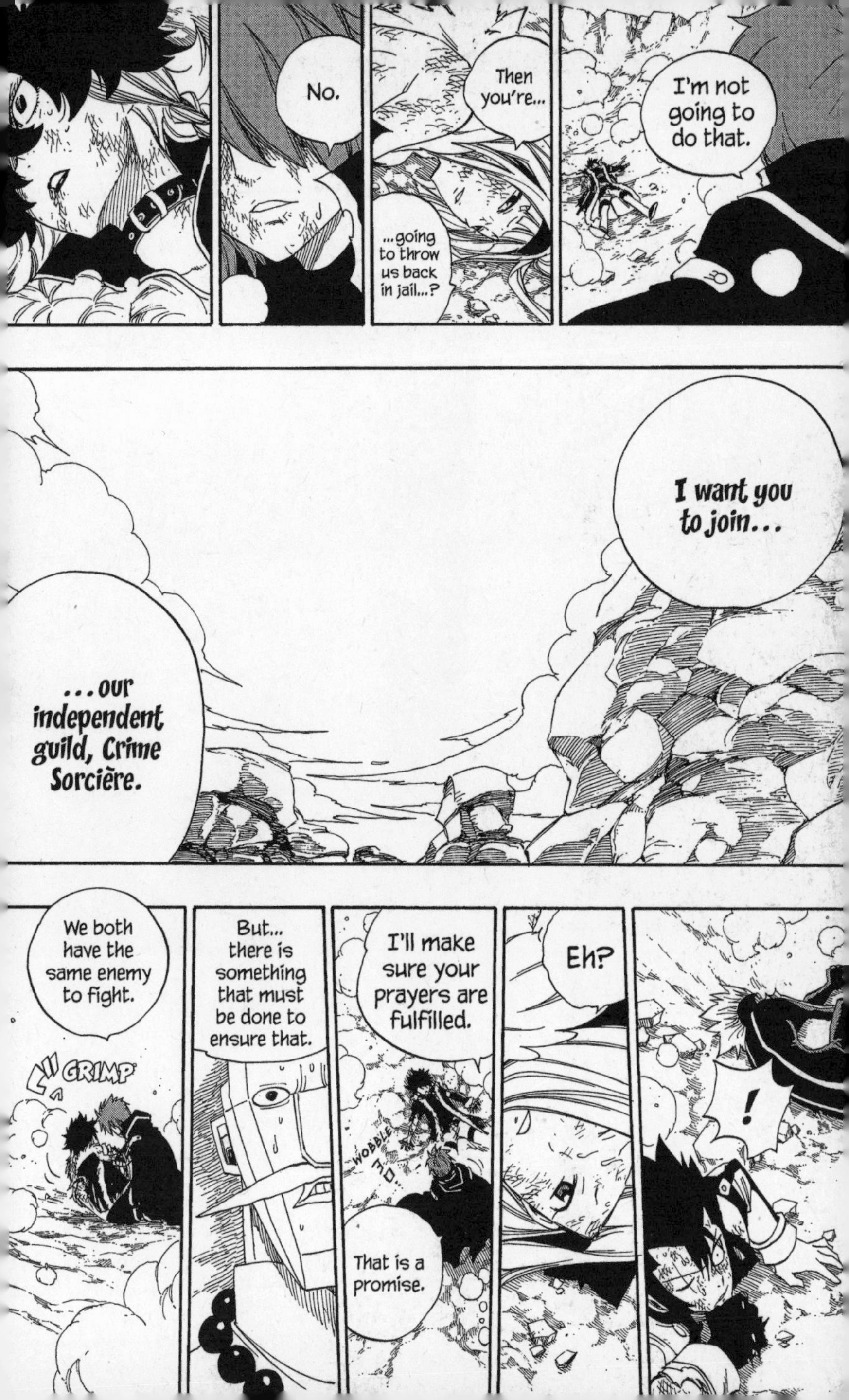
I'm not going to do that.
Then you're...
...going to throw us back in jail...?
No.
I want you to join...
...our independent guild, Crime Sorcière.
!
Eh?
I'll make sure your prayers are fulfilled.
WOBBLE
That is a promise.
But... there is something that must be done to ensure that.
We both have the same enemy to fight.
GRIMP

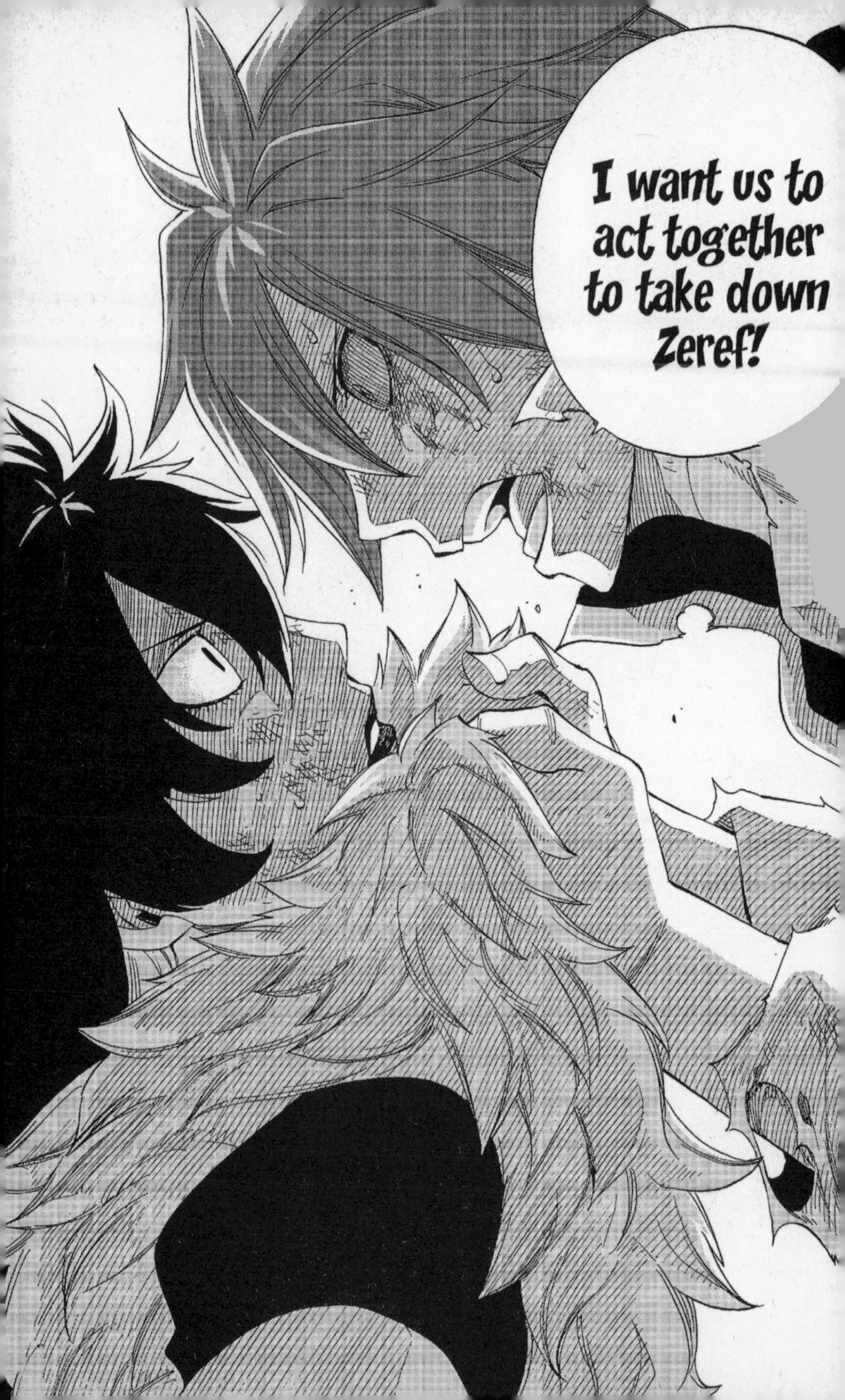
I want us to act together to take down Zeref!

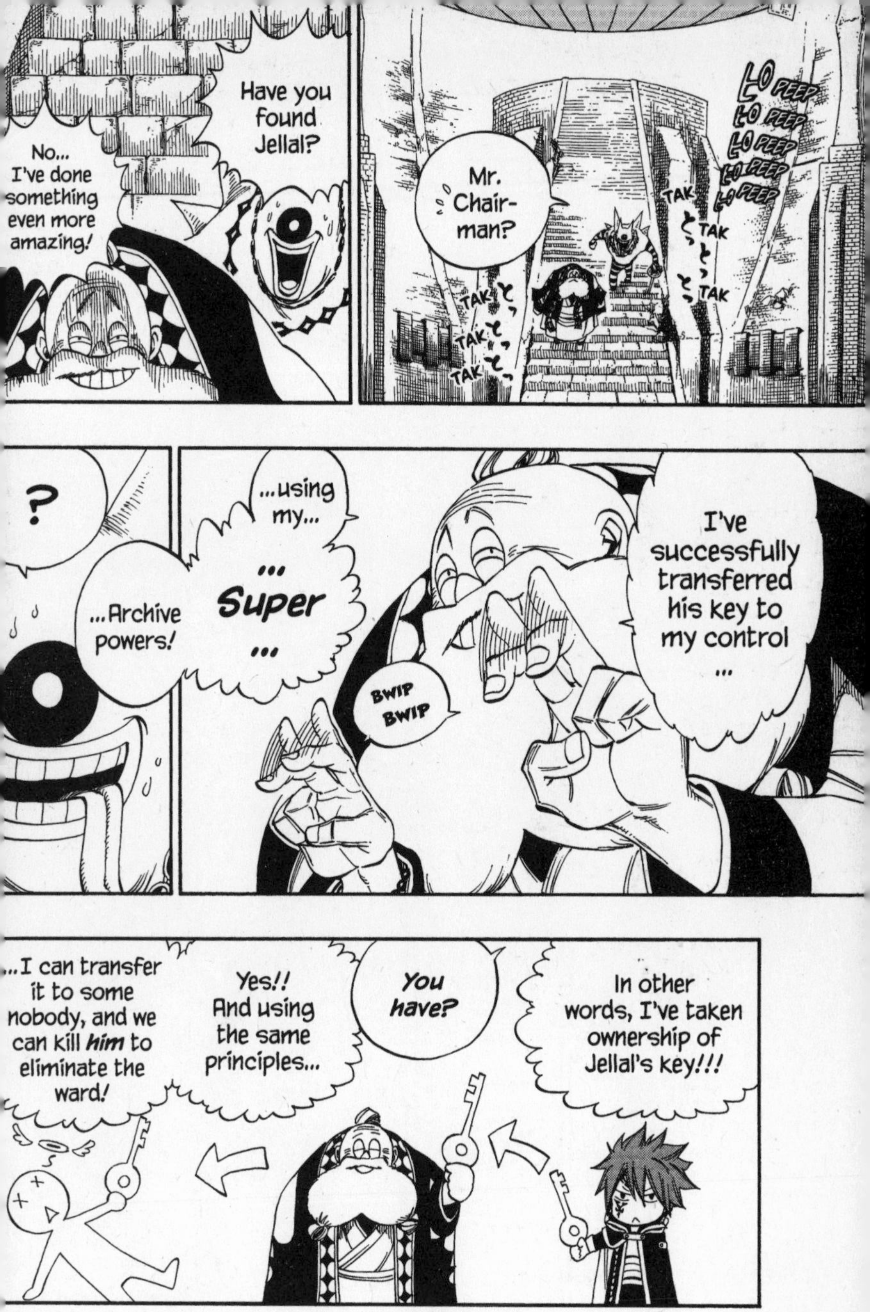
PEEP PEEP PEEP PEEP PEEP
TAK TAK TAK
Mr. Chair-man?
TAK TAK TAK
Have you found Jellal?
No... I've done something even more amazing!
I've successfully transferred his key to my control ...
BWIP BWIP
...using my...
... Super ...
...Archive powers!
?
In other words, I've taken ownership of Jellal's key!!!
You have?
Yes!! And using the same principles...
...I can transfer it to some nobody, and we can kill ***him*** to eliminate the ward!

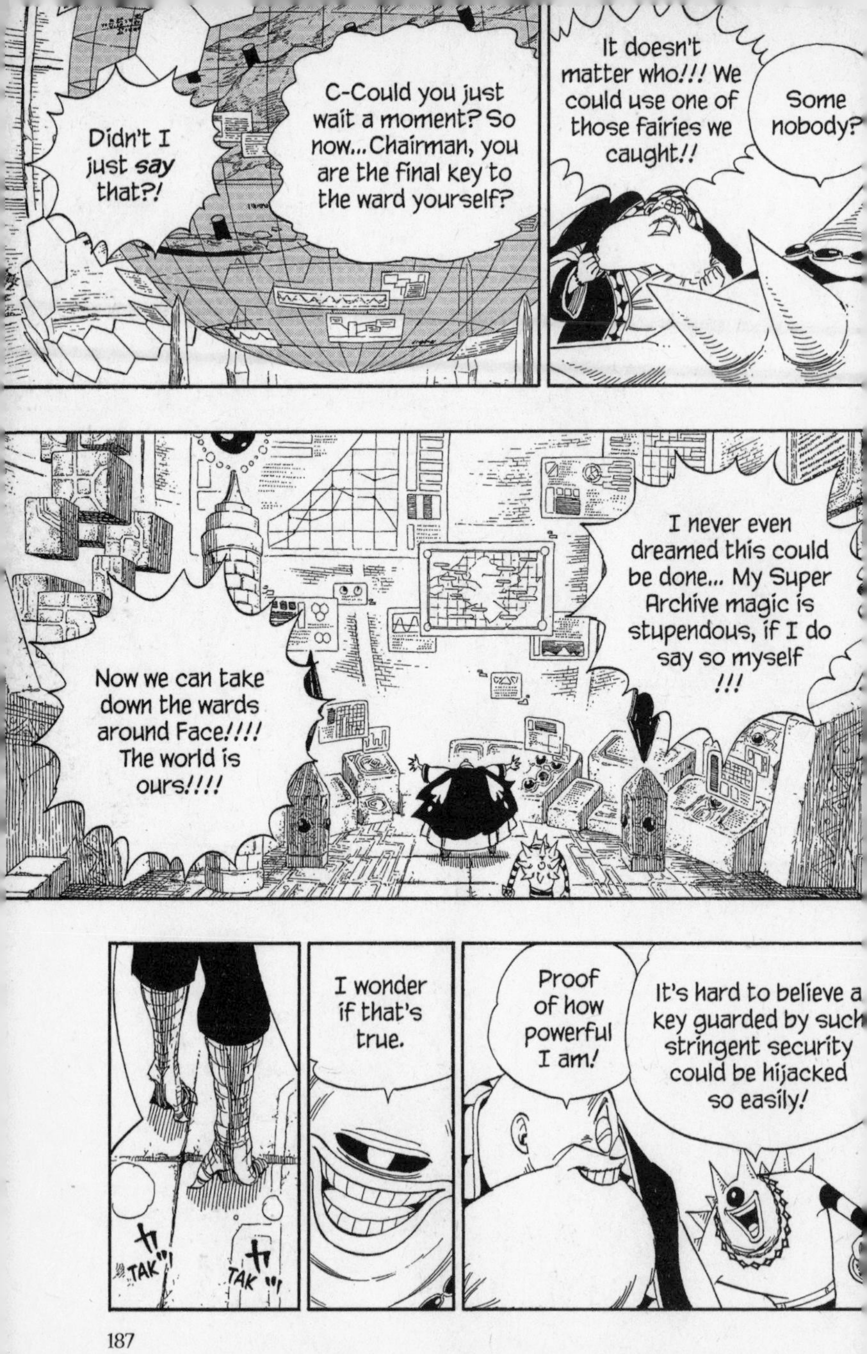
Some nobody?
It doesn't matter who!!! We could use one of those fairies we caught!!
C-Could you just wait a moment? So now...Chairman, you are the final key to the ward yourself?
Didn't I just say that?!
I never even dreamed this could be done... My Super Archive magic is stupendous, if I do say so myself!!!
Now we can take down the wards around Face!!!! The world is ours!!!!
It's hard to believe a key guarded by such stringent security could be hijacked so easily!
Proof of how powerful I am!
I wonder if that's true.
TAK
TAK

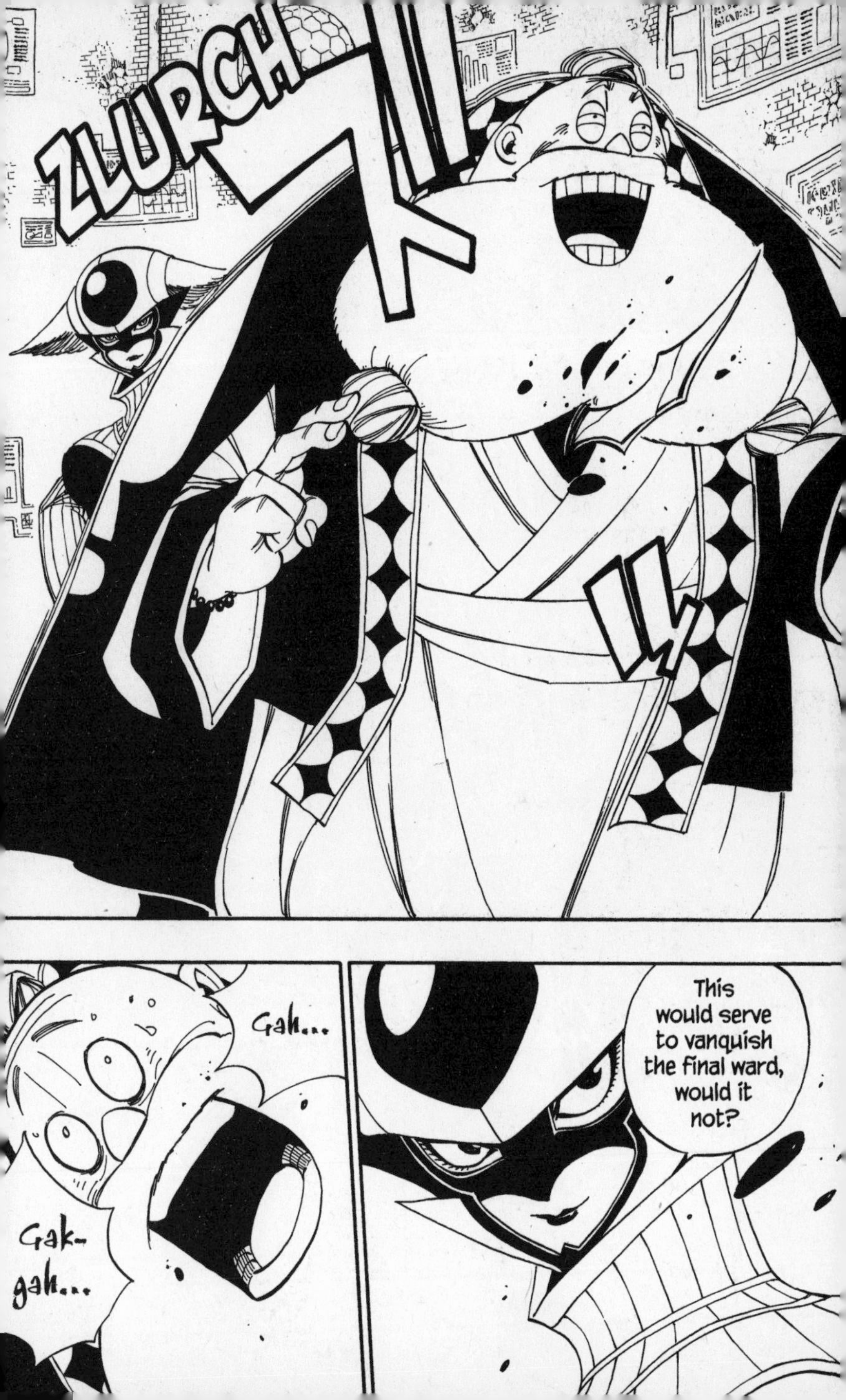
ZLURCH
This would serve to vanquish the final ward, would it not?
Gah...
Gak-gah...

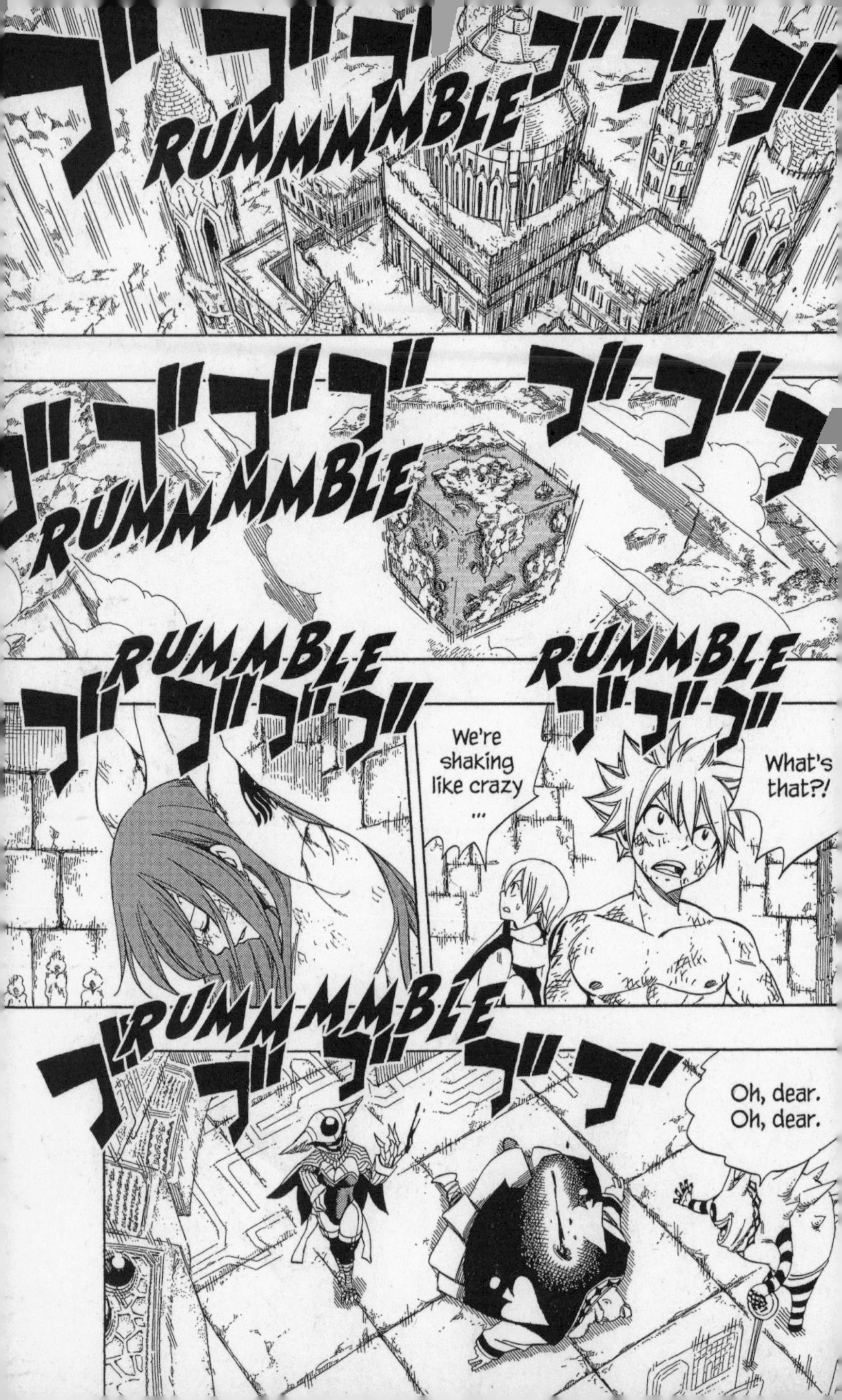
RUMMMMBLE
RUMMMMBLE
RUMMBLE
RUMMBLE
What's that?!
We're shaking like crazy ...
RUMMMMBLE
Oh, dear. Oh, dear.

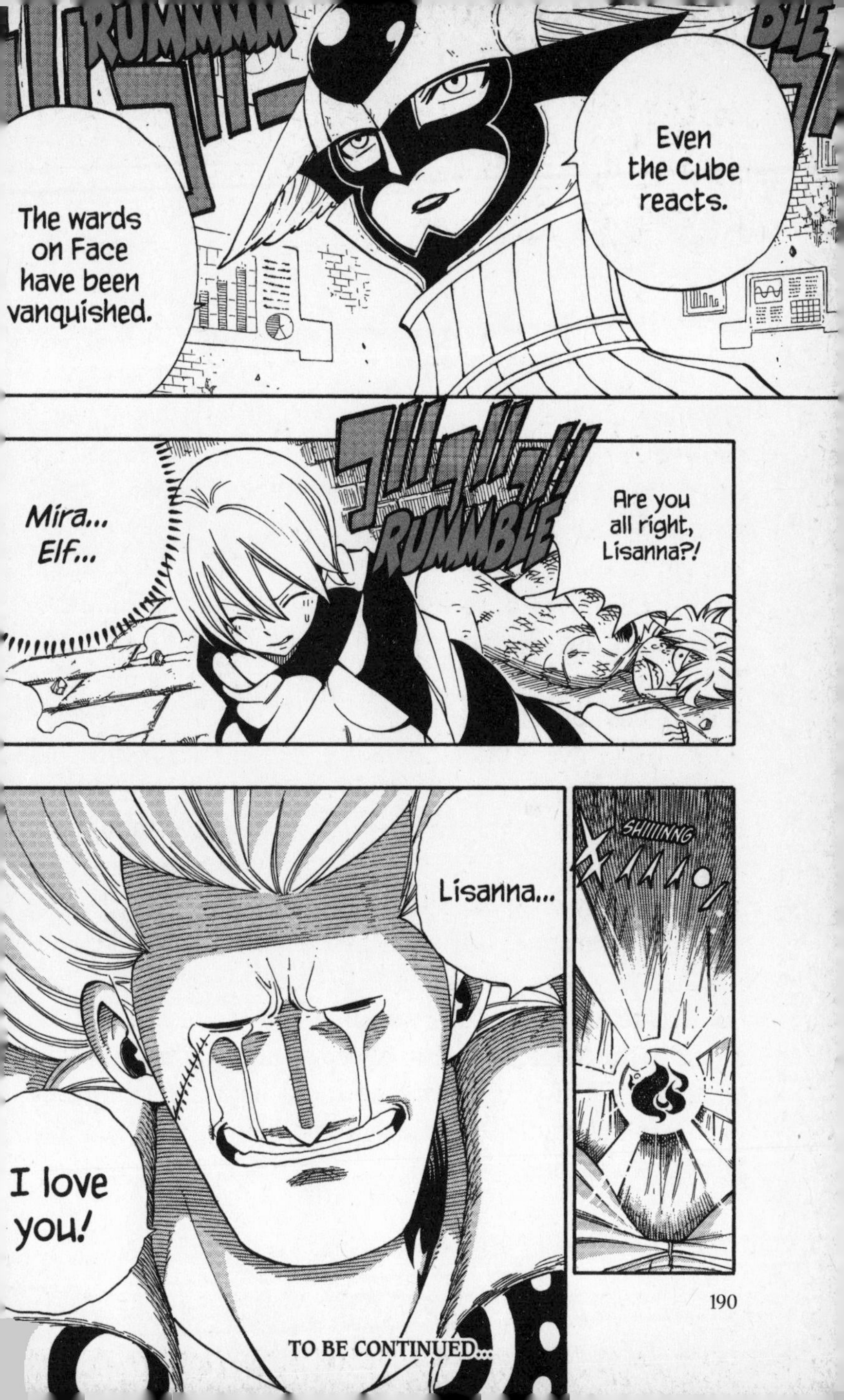
RUMMMM
BLE
Even the Cube reacts.
The wards on Face have been vanquished.
Are you all right, Lisanna?!
RUMMBLE
Mira... Elf...
SHIIIINNG
Lisanna...
I love you!
TO BE CONTINUED...

あとがき

Afterword

This time, because of the limitations of the number of pages allowed in the book, there are hardly any bonus pages. I'm sorry! Over and above that, I'm far more busy than I would have believed! Even apart from drawing a weekly manga, I've got to solve problem after problem... Hyaaahh!! But on a personal note, I'm really into the Tartaros Arc this time, and I'm getting all sorts of ideas piling on top of each other. There are some real surprising plot twists coming up, so be sure to look for them!

Now I think I've written about this somewhere before, but I'm not doing any of the drawing for the anime. There are a lot of animators putting in tons of hours and sweat to make it, and I really respect the work they're doing. They're taking pictures I only drew once and making them move, drawing picture after picture, and adding color until you get the feeling that the characters are alive! It's really incredible!

For that reason, instead of sending your impressions of the anime to the Magazine editorial department or through Twitter to myself, if you could send those impressions directly to the anime studio, I think that will help to cheer up and inspire all the the guys doing so much work! Please consider that, okay?

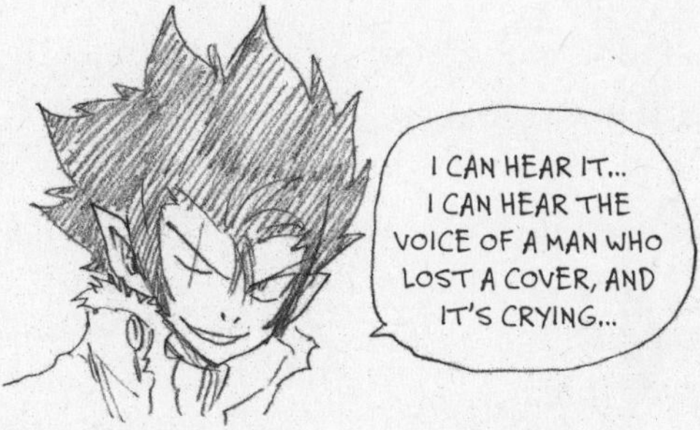
I CAN HEAR IT... I CAN HEAR THE VOICE OF A MAN WHO LOST A COVER, AND IT'S CRYING...

FAIRY TAIL

フェアリーテイル

43

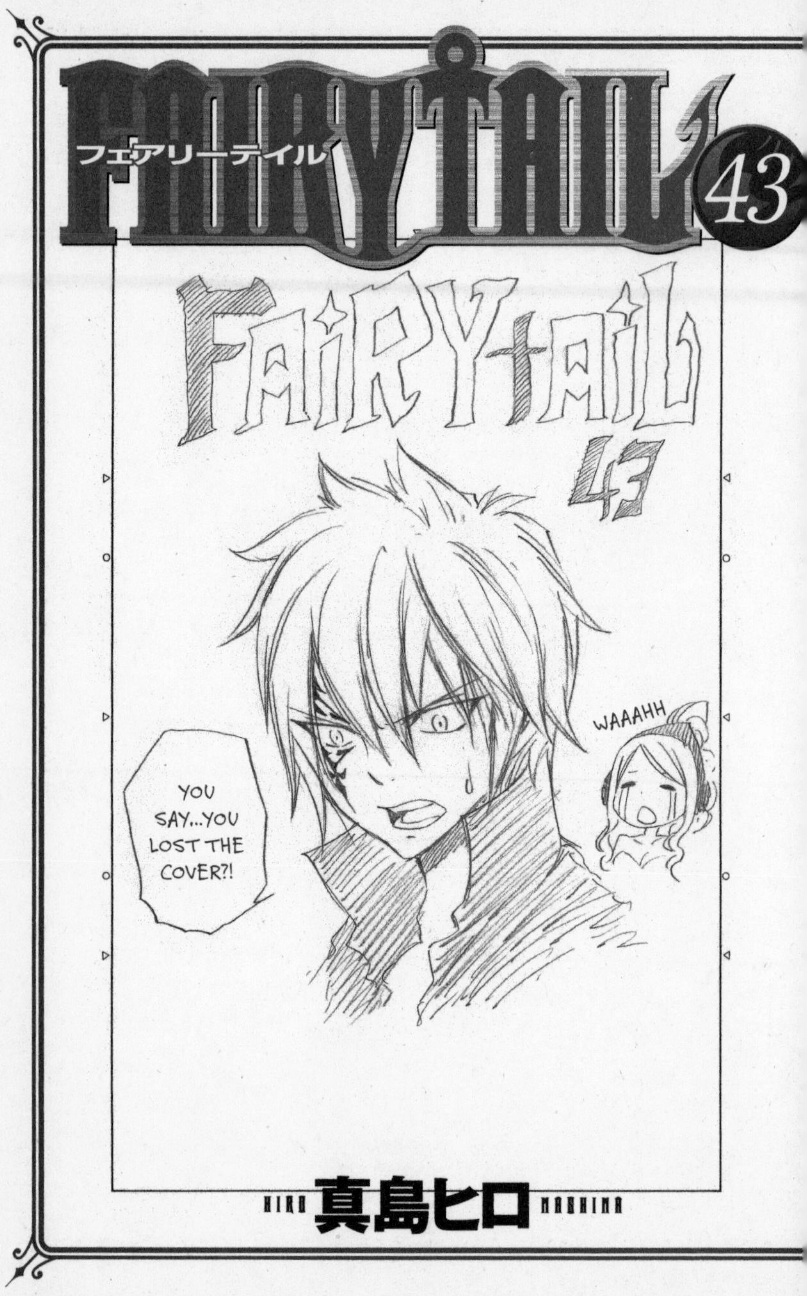

FAIRY tail
43
YOU SAY...YOU LOST THE COVER?!
WAAAHH

HIRO 真島ヒロ MASHIMA

FROM HIRO MASHIMA

I went to the Fairy Tail event called the Dragon King Festival 2014. I'm really not good at standing in front of crowds, but since the anime was starting up again after a year, I took part in the event. Since I was able to talk to the fans directly, I thought the event was incredibly fun! I hope there's a Dragon King Festival 2015!

Original Jacket Design: Hisao Ogawa

Translation Notes:

Japanese is a tricky language for most Westerners, and translation is often more art than science. For your edification and reading pleasure, here are notes on some of the places where we could have gone in a different direction with our translation of the work, or where a Japanese cultural reference is used.

Page 38, Magical Pulse Bomb

This is probably based on the electromagnetic pulse (EMP) that is said to occur wher a nuclear device is activated. Although a real pulse may cause damage aside from shutting down electronic devices (and in reality, not necessarily all electronic device are affected), in fiction the pulse simply shuts down all electric and electronic device for a period of time (for example, as used in the movie *Ocean's Eleven*) causing no othe damage.

Page 77, New Year's

There are several common trappings of Japanese New Year's celebrations on this page. The three bamboo stalks with a garland of pine are usually placed outside one's front door, but at times they also serve as interior decorations. Similarly, the gift tray to the left of the bamboo decoration has a traditional set of three *mochi* (rice paste) cakes topped by a mandarin orange. The *mochi* decoration is placed just inside the entrance to the home. The folding screen and *tatami* mats (rush mats) are not especially seasonal, but rather found in most traditional Japanese homes. Natsu, Master Makarov, Happy, Mirajane, Wendy, and Lucy are all wearing traditional Japanese clothes commonly worn on a first visit to a temple or shrine during New Year's (although normal clothes are perfectly acceptable).

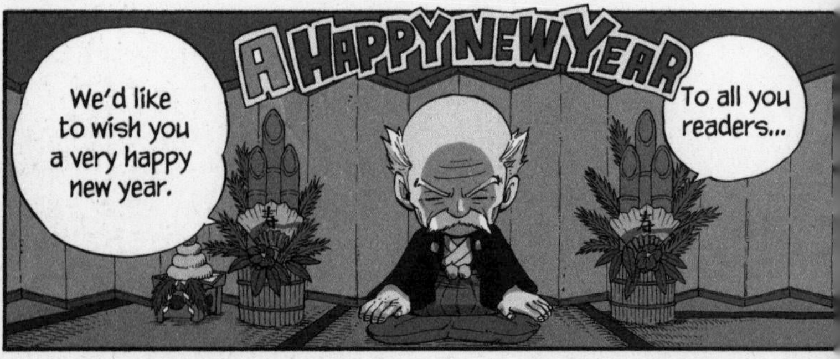
A HAPPY NEW YEAR
To all you readers...
We'd like to wish you a very happy new year.

age 151, Oden

a inexpensive stew, subtly flavored. It can feature fish, tofu, squid, octopus, *mochi* ce paste), seaweed, chicken, dumplings, eggs, radishes, potatoes, and other meats, getables, and concoctions. Although it is a stew, the elements (meat and veggies) are sually skewered on shish kebab-like sticks for easy access. Oden is served in restau- nts, but more commonly in convenience stores and sidewalk stalls.

age 151, Nattō

s mentioned in the notes for Volume 8, nattō is a strong-smelling fermented soybean sh in which beans are connected by a viscous, stringy fluid. The dish is very nutritious, d it contains nattokinase, a fibrinolytic enzyme which is said to prevent clotting the arteries. Still, nattō has a reputation for being loved by Japanese and hated by reigners (although there are foreign nattō lovers and Japanese detractors).

Preview of *Fairy Tail*, volume 44

We're pleased to present you with a preview from Fairy Tail, volume 44, now available digitally from Kodansha Comics. Check our Web site (www.kodanshacomics.com) for details!

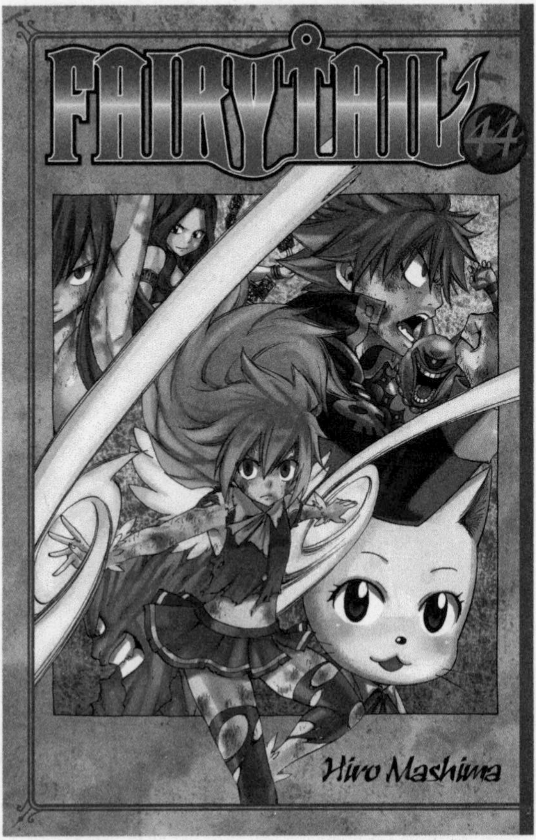
FAIRY TAIL
44
Hiro Mashima

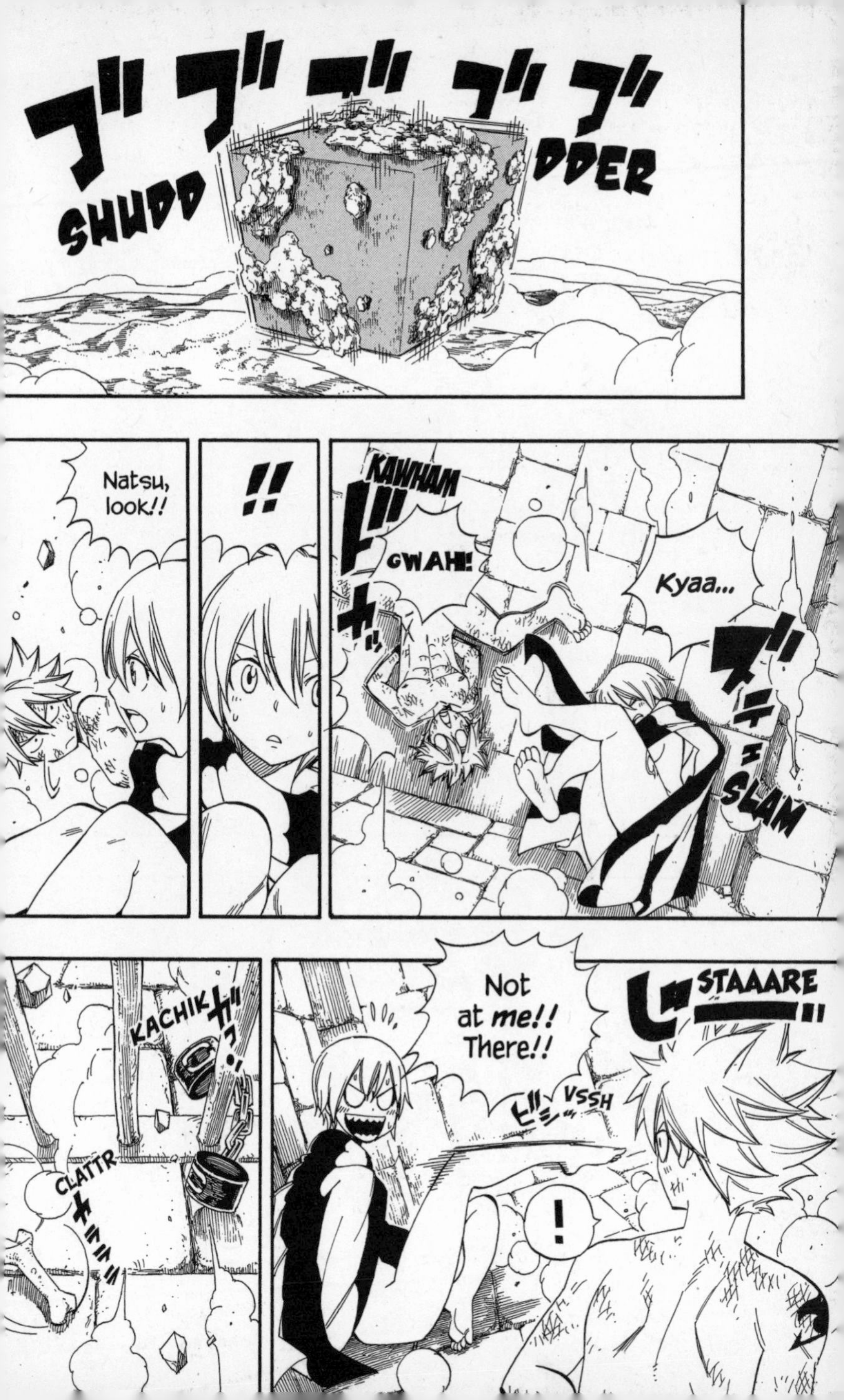
SHUDD
DDER
KAWHAM
Kyaa...
GWAH!
SLAM
!!
Natsu, look!!
STAAARE
Not at *me*!! There!!
VSSH
!
KACHIK
CLATTR

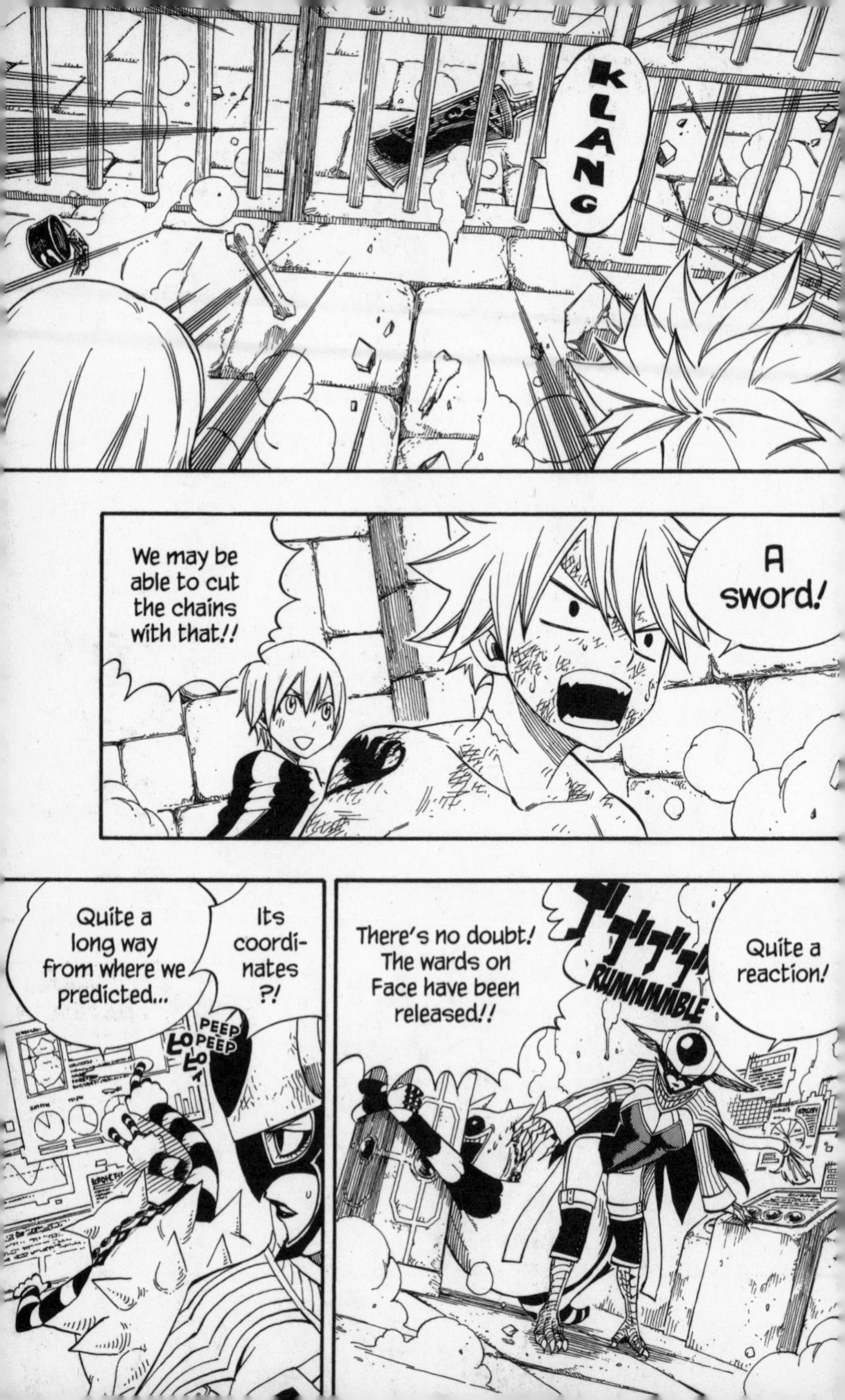
KLANG
A sword!
We may be able to cut the chains with that!!
Quite a reaction!
RUMMMMBLE
There's no doubt! The wards on Face have been released!!
Its coordi-nates?!
PEEP PEEP
Quite a long way from where we predicted...

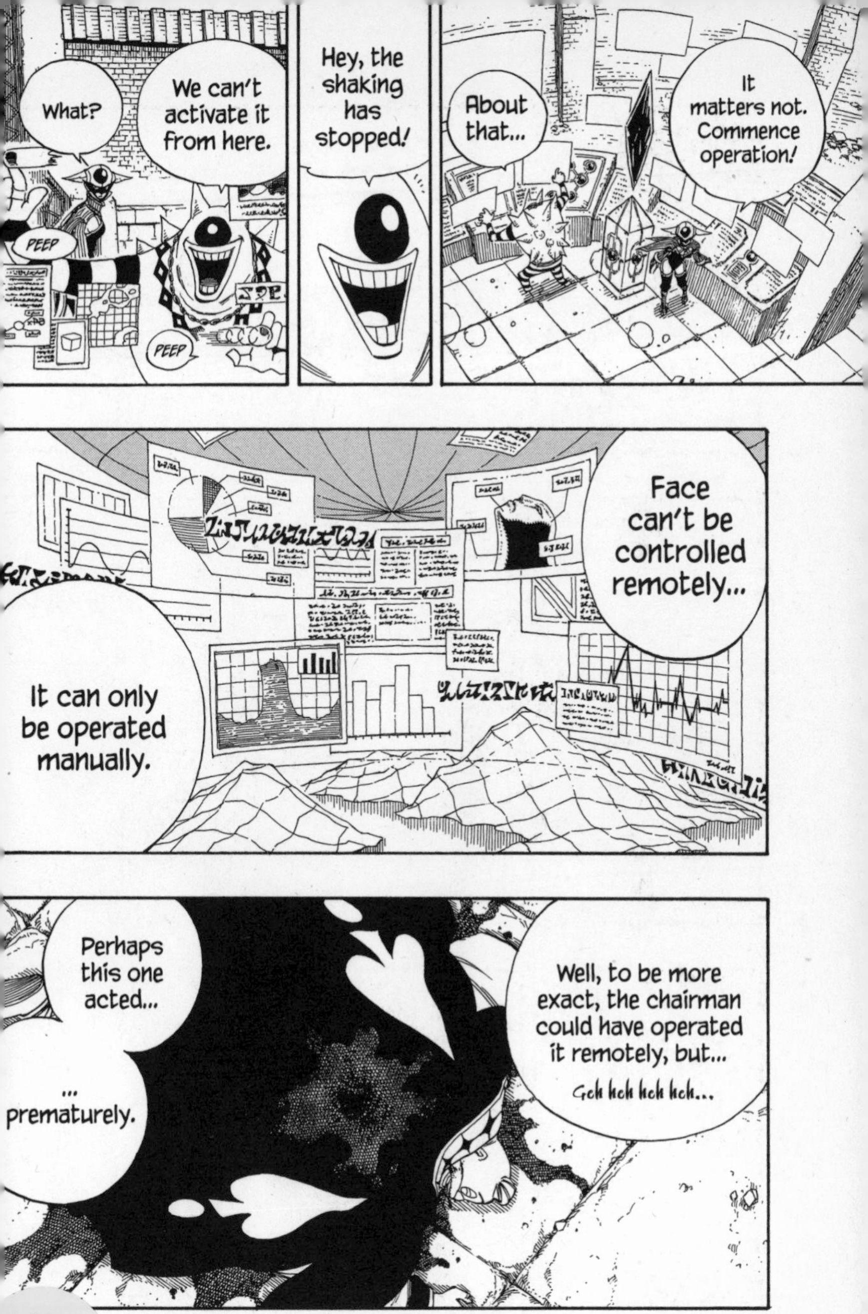
It matters not. Commence operation!
About that...
Hey, the shaking has stopped!
We can't activate it from here.
What?
PEEP
PEEP
Face can't be controlled remotely...
It can only be operated manually.
Well, to be more exact, the chairman could have operated it remotely, but...
Geh heh heh heh...
Perhaps this one acted...
... prematurely.

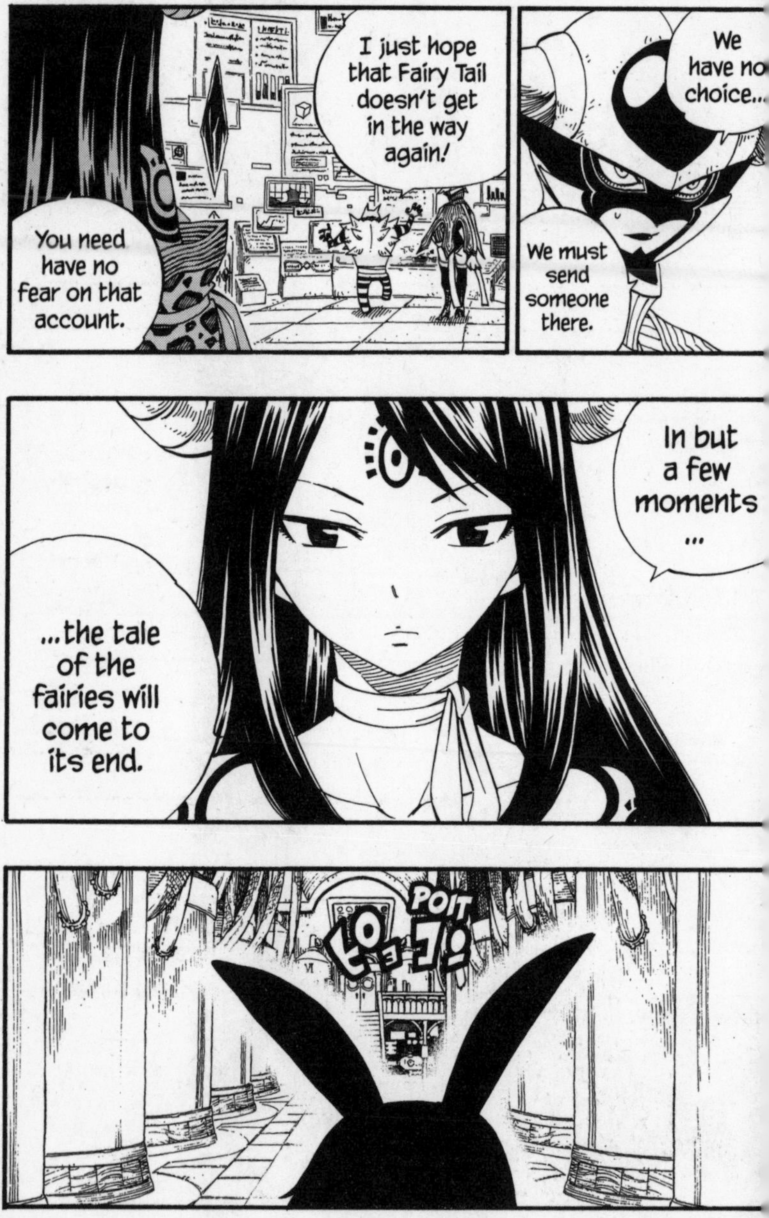
We have no choice...
We must send someone there.
I just hope that Fairy Tail doesn't get in the way again!
You need have no fear on that account.
In but a few moments...
...the tale of the fairies will come to its end.
POIT

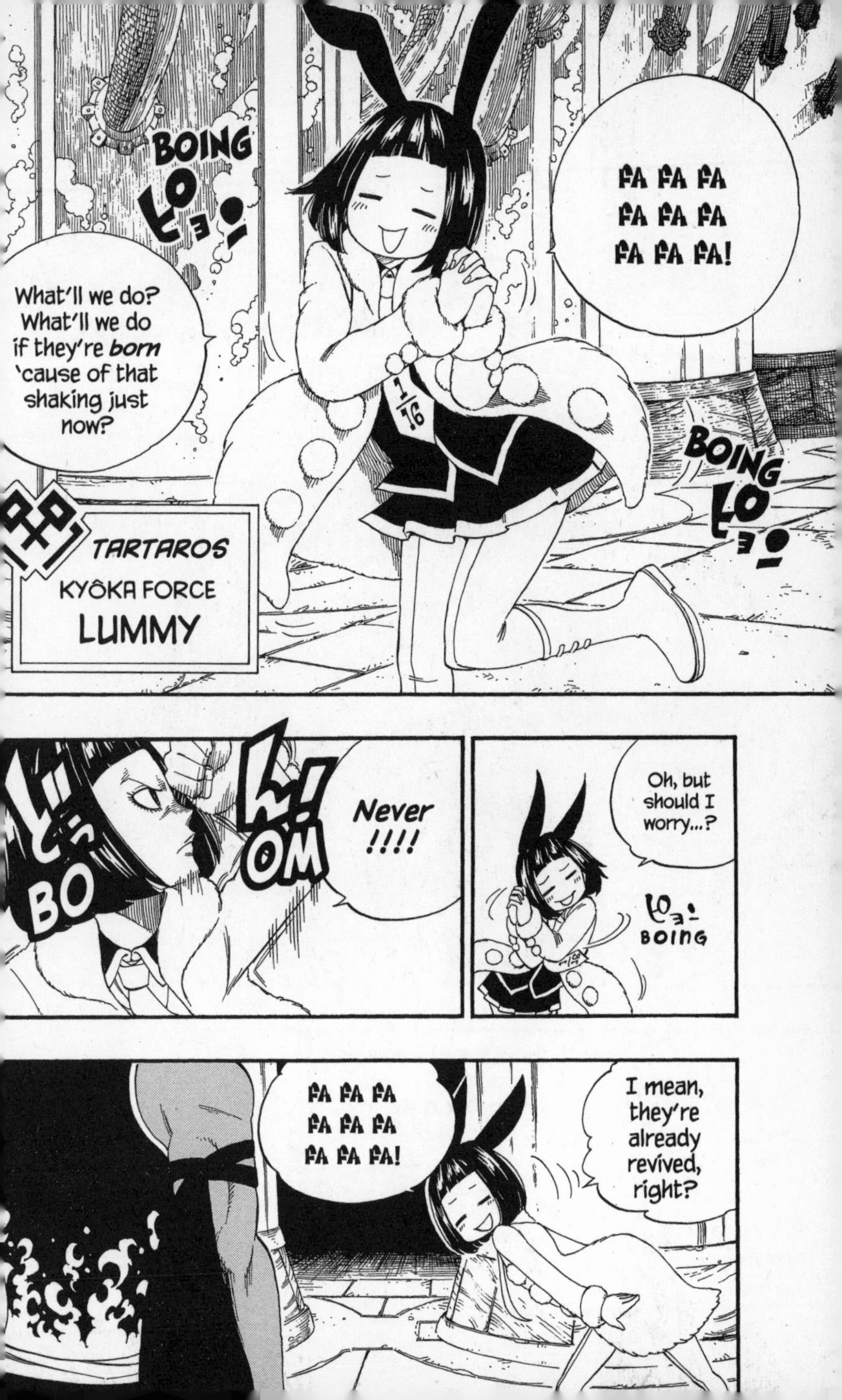
FA FA FA FA FA FA FA FA FA!
BOING
What'll we do? What'll we do if they're *born* 'cause of that shaking just now?
BOING
TARTAROS
KYÔKA FORCE
LUMMY
Oh, but should I worry...?
BOING
Never !!!!
BOOM
I mean, they're already revived, right?
FA FA FA FA FA FA FA FA FA!

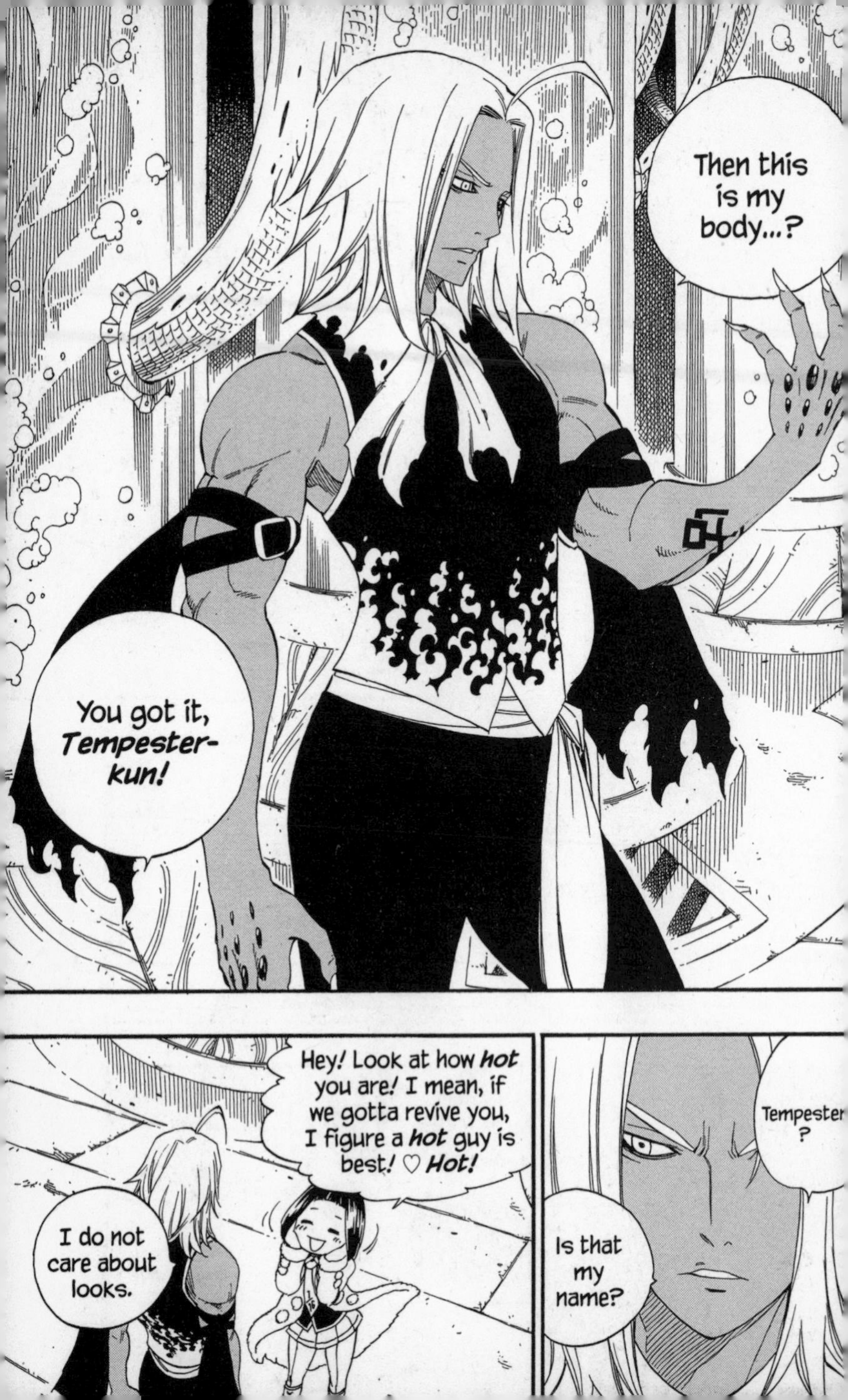
Then this is my body...?
You got it, *Tempester-kun!*
Tempester?
Is that my name?
Hey! Look at how *hot* you are! I mean, if we gotta revive you, I figure a *hot* guy is best! ♡ *Hot!*
I do not care about looks.

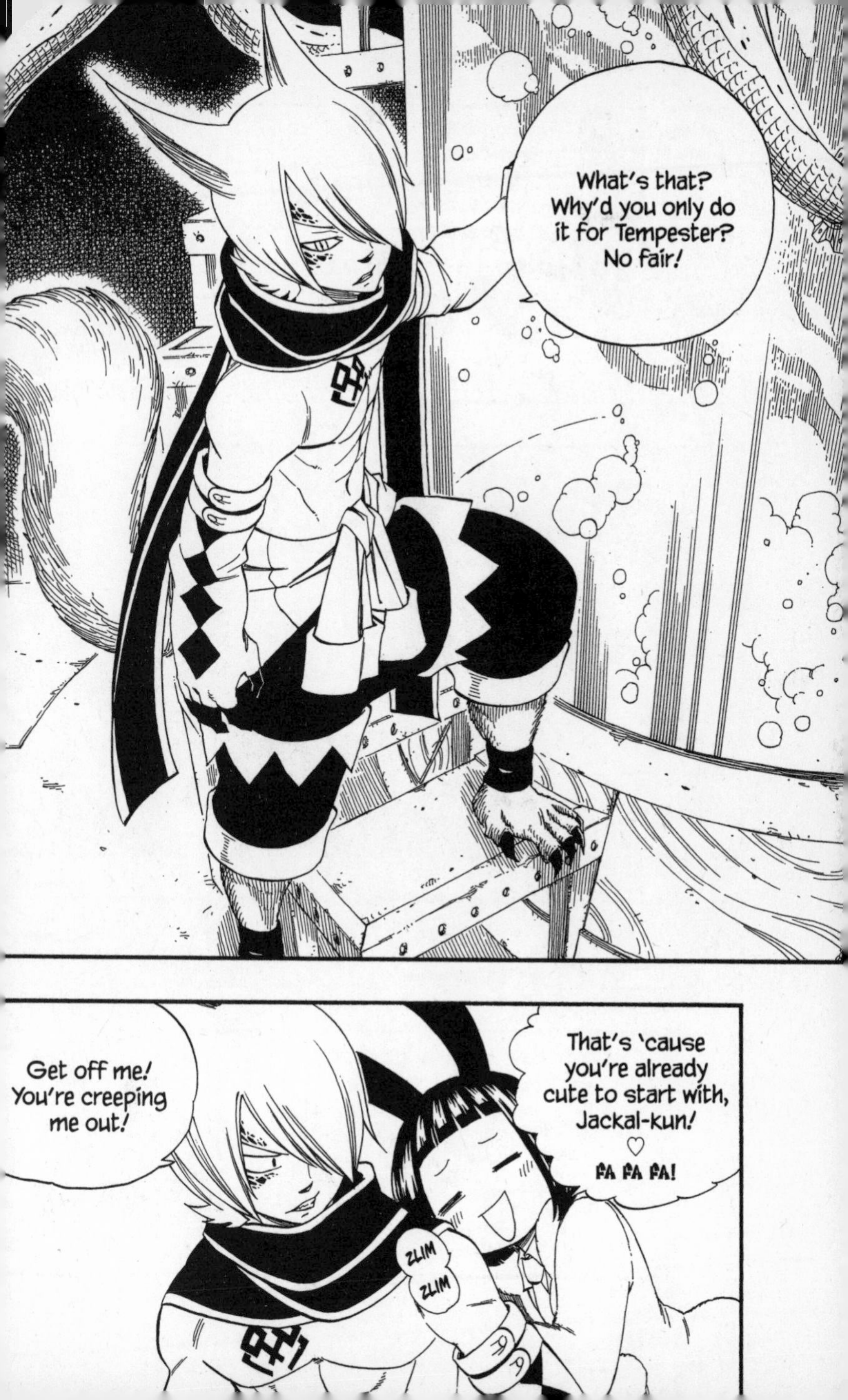
What's that? Why'd you only do it for Tempester? No fair!
That's 'cause you're already cute to start with, Jackal-kun! ♡
FA FA FA!
Get off me! You're creeping me out!
ZLIM
ZLIM

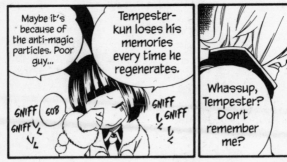

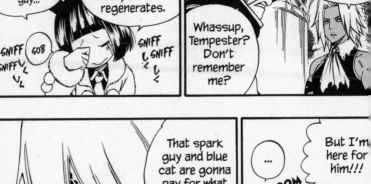

Jackal-kun...?
Whassup, Tempester? Don't remember me?
Tempester-kun loses his memories every time he regenerates.
Maybe it's because of the anti-magic particles. Poor guy...
SNIFF SNIFF
SOB
SNIFF SNIFF
But I'm here for him!!!
...
DOOM
That spark guy and blue cat are gonna pay for what they did!
I'm gonna crush them!
Your angry face is so ho It makes me come back t life!
Eugh! You're so annoying!!!
Who is that?
Hm? Who are you supposed to be?
Oh, I forgot!
TEE HEE

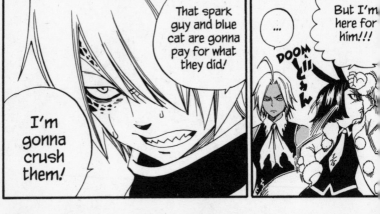

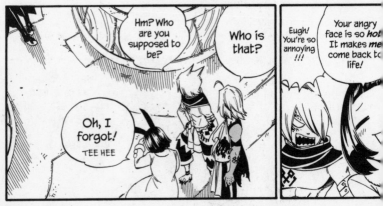

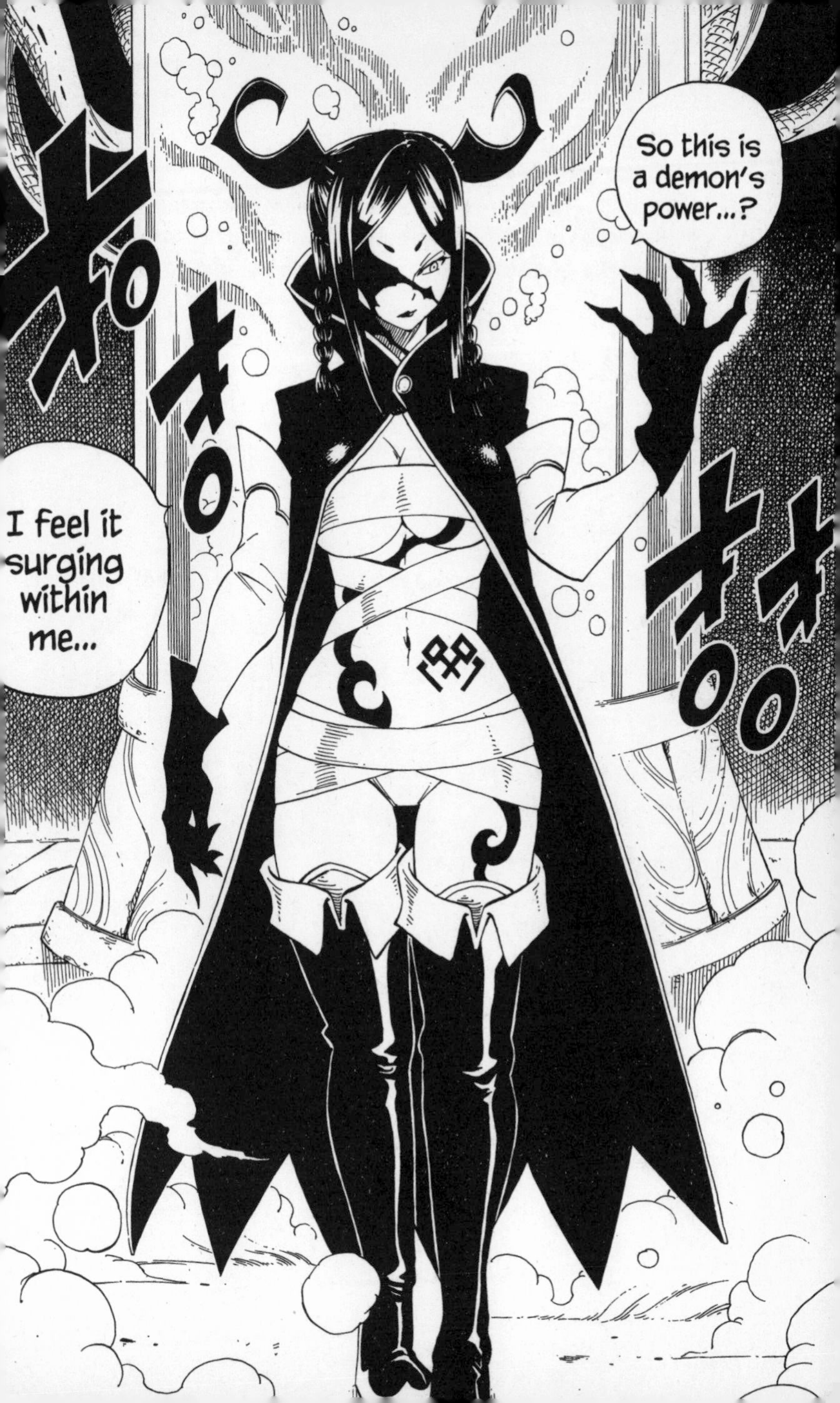
So this is a demon's power...?
I feel it surging within me...

A Kodansha Comics Trade Paperback Original.

Fairy Tail volume 43 copyright © 2014 Hiro Mashima
English translation copyright © 2014 Hiro Mashima

Published in the United States by Kodansha Comics, an imprint of Kodansha USA Publishing, LLC, New York.

Publication rights for this English edition arranged through Kodansha Ltd., Tokyo.

First published in Japan in 2014 by Kodansha Ltd., Tokyo
ISBN 978-1-61262-562-1

Printed in the United States of America.

www.kodanshacomics.com

9 8 7 6 5 4 3 2 1

Translation: William Flanagan
Lettering: AndWorld Design
Editing: Ben Applegate
Kodansha Comics edition cover design by Phil Balsman

TOMARE!

止まれ

[STOP!]

You're going the wrong way!

Manga is a completely different type of reading experience.

To start at the *beginning,* go to the *end!*

...at's right! Authentic manga is read the traditional Japanese way— ...om right to left, exactly the *opposite* of how American books are ...ad. It's easy to follow: Just go to the other end of the book and read ...ch page—and each panel—from right side to left side, starting at ...e top right. Now you're experiencing manga as it was meant to be!